THE CHEMICAL CAROUSEL

What Science Tells Us About Beating Addiction

BY DIRK HANSON

ISBN: I-4392-I299-6
ISBN-I3: 978I439212998

Visit www.booksurge.com to order additional copies.

ALSO BY DIRK HANSON:

The New Alchemists:
Silicon Valley and the
Microelectronics Revolution.

The Incursion:
A Novel

DEDICATION:

For Dick and Lou

TABLE OF CONTENTS

INTRODUCTION

"I feel that any form of so called psychotherapy is strongly contraindicated for addicts. The question "Why did you start using narcotics in the first place?" should never be asked. It is quite as irrelevant to treatment as it would be to ask a malarial patient why he went to a malarial area."

– William S. Burroughs

It was the late 1980s, and the "Decade of the Brain," sponsored by the National Institute of Mental Health (NIMH) and the Library of Congress, was still a few years away. I was sitting in a Clement Street diner in San Francisco, reading a book called *The Hidden Addiction*, by a Seattle M.D. named Janice Keller Phelps, and trying to understand why I could not stop drinking. Dr. Phelps was saying that most of what I thought I knew about alcoholism and other addictions was completely wrong.

Years earlier, I had written a nonfiction book about the rise of Silicon Valley, so I was under no illusions about the scientific learning curve involved in writing a book about the dawn of addiction medicine. But I had the means and the motivation: a background as a science and technology journalist, and a solid addiction to alcohol and cigarettes. So I wanted to learn, and I wanted to get well.

We're in Junior High, Randy and I, and it's the weekend. We're staying at Randy's, after a successful performance at a state swimming meet, and Randy's parent's are out for the night. A typical sleepover, stupid movies and all the cokes you can drink.

But this Saturday night turned out differently, and to this day I can't really say why. I remember Randy showing me his dad's stash of liquor bottles underneath the kitchen sink, and us laughing about it, and what would you pick, Scotch or Gin, and what the hell was Vermouth?

Amazingly, I don't recall what we picked, or exactly how much of it we drank. I remember that it went down okay, with the usual spluttering, and it was giggly and light-headed and fun.

And then, in my memory, a long, blurred period of time passing, and a sense of coming back into my body on a bed I did not recognize, face turned to the wall, Randy moaning quietly beside me. It was a sort of rolling blackout, sweet oblivion, the only one I have ever experienced. Suspended in time, as lost to ordinary chronology as I have ever been, before or since. And strangely, for all the drinking to come, I was never a blackout drinker again. No lost weekends, and no lost cars, dude.

"Come on," I remember saying to my friend, as I came unsteadily to consciousness on the rocking bed, "let's go have some more." Unbelievable. Randy and I had already drunk ourselves into a stupor.

Let's have some more. Good idea.

And then Randy saying, "Hi, mom," in the way you say it when you're trying to freak out your buddy and there's nobody really there, like looking over his shoulder and pretending to see somebody when your buddy is copping a quick piss in the bushes, and saying in a deep voice, "Hi there, sir, how's it going?" Just to watch him fumble with his zipper in a panic. So I roll over on the bed toward Randy, saying "Yeah, right, Randy, like I'm falling for that," and in that instant seeing Randy's mom standing speechless in the doorway of what turned out to be the master bedroom. Staring at us with shock. Or maybe I was the one who went into shock, as I remember very little of the rest of it. At some point Randy's mother called my mother, naturally, despite my fervent prayers designed to produce an intercession, and my dad drove over and took me home, where I fell asleep (it was Saturday) for most of the day. I woke up feeling like hammered dogshit, as they say. My father was sitting in a chair in my bedroom. "Well," he said, when I was as awake as I was going to get, "did you learn anything from this?"

It was no trouble admitting that I had. I had learned that alcohol was awful. Or at least, it led to awful things. And that was all true. Still, there was a small, calm center in the midst of the family hurricane, in which I thought I had learned something quite otherwise; something vital that made me nervous. Van Gogh, in and out of the asylum, insisted that there was "a calm, pure harmony, and music inside of me." I had discovered an odd sort of music inside of me, quite frightening and exhilarating at the same time.

Years later, I came across a study in the *Archives of Pediatrics and Adolescent Medicine*—"Age at Drinking Onset and Alcohol Dependence." The conclusion of this cross-sectional survey of more than 43,000 adults was stark and straightforward: "Relative to respondents who began drinking at 21 years or older, *those who began drinking before age 14 years* (my italics) were more likely to experience alcohol dependence ever and within 10 years of first drinking."

Randy and I were 13 years old.

I was lucky. After years of heavy drinking, I managed to quit. Genes are about risk, not about destiny. But bad genes and drunken uncles are not the whole story. Medical information about blood relatives is sometimes scanty. My late Norwegian grandmother wore hearing aids all the years I knew her, but I never heard anyone explain whether she was totally deaf in one ear, and if so what caused it, or whether it was viral, or the result of an injury, or something from birth—or what. Nobody seemed to know.

So, imagine the awkwardness and the lack of family medical records that can occlude the investigation of less straightforward arenas like alcoholism or drug addiction or depression. I had a great-grandfather who was an eccentric inventor and a trick-shot artist for Remington who encumbered the family with a pile of debts and of whom my late grandfather, who was his son, would never speak, at least to me. Like so many other families, the mental health and substance abuse histories of my forebears are lost to time, or wrapped up safely in received family folklore.

The first thing that science tells us about addiction is that the inclination over the past few decades to call it a disease has been the right way to go. Disease means medicine, and medicine means treatment—a yardstick for measuring the manifestations of addictive disease and the results of different forms of rehabilitation.

In essence, this book is the story of what happens to a molecule of cocaine, or a molecule of gin, or a molecule of THC, after it wends its way inside the human brain. Once that has happened, an alchemical combination of molecular messengers—serotonin, dopamine, norepinephrine, glutamate, corticotrophin-releasing factor (CRF)—operate at specific receptor sites, especially in the portion of the brain known as the limbic system. Everything that follows, from behavioral problems to broken marriages, from jail time to rehab, is a result of changes in infinitesimally small amounts of these chemicals in the brain.

A neurotransmitter is a chemical substance that carries impulses from one nerve cell to another. Neurotransmitters are manufactured by the body and are released from storage sacs in the nerve cells. A tiny junction, called the synaptic gap, lies between brain cells. (Think of Michelangelo's Sistine Chapel, with the finger of Adam and the finger of God not quite touching, yet conveying energy and information.) Neurotransmitters squirt across the synaptic gap, and this shower of chemical messengers lands on a field of tiny bumps attached to the surface of the nerve cell on the other side of the synaptic gap. These bumps are receptors, and they have distinctive shapes. Picture these receptors, brain researcher Candace Pert has suggested, as a field of lily pads floating on the outer oily surface of the cell.

Neurotransmitter molecules bind themselves tightly to these receptors. The fact that certain drugs of abuse *also* lock tightly into existing receptors, and send messages to nerve cells in the brain, is the key to the mystery of addiction.

The fact that certain drugs essentially "fool" receptors into receiving them is one of the most important and far-reaching discoveries in the history of modern science. It is the reason why even minute amounts of certain drugs can have such powerful effects on the human nervous system. The lock-and-key arrangement of neurotransmitters and their receptors is the fundamental architecture of action in the brain. Glandular cells are studded with receptors, and many of the hormones have their own receptors as well. If the drug fits the receptor and elicits a response, it is called an agonist. If it simply blocks the receptor site without stimulating a response, it is an antagonist. Still other neurotransmitters have only a secondary effect, causing the target cell to release other kinds of neurotransmitters and hormones.

Two of the most important neurotransmitters are serotonin and dopamine. The unfolding story of addiction science, at bottom, is the story of what has been learned about the nature and function of such chemicals, and the many and varied ways they effect the pleasure and reward centers in our brains.

In 1948, three researchers—Maurice Rapport, Arda Green, and Irvine Page—were looking for a better blood pressure medication. Instead, they managed to isolate a naturally occurring compound in beef blood called serotonin (pronounced sarah-tóne-in), and known chemically as 5-hydroxytryptamine, or simply 5-HT. The researchers determined that serotonin was involved in vasoconstriction, or narrowing of the blood vessels, and in that respect resembled another important chemical messenger in the brain—epinephrine, better known as adrenaline.

Even though there is at most 10 milligrams of the substance in our bodies, serotonin turned out to be one of nature's signature chemicals—a chemical of thought, movement and behavior, as well as digestion, ejaculation, and evacuation. The body's all-purpose neurotransmitter, involved in sleep, mood, appetite, among dozens of other functions. The cortex, the limbic system, the brain stem, the gut, the genitals, the bowels: serotonin is a key chemical messenger in all of it.

Another key neurotransmitter—dopamine—is considered to be one of the brain's primary "pleasure chemicals," and is found in areas of the brain linked to experiences of joy and reward.

Dopamine pathways play a role in carrying signals related to attention, movement, problem solving, pleasure, and the anticipation of rewarding experiences. Dopamine is one of the reasons why, after you have a pleasurable experience with food, drink, sex, or certain drugs, you are likely to feel a desire to repeat the experience. Dopamine is implicated in not just the drug high, but in the craving that accompanies withdrawal as well.

Feelings of pleasure, or joy, are natural drug highs. The fact that they are produced by chemical alterations in brain state does not make the fear or the pleasure feel any less real. The familiar "fight-or-flight response" triggered by extreme fright or excitement—rapid heartbeat, shallow respiration, elevated blood pressure, dilated pupils, and higher levels of glucose in the blood and muscles—is a function of the aforementioned norepinephrine/adrenaline system.

Pharmacokinetics, the study of how we metabolize drugs, has taken a quantum leap in recent years. So has the field of pharmacogenetics, the study of genetic differences in the way people respond to drugs. An area of the brain behind and below the cerebral cortex, known as the limbic system, is the primary site of action for addictive drugs. While the cerebral cortex is the seat of the higher faculties—logic and rational thought—the limbic system is the command and control center for the expression (or curtailment) of primal emotions—fear and joy. A subset of the limbic system—a set of various bodies and sites with names like the locus coeruleus and the nucleus accumbens—combine to form what is commonly referred to as the brain's pleasure pathway, or reward center. Addictive drugs, we now know, target this part of the brain, and we can now map these changes visually, with state-of-the-art scanning systems. We know for certain that there are well-documented neurochemical and genetic reasons why alcoholics and other drug addicts cannot, in so many cases, "just say no."

Almost nobody starts seriously smoking cigarettes after the age of 24. But somehow I managed it. Being a high school athlete, and an athlete on full scholar-

ship at college, eliminated the possibility of becoming a smoker. It didn't eliminate the possibility of being a smoker—a smoker in potentia. I was born to smoke.

And looking back, I can see how the pattern formed up. It was not as if I had never smoked a single cigarette until I turned 24. By no means. When I drank, I smoked, but in the convivial, loan-me-a-Marlboro style that goes with parties and overnights and road trips. By morning I would have forgotten all about cigarettes, and never felt tempted again until the next full bout of intoxication.

Recently, I ran across research suggesting that if a person smokes ten cigarettes, total, all at once or over a period of years, the chances of developing a full-blown daily addiction to nicotine is shockingly high.

Would it have made any difference to have known this at the time? I strongly doubt it. At the time, I blamed it on the numbing consequences of a bout of manual labor, and the fact that everyone planting trees around me was a smoker. Packs of cigarettes lay crumpled on the dashboard of every work truck.

One morning, at home, I noticed a pack of cigarettes left by a friend who'd visited the night before. Newports. Without any forethought, I reached down and fished one loose and lit it with a kitchen match. Within a few weeks, it was a pack of Camel straights a day.

I remember my wife looking at me, watching me light up in the living room. "What are you doing," she said.

For the next 24 years, until I quit smoking, I didn't have a very good answer. Now I do.

The science of neurology has created a paradigm shift in our basic understanding of the structure of the brain and the rest of the human nervous system. The emergence of a sound understanding of how this mechanism operates has helped explain why relapses on the part of recovering drug addicts and alcoholics have always been so distressingly common. Clearly some major piece of the puzzle had been missing. The real story of alcoholism and other addictions can now be couched in scientific terms, like any other medical disorder.

It has taken a long time, and a large group of doctors, clinicians, and assorted researchers to piece together the ways in which this new knowledge of the brain had direct application to the states of mind and body we call addiction, alcoholism, or drug dependency.

Addiction ranks as one of the world's major human health issues, and is recognized as a disease by the American Medical Association, the American Public Health Association, the World Health Organization, and the National Institute on Alcohol Abuse and Alcoholism (NIAAA), among other agencies and official bodies. And yet, well into the 1990s, treatment for alcoholism and other drug addictions consisted almost exclusively of detoxification, followed by a stint in Alcoholics Anonymous. "It was as if you had cancer," Dr. Janice Keller Phelps told me, "and your doctor's sole method of treatment consisted of putting you in a weekly self-help group." Dr. Phelps, then the director of the Alternatives in Medicine Clinic in Seattle, was the first physician to point out to me that physicians' feelings of therapeutic confidence are often threatened after they discover that addicts frequently do not get better under their care.

Despite decades of official recognition of the disease model of addiction, the traditional view of the addict as an immature and irresponsible person, short on will power, low on self-esteem, and forever at the mercy of his or her "addictive personality," is still alive and well. Moreover, this outmoded view works at cross-purposes with the goal of helping addicts recognize the need for treatment. Addicts have traditionally been taught to think of themselves the way Franz Kafka thought of himself in relation to his disease: "Secretly I don't believe this illness to be tuberculosis, at least not primarily tuberculosis, but rather a sign of my general bankruptcy."

As Keith Humphreys and Elizabeth Gifford write in their article, "Religion, Spirituality, and the Troublesome Use of Substances": "No scientific evidence supports the proposition that an effective social policy for promoting recovery from addiction should comprise belittling, shaming, and castigating addicted people; taking away their children and social benefits; and incarcerating them for extended periods."

We have become used to thinking of such conditions as alco-holism, drug addiction, depression, and suicide in terms of causes rooted firmly in the environment. What events in a person's life, what outside social factors, led to the problem? As Susan Sontag has written: "Psychological theories of illness are a powerful means of placing the blame on the ill. Patients who are instructed that they have, unwittingly, caused their disease are also being made to feel that they have deserved it."

No one knows how many addicts there are. U.S. public health officials commonly settle on a figure of between 10 and 15 per cent of the adult population. Whatever the actual frequency, addiction is a potentially lethal human health condition that is still frequently misunderstood. Up until the early 1990s, almost everyone had it wrong. Addiction wasn't what the experts said it was. Most of the doctors, parents, politicians, priests, and police officers charged with educating our children about the perils of drugs had gotten it wrong—and many of them are still getting it wrong.

Most of our current medical, legal, and psychiatric approaches to the prevention and treatment of drug addiction have failed—and are continuing to fail. In Samuel Butler's classic utopian satire, *Erewhon* sick people are thrown in prison, under a statute that makes it a crime to be ill. Is that our current approach to addiction? Does the drug problem belong in the Attorney General's office, as it now stands, or in the Surgeon General's office? In light of new medi-cal findings about addictive disorders, what is enlightened public policy, and what is not?

When I first began following the scientific research on addic-tion and alcoholism, the field was small, and the insights were ten-tative. Today, an interlocking maze of biomedical and psychiatric sub-specialties make up the world of addiction science. What I had originally viewed as a series of potential breakthroughs in addic-tion research very rapidly became the tip of an enormous iceberg: brain science, and the revolutionary new directions represented by modern biological psychiatry. Along the way, major breakthroughs took place. Prozac came along. So did smokeable forms of cocaine and methamphetamine. And the basic ying-yang debate over addictive drugs ran along the usual grooves. Either it was a medical disorder, or it was straighten up and fly right. In either case, as an addict, you were far more likely to end up in jail than in treatment. And you still are.

This is not a textbook, or a scholarly work. But the story is a scientific one, and can't really be made into anything else. Interested readers can track down additional material by consulting the selected bibliography.

I have also felt compelled to leaven the laboratory findings with what addicts themselves have to say about addiction. The common understanding and experience of addicts in Alcoholics Anonymous and Narcotics Anonymous is impressive, and much of it amplifies various strands of the medical research. Some of the most powerful insights into addiction come from addicts themselves. In the world of medical science, this is "anecdotal evidence," but I would feel remiss if I did not include it.

Most of the traditional thinking about addiction can be boiled down to three basic viewpoints:

1) *Psychological theories* focus on factors in early childhood or psychological and cognitive conflicts later in life, and hold that the secret to treating addiction is to be found in the mind of the addict. 2) *Sociological theories* assert that adverse societal conditions cause addiction, and that the cure lies in changing the social and environmental factors that mold the psyche. 3) *Biochemical theories* begin with the observation that key elements of drug withdrawal are distinctly physical in nature, and argue that the key to addiction is to be found in the structure of the drug molecule and its direct effect on certain cells in the central nervous system. The key to treating addiction, in other words, is chemical.

The biological view of addiction assumes the existence of metabolic individuality—some people are prone to addiction, and some people are protected from it, primarily, but not exclusively, because of their genetic endowment. For a minority of users, drugs that other people can easily manage to go without exert the kind of driving, compulsive control over behavior typically associated with the primary survival drives—food, water, and sex.

"Addiction," wrote David E. Smith and Richard B. Seymour of the former Haight Ashbury Free Medical Clinic, in their book *Drug Free*, "is a disease entity with its own psychopathology characterized by compulsion, loss of control and continued use in spite of adverse consequences. Addiction is progressive, potentially fatal if untreated, and incurable but remissible through abstinence and recovery."

Addiction, then, is not a single, monolithic condition triggered automatically by excessive use of mood-altering drugs. Only a little more than 15 years ago, brain scientists were arguing over whether to consider alcoholism a drug addiction. Cocaine, once considered by many drug experts to be a non-addictive substance, is now widely viewed as one of the most fiercely addictive drugs of abuse.

LSD, once assumed to be addictive, is not addictive at all. And hippies who scoffed at the notion of getting "hooked on pot" now routinely turn up at drug treatment clinics as self-confessed marijuana addicts, despite a relative lack of scientific evidence to support the notion of marijuana withdrawal.

Is sugar an addictive drug? Does it belong in the same category as Jack Daniels or crystal meth?

Perhaps a good place to start is to recognize that even a cursory investigation of drugs and addiction reveals that the line between legal and illegal substances is almost wholly arbitrary. Worse yet: From a hard science point of view, the distinction is completely misleading. There are crucial parts of the brain that do not know or care whether the drug in question is licit or illicit. As a prominent neuroanatomist at the National Institute of Mental Health once told me: "There's this arbitrary line drawn between legal and illegal drugs—and that line has nothing to do with addiction."

Tobacco kills as many as 400,000 people a year, according to the Journal of the American Medical Association. ("A thousand funerals a day," as former Surgeon General C. Everett Koop used to say.) Alcohol consumption accounts for as many as 100,000 deaths a year, and kills twenty times as many people as "hard drugs."

Most people understand that daily drinkers are not necessarily addicted to alcohol; that there is a difference between a drug habit, which non-addicts can develop, and a full-blown drug addiction. But many people have trouble extending this perspective to drugs like heroin, cocaine, and marijuana.

The drug trade, licit and illicit, is the largest, most lucrative industry in the world, and probably always has been, if you are willing to count spices. As a nation, our stance with respect to this industry has been wildly inconsistent: From real cocaine in turn-of-the-century Coca-Cola to the crack "epidemic" of the 1980s. From Carrie Nation and prohibition to the "romantic" alcoholic of the 1940s and 1950s. From "No Hope Without Dope" to "Just Say No" within the space of 25 years.

"If you're trying to come to a simple conclusion about all this," a scientist at the National Institutes of Health observed, "you've got a problem."

This book is divided into four parts:

—A history of drug use and abuse, with an emphasis on genetic studies.

—A look at the drugs themselves, and how they do what they do.

—An explanation of drugs of treatment and the emergence of anti-craving medications, or "fighting fire with fire." We will explore two case histories in particular: anti-craving drugs for cigarettes, the first success story in the field; and anti-craving drugs for carbohydrate overeaters, the first disaster in the field.

—Alternative approaches to addiction, from Alcoholics Anonymous to the war on drugs, with special emphasis on an approach called harm reduction.

If alcoholics and other addicts have specific chemical imbalances in the brain, and if these imbalances turn out to be reliable enough and measurable enough in sufficiently large numbers of human addicts, it is natural to wonder whether, eventually, you can find a way to correct them.

Some sort of neurotransmitter cocktail, maybe.

Or just possibly... a pill?

According to Dr. Steven Paul, formerly a leading addiction researcher at the National Institute of Mental Health (NIMH), before joining Eli Lilly and Company: "The exciting implication is that if we can understand the chemicals in the brain that alcohol and other drugs seem to work on, we can then start to modify these chemical systems—and modify the reinforcing properties of the drugs themselves."

Is it possible, I once asked Dr. Paul, that such research could result in the discovery of an "insulin shot" for alcoholics and other addicts?

"I think," said Dr. Paul, "that that's not a bad speculation."

For years, my primary hobby was fishing. Give me a lake, and, like Ratty in The Wind in the Willows, *I would happily mess about in boats for hours, catching and releasing whatever came to my hook. There is only one thing that can seriously mar the catch-and-release experience—the discovery that a fish has been "deep hooked," as the condition is commonly referred to.*

It's a hard feeling, pulling up a sizeable fish and seeing that your bait, or your artificial lure, is lodged deeply in the fish's gullet—sometimes completely out of sight. With a sinking feeling, you realize that anything you may do to remove the hooks may fatally injure the fish.

From time to time, it happens. What do you do about the dilemma of a deep hooked fish?

There are two schools of thought. The first is to declare that essentially nothing can be done; the fish is a goner and can't be saved whatever you do, and sometimes this turns out to be the case. The other approach is to dig deep in the tackle box for some tools, perhaps a long pair of pliers or hemostats, and, with the aid of fellow anglers, gently and patiently remove the barbed hooks with a minimum of damage. It requires some practice, patience, and persistence. Sometimes the fish jumps and writhes and make matters even worse for itself, getting hooked in an even less promising configuration of gristle, gill and barb.

With the right techniques and the proper equipment and support, the hooks can usually be removed in a way that does not kill the fish. But you are working with a living animal, and the clock is ticking.

Even if you are successful in removing the hooks with a minimum of damage, what comes next is just as essential. The fish has been roughly handled, after all. It is injured and exhausted and stressed. If you simply toss it back into the water, after finessing the deep hooking, the odds on your released fish are still not good. Instead, while supporting the fish with one hand under the belly or behind the neck, you use your other hand to grasp the tail or the back and gently wiggle the fish back and forth through the water, forcing oxygen through its gills and reviving it with this swimming motion, as if teaching it all over again how to go about its business.

And if your are lucky and diligent, at some point the fish will make an unexpected splash and become a ball of muscle, and disappear back into its home waters to live out its life.

This is not a book about why people occasionally drink more than they should, or why they can't seem to resist reaching for that extra fudge brownie. This is a book about why some people cannot stop compulsively drinking or taking drugs despite the ongoing physical and psychological toll it takes. The book itself, if it sells anything, sells the idea of objectivity as a way of looking at drugs, including alcohol—how people get hooked, and how they get free.

Obviously, addiction lies on some sort of spectrum, and this journey through the science of substance abuse centers on the hard end. If there are readers who are uncomfortable with the idea of addiction as a physical disease state, with root causes to be found in the central nervous system, let them read on, and decide, at the end, whether their notions remain valid.

My hope, in the end, is that addicts of every stripe, and the people who care about them, will read this book, recognize it as addressed to them, and find in it new and useful ways of viewing treatment and recovery.

For addicts, knowledge is always power.

PART ONE

ONE: THE ALCOHOLIC RATS OF DR. LI

"Theories that diseases are caused by mental states and can be cured by will power are always an index of how much is not understood about the physical terrain of a disease."

—Susan Sontag

In the early 1990s, it was safe to say that Dr. Ting-Kai Li was in possession of the largest and most famous collection of alcoholic rats in the world.

Housed in a laboratory near Dr. Li's office at Indiana University, the "P-line" of rodents were freely self-administering the body-weight equivalent of one bottle of whiskey a day for a 155-pound man; a blood alcohol concentration that would have gotten them arrested on any highway in America. The P-line rats were seriously addicted to ethanol, the purified form of booze known outside the laboratory as grain alcohol, or white lightning.

"It's actually the only line that's been well developed in the world," Dr. Li told me at the time, with justifiable pride. "And it has been developed through genetic selection for alcohol preference." In other words, Dr. Li did not teach these animals to drink. He didn't have to.

Dr. Li, who was then a professor of medicine and biochemistry at Indiana University, started out by patiently identifying those rare lab rats that were "predisposed toward alcohol preference." As it happens, such rats exist. Given exposure to alcohol, a subset of the lab rat population will consume it obsessively, in ever-increasing quantities. You just had to look for them. The Indiana group painstakingly identified such rats, and interbred them. Dr. Li, who is now the Director of the National Institute on Alcohol Abuse and Alcoholism (NIAAA), which is the alcoholism wing of the National Institutes of Health (NIH), makes it sound easy: "You take a stock with some genetic heterogeneity in it, and then you test it for drinking behavior, and there will be, say, two or three out of a hundred that like to drink, so you take those, and you breed them. And the ones that don't like to drink, you breed those, and within ten generations you start to have a very good separation between drinking scores."

A very good separation, indeed. When enough generations had passed, and enough stringent clinical conditions had been met, Dr. Li's P-line of alcohol-preferring rodents was a solid fact. They did not escape notice among the small but growing number of medical researchers and biochemists who fought over the minuscule grants available for researching alcoholism and other drug addictions.

Why would a rat drink alcohol, and why would anybody care? When I first spoke with Ting-Kai Li, the lack of suitable animal models of alcoholism and addiction was all too apparent. Without suitable strains of test animals, most genetic and neurobiological research would take centuries, and would involve ethical questions about human testing far stickier than the questions raised by the animal rights movement. Animal models are one of the primary pathways of discovery available to neurobiologists and other researchers. While working in an alcohol treatment clinic in Boston, it had become clear to Dr. Li that "if you want to understand alcoholism, you've got to understand the behavior of drinking. That's obvious, right? But there are certain aspects of drinking behavior you can't study in humans. So, you have to go to animal models.

I found that some people in Finland had developed a line of alcohol-preferring rats, and I didn't feel they were characterizing it as rigorously as I would have liked. But seeing that you could do it, anyway, we decided to do it ourselves."

The precisely spoken, self-effacing Dr. Li, along with neurobiology professor Dr. William McBride and their co-workers at Indiana University, were never really in the business of teaching rats to drink. They were in the business of discovering ways to make them stop.

Throughout the 1990s, other strains of alcoholic rats were developed, all genetically selected on the basis of their love for alcohol. There was the AA line of alcoholic rats developed by scientists in Finland, and the UChA line developed in Chile, and others in Italy—but the P-line of Dr. Li's "preferring rats" at the Indiana University School of Medicine, more than ten years in the making, became the focus of several provocative studies, made possible by the care with which the line had been characterized.

There are definite rules for animal models. There are various tests they must past to be considered reliable and robust. The P-line rats had to meet a number of scientific requirements in order to be truly useful. The idea was to insure that the P-line rats well and truly *needed* their daily alcohol fix, just like human alcoholics.

One of the rules was that the rats had to spontaneously consume enough alcohol to get drunk, even if ample supplies of normal food and water were available to them. Dr. Li believed the rats should show a strong dispensation for the voluntary oral consumption of ordinary water laced with a 10 per cent solution of ethanol. A stout whiskey and water, say. Given a choice between a dish of plain water and a dish containing 90 per cent water and 10 per cent ethanol, the rats should preferentially drink from the dish containing the alcohol. The P-line rats passed this test with ease.

Dr. Li had other behavioral criteria besides consumption. One of the trickiest aspects was the matter of deciding whether the P-line rats really "liked" the intoxicating effects of alcohol, the way human alcoholics do. Or had they simply learned to enjoy the taste, the smell, of alcohol?

Dr. Li did not want his rats to enjoy the taste or the smell. He wanted to demonstrate that the animals had an innate preference for alcohol. "Most humans do not particularly enjoy the taste of unchilled alcoholic solutions either," he pointed out, "since they have gone to great lengths to disguise the taste of alcohol in alcohol beverages." True enough: Most drinkers do not prefer theirs neat. The idea was to demonstrate that the P-line rats preferred alcohol for the specific purpose of getting drunk, so Dr. Li's rats did not always get to *drink* the alcohol, as such. More often, the animals took the alcohol through a tube directly connected to their stomachs. The rats were allowed to drink from one of two identically flavored containers of water. When the rats drank from one of the containers, all they got was an infusion of water directly into their stomachs. But when they drank from the other, they got a measured dose of white lightning straight to the stomach. So, the rats were not doing it for the taste. They were, it would seem, doing it for *the buzz.* Once the P-line rats got the hang of it, they drank from the container that triggered the alcohol infusion fourteen times more often than the normal rats.

So, it didn't have anything to do with the taste of alcohol. But what if the rats preferred alcohol because of its caloric value? When a rat or a human being metabolizes alcohol, many of the breakdown products can be used as energy sources—the body attempts to treat alcohol as food. What if the rats went for the ethanol because, unlike water, it was an additional source of nutrition?

To test for *that* possibility, the research group devised a system of pump catheters that allowed the P-line rats to administer themselves a straight brain infusion of alcohol by pressing a bar. No drinking, no tasting, no digesting, nothing but the immediate effect of alcohol on mammalian brain cells. And the P-line rats took right to it. They bar-pressed like crazy for alcohol infusions straight into the brain.

At that point, as Dr. Li emphasized, "there *are* no calories. There is simply no mechanism for metabolizing it directly in the brain."

Pure brain buzz. As we shall see, the brains of humans and the brains of rats are eerily similar at the neuronal level.

Dr. Li's genetically selected P-line rats appeared to ingest alcohol for the same reason human alcoholics do: They had a compelling need for its specific pharmacological effect on their central nervous systems. Both human and rat alcoholics drink in order to get intoxicated, and in order to stay that way as much of the time as possible.

"People ask whether the alcohol is truly rewarding for the rats," Dr. Li said back then. "Our preferring rats will work very hard to get that alcohol. They will sit there and press the bar *eight hundred times* in four hours. I mean, what do you think that is? If the infusion they get as a reward isn't alcohol, they won't do it. And if the rats get too much alcohol, it becomes aversive, and they stop."

To be like human alcoholics, the rats must also demonstrate both an increased tolerance to the effects of the drug, and the onset of physical dependence as manifested by withdrawal symptoms. And they do. The P-line rats develop tolerance, and they show acute withdrawal symptoms when researchers cut off their supply. The rats suffer tremors, seizures, and a rodent version of delirium tremens. They fall down a lot. They are also quick to avail themselves of a little "hair of the dog." After a period of abstinence, they take alcohol again to relieve the withdrawal symptoms.

Dr. Li has done a thorough job. The P-line rats meet every definition of alcoholism anyone could imagine, and the cause of their alcohol addiction appears to be strictly genetic. What was happening with the P-line rats was not explainable by resorting to arguments about simple learned behavior.

"How do you explain this difference?" said Dr. Li. "My explanation is that there are *genetic differences among different individuals.* You're making the assumption that you expose them to the same

environment, the same environmental influences, and yet they behave differently in terms of addiction."

Dr. Li and his colleagues first began working with animal
models of alcohol addiction back in the mid-1970s—a time when
the country was preoccupied with addiction of a different sort.
Americans tended to view the heroin, or "smack" problem of the
1970s as primarily a problem associated with inner city ghettos,
in the same way that they had viewed turn-of-the-century opium
addiction as a "Chinese problem." Throughout the 1970s, African-
American heroin addicts had been viewed as icons for property
crimes against the middle-class, a primary association that helped
perpetuate the popular notion that heroin addicts were black, and
belonged in prison. "Treatment" was a euphemism for letting them
off the hook. This prevailing view—that heroin addiction was
primarily a "Negro" problem, or, at the least, a problem of the
impoverished class—was severely challenged when soldiers began
returning in ever-greater numbers from Southeast Asia as the Vietnam War wound down. To its horror, the U.S. public slowly came
to realize that a significant number of GIs were returning as heroin
addicts—and while mostly male, they came in every sort of color.

It turned out that the American "heroin experience" in Vietnam was, to put it bluntly, harrowing. Naturally, Uncle Sam wanted
to know why.

Alcohol was not the emotional "hot zone" that the hard drugs
were in the 1970s. Alcoholism was, like cigarette smoking, a "public health problem." If so, it was a public health problem nobody
wanted to treat.

In 1971, under the direction of Dr. Jerome Jaffe of the Special Action Office on Drug Abuse Prevention, Dr. Lee Robins of
Washington University in St. Louis undertook an investigation of
heroin use among young American servicemen in Vietnam. Nothing about addiction research would ever be quite the same after the
Robins study. The results of the Robins investigation turned the
official story of heroin completely upside down. It was the same

kind off seismic shift that later took place when Solomon Snyder, Candace Pert, and others worked out the mechanics of neurotransmitters, or when Donald Goodwin, Robert Cloninger and Henri Begleiter, working from the findings of Dr. Li and others, traced out the broad outline of the genetics of addiction (to be more fully discussed later).

The dirty secret that Robins laid bare was that a staggering number of Viet Nam veterans were returning to the U.S. addicted to heroin and morphine. Sources were already reporting a huge trade in opium throughout the U.S. military in Southeast Asia, but it was all mostly rumor until Dr. Robins surveyed a representative sample of enlisted Army men who had left Vietnam in September of 1971—the date at which the U.S. Army began a policy of urine screening. The Robins team interviewed veterans within a year after their return, and again two years later.

After he had worked up the interviews, Dr. Robins found that almost half—45 per cent—had used either opium or heroin at least once during their tour of duty. 11 per cent had tested positive for opiates on the way out of Viet Nam. Overall, about 20 per cent reported that they had been addicted to heroin at some point during their term of service overseas.

To put it in the kindest possible light, military brass had vastly underestimated the problem. One out of every five soldiers in Viet Nam had logged some time as a junky. As it turned out, soldiers under the age of 21 found it easier to score heroin than to hassle through the military's alcohol restrictions. The "gateway drug hypothesis" didn't seem to function overseas. In the United States, the typical progression was assumed to be from "soft" drugs (alcohol, cigarettes, and marijuana) to the "hard" category of cocaine, amphetamine, and heroin. In Vietnam, soldiers who drank heavily almost never used heroin, and the people who used heroin only rarely drank. The mystery of the gateway drug was revealed to be mostly a matter of choice and availability. One way or another, addicts found their way to the gate, and pushed on through.

"Perhaps our most remarkable finding," Robins later noted, "was that only 5% of the men who became addicted in Vietnam relapsed within 10 months after return, and only 12% relapsed even briefly within three years." What accounted for this surprisingly high recovery rate from heroin, thought to be the most addictive drug of all? As is turned out, treatment and/or institutional rehabilitation didn't make the difference: Heroin addiction treatment was close to nonexistent in the 1970s, anyway. "Most Vietnam addicts were not even detoxified while in service, and only a tiny percentage were treated after return," Robins reported. It wasn't solely a matter of easier access, either, since roughly half of those addicted in Vietnam had tried smack at least once after returning home. But very few of them stayed permanently readdicted.

Any way you looked at it, too many soldiers had become addicted, many more than the military brass had predicted. But more of them had recovered on their own than anyone would have guessed. Somehow, the bulk of addicted soldiers toughed their way through it, without formal intervention, after they got home. Most of them kicked the habit. Even the good news, then, took some getting used to. The Robins Study painted a picture of a majority of soldiers kicking it on their own, without formal intervention. For some of them, kicking wasn't even an issue. They could "chip" the drug at will—they could take it or leave it. And when they came home, they decided to leave it.

However, there was that other cohort, that 5 to 12 per cent of the servicemen in the study, for whom it did not go that way at all. This group of former users could not seem to shake it, except with great difficulty. And when they did, they had a very strong tendency to relapse. Frequently, they could not shake it at all, and rarely could they shake it for good and forever. Readers old enough to remember Viet Nam may have seen them at one time or another over the years, on the streets of American cities large and small. Until quite recently, only *very* seriously addicted people who happened to conflict with the law ended up in non-voluntary treatment programs.

The Robins Study sparked an aggressive public relations debate in the military. Almost half of America's fighting men in Vietnam had evidently tried opium or heroin at least once, but if the Robins numbers were representative of the population at large, then relatively few people who tried opium or heroin faced any serious risk of long-term addiction. A relative small number of users were not so fortunate, as Robins noted. What was the difference? Was it a change in setting and circumstances that allowed most heroin users to quit? Or was it that the minority of soldiers who stubbornly became readdicted did so because, like Dr. Li's rats, they were *biochemically different* from their friends who stayed clean? Was it possible for people to find out which group they belonged to, before they got into trouble?

At roughly the same time, psychiatrist Norman Zinberg of Harvard, who was also studying heroin addiction, had concluded that heroin users tended to fall into one of two camps. Category 1 included hard-core addicts, prone to severe, even nightmarish withdrawal symptoms. Category 2 was composed of controlled, occasional users who led relatively normal lives, had normal jobs, and lived with normal families.

Zinberg attributed the phenomenon of "chipping," or regularly using highly addictive drugs without becoming addicted, to such factors as personality and the social setting in which the drug was used. Following Zinberg's lead, sociologists and psychologists began to focus on "set and setting"—the environmental and social circumstances within which social users do their drug taking. Set and setting definitely effect how people use drugs, as well as influencing the nature of their experience with drugs—but were set and setting the primary determinants of who got addicted, and who did not? Dr Li's rats seemed to suggest otherwise.

Faced with the reality of heroin chippers, researchers wanted to know how they did it. Very few researchers seemed intent on pursuing the obvious corollary: Alcohol is known to be highly addictive in the virulent form we call alcoholism. Most people can "chip" alcohol without becoming alcoholics. So how do casual drinkers get away with it?

Today, tobacco is widely considered to be as fiercely addictive as heroin or cocaine, yet in the late 1980s psychologist Saul Shiffman and co-workers at the University of Pittsburgh had no trouble rounding up a group of people who regularly smoked five or fewer cigarettes per day. Shiffman compared these nicotine chippers with a group of smokers who consumed the traditional 20 to 40 cigarettes daily. Shiffman verified that the chippers did not suffer any reportable signs of withdrawal when they were not smoking. They smoked just as often when alone as they did with others, casting doubt on the idea of chipping as a strictly social behavior. They also inhaled just as deeply as addicted smokers, casting equal doubt on the notion that chippers use different drug delivery approaches and thus achieve lower nicotine levels in the blood.

The study did, however, find one noteworthy difference, and it was a familiar one. Or perhaps familial would be the better word: Fewer of the chippers had first-degree relatives who smoked, and those relatives who did smoke had been more successful at quitting than the relatives of heavily addicted smokers. Were tobacco chippers genetically different from addicted smokers?

Well, yes, Dr. Li insisted. "That was the lesson of heroin use in Viet Nam. The ones who came home and got readdicted to heroin were the ones who were addictive to start with, mostly. With alcohol, if you take most college students, they are abusing alcohol while they're in college—but most of them grow out of it. Now, there is a group that doesn't grow out of it—they go on to become alcoholics. Those are the ones who are maybe more genetically susceptible in the first place."

What we need to remember is that alcohol, the drug, is an intimate part of the environment for most people, said Dr. Li. "Alcoholism, in those people who have a high susceptibility for it, is a *pharmacogenetic* disorder. There are many pharmacogenetic disorders. The more common ones are diseases like glucose-6-phosphate dehydrogenase deficiency." Dr. Li was referring to a common human enzyme deficiency that reduces the ability of red blood cells to carry oxygen, resulting in severe anemia. It is found predominantly in Jews and African-Americans. "People who have this disorder are *normal,*" Dr. Li insisted. "They don't get into trouble until they are exposed to a very particular kind of environmental insult; something that's an oxidative agent. Like eating fava beans, for example. They eat fava beans, and all their red blood cells go to hell."

And yet, how can something be a disease if the people who supposedly have it are perfectly normal until they start messing with alcohol or heroin? To some people, that just does not sound like a disease.

"People have all kinds of objections," Dr. Li went on. "They say, 'well, there are obvious environmental influences.' Of course there are. But there are also environmental influences on hypertension, on heart disease, on diabetes, and so on."

As it happened, black men in Viet Nam who suffered from glucose-6-phosphate dehydrogenase deficiency found out about it fast, whenever they took an anti-malarial medication called Dapsone, a drug now used to treat certain skin diseases similar to leprosy. Blacks with glucose-6-phosphate dehydrogenase deficiency would take Dapsone, which pulled the environmental trigger on their disease, and they would suffer acute hemolysis—the complete breakdown of their red blood cells. If they didn't take Dapsone, or eat fava beans, they were fine—you couldn't tell them from anyone else. "It's a good example of a pharmacogenetic disease where, if you're not exposed to the environmental agent, you don't get into trouble," said Dr. Li. "This is called inherited susceptibility. And in this case, we know the definite biochemical basis for it."

As another angle from which to view "inherited susceptibility," consider this alternative: What if eating fava beans for the very first time didn't make certain people sick—it made them feel incredibly good; better than they had ever felt in their life? Better than they ever thought possible. What if that first experience felt like a life truly worth living; a surcease from years of sadness, a miracle drug, the healing hand of God? What if certain people, for reasons of abnormal biochemistry, had never experienced the typical feelings of happiness and contentment most people take for granted—until they ate fava beans. And then, for the first time in their lives, they felt better than okay.

If fava beans were a rewarding stimuli instead of aversive, the disease would still be a pharmacogenetic disorder, hidden from view in the absence of the environmental trigger. Once having tasted the bean, however, a stubborn minority of people would be drawn to eat it repeatedly. And the more they ate the beans, the more their bodies would become dependent upon the artificial reward the beans provided—until they reached a point where they simply could not function unless they had their beans.

Here is how noted alcoholism researcher Dr. Donald Goodwin stated the hypothesis back in the 1980s:

> Alcoholics, or some alcoholics, lack the gene(s) for optimal production of Substance H (H for happiness). They are born, so to speak, unhappy. Sometime in their teens, they discover that having two or three beers or drinks makes them happy. Someone once said that you never feel better than when you start feeling good after feeling bad, and, for some alcoholics—those who start life feeling bad—drinking alcohol feels so good it becomes habit-forming. But not all is bliss. Ten minutes or so after the H-deficient person has a drink, he wants another. He is feeling unhappy again—unhappier than before he had the drink. The unhappiness now has a special quality sometimes called craving. A drink relieves this new unhappiness and even restores the original happiness, but just briefly. Another drink, and another, is needed to overcome the unhappy feeling produced by the same drug that produced the happy

feeling—alcohol. "It lifts you up and it lets you
down," as the saying goes, and some people are
lifted up and let down more than others, probably because of genes.

"Deranged Cellular Metabolism"

The idea of addiction as a disease first began to gain a tentative
foothold in scientific and government circles in the early 1960s, after the publication of E.M. Jellinek's *The Disease Concept of Alcoholism.*
Jellinek may not have invented the "alcohol science movement," as
he called it, and he may not have been much of a scientist himself
(the evidence suggests that he faked his doctorate), but he was the
first to describe the "disease syndrome" of alcoholism—chronic relapse leading to death by liver failure. A salesman by nature, Jellinek
ardently presented the disease model of alcoholism to the world
of the social sciences just as zealously as he had previously done
banana research in Honduras for United Fruit, and biostatistics
work for Worcester State Hospital in Massachusetts. The trouble
was that the "science" part of alcohol science was murky at best.
No real progress was made in loosening the grip that traditional
psychology exerted upon the prevailing public view of addiction.

A few years earlier, in 1959, a colorfully maverick dis-
senter named Roger J. Williams, professor of chemistry at the
University of Texas, had proposed a specific disease model of his
own; one that went all but unnoticed at the time. The late Roger
Williams was best known as the biochemist who discovered vitamin
B-5, better known as pantothenic acid, one of the so-called "anti-
stress" vitamins. This discovery produced a nice revenue stream
for Williams' home university through the patents he took out on
various processes for synthesizing B-5.

One of the problems with traditional theories of alcoholism, Williams believed, was that it was very difficult to identify the specific psychosocial pathologies psychiatrists insisted were behind alcoholism—such things as infantile regression and oral fixation. Those few researchers who did pay attention to alcoholism, he asserted, "have been so diverted by the rather vague and ill-defined personality disorders that alcoholics allegedly have that they have failed to concentrate upon the one thing that all alcoholics have—whether they are rich or poor... introverts or extroverts, dominant or submissive, repulsive or charming—*namely, an excessive appetite for alcohol.*" The idea of appetite was, for Williams, the essential semantic shift. As Williams insisted in his book, *Alcoholism: The Nutritional Approach*:

Alcohol is a physiological agent and the urge which the initial drink produces, in my opinion, arises because of *deranged cellular metabolism.* Except for the fact that derangement is involved, the urge is fundamentally similar to the urge we have for water when our tissues become dehydrated, for salt when our tissues become salt-hungry... or the unfortunate craving some diabetics have for sugar.... Those who have never had this specific craving for alcohol are unable to understand the problem that an alcoholic has, just as those who have never been morphine addicts cannot understand the craving that dope addicts possess.

The idea that the addict's urge to drink or take dope was primarily *physical* did not catch on in a hurry, the alcohol science movement notwithstanding. For the next twenty years or so, doctors and scientists who were inclined toward a disease model of the addictions did not always have an easy time of it, particularly in government circles. Lawmakers and educators tended to react with skepticism, if not outrage, to attempts to apply science to the matter of human vice. The disease model was an excuse for indolence and weak will. Some of this confusion is still with us. This is completely understandable, given the way bits and pieces of information on the subject have dribbled into the public press over the years.

Dr. Williams was saying that after a certain point, the burning urge for alcohol, or the insatiable craving for heroin became, for "addiction-prone" people, indistinguishable from the primal drives of food, thirst, or sex. "This is something that it is impossible to understand unless we take into account the *tremendous biochemical individuality* that exists." If alcohol and addictive drugs didn't effect you that way, well then, they just didn't, and you thanked your lucky stars for it, the way you would be thankful for not having allergies or diabetes. Blood composition, enzyme levels, endocrine activities, excretion patterns, and nutritional needs all vary from person to person, argued Williams, and the effect of any given addictive drug was going to vary widely from person to person. This neglect of biochemical individuality, Williams was convinced, was the reason physicians had no medical treatment to offer. They had the wrong paradigm—they were focusing on the drugs themselves, and not on the bodies and brains of the users.

Alcoholism, wrote Williams, "has come to be considered as in the domain of psychiatrists, many of whom could not be expected, because of the psychoanalytic flavor of their background, to be enthusiastic about biochemical and physiological approaches."

Alcoholics, Williams believed, responded to a specific strain of megavitamin therapy—large doses of amino acids, particularly glutamine, combined with loads of B vitamins, particularly thiamine—and no sugar. Ever since then, several generations of alternative and nutritionally based health therapists have worked variations on the basic Williams treatment protocol. It was one of the first alcoholism treatment programs that did not rely on other addictive drugs, or on general principles of psychotherapy.

There were, Williams insisted, periodic references in the literature to what he called the "X" factor—some particular defect, or excess, or absence, that was present in alcoholics, but absent in moderate drinkers and abstainers. The hunt for the X Factor, for Substance H, was fast becoming the Holy Grail of addiction research.

Williams thought the X factor was genetic.

"It's not going to be just one gene," Dr. Li told me, many years ago. And he was right. "It's not like cystic fibrosis, where they know it's one gene." The idea of addiction as a medical disease, genetic findings notwithstanding, is by no means a universally popular notion, even today. Given what is known at this point, can't alcoholism and other drug addictions all be accounted for simply by looking closely at environmental factors?

The round-faced, spectacled Dr. Li, whose broad vocabulary and precise diction I always found reassuring, typically had a dictionary near at hand for working out semantic arguments. "Disease," he read aloud during one phone conversation. "From the American Heritage Dictionary, 1981 edition. ' An abnormal condition of an organism, especially as a consequence of infection, *inherent weakness,* or environmental stress that impairs normal physiological functioning.' I mean, nobody would disagree that arteriosclerosis is a disease, even though there are both genetic tendencies and there are environmental things that cause it. And the idea with the public health approach to any disease, in the end, is to decrease the environmental effects as much as you can."

The alcoholic rats of Dr. Li are very different from normal rats, even before they are exposed to alcohol for the first time. From the moment of their birth, the central nervous systems of Dr. Li's alcohol-preferring rats are deficient in two essential neurotransmitters. These are serotonin and dopamine, two of the brain's most crucial chemical messengers. The brain of a rat or the brain of a human cannot function normally unless these chemicals are present in the appropriate concentrations.

Dr. Li's rats are low-serotonin, low-dopamine rodents.

Eventually, there were strains of mice that fell over when they drank too much, and strains that didn't fall over, and eventually a strain of so-called "knockout" mice, in which the absence of a single gene that codes for a particular form of serotonin leads to increased drinking among otherwise sober mice. Dr. Li's earlier conjectures about his alcoholic rats are now fact. In 1996, behavioral geneticists at a veteran's hospital in Oregon reported in the journal *Nature Genetics* that mice lacking a certain brain receptor for serotonin preferred ethanol-laced liquid to pure tap water. The knockout mice drink twice as much at a sitting as normal mice, yet are less tipsy and less prone to stumble. While the protocols might violate the need to design out alcohol preference based on taste, it seems safe to say that something distinctly *pharmacological* is going on here. "I think what you're looking at, if you want to take it to a more common level of brain function," said Dr. Li, "is that there is a so-called brain reward pathway which is responsive to a lot of things that are rewarding. If you want to look at it from an evolutionary standpoint, what was rewarding before was the sexual drive, and the drive toward food and water. The drugs that become addictive for certain people are the ones that utilize and work on these pathways. And these are the dopamine and serotonin pathways."

Why do alcoholics continue to drink? Why do junkies continue to use? Because there is something wrong with them, yes, that part is true. However, the "something" that is wrong with them appears to have its origins not in the psyche, but somewhere deep in the neurochemistry of the brain, beyond the reach of will power, group analysis, motivational exhortations, or even rock-solid logic and common sense. A stubborn minority of Dr. Li's rats in Indiana, and Dr. Robin's soldiers in Viet Nam, and Dr. Williams' alcoholic patients in Texas, all came "prewired" for addiction. Dr. Williams, among others, thought it had to do with biochemical individuality.

Dr. Williams was fond of making the analogy to allergies. (This was the position officially maintained by Bill. W., the cofounder of Alcoholics Anonymous—that alcoholism was "an allergy of the body and an obsession of the mind").

But what were any of these tentative insights worth? Why do addicts crave? Why doesn't everybody crave? Why were some people apparently protected from the siren call of addiction? What made the occasional users, the "chippers," different? Were they just made of sterner stuff? Possessed of iron will? How did they avoid taking up *the life*—the daily, sometimes hourly, search for drugs, the growing tolerance to their effects, the escalating patterns of usage, the seemingly uncontrollable nature of the urge, and all the damaging behavioral effects.

It seemed like you could peel the monkey off some people's backs with relative ease, while other people would go clean and then relapse in a continuing cycle, running through a cornucopia of addictive substances in the process. Depressed, insatiable, compulsive, unyielding, recalcitrant, sometimes suicidal, full-blown addicts were clearly dysfunctional, seemingly without the will or the inner resources to alter their self-destructive course.

Addictionologists, or addiction scientists, as they were sometimes being called, had been thinking along different lines. Addictive drugs performed a normalizing function on the central nervous systems of certain kinds of people. Long-term, recalcitrant addicts were people with inherent (and sometimes inherited) flaws in the basic chemistry of their central nervous systems. They had inherited a flawed metabolism, and then they had activated it through stress, negative environmental influences—and access to mood-boosting chemicals in liquid, powder, and pill form. As a result of intensive research on the mechanisms of withdrawal, craving, drug-seeking behavior, and relapse, investigators have opened the door to some informed speculation about a broader range of disorders that may lurk beneath the umbrella of the addictive disease concept.

TWO: THE DRUG DEAL

"In my judgment such of us who have never fallen victims [to alcoholism] have been spared more by the absence of appetite than from any mental or moral superiority over those who have. Indeed, I believe if we take habitual drunkards as a class, their heads and their hearts will bear an advantageous comparison with those of any other class."

— Abraham Lincoln

The history of brain science probably began about 4,000 B.C., somewhere in Sumeria, when human beings first discovered the extraordinary effects of the unripened seedpods of the poppy plant. Modern neuroscience owes a great debt of gratitude to this tame-looking plant drug and its sticky, incredibly potent byproduct called opium. Neuropharmacology—the study of the action of drugs on the nervous system—would never have advanced so quickly without it.

Historically, the emphasis has been on opium's cash value, not its value to science. A trade staple on the Silk Route for centuries, opium was very nearly the perfect business. The present-day drug companies, known collectively as Big Pharma, are not the first capitalists in the world to exert an unprecedented grip on drug retailing.

One of the less-civilized aspects of the early British Empire was its control of the opium trade in China and India. Perhaps the most sordid drug war in history was fought not to protect a nation from drugs, but for exclusive rights to market them. From roughly 1720 to the late 1800s, the merchants of the British East India Company ran a brisk and lucrative opium business with the Oriental "heathens." In 1839, the British went to war with China to maintain unlimited trading rights, and when the Chinese authorities seized and burned British opium shipments on the Canton River, the "street" price for addicts in China went up drastically—with no discernible effect on demand. The British won the war, retained unlimited marketing rights to opium in the Orient, and picked up the island of Hong Kong in the bargain.

It took the Chinese immigrant experience in America to bring home the true nature of opium's addictiveness. Americans and other "non-heathens" were not, as it turned out, immune to the spell of opium after all. By the mid-1800s, opium could be legally purchased in the United States as laudanum, patent medicines, and various elixirs. Opium was a godsend during the bloody years of the Civil War. Maimed and disabled soldiers found relief in morphine, the potent alkaloid of opium extracted by a German chemist, Friedrich Serturner, in the early 1800s. Named after Morpheus, Greek god of dreams, this drug, coupled with the fortuitous invention of the hypodermic syringe, meant that for all its bloody reputation, the American Civil War was the first war in which wounded soldiers could be offered effective pain relief. Used against constant, intractable pain, opium and its derivatives were among the most humane medical drugs ever discovered. How could a physician withhold it?

Americans, like others before them, soon discovered opium's major drawback. It was with the Civil War that the phenomenon of the addicted war veteran began, and addiction was sometimes known as "the soldier's disease."

The first law prohibiting the use of opium in so-called "dens" was passed in San Francisco in 1875, and it was distinctly racist in origin. According to San Francisco authorities, "many women and young girls, as well as young men of respectable family, were being induced to visit the dens, where they were ruined morally and otherwise." Congress followed suit, and in 1887 passed a law prohibiting the importation of opium by the Chinese. This resulted principally in soaring prices, and a resuscitation of the languishing arts of piracy on the High Seas.

By the late 1800s, homegrown opium had become a significant cash crop in several American states. As a Massachusetts government health official reported in 1871:

> Opium has been recently made from white pop-
> pies, cultivated for the purpose, in Vermont,
> New Hampshire, and Connecticut... It has also
> been brought here from Florida and Louisiana,
> while comparatively large quantities are regularly
> sent East from California and Arizona, where its
> cultivation is becoming an important branch of
> industry, ten acres of poppies being said to yield,
> in Arizona, twelve hundred pounds of opium.

The first designer drug of note was heroin, an analog, or close chemical equivalent, of morphine. It proved to be a multi-billion dollar medicine for Bayer Laboratories of Germany, starting in 1898. Marketed as a less addictive variant of the poppy, and hailed in the sales literature as a "heroic" drug (hence the name), it was used in many cough remedies of the day. The trade name was later dropped, and heroin entered the lexicon as a generic term.

As a percentage of the total U.S. population, there were undoubtedly more morphine and heroin addicts in the early years of the 20th century than there are today. By some estimates, one out of every 400 Americans was addicted to opium products in the early 1900s. Despite its connotation as a Chinese working-class vice, opium use was more common among the American upper classes than it ever was among the poor, presumably for reasons of cost. In 1908, *Putnam's* magazine reported that there were 40 institutions for the treatment of drug addiction, several of them having treated more than 50,000 patients, and none of them entirely cheap.

By 1914, despite more than thirty years of city, state and federal efforts to suppress opium smoking, "the amount smoked per year increased sevenfold—without taking account of smuggled supplies," according to Edward M. Brecher in his monumental 1972 study for Consumer Reports, *Licit and Illicit Drugs*.

The situation was much the same in Great Britain, even though the British had been shamed into abandoning the Far Eastern opium trade, and the British Navy now chased drug smugglers instead of doing the smuggling itself. Karl Marx, for one, decried the English working-class habit of "dosing children with opiates," referring to the 19th-century practice of quieting crying babies with laudanum.

In America, turn-of-the-century Sears Roebuck catalogs offered cures for both morphine addiction and alcoholism. The medicine being offered for morphine addiction consisted primarily of alcohol. The medical treatment offered for alcoholism, unsurprisingly, was tincture of opium. As the medical director of the notably named Brooklyn Home for Narcotic Inebriates put it in 1902, "The shore of the post-poppy land is strewn with wrecks of those who, after escape from narcotic peril, have taken to rum."

After the isolation of morphine from the poppy came other plant drug extractions: digitalis from foxglove, quinine from cinchona trees—and cocaine from the leaves of a squat bush found in South America. If the Orient was the center for opium products; if the ancient Arab world was largely responsible for popularizing coffee (the Persian philosopher Avicenna records its use in the Near East in the 11th Century); then historically South America had its distinctive offering as well. In the high Andes, the use and cultivation of coca by the native population of Incas had been commonplace since at least the 10th Century. This drug became better known in our time by the name of its primary active ingredient, cocaine. Historians suggest that cocaine was first brought to Europe by returning conquistadores, and ultimately became a popular anesthetic for cataract removal and dental surgery. Less than one hundred years later, it had become a seriously abused stimulant all over the world.

Cocaine was marketed legally in the late 1800s by Parke, Davis in the United States, and by Merck and Co. of Germany, among others. Touted as a general "brain tonic" and a non-addictive cure for depression, as well as an alternative to opiate and alcohol addiction, cocaine appeared in wines, chewing gum, powders—and in Coca Cola, the "temperance drink." (Reportedly, Coke contained 60 milligrams per eight-ounce serving, or roughly one modern snort). There were coca cigarettes, cordials, and salves. One bottling company even offered a soft drink simply named "Dope."

Opium, cocaine, and coffee were by no means the only plant drugs in use in the Americas. Datura, a weedy western species, had a reputation as a sedative and an aphrodisiac in small doses, but it was a poison at high doses. Datura nearly killed a number of the early colonists at Jamestown, Virginia, when they mistook the weed for wild spinach. Ever after, it was known as Jamestown weed, or Jimson weed. Almost 200 years later, Charlie Manson was rumored to have used Datura on his California girls. Don Juan the Mexican sorcerer allegedly used it on his student, Carlos Castaneda. There was also the occasional outbreak of "ergotism," or poisoning from a fungus commonly found growing on rye. This kind of outbreak plagued villages in medieval times, and may have been responsible for the "distempers" and "convulsive fits" of the Salem witch hysteria in 1691, some scholars argue. It is now known that ergot is one of the few substances in nature that chemically resembles LSD-25.

Either bad rye bread or Jimson Weed may have set the witches soaring, but in South America, magic of a different sort had been brewing for thousands of years. Ololiuqui (LSD-like morning glory seeds that fueled priestly hallucinations), Teonanacatl (psilocybin mushrooms), and Peyotl (mescaline-containing cactus) were all exclusively New World plant drugs used in religious rituals.

Historically, a few South American tribes also drank a potent brew distilled from the Ayuhuasca vine, a plant that contained a mind-altering compound called DMT. As unlikely as it sounds, DMT was to play a major role in fueling the neurotransmitter revolution of the 1990s. The effect of ingesting Ayahuasca, a foul stew of hallucinogenic alkaloids brewed up by jungle shamans, was so profoundly weird, so unsettling, so extrasensory, that the active ingredient, when isolated, was initially christened "telepathine."

"Drinking the Smoke"

The prototypically North American contribution to the world drug trade has always been tobacco. Tobacco pipes have been found among the earliest known Aztec and Mayan ruins. Early North Americans apparently picked up the habit from their South American counterparts. Native American pipes subjected to gas chromatography show nicotine residue going back as far as 1715 B.C. "Drinking" the smoke of tobacco leaves was an established New World practice long before European contact. An early technique was to place tobacco on hot coals and inhale the smoke with a hollow bone inserted in the nose.

The addicting nature of tobacco alarmed the early missionary priests from Europe, who quickly became addicted themselves. Indeed, so enslaved to tobacco were the early priests that laws were passed to prevent smoking and the taking of snuff during Mass. New World tobacco quickly came to the attention of Dutch and Spanish merchants, who passed the drug along to European royalty in the 17th Century. In England, American tobacco was worth its weight in silver, and American colonists fiercely resisted British efforts to interfere with its cultivation and use. Sir Francis Bacon noted that "The use of tobacco is growing greatly and conquers men with a certain secret pleasure, so that those who have once become accustomed thereto can later hardly be restrained therefrom." (As a former smoker, I am hard pressed to imagine a better way of putting it.)

Early sea routes and trading posts were determined in part by a desired proximity to overseas tobacco plantations. The expedition routes of the great 17th and 18th Century European explorers were marked by the strewing of tobacco seeds along the way. Historians estimate that the Dutch port of Amsterdam had processed more than 12 million pounds of tobacco by the end of the 17th Century, with brisk exports to Scandinavia, Russia, Prussia, and Turkey. (Historian Simon Schama has speculated that a few enterprising merchants in the Dutch tobacco industry might have "sauced" their product with cannabis sativa from India and the Orient.) Troubled by the rising tide of nicotine dependence among the common folk, Bavaria, Saxony, Zurich, and other European states outlawed tobacco at various times during the 17th Century. The Sultan Murad IV decreed the death penalty for smoking tobacco in Constantinople, and the first of the Romanoff czars decreed that the punishment for smoking was the slitting of the offender's nostrils. Still, there is no evidence to suggest that any culture that has ever taken up the smoking of tobacco has ever wholly relinquished the practice voluntarily. A century later, the demand for American tobacco was growing steadily, and the market was worldwide. Prices soared, with no discernible effect on demand. "This demand for tobacco formed the economic basis for the establishment of the first colonies in Virginia and Maryland," according to drug researcher Ronald Siegel. Furthermore, writes Siegel:

The colonists continued to resist controls
on tobacco. The tobacco industry became as
American as Yankee Doodle and the Spirit of
Independence.... In 1776 the American tobacco
industry was strong enough to help finance the
Revolution. So England tried to eradicate the

crop. British armies, trampling across the South, went out of their way to destroy large inventories of cured tobacco leaf, including those stored on Thomas Jefferson's plantation. But tobacco survived to pay for the war and sustain morale.

In many ways, tobacco was the perfect American drug, distinctly suited to the robust American lifestyle of the 18th and 19th Centuries. Tobacco did not lead to debilitating visions or rapturous hallucinations—no nodding out, no sitting around wrestling with the angels. Unlike alcohol, it did not render them stuporous or generally unfit for labor. Tobacco acted, most of the time, as a mild stimulant. People could work and smoke at the same time. It picked people up; it lent itself well to the hard work of the day and the relaxation of the evening. It did not act like a psychoactive drug at all. As with plant drugs in other times and cultures, women generally weren't allowed to use it. Smoking tobacco was a man's habit, a robust form of relaxation deemed inappropriate for the weaker sex. (Women in history did take snuff, and cocaine, and laudanum, and alcohol, but mostly they learned to be discreet about it, or to pass it off as doctor-prescribed medication for a host of vague ailments, which, in most cases, it was.)

Demon Rum

Let the record show that Colonial Americans did not stint on the rum, in addition to their native plant drugs. The Orient had its rice wines; the Middle East had its date wines. Scandinavia had mead from fermented honey; Mexico had its pulque. The ancient Romans probably learned the art of brewing from the Greeks, who picked it up from the Egyptians, who may have gotten it from the Babylonians.

While ancient meads and other brews were meant primarily as food, wines and distilled spirits were not. When yeasts consume the sugar found in certain foods, like grains, one of the byproducts is ethanol—the kind of alcohol you can drink. All you need to do is smash some grain, moisten it, cover it, and come back later. But natural fermentation only takes you so far—to about 14 per cent, specifically. For stronger brews than that, the process of distillation must be employed. We know that the vapors from boiled wine were used to treat the sick in the Middle Ages. Eventually, those concentrated vapors became available on a day-to-day basis, as brandy.

And so it has been throughout history. The use of wine is pre-biblical; animals seek out plant drugs and eat them; native peoples in all lands discover and use drugs for their mind-altering properties. Children in South American slums inhale benzene fumes—the quickest, cheapest high they can get. If there were a gateway experience—a gateway brain state rather than a gateway drug—it would likely be the common childhood experience of twirling in circles to induce dizziness. The famed whirling dervishes of Turkey refined the technique and incorporated it into their religious rituals.

Some anthropologists have speculated that alcohol and nicotine addiction may have been a crucial factor in converting hunting and gathering cultures to agriculture. Early man's discovery of how to produce alcohol through fermented grains may have been an important step toward village-based agriculture. Similarly, early cultures that had learned to cultivate tobacco may have become highly reluctant to wander too far afield of their supply. Unwilling to migrate to distant hunting grounds because of their fondness for tobacco, they may have learned to cultivate other crops in order to survive in their newly fixed abodes.

The "Good Creature of God," as the Puritans referred to alcohol, was the social centerpiece in taverns throughout the colonies. The phenomenon of the village drunkard was easily understood: He was simply the person in town of the lowest moral fiber.

One of the first physicians to argue that habitual drunkards were "addicted" was Dr. Benjamin Rush, a signer of the Declaration of Independence, America's first professor of chemistry, a fervent believer in copious blood-letting, and the author of the 1812 treatise, *Medical Inquiries and Observations upon the Diseases of the Mind*, for which he is considered by some to be the father of American psychiatry. Rush was another controversial figure, touted by many as a heroic innovator and by others as something of a quack. Rush strenuously emphasized "depletive" remedies—anything that made the patient bleed, sweat, retch, or blister.

As for alcoholism, Dr. Rush considered it a "disease of the will" resulting in loss of control over drinking behavior, and curable only through abstinence. He recommended the creation of "sober houses" where drunkards could acquire the habit of abstinence. John B. Gough, a well-known presence on the temperance lecture circuit, called alcoholism a sin, "but I consider it also a disease. It is a physical as well as moral evil." The drunkard's confession was a popular literary motif in the mid-19th Century. The only novel Walt Whitman ever wrote was called *Franklin Evans, or The Inebriate*. If Carrie Nation became the strident public face of the American Temperance Movement, Benjamin Rush was its patron saint.

Nonetheless, the temperance movement remained largely committed to the notion that habitual drunks could quit if they wanted to. All they really needed was a good dose of Emersonian self-reliance. The temperance movement soon switched to an obsession with nationwide prohibition, and treating alcohol addiction gave way to activist politics and battles with the "liquor trust." Addiction once again transmogrified into a condition brought on exclusively by opium products. The idea of alcoholism and all other substance addictions as recognizable disease states did not significantly reemerge until the founding of Alcoholics Anonymous in the late 1930s.

As the 20th Century began, America's drinking habits were undergoing a thorough review. A newly industrialized nation with expanding populations, newfound mobility, and loosened family structures brought social problems into sharper focus—crime and mental illness in particular. Alcohol, in and of itself, was again considered to be a substance capable of enslaving anyone and everyone. Temperance movement leaders were opposed to the idea that some people could control their drinking, and imbibe moderately for a lifetime, the same way many people today are incensed by the notion that some people can dabble recreationally with illegal drugs and not suffer the consequences of addiction.

In late 1914, while the prohibition battle raged, the government took aim at non-alcoholic drugs. The legal status of heroin and cocaine changed overnight with the passage of the Harrison Narcotic Act. The U.S. Congress, with the vociferous backing of William Jennings Bryan, the prohibitionist Secretary of State, voted to ban the "non-medical" use of opiates and derivatives of the coca plant. Under the Harrison Act, physicians could be arrested for prescribing opiates to patients. "Honest medical men have found such handicaps and dangers to themselves and their reputation in these laws," railed an editorial in the journal *American Medicine*, "that they have simply decided to have as little to do as possible with drug addicts..." The Harrison Act did have the effect of weeding out casual users, as opium became dangerous and expensive to procure. Housewives, merchants, salesmen, and little old ladies who had been indulging in the "harmless vice" now gave it up.

By 1919, continued pressure from the alcohol temperance movement culminated in Congressional passage of the Volstead Act, which provided for federal enforcement of alcohol prohibition. The temperance activists had pulled it off, though there is nothing very "temperant" about total prohibition. A year later, the states ratified the 18th Amendment. Within a five-year period, morphine, cocaine, and alcohol had all been banned in America. The Prohibition Era had begun. At roughly the same time, alcohol prohibition movements were sweeping across Europe, Russia, and Scandinavia.

It is hard, from the modern vantage point, to imagine how anybody thought they could get away with it. As we know, organized crime syndicates took control of bootleg alcohol distribution, law enforcement agencies received "protection" money, and millions of Americans became criminals by continuing to drink in "Speakeasies." As the Dutch philosopher Baruch Spinoza noted almost three centuries earlier, "He who tries to determine everything by law will foment crime rather than lessen it."

Prohibition and the passage of the Harrison Narcotics Act coincided, as well, with a short-lived effort to prohibit cigarettes. Leaving no stone unturned in the battle to eliminate drugs and alcohol from American life, Henry Ford and Thomas Edison joined forces to wage a public campaign against the "little white slavers." Edison had shown an earlier fondness for Vin Mariani, a French wine laced with prodigious amounts of cocaine, but he and Ford wanted to stamp out cigarette smoking in the office and the factory. Although that effort would have to wait another 75 years or so, and may yet become the next large-scale test of federal prohibition, New York City did manage to pass an ordinance prohibiting women from smoking in public. Fourteen states eventually enacted various laws prohibiting or restricting cigarettes. By 1927, all such laws had been repealed.

As Prohibition continued, police and federal law enforcement budgets soared, and arrest rates skyrocketed, but no legal maneuvers served to make alcohol prohibition effective, once "respectable" citizens had chosen not to give up drinking. Whether or not Prohibition reduced the incidence of alcoholism in America continues to be debated to this day. What is not debatable is that alcohol was freely available in the United States throughout the prohibition years. Nonetheless, the alcohol ban stayed in force until 1933, when the 18th Amendment was repealed by popular acclaim. The experience was so repellent that even today, when drug legalization is considered a legitimate topic of debate, most American reformers are unwilling to argue the case for neo-prohibitionism. (America's ambivalence over alcohol is still evident in some states, where "dry" counties have made the sale of liquor illegal from time to time.)

As the temperance crusaders faded away, politicians and the public turned their attention back to heroin addiction, as the opiates became the official villains again. However, one practice that remained quietly popular with an older generation of physicians well into the 1940s was the conversion of alcoholics into morphine addicts. The advantages of alcohol-to-morphine conversion were spelled out by the Assistant Surgeon General of the U.S. Public Health Service: "...Drunkards are likely to be benefited in their social relations by becoming addicts. When they give up alcohol and start using opium, they are able to secure the effect for which they are striving without becoming drunk or violent." Perhaps so, but there were plenty of doctors who did not believe that addiction of any kind fell within the scope of medical practice in the first place. Subsequent laws tightened up the strictures of the Harrison Act. Mandatory life sentences were imposed in several states for simple possession of heroin. The first addict sentenced to life imprisonment under the new laws was a twenty-one year-old Mexican-American epileptic with an I.Q. of 69, who sold a small amount of heroin to a seventeen year-old informer for the FBI. (In 1962, the U.S. Supreme Court ruled that imprisonment for the crime of simply *being* an addict, in cases where the arrest involved no possession of narcotics, was cruel and unusual punishment in violation of the Bill of Rights.)

The Prohibition Years also sparked a rise in marijuana use and marijuana black marketeering. To checkmate the migration toward that drug, Congress passed the Marihuana Tax Act of 1937, modeled closely after the Harrison Act. The American Medical Association opposed this law, as it had opposed the Harrison Act, but to no avail. The assault on marijuana was led by Harry J. Anslinger, the indefatigable U.S. Commissioner of Narcotics who served a Hoover-like stretch from 1930 to 1962. At one point, Anslinger announced that marijuana was being taken by professional musicians. "And I'm not speaking about good musicians," he clarified, "but the jazz type." Due in no small part to Anslinger's tireless public crusade against "reefer madness," additional state and federal legislation made marijuana penalties as severe as heroin penalties. The most famous early victim of Anslinger's efforts was screen actor (and reputed jazz fan) Robert Mitchum, who was busted in 1948 and briefly imprisoned on marijuana charges.

American cannabis hysteria was in marked contrast to marijuana attitudes in other parts of the world. A British customs agent, attempting to catch the flavor of cannabis use in India during the early 1900s, explained that, for Muslims, marijuana is "the spirit of the great prophet Khizr or Elijah." Islamic poets, the customs officer writes, honor marijuana with the title of *Warak al Khiyall*, or Fancy's Leaf, "from its quickening the imagination." Some historians claim to have traced the medicinal use of marijuana back at least as far as the 1st or 2nd Century C.E., when the Chinese physician Hua T'o allegedly used a boiled hemp decoction to anesthetize patients during abdominal surgery.

One highly addictive drug that did not immediately fall under the proscriptions of the Harrison Act was a cocaine-like stimulant called amphetamine. Originally intended as a prescription drug for upper respiratory ailments and the treatment of narcolepsy (sleeping sickness), the drug was first synthesized in 1887 by a German pharmacologist. It was a British chemist named Gordon Alles, however, who showed everyone just what amphetamine could really do. There was no direct analog in the plant kingdom for this one. Alles, who also worked at UCLA and Caltech, documented the remarkable stimulatory effect of "speed" on the human nervous system—research that led directly to the commercial introduction of amphetamines in the late 1930s under the trade name Benzedrine. Once it became widely available over the counter in the form of Benzedrine inhalers for asthma and allergies, it quickly became one of the nation's most commonly abused drugs, and remained so throughout the late 1950s and 1960s.

For people suffering from depression, an oral dose of amphetamine lifted their mood even better than cocaine had lifted the morose spirits of Sigmund Freud. During World War II, American, British, Japanese and German military commanders frequently ordered the use of Benzedrine and the newer Dexedrine for "non-medicinal" purposes by their respective soldiers. The effects lasted eight hours or more, and the drug proved especially useful for long-distance aerial bomber crews and fighter pilots.

In the end, users paid dearly for the energy surge provided by speed. Anxiety, confusion, inability to concentrate, prolonged exhaustion, and severe depression were all common symptoms of amphetamine withdrawal. Chronic use resulted in paranoia, delusion, and psychosis. In Japan, the practice of providing government amphetamine to civilian factory workers during World War II led to serious social disruptions by war's end. By some estimates, 2 per cent of Japanese adults were addicted to amphetamine.

A number of world leaders during the war years resorted to addictive drugs. The most notorious case was Adolph Hitler, whose personal physician supplied him with more than seventy medications, ranging from powerful painkillers like Percodan, to hormones from the testes of young bulls. Along the way, Hitler took various barbiturates, amphetamines, and, starting in 1944, daily cocaine treatments for chronic sinusitis. From the point of view of drug use, Hitler was the Elvis Presley of his day. Mercifully, Winston Churchill's drug use did not become problematic until after the war, when his erratic behavior and impaired decision-making as prime minister in the 1950s were effectively hidden from public view. Churchill's drug of choice was cognac, but he became increasingly dependent on "reds," or Seconal, a powerful and addictive barbiturate. Anthony Eden, Churchill's successor, was heavily addicted to amphetamines, a fact that may have played a role in the disastrous Suez Crisis, according to biographer William Manchester.

Postwar Chemistry

Overseas, the results of Prohibition and the Harrison Act had been watched closely for decades by British politicians and health officials, who were appalled by what seemed to be the result: The creation of an unprecedented American black market for heroin, alcohol, and other addictive drugs. An advisory group to the British government, the Rolleston Committee, recommended that heroin addiction be treated as an "illness" for which physicians would be allowed to prescribe opiates. Periodic pleas for similar treatment were put forth by the American Medical Association and the American Bar Association, only to be squelched by the FBI and other federal law enforcement agencies. The American emphasis was on law enforcement, but no matter how stern the strictures of the Harrison Act, there was still an intractable subgroup of opiate addicts who simply would not, or could not, give it up—a group of users who would go to great lengths, involving much time and danger and expense, to procure a continuing supply of it. They would lie, cheat, and steal, even though they were not by nature chronic liars, cheaters, or thieves.

By the 1950s, doctors at a federal treatment center in Lexington, Kentucky, recognized that "pathological addicts," unlike casual users, never wholly seemed to lose their craving for the drug, no matter how long they went without it. Like furnaces with the pilot light burning steadily, chronic addicts were ready to ignite at a moment's notice. Doctors in these institutions also got a close look at the phenomenon of opiate withdrawal. Physical dependence was graphically associated with alcohol withdrawal as well. Nonetheless, alcoholism and drug addiction continued to be treated as two separate afflictions. Alcohol had clearly emerged by this time as America's most popular legal vice, and a certain logic seemed to prevail. Alcoholics had a "problem," but junkies were criminals of the lowest sort.

The prevailing psychological paradigms of the day did not exactly encourage scientists and physicians to look for biological parallels. Alcohol, according to one Freudian textbook used in the 1960s, "produces pleasure, elation and a retreat to the original infantile state. The rejecting mother is often relinquished as a potential provider and the father is turned to as a substitute, in a passive, longing, more or less homosexual way." This classical view of alcohol abuse as a psychological problem, a working-through-Freudian-difficulties kind of illness, was by no means unanimous. Dr. Robert J. Campbell of Fordham University, who believed that alcoholics, as a group, exhibited symptoms more in line with classic physical brain disorders, wrote in 1962: "Results obtained with reconstructive types of psychotherapy have been disappointing and are inconsistent with the view that this is a wholly psychogenic disorder."

The problem was that addiction didn't really fit very well into the schema of symptoms for classic mental illnesses. Other than obsession and compulsion, drug craving didn't match up very vigorously with known mental disorders at all—unless you simply classified alcoholism and drug addiction as two separate but strictly mental illnesses, as the former Soviet Union chose to do.

In the 1960s, marijuana emerged from the alleys and swing clubs to become America's "second most popular drug." Amphetamine and methamphetamine, previously the sole concern of fighter pilots, truckers, bikers, and assorted bohemians, became available to ordinary housewives as prescription diet pills. German scientists managed to spin off a psychoactive cousin of amphetamine, called MDMA, which started out life as an appetite suppressant, and which enjoyed some 1960s popularity as the "love drug." MDMA surfaced 30 years later as the "empathy drug" known as Ecstasy, or X.

PCP was an early example of a designer drug gone bad; a legal anesthetic from the 1950s that proved so notoriously unreliable, with so many patients coming out of anesthesia disoriented and hallucinatory, that it eventually found a niche primarily as a hog tranquilizer in veterinary medicine. Rediscovered by hippies and hoodlums in the 1970s, "Angel Dust" enjoyed early notoriety for its hallucinations and body-slam physicality. The dose had to be just right, however, because an overdose of PCP brought on symptoms of acute schizophrenia, coma, and death. There were also vague rumors about ketamine, or Vitamin K, a dissociative anesthetic which, like PCP, was formerly of interest only to equine veterinarians,

LSD and addictive tranquilizers like Valium were suddenly available to ordinary citizens in mass quantities. Cocaine made a reappearance, while cigarettes and coffee remained as popular as ever. Even President John F. Kennedy, so the rumors went, received occasional injections of amphetamine from Max Jacobson, the notorious "Dr. Feel-Good" who supplied speed to an endless procession of celebrities in the 1960s. Very few of these drugs were unanimously considered addictive. The greatest fear was that the use of drugs like LSD and marijuana would lead, inevitably, to heroin addiction. Drug experts generally conceded that marijuana, cocaine, Valium, coffee and tobacco could be "psychologically habit-forming," but not truly addicting.

Even at the height of the "Drug Culture," the cocktail party remained the most popular form of mass drug high in America. What seemed so puzzling to so many adults was that the kids were adamantly rejecting their parents' time-honored stimulant in favor of a long list of scary, exotic, and illegal substitutes. One useful fact that came to greater public awareness during the battle of the generations was the reality that alcoholism could strike at any age, and often where it was least expected. This was the shocking aspect of Blake Edwards' film, "The Days of Wine and Roses," which featured the first objective cinematic depiction of the organization known as Alcoholics Anonymous.

One of the oldest and allegedly one of the most successful approaches to alcoholism, Alcoholics Anonymous was also the most curious and controversial. Based on a mixture of unproven medical theory and quasi-religious nostrums, the movement arose in 1935 when an Ohio alcoholic named Bill Wilson teamed up with a physician, Robert Smith, to form the amateur self-help program better known as A.A. Using a Twelve Step program of mental, physical, and spiritual recovery, A.A. was a loose association of peers seeking to combat what its two founders referred to as "an allergy of the body and an obsession of the mind."

At first glance, A.A. did seem like something of a throwback to the early days of the temperance movement, when only God his mighty Self could rescue the wretched sinner from the clutches of Demon Rum. But Alcoholics Anonymous was not a disguised religious cult, or a last-chance haven for terminal street winos. It was not Norman Vincent Peale or Dale Carnegie, either. Bill Wilson was a sharp thinker who corresponded with C.G. Jung, studied philosopher William James' *Varieties of Religious Experience*, and openly despaired over psychiatry's inability to do anything useful for alcoholics.

By floating the notion that hardcore alcoholics were "allergic" to alcohol, Wilson wasn't trying to say that they could deny responsibility this way. To Wilson, alcoholics were not so much morally bankrupt as they were metabolically compromised. The allergy metaphor wasn't perfect, but it was basically the first medical model of addiction to gain any kind of serious foothold in America. By insisting that alcohol affected certain people, and certain people only, in addictive ways, the founders of Alcoholics Anonymous were among the pioneers of biological psychiatry.

A.A. wasn't really a medical treatment, and it wasn't a formal psychiatric program, either. It predated the 1960s mania for encounter groups by decades. A.A. took no official position whatsoever about the ultimate causes of alcoholism, let alone the political issues of the day. You could show up at an Alcoholics Anonymous meeting convinced it was a disease, or convinced that the devil made you do it. A.A. didn't care.

One of the most courageous proponents of Alcoholics Anonymous in the 1960s was Iowa Governor Harold Hughes, who started out life as an alcoholic truck driver and all-around badass who could rival Johnny Cash for meanness and rugged good looks. One day, the drunken future governor climbed into a bathtub with a loaded shotgun, and prepared to end it all—only to experience a religious epiphany that was to last him the rest of his life.

In a successful 1964 bid for re-election, Governor Hughes was accused by his opponent of having had relapses. Hughes said: "I am an alcoholic and will be until the day I die... But with God's help I'll never touch a drop of alcohol again. Now, can we talk about the issues of this campaign?" Harold Hughes came clean in public about his alcoholism at a time when such supposedly career-ending admissions were simply never made. He later served as an Iowa Senator, and became a candidate for President of the United States. The Comprehensive Alcohol Abuse Act of 1970, better known as the Hughes Act, ushered in the National Institute on Alcohol Abuse and Alcoholism (NIAAA), and made grants available to the states for community-based treatment programs. The legislation also provided incentives for hospitals to admit alcoholics, and came down strongly in favor of the confidentiality of patient records. Senator Hughes was concerned about drug addiction as well, fretting that "treatment is virtually nonexistent because addiction is not recognized as an illness." Four years later, legislation was passed creating the National Institute on Drug Abuse (NIDA), which continues to conduct useful research to this day.

The starting date for modern brain science is usually pegged to the discovery of the anti-psychotic effects of chlorpromazine, approved for use in 1954 under the trade name Thorazine. Despite this, a strong case can be made that the discovery of lysergic acid, or LSD-25, by the Swiss chemist Albert Hoffmann in 1947 might be the most telling milepost of all. At the Sandoz Laboratories of Switzerland, Hoffman was the first person to successfully synthesize the particular molecule known as LSD-25, while searching for a new drug to use against migraine headaches. Dr. Hoffman first tested the drug on himself, by accident, after a small amount of water-soluble LSD came into contact with his skin. Albert Hoffman took the world's first LSD trip while riding his bicycle through the streets of Basle one afternoon in 1943.

If ever there was a substance that demonstrated the power of brain chemistry, LSD was it. LSD was in fact the most powerful drug ever discovered; a thousand times more potent than drugs like Thorazine and the tranquilizing drugs. It was vastly more potent than the classical hallucination-inducing drug families: the phenethylamines like mescaline, the indole alkaloids like psilocybin and DMT, the dissociative anesthetics like ketamine, and the amphetamine derivatives like MDMA (Ecstasy). LSD either bedazzled researchers, or scared the living bejesus out of them. It was either the Devil's Brew or the Second Coming.

As Stanislov Grof, one of the early LSD investigators, has written:

> For neuropharmacologists and neurophysiologists, the discovery of LSD meant the beginning of a golden era of research that could solve many puzzles concerning the intricate biochemical interactions underlying the functioning of the brain.... as well as extending the range of applicability of psychotherapy to categories of patients that previously had been difficult to reach such as alcoholics, narcotic drug addicts, and criminal recidivists...The spiritual experiences frequently observed in LSD sessions offered a radically new understanding of a wide variety of phenomena from the world of religion...

Psychedelic drugs such as LSD had been in use for centuries, extracted from the plant cornucopia through painstaking trail-and-error, and incorporated into religious and mystical traditions. A non-threatening combination of "set and setting" was considered immensely important to the success of the experience with these psychedelics, now sometimes referred to as "entheogens," a Greek coinage meaning "to realize the divine within." For all its microdose power, its reputation for producing intense polychromatic imagery, LSD proved remarkably safe in early clinical trials. The altered sensorium typical of LSD could be intense, overwhelming, and frightening—colors and geometry and music shifted and blended; walls and rugs melted and fractured into a thousand kaleidoscopic rearrangements. When the user waved a hand, the hand "traced" it's way across the field of vision, much like the stroboscopic photography of Harold "Doc" Edgerton. Beyond these alterations of form and perception, a bit deeper into the works, one's sense of self became more mutable as well. Sometimes, if conditions were right, users would experience empathetic perceptions of a seemingly deeper, truer, more resonant self or essence.

Alternately, nothing very interesting at all would happen for long periods. Bad trips were usually the result of an overdose, or a surprise dose without prior consent, and were generally amenable to the soothing ministrations of a "guide," or, failing that, an injection of Thorazine.

Generally safe and non-lethal did not mean trivial, however. It is safe to say that a trip on a powerful psychoactive drug like LSD (or its chemical cousin, Ecstasy) is not to everyone's taste, and cannot be recommended, like aspirin, as some sort of general panacea. LSD was nothing like an alcohol or marijuana high. It was far more "mind-altering" than any other drug.

The most powerful drug ever discovered was not likely to remain a secret for long. The CIA, not surprisingly, had shown considerable interest in the new mind-altering drugs. Quite a few people already knew about LSD-25. For years, a small coterie of accomplished men and women met quietly in Los Angeles for long, talk-fueled LSD sessions. Participants included Aldous Huxley, Gerald Heard, Alan Watts, Sidney Cohen, Oscar Janiger, Anais Nin, and many others. These get-togethers seem to be the first example of LSD escaping the lab and being used in casual social circumstances, as Martin Lee and Bruce Shlain point out in their book, *Acid Dreams*.

Psychologist Timothy Leary of Harvard certainly knew about it. The scientists, therapists, and artists who experimented with LSD therapy in the late 1950s were not prepared for the likes of Leary, novelist Ken Kesey, poet Allen Ginsberg, and the assorted freaks, pranksters, con artists and runaways of the Woodstock Generation. Ken Kesey, in particular, delighted in stinging the Feds by insisting that it was Uncle Sam who first got him high, paying Kesey and others to take LSD, guinea pig-style, in certain government-funded research programs in Palo Alto and at Stanford University in the early 1960s.

It made a great story, and it happened to be true. However, the original chapter of the acid story began ten years earlier, when a former intelligence agent, rogue businessman, and general intellectual gadfly named Al Hubbard took his first LSD trip. Captain Alfred M. Hubbard, who has been dubbed the "Original Capt. Trips," was part of a select cadre of World War II veterans who had been involved in creating intelligence institutions like the Office of Strategic Services and the CIA, and who had immersed themselves in cryptology and truth serums and interrogation drugs in the service of the war effort. (Thomas Pynchon caricatured some of this work in his novel, *Gravity's Rainbow.*) Hubbard broke ranks with the intelligence community early on, but continued to share his clandestine stash of LSD with certain friends and acquaintances. This odd and extraordinary businessman is said to have arranged private LSD sessions in the late 1950s for scientists, captains of industry, members of the British parliament, UN representatives, prime ministers, and various artists. For a time, Al Hubbard settled in Vancouver, where he became Canada's only legally licensed, FDA-approved importer of Sandoz LSD. In certain North American research circles, Al became a very popular man

Hubbard is credited by various parties with being the man who put together the basics of the North American psychedelic therapy sessions and hippie acid tests to come—high doses of LSD, amplified music, strobe lights, and experiments with ESP. Along with Huxley, Hubbard came to believe that the more mystical or "transpersonal" experiences LSD sometimes afforded might hold considerable psychotherapeutic potential. With LSD provided by Hubbard, Canadians Abram Hoffer, Ross Mclean, and Humphrey Osmond pursued the idea of LSD as a treatment for alcoholism. In the U.S, research on LSD and alcoholism was undertaken by Oscar Janiger, Sanford Unger, and others on the West Coast.

Throughout this period, there were LSD clinics operating in England and Europe. European LSD therapists tended to use very low doses as an adjunct to traditional psychoanalytic techniques. But North American researchers took a different, bolder approach. When "psychedelic" therapy began to catch on in Canada and the United States, therapists typically gave patients only one or two sessions at very high doses. These early efforts were aimed at producing spontaneous breakthroughs or recoveries in alcoholics through some manner of religious epiphany or inner conversion experience. The only other quasi-medical approach of the day, the Schick Treatment Center's brand of "aversion therapy," was not seen to produce very compelling long-term recovery rates, and subsequently fell out of favor. In this light, the early successes with LSD therapy, sometimes claimed to be in the 50-75 per cent range, looked noteworthy indeed. However, the design and criteria of the LSD/alcoholism studies varied so widely that it has never been possible to draw definitive conclusions about the work that was done, except to say that LSD therapy seemed to be strikingly effective for certain alcoholics. Some patients were claiming that two or three trips on LSD were worth years of conventional psychotherapy—a claim not heard again until the advent of Prozac thirty years later.

"I've taken lysergic acid several times, and have collected considerable information about it," Bill Wilson, the co-founder of Alcoholics Anonymous, disclosed in a private letter written in 1958. "At the moment, it can only be used for research purposes. It would certainly be a huge misfortune if it ever got loose in the general public without a careful preparation as to what the drug is and what the meaning of its effects may be." Like many others, Wilson was excited by LSD's potential as a treatment for chronic alcoholism. Even Hollywood was hip to the new therapy. Cary Grant, among others, took LSD under psychiatric supervision and pronounced it immensely helpful as a tool for psychological insight. Andre Previn, Jack Nicholson, and James Coburn agreed. (It could be argued that the human potential movement began here).

No drug this powerful and strange, if American history was any guide, could remain legal for long. Unlike their colleagues in the intelligence agencies, politicians and law enforcement officers didn't know about Mongolian shamans and their fly agaric mushrooms; about European witches and their use of psychoactive plant drugs like nightshade and henbane; about Persian sheiks with their cannabis water pipes; Latin American brujos with their magic vines.

But for the CIA, the big fish was always LSD.

What interested the Central Intelligence Agency about LSD was its apparent ability to produce the symptoms of acute psychosis. Operation ARTICHOKE was designed to ferret out LSD's usefulness as an instrument of psychological torture, and as a possible means of destabilizing enemy forces by means of aerosol sprays or contaminated water supplies. (The drug's overwhelming potency made such parts-per-billion fantasies a possibility.)

The agency knew where to turn for a secure American source of supply. Eli Lilly and Co., the giant drug manufacturer, was already involved in LSD research on behalf of the U.S. government. The trouble was that LSD was expensive, and all roads led to Sandoz Laboratories in Switzerland. Organic LSD had to be painstakingly extracted from ergot, a fungus that grows in kernels of rye. Eventually, Sandoz and Eli Lilly successfully synthesized LSD in their own laboratories. With the advent of a reliable domestic supplier of synthetic LSD, the CIA under Allen Dulles was assured of a steady source for experimental purposes.

When LSD did not pan out as a reliable agent of interrogation, CIA investigators turned their attention to its purported ability to mimic acute psychosis—its "psychomimetic" aspect— which researchers were praising as a new avenue toward a biological understanding of schizophrenia. The CIA funneled grant money for LSD research into the academic and commercial R&D world through a host of conduits. Various experiments with non-consenting subjects—typically military or prison personnel—showed that LSD could sometimes break down established patterns of thought, creating a "twilight zone" during which the mind was more susceptible to various forms of psychological coercion and control. Perhaps, under the influence of LSD, prisoners could be transformed into counter-espionage agents. It also occurred to the CIA that the same drug could be used on their own agents for the same purposes. Numerous CIA agents took LSD trips in order to familiarize them with acid's Alice-in-Wonderland terrain. Some of these unusual experiments were captured on film for use in military training videos.

One place where ARTICHOKE research took place was the Addiction Research Centre at the Public Health Service Hospital in Lexington, Kentucky—the same hospital that specialized in the treatment of hardcore heroin addicts. Lexington was part hospital and part penitentiary, which made it perfect for human experimentation. The addict/inmates of Lexington were sometimes given LSD without their consent, a practice also conducted at the federal prison in Atlanta, and at the Bordentown Reformatory in New Jersey.

In 1953, then-CIA director Allen Dulles authorized Operation MK-ULTRA, which superseded earlier clandestine drug investigations. Under the direction of Dr. Sidney Gottlieb, a chemist, the government began slipping LSD and other psychoactive drugs to unwitting military personnel. During a work retreat in Maryland that year, technicians from both the Army and the CIA were dosed without their knowledge, and were later told that they had ingested a mind-altering drug. Dr. Frank Olson, a civilian biochemist involved in research on biological warfare, wandered away from the gathering in a confused state, and committed suicide a few days later by leaping to his death from an upper floor of the Statler Hilton in New York City. The truth about Olson's death was kept secret from his family, and from the rest of the nation, for more than twenty years. In 1966, LSD was added to the federal schedule of controlled substances, in the same category as heroin and amphetamine. Simple possession became a felony. The Feds had turned off the spigot, and the research came to a halt. Federal drug enforcement agents began showing up at the homes and offices of well-known West Coast therapists, demanding the surrender of all stockpiles of LSD-25. The original acid elite was being hounded, harassed, and threatened in a rancid atmosphere of pharmaceutical McCarthyism. Aldous Huxley, Humphrey Osmond, even father figure Albert Hoffmann, all viewed these American developments with dismay. The carefully refined parameters and preparations, the attention to set and setting, the concerns over dosage, had gone out the window, replaced by a massive, uncontrolled experiment in the streets. Small wonder, then, that the circus atmosphere of the Haight-Ashbury "Summer of Love" in 1967 seemed so badly timed. Countercultural figures were extolling the virtues of LSD for the masses—not just for research, not just for therapy, not as part of some ancient religious ritual—but also just for the free-wheeling American hell of it. What could be more democratic than the act of liberating the most powerful mind-altering drug known to man?

It is at least conceivable that researchers and clinicians eventually would have backed away from LSD anyway, on the grounds that the drug's effects were simply too weird and unpredictable to conform to the rigorous dictates of clinical studies. Nonetheless, researchers had been given a glimpse down a long, strange tunnel, before federal authorities put an end to the research.

LSD and Serotonin

What did LSD do to the brain, exactly, in order to set off the fireworks that so fascinated brain scientists, hippies, and government spies? And why, after years of massive, unauthorized field-testing, so to speak, was there so little evidence implicating LSD as an addictive drug? Powerful as it was, LSD did not show any of the classic attributes of addiction, such as withdrawal or craving, although it was possible to build up a tolerance to its effects with repeated dosings.

A novel brain chemical, discovered less than a year after LSD, proved to be a crucial piece of the puzzle.

According to an early theory, the aberrant mental functioning produced by the tiniest dose of LSD was due to interference with normal levels of serotonin in the brain. In 1954, chemists D.W. Woolley and E. Shaw had published an article in *Science* strongly arguing that serotonin was the likely biochemical basis for major mental disorders. Wooley and Shaw confirmed that the most acutely serotonin-active substance known to man was the ergot derivative known as LSD. LSD's chemical architecture looked eerily similar to serotonin's.

While the idea of LSD as a "model" of psychosis did not hold up, the link between serotonin and mental disorders was there all along. The strongly serotonin-mediated mental disorders, researchers ultimately discovered, were depression, drug addiction, and alcoholism. LSD was not the only drug in town—underground chemists were dabbling with psychoactive compounds found outside the tryptamine family, the chemical group that included LSD, DMT, and psilocybin. There was a very strange "indole alkaloid" group that included harmaline, a substance found in a plant called Syrian Rue. There was a similar substance called ibogaine, extracted from an African shrub. In 1957, two scientists in the research department of CIBA Pharmaceutical Products in New Jersey, reported on "an indole alkaloid with central-stimulant properties" used by native peoples in the Congo: "The crude extracts of Tabernanthe iboga caused a feeling of excitement, drunkenness, mental confusion, and, possibly, hallucinations." The CIBA researchers were working from early reports by French and Belgian explorers in the 1800s, which had noted the use of this remarkable shrub in the Congo and surrounding regions. A few researchers had begun to wonder whether harmaline and ibogaine might not harbor LSD-like properties that could be used in psychiatry and the treatment of addiction.

In the 1970s, addiction research was stuck in an impossible situation. The best tools for studying the workings of the human brain were the very drugs now completely prohibited under state and federal law: heroin, cocaine, PCP, LSD, marijuana. President Richard Nixon inaugurated the 1970s with a new war on drugs, the Comprehensive Drug Abuse Prevention and Control Act. This omnibus bill replaced all previous federal drug statutes and classified illegal drugs according to five different "controlled substance" schedules. Heroin, marijuana and LSD were lumped together as Schedule I drugs, the most prohibitive category of all. Nixon and his successor, President Ford, added a new wrinkle by bringing a multiplicity of new agencies into the fray—the U.S. Customs Service, the Immigration and Naturalization Service, the Internal Revenue Service, the U.S. Coast Guard, the Federal Aviation Administration, and the Bureau of Alcohol, Tobacco and Firearms. Predictably, widespread heroin busts simply forced prices up, causing more street crime by low-income addicts.

In the 1980s, during the Reagan-Bush years, Americans were confronted—quite suddenly, it seemed—with yet another drug "epidemic." The resulting media fixation provides a fascinating example of what Dr. Janice Keller Phelps has referred to as "drug education abuse." This new drug war took off in earnest under the direction of President Ronald Reagan, after Congress and the media discovered that an inexpensive, smokable form of cocaine was appearing in prodigious quantities in some of America's larger cities. Crack was a refinement to freebasing, which was, in turn, a much more expensive form of coke smoke that blew up, quite literally, in comedian Richard Pryor's face years ago. Crack was a drug dealer's dream. The "rush" from smoking crack was more potent, but even more transient, than the short-lived high from nasal ingestion

Coupled with this development were the cocaine-related deaths of two well-known athletes, college basketball star Len Bias and defensive back Don Rogers of the Cleveland Browns. Bias played for Maryland, a home team in Washington, D.C. Then-president Reagan, an ardent sports fan, went on television to publicly pledge almost a billion dollars for drug interdiction along the Southwest border. The President also ordered urine testing for all government employees in "sensitive" positions.

Six months earlier, Reagan had signed a directive bringing the military into the drug wars for the first time. The initial test of the directive was Operation Blast Furnace, a no-holds-barred attack on cocaine laboratories in the jungles of Bolivia, using 160 U.S. troops and six Black Hawk helicopters. The foray resulted in exactly one arrest. Everyone else had been tipped off. Even as a photo opportunity, the project turned out to be a complete disaster. President Reagan went on to endorse mandatory sentences for simple possession. The idea of "zero tolerance" has been widely endorsed by every administration since.

The death of Len Bias elevated the current cocaine paranoia to the realm of the mythic. Cocaine became America's first living-room drug, courtesy of the nightly news. The summer of 1986 will be remembered as the season of the "crack plague," as viewers were bombarded with long news stories and specials. NBC Nightly News offered a special report on crack, during which a correspondent told viewers: "Crack has become America's drug of choice... it's flooding America...."

The hyperkinetic level of television coverage ultimately led *TV Guide Magazine* to commission a report from the News Study Group, headed by Edwin Diamond at New York University. The investigators quickly demolished the notion that cocaine had become America's "drug of choice," and were at a loss to account for where the networks had come up with it: "Statistically, alcohol and tobacco are the legal 'drugs of choice': 53 million people smoke cigarettes; 17.6 million are dependent on alcohol or abuse it. Marijuana still ranks as the No. 1 illegal drug. According to NIDA, 61.9 million people in the United States have experimented with marijuana." The study group went on to note that the often-deadly "Black Tar" heroin had hit the streets of American cities the same summer. "Why was crack a big story [that summer] while Black Tar was not? One reason [is that] crack is depicted as moving into 'our'—that is, the comfortable TV viewers'—neighborhood."

For the past hundred years or so, America has *always* been por-trayed as being on the verge of, or in the throes of, one drug epi-demic or another. Throughout the 1990s, America began a rerun of the amphetamine problem, including a new and dangerous twist. As nasally ingested cocaine became smokable crack, so the oral ad-ministration of amphetamine in pill form evolved into a smokable variant sometimes known as "ice" or "glass." In the terminology used by behavioral psychologists, crack and ice are highly rewarding and reinforcing. When the crack epidemic first became news, it was clear that the old specialty of free-basing was now within reach of existing cocaine users. No paraphernalia needed except for a small pipe; no more butane and mixing; no muss, no fuss. As Dr. David Smith of the Haight Ashbury Free Clinic in San Francisco has pointed out, rampant amphetamine abuse was a major contributor to the downfall of the Haight Ashbury counterculture in 1960s San Francisco. Present-day rampant production of "biker speed" has inspired a heightened level of law enforcement in the West and Midwest not seen since the days of Bonnie and Clyde.

After having spent more than $100 billion dollars over the preceding ten years, the Reagan-Bush drug war had almost no last-ing successes to report. Interdiction at the border was a joke, co-caine and heroin were cheaper than ever, and the majority of violent crimes were still being committed by people addicted to alcohol, cocaine, and other drugs. Treatment for drug and alcohol addiction in prison was still an afterthought. After the "just say no" years of the Reagan administration, and the "lock 'em up," policy thrust of the senior Bush years, many policy reform advocates were buoyed by Bill Clinton's election and his ardent backing of treatment on demand (which never came to fruition).

A decade down the road, not much has changed politically. Treatment still doesn't work, and addiction is as firmly criminal-ized as ever. Statistical blips on the graph are treated like major news stories, as when teenage girls took up smoking in large num-bers (early 1990s), only to be followed by a cohort that reversed the trend (late 1990s). Meanwhile, studies casting doubt on the effectiveness of America's favorite drug programs, like DARE and the Alliance for a Drug-Free America, are buried or ignored.

The Fourth Drive

The lesson learned from previous attempts to extinguish drug use is reasonably clear: Drug wars never succeed. Even when drug wars seem to be working, and demand goes down, lowered usage of a particular drug often disguises the fact that a new drug has replaced it. Demand for drugs is like a balloon—squeeze it in one place, and it bulges out somewhere else. As Dr. Ronald Siegel argues in his book, *Intoxication*:

> The major primary drives, those associated with survival needs and part of the organism's innate equipment, include the drives of hunger, thirst, and sex.... Unlike other acquired motives, intoxication functions with the strength of a primary drive in its ability to steer the behavior of individuals, societies, and species. Like sex, hunger, and thirst, the fourth drive, to pursue intoxication, can never be repressed. It is biologically inevitable.... There is a pattern of drug-seeking and drug-taking behavior that is consistent across time and species.

Siegel uses the idea of the "fourth drive" to describe drug intoxication as a whole. For most people, however, the drive to use mind-altering drugs is simply not that powerful. Only in the case of addiction does the urge to use drugs become strong enough to be considered an artificial primary drive. Incredibly enough, the specific changes in brain chemistry that lay behind the behavioral manifestations of reinforcement and reward—the active engine of drug addiction—have been mapped out in essential outline over the past two decades. Drug wars come, and drug wars go, but the essential question never changes: Who gets addicted, and why?

The breakthrough that laid the groundwork for the first truly scientific understanding of addictive drugs took place in 1972, when researchers discovered the existence of specific receptor sites in the brain for the opium molecule. Scientists had long suspected that a substance as powerful as opium could only accomplish its dramatic effects through some highly specific mechanism of action in the brain. A dart laced with etorphine, a lab-enhanced form of opium, can knock a charging elephant to the ground in seconds. Any drug with that kind of immediate physical power, the thinking went, had to work by somehow binding directly to the membranes of specific nerve cells. Thirty years later, the implications of this new way of thinking are still rippling through biology and neurology, creating entirely new disciplines, like neuropsychopharmacology—the study of the molecular mechanisms of action that allow some drugs to have such powerful effects on the mind.

At roughly the same time, emergency room doctors were baffled to discover that timely injections of a drug called naloxone *completely reversed* the effects of heroin intoxication. Minutes after an injection of naloxone, heroin addicts were awake, fully recovered, and instantly into the rigors of heroin withdrawal. Naloxone, and a similar drug called naltrexone, rescued O.D. victims from respiratory failure. Like a magic bullet, naloxone—trade name Narcan—blocked the effects of heroin. The existence of a compound capable of blocking the effects of one of the strongest drugs known to man led Dr. Avram Goldstein of Stanford University to formally propose that the brain contained specific receptor sites for the opium molecule.

At Johns Hopkins University School of Medicine in Baltimore, Dr. Solomon Snyder and a young doctoral candidate named Candace Pert devised a method for testing this theory. By making molecules of naloxone radioactive, and following the course of the molecules with the aid of a radiation counter, Snyder and Pert were able to show that naloxone attached itself very specifically to certain neurons in certain parts of the brain. If naloxone molecules were capable of locking into specific sites, then presumably these were the same sites in the brain where the opiates did their work. Further experimentation proved that this was definitely the case. Naloxone was a heroin *antagonist*—it blocked the effect of the drug at specific sites on nerve cells in the brain. (If the drug fits the receptor and elicits a response, it is called an agonist. If it simply blocks the receptor site without stimulating a response, it is an antagonist.)

The Snyder-Pert experiment was the first solid proof that receptors for certain brain chemicals existed, and it provided the first evidence for the "lock-and-key" mechanism by which they work. It was one of the 20th Century's most revolutionary scientific discoveries, and like most such discoveries, it was not easy to understand. It was as if people were born with specific receptor sites in the brain for opium. What sense did that make? Animals had these sites, too. Why would there be specific regions in the mammalian brain primed to be activated specifically by the distilled essence of the poppy plant?

The only explanation that seemed plausible was that substances like heroin and naloxone were artificially stimulating neuronal receptors designed for some other internal chemical altogether. Scientists concluded that what they had discovered was an accident of nature, and that there had to be a natural chemical compound, manufactured in the body, which attached to those sites in the first place. Two scientists in Scotland, Dr. Hans Kosterlitz and Dr. John Hughes, proved this supposition correct. The brain manufactured its own natural painkillers, known collectively as endorphins. The purpose of these exceedingly strong chemical messengers was to block pain in times of stress. They also helped generate feelings of well being at other times. Endorphins were apparently the reason soldiers in the stress of battle could sometimes continue to fight after receiving terrible wounds that would have incapacitated them under normal circumstances.

The substances known as endorphins were deceptively simple compounds composed of amino acid chains. They were not chemically related to heroin, but they were the body's natural painkillers, an internal reserve supply of natural opiates. The only reason opium worked so dramatically to relieve pain was because a part of the opium molecule was *similar in shape* to the naturally occurring endorphins. Heroin "fooled" the receptors designed for the shape of an endorphin molecule. Not only that, but heroin and the other opiates stimulated these receptors just as effectively as the natural endorphins did.

The stunning power of the opiates had been revealed as an architectural quirk of nature.

The naloxone molecule bore an uncanny resemblance to the shape of natural endorphin molecules, and when doctors gave an O.D. victim a shot of naloxone, the naloxone molecules knocked the opium molecules right off their receptors. Then they bound themselves to the endorphin sites even more tightly than the heroin molecules did. Naloxone was capable of snapping onto the receptor sites without triggering the release of endorphin. Their shape was right for occupying, but not activating, the endorphin sites. Naloxone prevented any stray heroin molecules from getting a chance to activate the endorphin sites. As a heroin antagonist, naloxone dramatically reversed the effects of a heroin high, but didn't produce a high of its own.

The brain scans developed for studying this chemical activity were produced by introducing radioactive atoms into naloxone. Wherever naloxone stuck to a receptor site in the brain of a rat, the "hot" connection lit up on special film. These maps of receptor geography in the brain led Dr. Pert and her colleagues to christen the new science "receptorology." Likening these snapshots to "tiny sparkling grains in a sea of colorfully stained brain tissue," Pert was helping to invent a new field of study. It was similar in some ways to endocrinology (the study of ductless glands and their secretions). Biology, pharmacology, and brain studies were all highly compartmentalized disciplines in the 1970s, and break-throughs in one field often went unnoticed in the others. "Recep-torology" came to be known as neuroscience, or neuropharmacol-ogy, and operated under a deceptively simple premise: If it is a drug, and if it has an effect on the brain, then it must have a brain receptor site to which it binds. Find its site of action, and you find out what it is, what it does, and where it does it. For psycho-active drugs, this meant finding out chemically how they altered *consciousness*.

The neuroscientists kept refining the art, experimenting with radiosensitive film and other radiographic techniques for enhanc-ing the receptor maps of the brain. One of Pert's postdocs was assigned the task of locating a receptor for PCP, and found it in short order. They were living through heady times. Once the images moved from film to computer, color-coding became possible, and the receptor maps began to resemble heat sensitive photography. In her autobiography, *Molecules of Emotion*, Dr. Pert writes: "When I looked at the images, I thought they resembled colorful butterflies, and I couldn't resist making some of them into posters to grace the otherwise sterile hallway walls. I fantasized that we'd invented a new art form called 'photoneurorealism'...

By the early 1990s, the dirty little secret was a secret no longer: Most addiction treatment programs were failing. In the case of the newly arrived crack cocaine, relapse rates after formal treatment sometimes approached one hundred per cent. Clearly, a piece of the puzzle was missing. If receptors were the sites that controlled how drugs affected the mind, and if genes controlled how receptors were grown, then it made sense to examine the question of whether alcoholism and other addictions could be inherited.

One implication of the receptor theories was that sensitivity to addictive drugs could conceivably have a genetic basis. It was a large step in the right direction, because there were already good reasons for seeing alcoholism and other addictions as inherited dysfunc-tions in brain chemistry.

THREE: "SISS IM BLUT"

"It's in the blood."

—old Amish saying

It is no secret that alcoholism tends to run in families.

The behaviors known as pan-addiction and substitute addiction seemed to demonstrate that some addicts were vulnerable in an overall way to other addictive drugs as well. If it was one addiction at a time, that was known as substitute addiction. If it was many addictions simultaneously, researchers called it pan-addiction. The fact that a striking number of alcoholics also had cigarette addictions, and were heavy coffee drinkers, or had been addicted sequentially or simultaneously to various illegal addictive drugs—this was no great secret in the addiction therapy community.

Addicts showed a remarkable ability to shift addictions, or to multiply them. Many addicts seemed to be able to use whatever was readily at hand—alcoholics turning to cough syrup or doctor-prescribed morphine; pill poppers switching to alcohol; cocaine addicts turning to pot. If addiction was really, at bottom, a metabolic tendency rather than a sociological aberration, then it could conceivably express itself as a propensity to become seriously hooked on *any* drug that afforded enough pleasurable reinforcement to be considered addictive.

Treatment therapists have known for years that the children of alcoholics are far more likely to become abusive drinkers, compared with the children of non-alcoholic parents. This alone does not prove the case for a genetic link in alcoholic families, because other factors—environmental influences, learned behaviors, parental abuse—all might combine to explain why the siblings of alcoholics so frequently become alcoholics themselves. In hindsight, researchers might have been better off looking for genetic clues to heroin addiction, or cigarette smoking, rather than alcoholism. In some ways, it is unfortunate that the addictive drug involved in the detective hunt for genetic factors was alcohol—a drug whose effects in the brain and body are diffuse, and over which there is a great deal of traditional confusion about what actually constitutes addiction.

Nonetheless, it made sense to investigate the possibility of direct genetic influences on alcoholism. Biologists and neurochemists already had strong reasons for believing that a number of classic mental illnesses, particularly schizophrenia and depression, had firm physical *and* genetic underpinnings. Alcoholism and drug addiction, often considered strictly mental aberrations, might turn out to be similar cases.

Genetic researchers scored their most notable early success by proving the inheritability of Huntington's chorea, a rare disorder characterized by rapid, involuntary movements and dementia. Folk singer Woody Guthrie was one of its victims. Huntington's eventually drove its victims insane, but it was a form of insanity with a distinctly genetic origin. It was transmitted as an autosomal trait, meaning that if one parent died of the disease, a child of that parent had a fifty per cent chance of inheriting the dominant gene and dying from it as well. However, it was not until 1993 that a large group of scientists announced they had isolated the defective gene responsible for Huntington's, on the tip of chromosome 4. While the disease cannot presently be cured, it can now be identified. The best-known single-gene disorder, Cystic Fibrosis, took decades of research to pin down, and the finding has not yet yielded a cure, either.

Scientists also began speculating about a possible genetic basis for that most dramatic of all mental illnesses, schizophrenia. With its disassociations and delusions—hearing voices from Mars, posing as Napoleon—schizophrenia defines for most people the essence of what it is to be insane. The classical view was that something *happened* to people that made them schizophrenic. Something drove them mad. "Double binds," where parents tell their children that they love them while doing unlovable things to them, were once popular culprits. Radical British therapist R.D. Laing made a splash in the 1960s with his theory that schizophrenia was in essence a sane response to an insane world. Overlooked in all this was a steady and tantalizing accumulation of evidence that even schizophrenia had a genetic component.

In 1962, Dr. James Shields and Dr. Irving Gottesman began a study of psychiatric patients in a London Hospital, reasoning that a study of identical twins might shed light on the genetic theory of schizophrenia. From some 45,000 patient records, the researchers unearthed the fact that a clear majority of the identical twins of the hospitalized schizophrenics were schizophrenics themselves. Two years later, Dr. Seymour Kety of the National Institutes of Mental Health (NIMH) published the results of a seminal adoption study based on Danish health and population statistics, which concluded that the children of schizophrenics ran a markedly greater risk of becoming schizophrenics themselves, even when the children were raised out of the home.

This kind of research is always controversial. Eugenics, a pseudo-science that lay behind the appalling genetic experiments undertaken by the Nazis, had claimed in its day that such conditions as drunkenness and feeble-mindedness were simple Mendelian inheritance traits. The very idea of genetic explanations for mental illnesses brought to mind earlier calls for the sterilization of criminals and alcoholics. For most of its existence, the science of behavioral genetics has been associated with the dreams of Aryan purity, or else the cloned dystopia of *Brave New World*.

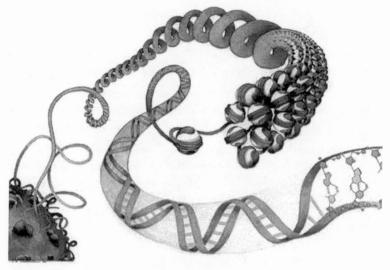

The Genetic Puzzle

Fathers and Sons

The hunt for genetic influences on alcoholism derives largely from the work of Dr. Donald W. Goodwin, chair of the Department of Psychiatry at the University of Kansas Medical Center. Starting in the early 1970s, Dr. Goodwin and co-workers, using computer technology and a detailed database of Scandinavian health records, scrutinized the results of 5,000 adoption cases in Copenhagen. The results of the initial study stunned alcoholism experts around the world. The sons of alcoholics were more likely to become alcoholics themselves, as many had expected. But the relationship held true even when the children of alcoholics were separated from their natural parents shortly after birth, and subsequently raised by foster parents.

As often happens, the studies were confined to males. In Phase 2 of the Danish studies, Goodwin selected only alcoholic families in which one son had been raised by his biological parents, while the other son had been adopted away early in life. Raised in separate environments, twins of this sort are highly prized for genetic research. Goodwin compared the sons who had been raised by their alcoholic birth parents to their adopted-away brothers. It didn't seem to make any difference: Rates of alcoholism were roughly the same. Environmental factors alone did not seem to account for it. "By their late twenties or earlier," Goodwin wrote, "the offspring of alcoholics had nearly twice the number of alcohol problems and four times the rate of alcoholism as the children whose parents had no record of hospitalization for alcoholism." The same relationship was unearthed in studies of schizophrenic twins: It did not look like family environment was the primary determinant.

Perhaps some of the children simply ended up with less effective foster parents, detractors pointed out. Alternatively, some unknown trauma might have been inflicted in the womb. Maybe the pregnant mother drank. Environmental factors can never be ruled out. Nonetheless, the basic implications of Goodwin's work could not be shaken off. The Danish adoption studies were the first major scientific papers to establish a firm link between heredity and alcoholism.

Beginning in the 1980s, Dr. C. Robert Cloninger, professor of psychiatry and genetics at Washington University in St. Louis, and Michael Bohman, a Swedish pediatrician, began a broader series of adoption studies. The Stockholm Adoption Study made Cloninger a heavyweight in the growing field of behavioral genetics. The Cloninger team studied the records of more than 3,000 adopted individuals, and the Stockholm Adoption Study confirmed the Danish studies: The children of alcoholics, when compared with the children of non-alcoholic parents, were far more likely to become alcoholics themselves—even if they were adopted away. Moreover, "Alcohol abuse in the adoptive parents was not associated with an increased risk of abuse in the children they reared," Cloninger later reported in the journal *Science*, "so there was no evidence that alcoholism is familial because children imitate their [non-biological] parents."

The alcoholics in the Cloninger-Bohman studies fell into two distinct categories. Type I, the more common form, developed gradually, later in life, and did not necessarily require structured intervention. Type I alcoholic men did not always experience the dramatic declines in health and personal circumstances so characteristic of acute alcoholism. These people sometimes straddled the line between alcoholism and "problem drinking." For Type I alcoholics, the genetic inheritance was more like a latent tendency; a propensity that did not automatically show up in every case. It was as if some environmental triggering mechanism, some outside set of circumstances, was required for the inheritance to express itself.

Type 2 alcoholism was a different story altogether. It was bad business from the start; a very unlucky roll of the dice indeed. Type 2 alcoholics were in serious trouble starting with their first taste of liquor during adolescence. Their condition worsened with horrifying speed. They frequently had a history of violent and antisocial behavior, and they often ended up in prison. They were rarely able to hold down normal jobs or sustain workable marriages for long. Type 2s, also known as "familial" or "violent" alcoholics, were even more likely to have had an alcoholic parent. They were, in short, severely addicted to alcohol.

Almost 20 per cent of children born to Type 2 alcoholics became alcoholics themselves. At first glance, this rate does not seem particularly high, when compared to Huntington's chorea. The numbers are not as neat and clean as classic Mendelian genetics would have it. But recessive traits are like that. In the case of a recessive gene, inheritance rates are much lower. "Most behaviors," writes Tabitha Powledge in *Bioscience*, "do not wend their way through generations in the manner of Mendel's smooth and wrinkled peas." Viewed in that light, 20 per cent is a very high number, and the Stockholm Adoption Study constituted strong evidence for the inheritability of the condition known as alcoholism.

Goodwin's Danish studies and the Cloninger-Bohman studies were not the only evidence for a genetic connection in at least some cases of alcoholism. In the United States, Remi Cadoret and a team at the University of Iowa studied Iowa adoptees, and came up with similar results. In fact, more than a dozen major studies of twins pointed to the same conclusion: In alcoholic families, there is a marked difference in alcoholism rates when identical twins (who share the same genes) are compared with fraternal twins (whose genetic makeup differs). If one identical twin is alcoholic, the likelihood that the other identical twin is also alcoholic turns out to be nearly twice as high as it is with fraternal twins. Alcoholism begets alcoholism, even when the alcoholic parent is nowhere on the scene.

But enough about men. It is clear that a genetic propensity for alcoholism is not limited to males. To jump ahead of the story for a moment, *The Journal of the American Medical Association* (JAMA) published studies of female twins which showed the same sorts of relationships, and another twins study in 1994 showed that familial transmission of female alcoholism owed a lot to heredity and very little to the usual suspects: home life, schools, neighborhood, and so on. Female alcoholics show higher levels of depression and prescription drug abuse than male alcoholics do. It is conceivable that women may preferentially inherit a tendency toward depression rather than alcoholism. There are more female depressives than males, and there are more male alcoholics than female. Recent studies of the correlation between mood disorders and women writers show that more than half the female writers in the studies suffered from depression. They did not, however, show a higher than usual rate of alcoholism, compared to an alcoholism rate in comparable studies as high as 30 per cent for male writers.

In later phases of his studies, Goodwin did not find the same straightforward relationship for the daughters of alcoholics, but recent discoveries about male-female differences in the enzymes that metabolize alcohol might help clear up these discrepancies. Women, in general, are more affected by alcohol, metabolize it less quickly, and may seek out other forms of addiction that have fewer immediate adverse effects.

Do the same genetic relationships demonstrated in the alcohol adoption studies prove true for other drugs? Was it conceivable that heroin addiction or cigarette smoking could be traits (disorders, really) that men and women inherited?

"There have been a number of animal studies showing genetic differences in sensitivity to nicotine," said Dr. Neal Benowitz of the Clinical Pharmacology Unit at San Francisco General Hospital, one of the nation's premier nicotine research centers. And Professor Ovide Pomerleau, the Director of Behavioral Medicine at the University of Michigan Medical School, who collaborated with Cloninger's group on genetic studies of nicotine and alcohol, told me: "Some people are drawn to smoking, and some people are not. Everybody pretty much goes through the same kind of peer pressures, the same kind of socialization pressures, and then you have some people who emerge as smokers, and some people who don't. Some people who start smoking give it up easily, and there are others who can't. Well, why? My answer is that I think there are innate differences in susceptibility."

The Cadoret group looked into the question and reported in the *Archives of General Psychiatry* in 1986 that alcohol problems in biological relatives appeared to correlate highly with drug abuse in siblings. "Some theorists have suggested that multiple addictions to a wide variety of substances constitute evidence against a genetic interpretation of addiction," wrote Cadoret. "The present data appear to refute that position, suggesting instead some underlying biochemical foundation involved in all of the substances abused...."

Dr. Janice Keller Phelps, the drug treatment specialist from Seattle, maintained that "a large number of addicted people I have treated over the years had strong family histories of addiction. Time and again I encountered heroin addicts, cocaine addicts, or speed addicts with one or both parents addicted to alcohol, for example, or with one or more brothers or sisters also addicted—though not necessarily to the same drug. It is known and acknowledged that many alcoholics have one or more alcoholic parents; the large number of children of alcoholics who are *not* alcoholic but instead are addicted to other substances, however, is not so well recognized."

In many ways, the genetic findings by Goodwin, Cloninger, and others were as far from the old problems-in-living approach, the Freudian approach, as it was possible to get. As Dr. Edward Sellers, who directed the psychopharmacological research program at the University of Toronto's Addiction Research Foundation during the 1990s, explained to me: "One simplified way of looking at it is that every cell, every hormone, every membrane in the body has got genetic underpinnings, and while many of the genetic underpinnings are similar in people, in fact there are also huge differences. So on one level, the fact that there is a genetic component to addiction is not very surprising. What *is* surprising is that you could ever have it show up in a dominant enough way to be something that might be useful in anticipating risk."

If there existed a set of genes that predisposed people to alcoholism, and possibly other addictions, then these genes had to control the expression of something specific. That's what genes did.

However, addiction researchers could not even agree on the matter of where they should be looking for such physical evidence of genetic difference. In the brain? Among the digestive enzymes? Blood platelets? A gene, or a set of genes, coding for...what? Substance H? Production of certain neurotransmitters? What was it they were supposed to be looking for?

What set of genes coded for happiness?

Henri Begleiter and the P3 Wave

Researchers hunting for biological markers and abnormalities met with mixed success. There was already evidence that enzymes of metabolism could make a difference in drinking behavior. For example, many people of Asian descent experience the so-called "alcohol flush reaction" when they drink. This unpleasant response to alcohol visibly reddens the skin and makes sufferers feel ill. The alcohol flush reaction is a dominant genetic trait. Approximately 50 per cent of Asian men are deficient in one of the enzymes that metabolize alcohol. They are genetically protected against alcoholism due to a built-in defect.

Thus, there were good reasons to pursue enzymes as possible markers. When drinkers drink, the first thing that happens is that enzymes go to work converting the alcohol into a breakdown product called acetaldehyde. Dr. Marc Schuckit, a professor of psychiatry at the University of California's San Diego Medical School, has been prominent among researchers studying the genetic control of enzymes involved in alcohol metabolism. Dr. Schuckit conducted studies of subjects with alcoholic relatives, and found that they exhibited acetaldehyde levels well above normal. Their bodies were more efficient at metabolizing alcohol, it seemed.

The siblings of alcoholics also showed what Dr. Schuckit calls a "decreased intensity of reaction" to alcohol. Measurements of "static ataxia"—the degree to which people's bodies begin to weave and sway when they get drunk—show quite clearly that drinkers with alcoholic relatives sway much less than drinkers with no family history of alcohol problems. These drinkers also reported fewer unpleasant reactions to very high doses of alcohol. In short, drinkers from families with a history of alcoholism seemed to have a higher tolerance for alcohol. They can "hold their liquor." The tolerance appeared to be innate, rather than the sole result of years of abusive drinking.

The amazing tolerance that Dr. Li's rats develop for alcohol dovetails with Schuckit's findings, too. Dr Li's animals, he told me, "started to develop tolerance to the effects of alcohol after a single dose. Most animals lose their tolerance in two days, but these guys are tolerant ten days later. That's a very marked difference. If you look at Schuckit's data, one way to interpret it is that the children of alcoholics who are more susceptible are the ones who are less affected by alcohol."

Drug intoxication produces characteristic waveform signatures in the mammalian brain. The search for specific biological markers in the brain was made possible by positron emission tomography, better known as the PET scan. The idea is simple: Doctors inject test subjects with radioactively tagged glucose, which passes the blood-brain barrier with ease. The more electrochemically active portions of the brain burn extra glucose for energy. By noting precisely where the tagged glucose has gone, and converting that information into a digital two-dimensional array, a PET scan serves as a neurobiological map of brain activity in response to specific stimuli. Functionally, PET scans are pictures of the brain, showing specific areas that "light up" during the performance of a task, or in response to a drug, as we saw in the Snyder-Pert experiments.

Neuroimaging techniques like nuclear magnetic resonance imaging, or MRI, provide another level of detail. With MRIs, scientists could study the brain as a living work in progress. They could create a three-dimensional picture of the brain, with the sagittal, transaxial and coronal planes all visible at once—almost a brain hologram. For the first time, addiction scientists could watch areas of the brain light up with activity under the influence of specific mood-altering chemicals. Two areas were of particular interest. One was the nucleus accumbens, which was involved in the regulation of dopamine and serotonin synthesis. The other was the locus ceruleus—a tiny area of the brain saturated with cells involved in the production and release of the neurotransmitter norepinephrine. Norepinephrine is another important neurotransmitter in the story. It is also known as noradrenaline, and is essentially identical to adrenalin (the latter also called, confusingly, epinephrine). For practical purposes, the four terms are essentially synonymous.

Alcohol, cocaine, the opiates, and other drugs made these two areas of the brain bloom with activity on the MRI and PET scans. These snapshots of your brain on drugs specifically showed that psychoactive drugs of abuse, the ones that altered mood and emotion, did so at the very sites in the brain known to be involved in regulating emotional states. As a general rule, the same areas of the brain tended to light up no matter what addictive drug was under study. Whether it was a molecule of rapture, or a molecule of sorrow, sooner or later it went surging through the brain's limbic system—a diffuse aggregation of mid-brain structures involved with emotion, memory, mood, sleep, and a host of specific behaviors ranging from appetite to risk-taking.

That the subjects also showed characteristic brain activity when they *quit* doing drugs was of equal interest. Dr. Kenneth Blum and his coworkers at the University of Texas Health Science Center demonstrated that certain waveforms occur in the locus ceruleus when abstinent addicts experience cravings. The locus ceruleus helps control levels of the original "fight or flight" chemical, norepinephrine, and when an addict in withdrawal panics, the locus ceruleus lights up like the Fourth of July. Other studies of the nucleus accumbens showed abnormal firing rates in scanned addicts who were deep into an episode of craving. Drug hunger in abstinent addicts, it appeared, was not all in the head, or strictly psychological. Craving had a biological basis.

Something about modern genetic research breeds a strong jolt of excitement. There is the promise of sudden discoveries, headlines, and great leaps forward toward cures for stubborn diseases. Even the most sober scientists seem to get enthused about gene hunting. The idea of curing a disease by locating a defective gene and repairing it is one of the brightest and fondest hopes in medicine. At least 3,000 medical disorders, including diabetes, cystic fibrosis, and some forms of Alzheimer's are inherited diseases caused by defective genes passed on from generation to generation.

Dr. Kenneth Blum of the University of Texas Health Sciences Center, and Dr. Ernest Noble, director of the UCLA Alcohol Research Center, were interested in the gene responsible for a specific kind of dopamine receptor. In 1990, the team reported in the *Journal of the American Medical Association* that a particular variant of the gene responsible for the production of the dopamine D2 receptor was three times as common in the brains of deceased alcoholics. Blum and Noble found the aberrant form of the gene, called the A-I allele, in 77 per cent of the alcoholics, compared with only 28 per cent of the non-alcoholics. Unfortunately, the study involved the use of extracted DNA from the preserved brains of only 35 people believed to have been alcoholics. This DNA was compared with genetic material taken from 35 supposedly non-alcoholic brains. Early attempts to replicate the research did not meet with much success. "We may have found a gene that modifies, rather than causes alcoholism," psychiatrist Ernest Noble speculated. The AI allele also turned up in people suffering from Tourette's syndrome, autism, and other disorders. In addition, a 1996 article in *Pharmacogenetics* claimed that compulsive gamblers with no associated substance abuse history were more likely to carry the AI variant than non-gamblers.

Eventually, the NIMH did its own study, and could not support the Blum/Noble conclusions. Geneticists began to shy away from the D2 hypothesis, on grounds that nothing in genetics ever turns out to be that simple. Still, it was logical to ask whether the children of alcoholics, having in some cases inherited a genetic susceptibility toward the condition, might also show characteristic and identifiable brain abnormalities at an early age. Was it possible that people who became addicted to alcohol or some other drug exhibited certain differences in brain chemistry even before they ever took a drink, a toke, or a snort?

At the State University of New York's Health Science Center in Brooklyn, Dr. Henri Begleiter, a professor of psychiatry, began investigating the brain wave activity of alcoholics in the early 1980s. People have heard of alpha waves and theta waves, but there are many other brain waves, evoked by various kinds of stimulation. Scientists can now measure electrical phenomena called evoked potentials (EPs), and event-related potentials (ERPs). For example, certain characteristic waveforms occur when the brain reacts to visual and auditory stimuli—when a person sees flashes of light, for example, or hears a clicking noise. As the signal of the flashing light makes its way from the retina of the eye to the cortex of the brain, electrodes placed on the scalp record the nerve impulses.

Begleiter and his coworkers recorded various event-related potentials, using scalp electrodes. The result was a series of sine wave-like printouts measuring amplitude and elapsed time for any given brain wave. The so-called P3 voltage, a measure of reaction time invoked by such stimuli as flashing lights or clicking noises, especially interested the researchers. Prior testing had shown that people suffering from schizophrenia or attention deficit disorder exhibited low P3 amplitudes. When Begleiter's team tried recording P3 waves, something odd turned up. Diminished P3 waves were characteristic of an overwhelming majority of practicing alcoholics. As it turned out, the same event-related P3 wave abnormalities could be found in *recovering* alcoholics—even when they had been abstinent for years.

It was left for Begleiter's team to round up a group of children ranging in age from six to eighteen, all of whom had an alcoholic parent, and all of whom, as Begleiter's team documented, showed the same diminished amplitude in P3 waves. None of the children had ever been exposed to alcohol before. Nonetheless, there it was: The P3 waves of these children exhibited exactly the same waveform abnormalities as their actively alcoholic parents.

When Begleiter limited the pool of brain scan volunteers to the sons of fathers who had been diagnosed as Type 2 alcoholics, and compared their P3 waves with the P3 waves of a control group, he was able to correctly identify the children of Type 2 fathers almost 90 per cent of the time. Begleiter had discovered an organic impairment in the brains of non-drinking siblings of alcoholics.

Begleiter's work caught most genetic researchers by surprise. Numerous laboratories raced to replicate Begleiter's findings—and consistently succeeded. The P3 deficit was verifiable, and repeatable. Addiction researchers sat up and took notice: Here was compelling evidence of a marker for alcoholism; a specific abnormality in the brain which was apparently passed on genetically in alcoholic families.

"Because of the D2 business, we are going to make triple sure that something we report is in fact real," Begleiter told *Science* magazine. The initial findings from Begleiter's Collaborative Study on the Genetics of Alcoholism were not supportive of Blum and Noble's

D2 hypothesis. ("We believe it doesn't increase the risk for any-thing," one researcher said bluntly.) Robert Cloninger weighed in with a paper demonstrating that when you broadened the samples and took another look, the D2 connection faded away. Very prob-ably, the D2 allele plays a second-order role of some sort; a piece, perhaps, of the larger puzzle of gene interactions for alcoholism and other addictions.

"The only markers which are currently reliable are the elec-trophysiological brain abnormalities we have found in the kids of alcoholics," Begleiter told me at the time. "Actually, it's more than just the P3." A colleague of Begleiter's, neuroscientist Ber-nice Porjesz, found that an additional neurological oscillation, the N400 waveform, was markedly different in the children and fami-lies of alcoholics. The children with abnormal P3 or N400 waves were more likely to abuse drugs and tobacco in later years. The P3 findings have been thoroughly verified in other laboratories all over the country. There have been no retractions, and little difficulty in duplicating the findings. Begleiter's markers are solid.

Begleiter bracketed his results with careful qualifiers, but re-searchers could see that the field of addiction medicine had just gotten a big boost. The Scandinavian studies had shown that there were good grounds for viewing alcoholism and possibly other ad-dictions as disorders with genetic components. Dr. Begleiter's stud-ies proved that you could look for evidence of this inheritability in the brain itself. Whatever flaw was being inherited left detectable tracks, and the P3 wave differentials represented the first confirmed example of this.

When I spoke with Dr. Begleiter shortly after he first pub-lished his discoveries, he made it clear that the drive to understand addiction was tied tightly to the emerging precepts of biological psychiatry. Many of the traits we consider central to our person-ality—one's behavioral repertoire, as it were—may have genetic origins. Aggression, impulsivity, thrill seeking, eccentricity, shyness, depression—biological psychiatrists believed that genetic factors partially account for the appearance of traits like these. "My bias is that what is inherited is a predisposition, a very general predis-position," Begleiter said, "and it is not specific to alcoholism. It is not even specific to addictive drugs. Instead of looking at just one disease entity, we may be looking at a predisposition to many diseases."

On the face of it, the work of Cloninger, Begleiter, and others had little to do with anything that could rightly be called an "ad-dictive personality." Nevertheless, if there are biological differences in brain function, then these differences can conceivably lead to observable differences in behavior. With other brain diseases— epilepsy, Tourette's syndrome—this is taken for granted. This knowledge has led addiction researchers to pursue the possibility of identifying *behavioral* markers for addiction, as well as physiologi-cal ones like P3 waves and the genes that codes for them.

Dr. Cloninger has asserted that children who show a high pro-pensity for risk-taking, along with impulsivity, or "novelty-seeking," are more likely to develop alcoholism and other addictions later in life. Cloninger has put together a complicated and controver-sial classification system of neurotransmitter/behavioral corre-spondences, the intent of which is to demonstrate that inheritable chemical imbalances are the motive agent behind these behaviors.

Begleiter, for his part, believes that drinking by young people with conduct disorders can be predictive. The younger you start drinking, the greater the chance of becoming an alcoholic. Drink before age 15, and the odds are four times as high.

Throughout the 1990s, the scope of the research changed from genetic population studies to high-tech neuroanatomy. The work of Henri Begleiter and Bernice Porjesz at the SUNY Health Science Center formed the core of a decade-long, six-university research program called the Collaborative Study on the Genetics of Alcoholism (COGA), under the auspices of the NIH. Many of the researchers cited by name in this book are contributors to the multi-faceted study. In 1998, the investigators successfully traced Begleiter's P3 waves to the chromosomal regions responsible for them. The regions that coded for P3 waves also turned out to be rich in genes for the production of glutamate and acetylcholine receptors. The body uses glutamate, another common amino acid, to synthesize glutamine, which detoxifies ammonia and combats hypoglycemia, among other things. Glutamine carries messages to brain regions involved with memory and learning. An excess of glutamine can cause neural damage and cell death, and it is a prime culprit in ALS, known as Lou Gehrig's disease.

Even though glutamine is an "excitatory" neurotransmitter, it is, paradoxically, the material from which the inhibitory neurotransmitter GABA is synthesized. Short for gamma-amino butyric acid, GABA's job is to slow things down; to serve as a speed governor. It is the opposite of norepinephrine, which revs things up. GABA is found in high quantities in the hippocampus, an area of the brain associated with memory. As will become clear, alcohol has a profound effect on the brain's GABA system, often with "memorable" results.

Dr. Roger Williams of Texas always argued that most alcoholics were functionally hypoglycemic and would respond to medical treatments, chiefly nutritional supplements of the B vitamins and glutamine. As for acetylcholine, this excitatory neurotransmitter plays an important role in tobacco addiction, and will be discussed later.

Behaviors, then, can be symptoms of addiction—possibly even precursors of addiction. But can a behavior *be* the addiction? Can people become addicted to activities, the same way they become addicted to drugs? Is compulsive gambling a legitimate addiction?

Addiction to drugs, addiction to carbohydrates, and addiction to behaviors such as gambling and skydiving may be related diseases with the same biological underpinnings. Behavioral traits like impulsivity apply equally to compulsive gamblers, Begleiter maintains. A person with a predisposition for addiction might end up becoming addicted to gambling rather than, or along with, an addiction to alcohol. A person born with a biochemical predisposition for addiction, who happened to live in a country where addictive drugs were absolutely unavailable, might end up addicted to a high intake of sugar foods instead. I asked Begleiter if he was saying that addiction to certain behaviors might serve to normalize the central nervous systems of addictive people the same way certain drugs do.

"Correct," he said.

Cloninger's categories suggest that our behaviors and our innate temperaments are, at any given moment, the result of a precise intermixing of chemical saturation and release levels in the central nervous system. To be completely reductionist about it, we are the way we are because of the way the surfaces of our nerve cells are constructed. Novelist William Burroughs once declared that the real war was the one going on "in the space between our cells." Nowadays, we can speculate that the war going on in the spaces between our cells is the chemical war being constantly waged among our personalities, behaviors, moods, and appetites.

If Li, Begleiter, Cloninger, and the others had gotten it right, for all their scientific disagreements over "hard" medical science and "soft" psychology, addicts were stuck with a package of symptoms Begleiter calls behavioral *dysregulation*. It is a good word for what Begleiter the psychologist is trying to describe.

"Disinhibition, impulsivity, trouble fitting into society—you have certain behavioral disorders in kids who later develop into alcoholics and drug addicts," he said. The behavior itself doesn't cause the addiction. The dysregulated behavior is a symptom of the addiction.

"When you talk to these people, as I have," Begleiter said, "you see that the one thing they pretty much all report is that, under the influence of the drug, they feel much more *normal*. It normalizes their central nervous systems. Initially, what they have is a need to experience a normal life." So, it wasn't ducktails, pool halls, tattoos, casual sex, or lack of parental involvement that caused addiction to alcohol and cigarettes and pot, and maybe cocaine and speed and heroin. It wasn't just the "bad kids." Irrational anger, certain forms of overeating, certain compulsive behaviors like gambling—these behaviors were symptoms of the same group of related disorders that included drug and alcohol addiction, and which involved specific chemicals and areas of the brain related to reward, motivation, and memory.

The trait of impulsivity—Cloninger's novelty-seeking—is a possible marker for addiction that may help explain why it is usually impossible to persuade addicts to give up their drugs by sheer force of logic—by arguing that the drugs will eventually ruin their health or kill them. "They tell me it'll kill me," sang Dave Van Ronk, "but they don't say when." Consider the always-instructive case of cigarette smoking. In 1964, the Surgeon General's Report on Smoking and Health laid out the case for the long-term ill effects of nicotine quite effectively—and millions of people quit smoking. A stubborn minority did not, and many of them still have not. Are they simply being hedonistic and irresponsible? Or are the long-term negative consequences, so dramatically clear to others, simply not capable of influencing their thinking to the same degree? Biochemical abnormalities similar to those predisposing certain people to addiction may also prevent them from comprehending the long-term results of their behavior.

"Once the addictive process has taken over," as Dr. Begleiter explained it, "addicts know that if they take a glass of this stuff, they are going to feel better. And indeed, they are. It is foolish to deny the fact that they are going to feel better. Now in the long run, sure, it is going to kill them. But this is very much a part of this impulsivity, this behavioral dysregulation. These people can never think long term. The long term, both positive and negative, is totally foreign to them. And this is one of the reasons that they get addicted to drugs which are very fast acting—the faster the better. Because if you say to them—let's make up an example—if you say 'I'm going to give you alcohol, but it's only going to make you feel better three hours from now,' they won't touch the stuff. It may be the same substance, but if it doesn't act immediately, they don't want it."

The brooding, antisocial loner, the one with impulse control problems, a penchant for risk-taking, and a cigarette dangling from his lip, is a recognizable archetype in popular culture. From Marlon

Brando to Bruce Lee, these flawed heroes are perhaps the ones with restless brain chemicals; the ones who never felt good and never knew why ("What are you rebelling against?" "What've you got?"). They were the ones deficient in Substance H, for Happiness. They were the people who, in Begleiter's phrase, lacked the chemicals for long-term thinking. Talented or not, bohemian or straight-laced, they tended toward low self-esteem and high rates of suicide. They were frequently Cloninger's Type 2s.

Along the way, then, highly addiction-prone people discover their drug of choice. They find a medicine that actually *does* something. They feel better for a while. Normal, even.

As Begleiter described it, "anything which is personality is biological as well." But does environment matter? Indeed it does, agreed Begleiter. "Environmental factors are critical, and I would in no way underestimate them."

Different cultures have traditionally exhibited different rates of alcoholism. Irish immigrants have a high rate, Jews have a low rate, and cultural factors, not genetic theories, would seem to explain the difference. "There are many reasons why you become an alcoholic," Begleiter said, "but one of them is that alcohol is available—it's part of the environment. So obviously, you don't become an alcoholic in Saudi Arabia even though you may have the genes for it. Environmental factors, whether they are social, or purely behavioral, or developmental in character, play a major role in shaping the manifestation of the disease."

This leads us back in the direction of Dr. Li's pharmacogenetic diseases. Phelylketonuria, or PKU, is another good example of how it sometimes works with genetic illnesses. Children born with PKU have an inherited disability—they cannot properly digest the amino acid phenylalanine. The dietary mechanisms for redressing the disorder were well understood, even though the genetics of PKU were not. Environmental influences—diet, in this case—can strongly influence genetic diseases. Choosing to experiment with strongly addictive drugs like cocaine and speed and cigarettes is not dangerous because everyone who does so will become addicted. It is dangerous because a *certain percentage* of those who do will become addicted, and, because of the nature of recessive genes and the plethora of environmental influences, it will be hard to identify potential alcoholics *in utero* by means of some genetic test. At this stage, there is no reliable way of determining the at-risk percentage in advance.

Many observers have noted that writers, to cite one well-known example, seem to be highly prone to alcoholism. At first glance, this observation seems to fly in the face of the theory that innate biochemistry plays a role in addiction. Of America's seven Nobel Prize winners in literature, as Donald Goodwin notes, at least four of them—Hemingway, Faulkner, Sinclair Lewis, and Eugene O'Neill—were clearly alcoholic.

There are at least two ways of looking at this example. It may be that famous writers who are also famous alcoholics have led people to the conclusion that a majority of working writers are alcoholics. If carpenters, as a precisely defined group, were as intensely studied as Nobel Prize winning writers, rates of addiction might turn out to be roughly the same.

The more likely explanation has to do with tentative links between mental disorders and creativity. Creative artists seem to suffer from high rates of depression as well as addiction. Henri Begleiter's list of potential behavioral markers for addiction includes such things as impulsivity, and trouble fitting into society. Artists are the classic "outsiders" of society. Behavioral dysregulations that accompany addiction, if such is the case, might also aid creativity in some unknown way.

Proving that a condition is sometimes an inherited disease is an important step, but it is not the whole story. It is one thing to discover genetic evidence for a mental disorder, and quite another to locate the gene or genes responsible for it. And even if that can be accomplished, it does not automatically lead to a cure, or even a more effective treatment. Researchers well remember the cautionary tale of a medical sociologist named Janice Egeland, who went looking for genetic evidence related to manic depression in the 1980s. She chose to do her detective work among the genes of the Old

Order Amish of Pennsylvania, a Mennonite sect dating back to the 17th Century. The Amish, like the Scandinavians, kept detailed genealogical and health records.

Because of the Amish lifestyle and history, the existence of manic depression in families stood out more clearly against the sociological landscape. The 12,500 Amish in Lancaster County, Pennsylvania are, with few exceptions, descended from the same 30-odd couples who emigrated from Europe in the early 1700s. Egeland's team of scientists from Yale University and M.I.T. painstakingly verified what the Amish already knew: Of 32 active cases of manic depression identified by the researchers, every one of them belonged to families with histories of the disorder stretching back for generations. Moreover, all of the suicide victims since 1880 had been members of the same four families.

Janice Egeland was looking for the actual gene itself, and initial news reports indicated that she had found it. A gene predisposing its victims to manic depression could be traced in one Amish family to a specific region on human chromosome 11.

Then, disaster struck. Closer scrutiny of the data showed that the incredibly complex statistical analyses performed by Egeland's group were thrown off when additional manic-depressives were discovered and factored into the study. According to Dr. Steven Paul, then of NIMH, the revised analysis did not cast any doubt whatsoever on the basic finding that at least some forms of manic depression have a genetic basis. But the single gene on chromosome 11 was not the culprit.

A similar public setback took place in the case of schizophrenia, when a group of researchers in London, and another group at Yale, demonstrated that some cases of schizophrenia were apparently linked with genetic defects on chromosome 5. Once again, retractions were soon in order. Attempts to duplicate the findings by several international research terms were unsuccessful. Schizophrenia is undoubtedly too complex to result from a single genetic defect, or it may be that the gene in question only accounts for a fraction of the cases of schizophrenia. In any event, the gene on chromosome 5 no longer appears to be the primary culprit.

Single-gene strategies have not fared well. "Molecular geneticists were bumping their heads against a fundamental problem," writes Dr. Nancy Andreasen, Chair of Psychiatry at the University of Iowa College of Medicine. "Most human diseases are 'complex illnesses.'"

Diabetes, heart disease, and cancer are complex illnesses. As Alan Leshner of the National Institute on Drug Abuse has written, "Addiction is a brain disease—but not just a brain disease." Leshner defines it as a "psychobiological illness with critical biological, behavioral, and social-context components."

If it is all of these things, then what is it? Leshner could be offering up a definition of fibromyalgia, or chronic fatigue syndrome, or anxiety, for that matter. On the other hand, diseases are like that. And a host of factors conspires to make addiction a special case in the annals of medicine.

Epigenetics

If psychiatric disorders, including depression and addiction, are rooted in nature, but modified by nurture, some better way of viewing the interaction between genes and the environment is desperately needed.

Enter "epigenetics," defined as the study of how gene expression can be modified without making direct changes to the DNA. Writing in *Science News*, Tina Hesman Saey explains that "epigenetic mechanisms alter how cells use genes but don't change the DNA code in the genes themselves.... The ultimate effect is to finely tune to what degree a gene is turned on or off. Often the fine tuning is long-lasting, setting the level of a gene's activity for the lifetime of the cell."

A common form of epigenetic modification involves adding molecules to the DNA structure. Adding molecules from a methyl group or an acetyl group can change the manner in which genes interact with a cell's transcribing system. Cells can "mark" specific genes by attaching a methyl group consisting of three hydrogen atoms and one carbon atom to cytosine in the DNA base, effectively turning genes on or off without making major alterations to genetic structure. (Gene mutations or insertions, on the other hand, are capable of fundamentally altering the DNA protein structure.)

Scientists have learned that epigenetic changes can be caused by environmental impacts, but the details are not well understood. We have not yet reached the point of being able to link a specific experience of stress or infection or chemical exposure to specific epigenetic alterations.

What does any of this have to do with drug addiction or depression? One of the environmental impacts researchers have linked to epigenetic changes is drug addiction. The DNA double helix is packaged in proteins collectively called chromatin. One set of proteins, the histones, is a frequent site of epigenetic modification. Eric Nestler and co-workers in the Southwestern Medical Center at the University of Texas found that alterations in chromatin packaging were tied up with the dopamine release caused by cocaine addiction. In a paper published in *Neuron*, the researchers concluded that chronic cocaine use was influenced by "chromatin remodeling." Specifically, modulating histone activity "alters locomotor and rewarding responses to cocaine."

How does this work? As Saey writes: "Another gene, known as delta-FosB, also switches on when a wave of dopamine washes over the nucleus accumbens.... Delta-FosB teams up with other transcription factors and recruits enzymes that acetylate histones and remodel control regions of some genes..... Such findings suggest that medicines that interrupt or reverse epigenetic changes caused by drugs of abuse could one day prevent or cure addiction."

In the end, what can we say with any certainty about the genetics of alcoholism and other addictions?

There is no single gene for alcoholism, and no likelihood of a quick fix. Addiction probably results from a complex interaction of several genes. It is possible to have the genes without having the disorder. Part of the problem has to do with the immensely subtle and difficult mathematics of the whole genetic enterprise. The literature is rife with procedural difficulties and qualifiers ("The inverse of the asymptotic variances of the correlations are used as weights.") Drawing generalizations from genetic research is immensely difficult, and it is one reason why science journalism so often goes so far astray. Gene hunting is exciting work, but rather than trying to find the genes for addiction, many researchers have been looking instead at the level of the central nervous system—the physiology and chemistry of neurons in action. Rather than chase the genes thought to be responsible for a susceptibility to alcohol and drug addiction, recent research has focused more keenly on the influence of drugs on the action of neurotransmitters at their receptor sites. What they have learned thus far throws new light on the nature of human motivation and desire.

FOUR: THE REWARD PATHWAY

"Drunkenness is a purely accidental susceptibility of a brain, evolved for entirely different uses, and its causes are to be sought in the molecular realm, rather than in any possible order of 'outer relations.'"

—William James, 1909

The human brain, once touted as a sort of organic digital processor, was revealed during the Decade of the Brain as something more closely resembling a bucket of organic soup capable of transmitting a weak electrical potential at lightning speed. The soup was composed of peptides, neurotransmitters, hormones, and other "information substances."

The key to all this, as we have seen, was humanity's ancient friend and foe, opium. One of the first observations teased out by Pert, Snyder and Kuhar back at Johns Hopkins was that the opiate receptors they had discovered were densely concentrated in areas of the brain known collectively as the limbic region. It was the same with Dr. Li's rats: The effect of alcohol on serotonin and dopamine transmission was most noticeable in the limbic system. Over the years, other neuroscientists discovered specific receptors for dozens of messenger molecules in the central nervous system. Like Christmas tree lights beaming forth from a tangle of branching nerve pathways, radioactively tagged molecules lit up on digital scans, revealing a sparkling map of receptor distributions in the brain.

From an evolutionary perspective, the human brain is a famously three-part organ. Typically, these parts are thought of as the reptilian brain, the mammalian brain, and the primate brain. Different parts of the brain control different functions. There are movement centers, centers of emotion, centers for memory, and centers for pleasure and reward. The first brain to evolve in animals was the brain stem, the center of control for vital processes such as breathing and cardiovascular control. We share this part of the brain with the reptiles. The mid-brain, or limbic system, is the seat of appetite, emotion, reward, and pleasure. The limbic system is most highly developed in mammals. Finally, primate evolution resulted in a third brain, the cerebrum, on top of the older two. In time, human evolution resulted in an addition to the cerebrum—a thin, folded layer of nerve cells called the cortex. Humans being humans, we tend to focus our attention primarily on this crowning cerebral development, forgetting that the reptilian and mammalian brains lie buried beneath the cortex, controlling many of our behaviors and emotions.

Scientists learned that the neurotransmitters dopamine and serotonin were involved in a dazzling variety of brain activities. Acetylcholine, another of the major excitatory neurotransmitters in the brain, turned out to be involved in arousal, and carries messages from the brain to the muscles. Curare, the deadly poison used by Amazon Indians, works because it blocks the transmission of acetylcholine, resulting in paralysis and respiratory failure. Norepinephrine is an energizer, carrying the message we commonly refer to as an adrenaline surge. It is the brain's "go" signal. It is also involved in certain forms of memory.

A receptor site exists for the benzodiazepines, the class of tranquilizer drugs to which Valium belongs. When activated, it generates feelings of contentment, and suppresses feelings of anxiety.

There was also a receptor site for PCP, the animal tranquilizer. Scientists speculated that the natural substance designed to fit the PCP receptors would be the chemical reason why people are sometimes capable of extraordinary feats of strength, such as lifting a car off a trapped child in an emergency. In addition, scientists discovered a receptor for DMT, a hallucinatory chemical found in South American vines. Recent research suggests that the natural chemical in the brain that fits into the DMT receptors is... DMT itself. Although it was synthesized years ago, DMT appears to have been a natural substance in the brain all along.

Most of these substances will make a pass through the limbic system on their journey through the body. The limbic system is a U-shaped aggregation of structures located below and behind the prefrontal cortex. This is where the brain processes much of the information it receives about events, perceptions, and memories. The information ultimately goes to the autonomic nervous system as some form of emotion, arousal, or action. The limbic system as a whole comprises the center of control for basic survival behaviors. This older chemical self, residing in the midbrain, mediates between higher cortical functions and back brain life support functions. The limbic region serves as a sort of stimulus filter for assessing and reacting to the world. Here we find the hippocampus, where memories are formed, and the amygdala, the generator of feelings of fear and aggression—the fight-or-flight box. Connected via the ventral tegmental area, there is the dopamine-rich nucleus accumbens, a significant site of action for addictive drugs. The limbic system also includes the hypothalamus, which is involved in arousal and temperature control.

Finally, there is the locus coeruleus, a tiny nucleus of cells located near the brain stem, and increasingly implicated in the stress reactions characteristic of drug withdrawal. During withdrawal, the amount of functional dopamine, endorphin, and serotonin at the locus coeruleus is markedly reduced. Stress levels soar.

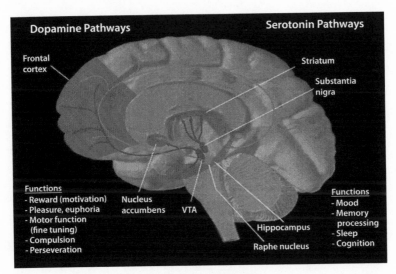

Dopamine Pathways

Serotonin Pathways

Frontal cortex

Striatum

Substantia nigra

Functions
- Reward (motivation)
- Pleasure, euphoria
- Motor function
  (fine tuning)
- Compulsion
- Perseveration

Nucleus accumbens

VTA

Hippocampus

Raphe nucleus

Functions
- Mood
- Memory
  processing
- Sleep
- Cognition

The Reward Pathway

A good way to remember the survival functions of the limbic system is to think of the "four Fs"—feeding, fighting, fleeing, and.... sexual reproduction. Leaving aside the fight-or-flight response, these survival behaviors are typically referred to as the drives for food, water, and sex. A rat, or a human being, will work very hard for food, water, and sex, because these things are pleasurable. They are highly rewarding. And because they are, the survival of the species is protected.

The limbic system is also the center for feelings and moods like pleasure, pain, anger, alertness, desire, hunger, arousal, and attention. In broad strokes, and in common with other mammals, it mediates many of our fears and pleasures. Its activities are deep-rooted, ancient, and pre-verbal. Language is unnecessary in the limbic world of sense and response, action and reaction. The actions of the limbic system undergird everything we think we know about ourselves, challenging our image of who we are, and calling into question the degree of direct control we exercise over our emotions. We speak of "chemical" rage—and sometimes the image is all too apt.

The limbic system is *changed* by addictive drugs. The basic destination of a molecule of alcohol or a molecule of cocaine is the nucleus accumbens in the limbic system—the so-called "pleasure center" of the brain. Drug molecules train the brain, and when this process of change reaches a certain point, the pathology is no longer drug abuse, but drug addiction. Addicts sometimes speak of having a monkey on their back, or of feeding the monkey. The monkey is there, all right, buried in the limbic part of the brain that we share with the other mammals.

The reward pathway is semantic shorthand for a series of intricate processes; a limbic blueprint outlining the neural basis of drug reinforcement. Drugs of abuse ultimately render neurotransmission along the reward pathway dysfunctional through repeated or continuous excitation. Randolph Nesse of the University of Michigan's Department of Psychiatry explains that addictive drugs "create a signal in the brain that indicates, falsely, the arrival of a huge fitness benefit. This changes behavioral propensities so that drug-seeking increases in frequency and displaces adaptive behaviors." What this means is that the brain begins to consider drug taking a vital activity accompanied by significant and immediate rewards, thereby displacing other activities—social, familial, and professional—that are more beneficial in the long run.

The Chemistry of Need

The molecules that drive the reward pathway are ancient. Receptors for serotonin and dopamine, the brain's primary pleasure chemicals, can be found in mollusks and arthropods that diverged from main prevertebrate lines more than 600 million years ago. Serotonin, also known as 5-HT, occurs in nuts, fruit, and snake venom. It is found in the intestinal walls, large blood vessels, and the central nervous system of most vertebrates. The body normally synthesizes 5-hydroxytryptamine, as serotonin is formally known, from tryptophan in the diet.

Serotonin and dopamine are part of a group of compounds called biogenic *amines*. In addition to serotonin and dopamine, the amines include noradrenaline, acetylcholine, and histamine. This class of chemical messengers is produced, in turn from basic amino acids like tyrosine, tryptophan, and choline. The amines are of great interest, because mood-altering drugs and addictive drugs both show a straightforward affinity for receptors designed for the brain's own amines.

"The factors governing drug-taking behavior are not unique to humans," writes M.A. Bozarth of the department of Psychology at the State University of New York. "They involve biobehavioral processes shared across mammalian species. Indeed, drug addiction might be considered a phylogenetically primitive behavior. The brain systems mediating the addictive properties of drugs evolved early and have a central role in promoting survival of the organism."

No other substance found in the central nervous system has as many diverse functions as serotonin. The substance is involved in regulating appetite, sleep, mood, memory, learning, endocrine regulation, smooth muscle contractions, migraine headaches, motility of the GI tract, and blood platelet homeostasis. Serotonin also plays a large role in initiating and shaping behaviors of a sexual or hallucinatory nature. In animal models, and in some human studies, lower serotonin levels correlate with higher levels of violence.

A serotonin-selective agent like sumatriptan, a popular migraine medication, works by binding selectively to a serotonin receptor subtype involved in arterial circulation and dilation. The difference between serotonin-active drugs like sumatriptan, and similarly serotonin-active drugs LSD or Ecstasy, is that the former locks exclusively into these "5-HT1" receptors, and nowhere else. Psychedelic drugs like LSD and Ecstasy are both partial agonists at 5-HT receptors, boosting serotonin in the cerebral cortex, and also in the locus coeruleus. Other 5-HT agonists like ondansetron do not have that effect. Ondansetron (trade name Zofran) helps reduce the nausea of chemotherapy and works as a general anti-emetic by blocking serotonin activity of the 5-HT3 receptor subtype in the GI tract. (Vomiting is another serotonin-mediated reflex.)

Dopamine, like serotonin, also mediates drug hunger. When addiction scientists blocked dopamine production in test animals for extended periods, they can even get extremely hungry rats to ignore food altogether. The progressive disruption of normal dopamine production and normal dopamine receptor arrays produces what researcher George Koob has dubbed "spiraling distress." It is extraordinary to discover that scientists have now located, quite precisely, the physical location of all this spiraling distress in the form of drug dependence, craving, and relapse. All the addictive drugs we have examined effect neurotransmitters and receptors for dopamine, serotonin, GABA, glutamate, opiate peptides, and others. More precisely, all this happens along pathways connecting the nucleus accumbens to other parts of the brain.

Alcohol, heroin, cigarettes, and other drugs caused a surge of dopamine production, which was then released into the nucleus accumbens. The result: Pleasure. The nucleus accumbens has been called the engine of the reward response. When scientists pipe a dopamine-mimicking substance into the nucleus accumbens, targeting dopamine D2 receptors, withdrawal symptoms are blocked in morphine-addicted rats. Similarly, when scientists block dopamine receptors in the accumbens, the morphine-dependent rats exhibit withdrawal symptoms.

More recently, scientists have managed to record a rise in dopamine levels in lab rats by cueing the rats to anticipate a pleasurable event—food, sex, or sweet drinks. When you conditioned the rats to a ringing bell before dinner, soon the rats would be showing elevated dopamine levels at the sound of the bell only. Anticipation of reward was all it took. Or you could give one of the male rats a good close look at a suitable female through a mesh panel, and the male rat's dopamine levels would surge, presumably in anticipation of possible carnal pleasures, and dopamine levels would spike even higher, of course, once the divider was removed.

This helped explain one of addiction's central mysteries, which is relapse. Why would an active addict, an alcoholic, ever go back? The more so since the adverse effects of continued use have long ago swamped whatever euphoric sense of well being, or even just plain normalcy, the drug once provided? One answer might be that dopamine causes human beings to pay attention to stimuli that are potentially rewarding. Even in the absence of any possibility of reward—on a desert island, in a rehab clinic—dopamine dysregulation could kindle episodes of fierce craving, precisely because such episodes of craving had often been rewarded by the experience of the drug in question: drug hunger followed by temporary drug satiation. The hunger burned even more fiercely when the addict was exposed to direct cues, like seeing the drug, or being in places where the drug was previously used, whether a neighborhood tavern or a crack house.

What we know is that *all* addictive drugs produce their effects by impinging upon the normal operation of the branching pipeline of limbic reward, and that these effects ultimately involve the frontal cortex as well. Take the drug away, and the brain begins its complex and minutely ordered repertoire of compensatory effects, causing physical discomfort, depression, and irritability.

The craving for a reward denied causes dopamine levels in the nucleus accumbens to crash dramatically, as they do when users go off drugs. Dopamine, serotonin, and norepinephrine activity soars just as dramatically when a drug user relieves withdrawal symptoms by relapsing. The release of dopamine and serotonin in the nucleus accumbens appears to be the final destination of the reward pathway—the last act in the pleasure play. If you think about a drug, take a drug, or crave a drug, you are lighting up the nucleus accumbens with a surge of electrochemical activity. These are essentially the same pathways that regulate our food and water-seeking behavior. By directly or indirectly influencing the molecules of pleasure, drugs and alcohol trigger key neurochemical events that are central to our feelings of both reward and disappointment. In this sense, the reward pathway is a route to both pleasure and pain.

Detox and withdrawal does not mean that the brain of the addict has returned to normal. Not only does addiction change things, but the changes wrought by drug and alcohol abuse persist long after the drugs have been withdrawn. Thus, detox and withdrawal do not end the matter. After that comes the behavioral and social-context components: The craving to use. The drug-seeking behavior. Chronic exposure to cocaine in lab rats produces a characteristic supersensitivity of the dopamine receptors found in the nucleus accumbens. Increased GABA release during withdrawal reduces the firing of dopamine and serotonin-producing neurons. The result: what psychologists call an "aversive state," which is more or less the same state lab rats are in if you knock out their pleasure pathways.

Finding a way to override serotonin- and dopamine-mediated mid-brain commands is the essential key to recovery from addiction. One of the aims of a biological understanding of addiction is to tease out the mechanisms by which the reinforcing effects of addictive drugs become transformed into long-term adaptive changes in the brain. "Why are we so surprised that when you take a poison a thousand times, it makes some changes in your head?" said James Halikas, who was co-director of the chemical dependency treatment program at the University of Minnesota during the crack heyday of the late 1980s and early 1990s. "It makes *sense* that poisons change things."

The fact that certain drugs mimic the shapes of certain neurotransmitter receptors, and essentially "fool" receptors into receiving them, is one of the most important and far-reaching discoveries in the history of modern science. It is the reason why even minute amounts of certain drugs can have such powerful effects on the human nervous system. When a properly shaped neurotransmitter molecule hits its target receptor, it snaps into place. Many different neurotransmitters can squirt across the gap all at once, but which ones are taken up, and in what amounts, depends upon the particular array of receptors waiting for them across the gap. Neurotransmitters are not always rendered into an inactive form and swept away after stimulating the proper receptor. Some of the molecules are recaptured and stored in special sacs, to be used again as needed. This process became known as "reuptake."

One way to grasp the complexity of neurotransmitter activity in the brain is to think of the transportation infrastructure of a large city, its several neighborhoods connected by a maze of intersecting highways, cloverleaves, and merge lanes—from eight-lane freeways to one-way city streets. Moving vehicles have different purposes, and there are many different subtypes of each vehicle. An excess of traffic on one road influences the flow of traffic on distant thoroughfares. The highways and streets intersect, combine, and divide in a pattern that looks inherently chaotic when viewed from above. There are all sorts of indirect ways to influence traffic flow—cellular telephones, radio transmitters, and pagers, to name a few. One message might order a squadron of yellow taxis to the L.A. Coliseum, but when the taxis arrive, the number of them that can pick up passengers is affected by the number of parking spaces already in use.

The city's traffic system is seemingly beyond comprehension, but at any single point in the interlocking system of individual components, everything is (relatively) orderly and understandable. Most of the time, the vehicles get where they are going. When all is going well inside our brains, the neurotransmitter systems are in exquisite balance, producing just the right amount of chemicals at the right time and in the right places. The substances that help us sleep; that tell us to eat when we're hungry; that allow us to feel pleasure when we do something pleasurable or restrain us from self-inflicted pain, are all doing their jobs. But that is not always how it goes. By affecting cell receptors, mind-altering drugs also alter the biochemistry of the cells themselves. Once this exquisite equilibrium is disrupted, there are many possible ramifications—and drug addiction is one of them.

The best current view of addiction can be encapsulated in the popular "4 Cs," otherwise known as the Cardinal symptoms of addiction: loss of Control over use of the drug, Continued use despite adverse consequences, Compulsive use, and Craving in the absence of the drug. With the help of Dr. Goodwin, alcohol specialists have formulated their own definition: Alcoholism is defined as a "primary, chronic disease, characterized by.... impaired control over drinking, preoccupation with alcohol, use of alcohol despite adverse consequences, and distortions in thinking, most notably denial."

The two definitions sound about the same.

Pan-Addiction

The newer views of addiction as an organic brain disorder cast strong doubt on the longstanding assumption that different kinds of people become addicted to different kinds of drugs. By 1998, the *Archives of General Psychiatry* flatly stated the reverse: "There is no definitive evidence indicating that individuals who habitually and preferentially use one substance are fundamentally different from those who use another." This quiet but highly influential breakthrough in the addiction paradigm has paid enormous dividends ever since.

From a genetic standpoint, the implication was that an addiction to alcohol, heroin, or speed did not necessarily "breed true." The sons and daughters of alcoholics could just as easily grow up to be heroin addicts, and *vice versa*, due to the same brain anomalies.

In her book, *The Hidden Addiction*, Dr. Janice Keller Phelps writes: "The idea of pan-addiction—addiction to anything as a manifestation of an inheritable biochemical flaw—is borne out by my repeated clinical observation that addiction to one substance is basically the same as addiction to another. The underlying pathology is the same in every case."

There are numerous examples at hand. Recovering alcoholics and heroin addicts tend to be notorious chain-smokers, for one.

Professor Pomerleau, among others, leans toward the theory that those Americans who continue to be hard-core smokers, unwilling or unable to stop, may represent a biological pool of people who are genetically prone to addiction. Alcohol researcher George Vaillant, who directed the seminal Harvard Medical School longitudinal studies (to be treated in detail later), sees it the same way: "Alcoholism is a major reason that people don't stop smoking. Those who keep on smoking after age 50 tend to be alcoholics."

There you have it. Throw a lasso around America's cigarette smokers, and you are likely to snare the lion's share of "drug abusers" and "problem drinkers" as well. This may also explain why there is such a huge overlap between gamblers and alcoholics, and between gambling and cigarette addiction. It is no secret to anyone who has been inside a casino that a striking percentage of the patrons are also smokers and drinkers. If gambling were truly capable of releasing enough Substance H to produce the hallmark symptoms of addiction, we would also expect to see such manifestations as continued use despite adverse circumstances, escalating use, and various forms of self-destructive behavior. It depends on whether the dopamine/serotonin patterns produced by addiction, involving midbrain dopamine neurons with divergent connections to the frontal cortex and other forebrain regions, are the same in compulsive gamblers as in alcoholics and other addicts. Many researchers at NIDA do not believe that the alterations in neurotransmission brought about by behaviors are nearly as powerful as the chemical surges produced by drugs, and therefore cannot result in a state technically called addiction.

Nonetheless, human neurostudies continue to show intriguing dopamine patterns during gambling and certain other forms of game playing. A study at Massachusetts General Hospital in Boston, published in the journal *Neuron*, used MRIs to map the brains of male volunteers engaged in a roulette-style gambling game. Sure enough, the expected dopamine-rich neural circuitry that lights up with drug use also showed increased activity during the gambling game. Part of what drives the destructive gambling cycle appears to be the intense, dopamine-driven arousal produced by the anticipation of reward—the jackpot. Recent research has focused on the part played by midbrain dopamine in the anticipation of reward, otherwise known by addicts as "waiting for the man." In the world of gaming, it is known as the classic "gambler's fallacy—the expectation that after a series of losses, a win is "due." Statistics say otherwise, and gamblers certainly know all about house percentages. Yet, the expectation effects of beating those odds may produce the same anticipatory effect on a disordered metabolism as drug-related activities. A very small, speculative, and intriguing study at Duke University suggested that dopamine agonists given for Parkinson's disease might sometimes be a catalyst for excessive gambling behaviors in elderly patients, even those who had never shown an interest in gambling before. As for shopping and sex, even an informed guess seems premature at this point.

Addicts, alcoholics, compulsive gamblers, bulimics—they all liked to smoke, and perhaps that was because they lacked something other people had in relative abundance. I have called it Substance H, in honor of Dr. Goodwin. Substance H stands revealed as a mix of key neurotransmitters operating on the reward pathway of the brain. This is the physical machinery of drug abuse—the mechanics of mundane rapture. Substance H is composed of the joy molecules; the elixir that ties together opium, god, and madness. Substance H for contentment, for peace of mind.

Substance H for happiness.

Without a sufficient amount of joy molecules coursing through your brain and body, showing up at just the right time, in just the right amounts, and in all the right locations, you would walk much more than a mile for that Camel. In much the same way that you would walk much farther than a mile to eat when hungry, drink when thirsty, or to consummate sexual lust, you will do it to get more of the drug, or more of the activity, that provides you with an equivalent jolt of Substance H. In the case of active drug addiction, the drug has sensitized things. The brain has diddled with itself. It has grown new receptors and altered the layout of existing receptor arrays because of the near-constant presence of the drug.

The metabolic disorder we call addiction is a manifestation of an "impaired reward cascade response." This is where and how addiction happens. It is understood that addiction has its cognitive and environmental aspects as well, but the scientific mystery of how normal people become uncontrollable addicts has been substantially explained. Addictive drugs are a way of triggering the reward cascade. Cocaine, cocktails, and carbo-loading were all short-term methods of either supplying artificial amounts of these neurotransmitters, or sensitizing their receptors, in a way that produced short-term contentment in people whose reward pathway did not operate normally. Naturally, you had to allow for environmental and social factors, but no matter how you added it up, a certain number of people were going to get into trouble with drugs and alcohol. It was human nature. And a percentage of that percentage was going to get into trouble very quickly. These were the people who were hard to treat, and seriously prone to relapse. They would get into trouble because the drug did not have the same effect on them that it had on other people. Like a virus infecting a suitable host, drugs went to work on those kinds of addicts in a hurry.

Most of what has taken place in addiction medicine over the past fifteen years has gone on while very few people were looking. Many Americans had never heard of the NIH, or the CDC, or any of the rest of the government's alphabet soup of medical research agencies, until the public spotlight fell on AIDS research.

Nonetheless, a major paradigm shift was underway. Researchers were seeing that certain people were *inherently* vulnerable to the rewarding effects of the drugs, and highly vulnerable to the dangers of long-term addiction. The drugs themselves were only a substantial threat for these kinds of people.

Even food alters neurotransmission, but the alterations produced by psychoactive drugs amounts to something quite different. In the beginning, the brain does not have a strategy for dealing with a neurotransmitter flood of this magnitude. But it learns. It adjusts, working toward homeostasis by altering the manner and the quantity in which receptors are arrayed. It does this whether the drug in question is cocaine or Prozac. With addictive drugs, though, the task is unique. "The addicted brain is distinctly different from the nonaddicted brain," writes Alan Leshner, the former director of NIDA. "Changes in brain structure and function is what makes it, fundamentally, a brain disease. A metaphorical switch in the brain seems to be thrown as a result of prolonged drug use."

Addiction is both a cause and a consequence of these fundamental alterations in brain function. If physical abnormalities in the brain are at the root of the problem, then any treatment program worth its weight ought to be dealing—directly or indirectly—with these differences in brain state. The goal of treatment, according to Leshner, "must be either to reverse or to compensate for those brain changes." However, for the public, and for many health care professionals, addiction as "a chronic, relapsing disease of the brain" is still an unfamiliar concept.

Writing in *Lancet*, researcher Charles O'Brien has suggested a similar orientation: "Addiction must be approached more like other chronic illnesses—such as diabetes and chronic hypertension—than like an acute illness, such as a bacterial infection or a broken bone."

Other novel aspects of the modern environment have a significant but less dramatic effect on neurotransmission. Playing video games and watching bad television displaces more useful and adaptive behaviors. Snacks high in fat, salt, and sugar tend to displace more nutritious foods in the diet. We are vulnerable to such fitness-decreasing incentives because our brains are not designed to cope with continual access to pure drugs, video games, and snack foods. Hundreds of generations of exposure would likely be needed to shape resistance to their allure. The mismatch between our bodies and our modern environments is a major cause of behavioral and medical problems. Why isn't it simply enough to say that the allure of drugs lies in their ability to produce pleasure? Because, as

Randolph Nesse points out, "As addiction develops, drug-induced pleasure declines or remains constant, even as cravings increase and maladaptive consequences accumulate, thus making it clear that the pursuit of pleasure is an insufficient explanation." And it could get worse before it gets better, from an evolutionary point of view. Nesse offers this discomfiting thought: "The mismatch between novel pharmacological hyperincentives and ancient brain mechanisms is likely to worsen with the discovery of new [addictive] drugs and new routes of administration." All of this suggests that we are not likely to win a war on drugs, achieve zero tolerance, or become chemical-free any time soon. The drug problem is an artifact of the basic design of the mammalian brain. Humankind is extraordinarily susceptible to drug abuse anywhere and everywhere certain drugs are widely available—and all because of a "design quirk" in the reward pathways of the central nervous system.

What would happen to addiction-prone men and women if they never managed to discover the drugs? Would they be "normal"? Depending on the specific mix of these receptor-specific tendencies, the specifics of the chemical disorder—the actual matter of individual cases—could play out in a number of ways. They certainly were not likely to be, in the words of a song by R.E.M., "shiny happy people." Abstinent addicts could manifest a host of other symptoms: depression, aggression, sleep disorders, emotional hypersensitivity, suicide, obsessive-compulsive disorder, overeating, panic reactions, and body dysmorphic disorder (a tendency to see a less attractive person in the mirror than is objectively the case). They might engage in certain high-risk behaviors (gambling, skydiving, or sexual experimentation). Addiction might be only one form of an organic brain disease marked by a genetic tendency toward a chemically disordered reward pathway in the central nervous system. The disorder's salient characteristic is an organic instability in the transmission and supply of one or more of the major pleasure chemicals.

Hedonism, the pursuit of pleasure for its own sake, is not really the answer to these riddles. The pursuit of pleasure does not explain why so many addicts insist that they abuse drugs in a never-ending attempt to feel *normal*. With compulsive use and overuse, much of the pleasure eventually leaches out of the primary dysphoria-relieving drug experience. This does not, however, put an end to the drug-seeking behavior. Far from it. This is the point at which non-addicts tend to believe that there is no longer an excuse—the pleasure has dribbled away, the thrill is gone—but even when addicts aren't getting the full feel-good benefits of the habit, they continue to use.

And now we know why. Any sufficiently powerful receptor-active drug is, in its way, fooling Mother Nature. This deceit means, in a sense, that *all* such drugs are illicit. They are not natural, however organic they may be. Yet, the human drive to use them is all-pervasive. We have no real built-in immunity to drugs that directly target specific receptors in the limbic and cortical pleasure pathways. The act of "liking" something is controlled by the forebrain and brain stem. If you receive a pleasant reward, your reaction is to "like" it. If, however, you are anticipating a reward, and are, in fact, engaging in behaviors motivated by that anticipation, it can be said that you "want" it. The wholly different act of wanting something strongly is a mesolimbic dopamine-serotonin phenomenon. We like to receive gifts, for example, but we *want* food, sex, and drugs. As Nesse and Berridge put it, "The 'liking' system is activated by receiving the reward, while the 'wanting' system anticipates reward and motivates instrumental behaviors. When these two systems are exposed to drugs, the "wanting" system motivates persistent pursuit of drugs that no longer give pleasure, thus offering an explanation for a core paradox in addiction."

The absence of pleasure does not mean the end of compulsive drug use. Researchers are beginning to understand how certain drugs can be so alluring as to defeat the strongest of people and the best of intentions. It certainly does not eliminate the pain of drug hunger, of craving, to know that it is physically correlated with "a pathological overactivity of mesolimbic dopamine function," combined, perhaps, with "increased secretion of glucocorticoids." For such a wide variety of drugs, exhibiting a wide variety of effects, the withdrawal symptoms, while varying by degree, are nonetheless quite similar. The key, as we have seen, is that the areas of the brain that control "wanting" become sensitized by reward pathway drugs.

Under the biochemical paradigm, a runaway appetite for nonstop stimulation of the reward pathway is a prescription for disaster. The harm is physical, behavioral, and psychological—as are the symptoms. Peer pressure, disciplinary difficulties, contempt for authority—none of these conditions is necessary for drug addiction to blossom. What the drug itself does to people who are biologically vulnerable is enough. No further inducements are required.

Dr. James Halikas: "For a drug which is addicting, I can addict one hundred percent of the population at any given time. I may have to tie them into a bed, give them alcohol intravenously, force crack smoke into their lungs, but I can create the physical event, and that's part of the definition of addiction. Now, after they're no longer physically addicted, who will return to the use of the substance? What happens after you wring them out? And there are at least two groups then. There are those who tend to have reoccurrences and relapses, who will be drawn back to it, and I think that's largely biological and genetic. And there are others who are probably at relatively low risk of that kind of relapse, and that probably is also biologic and genetic. And then there's a third group in the middle that, depending on the vicissitudes of the remainder of their life, will either go back to it, or not. It's not the addictive part that's in question, it's what happens after."

Even this brief summation of the ways in which addictive drugs alter neurotransmission should serve to demonstrate that these substances have more in common than we ordinarily assume. All these drugs are of course rewarding, so it is perhaps not too surprising, for all their differences, that they work the limbic reward pathways. All these drugs share common mechanisms of action, which is why they are addictive. As we will see, there are striking similarities in the neurotransmitter alterations caused by almost all psychoactive drugs, even though the effect of the drugs, as well as their addictive potential, varies widely.

There is more to addiction than the matter of brain chemistry, of course. Nonetheless, the neuropharmacology of addictive drugs can be spoken of with a specificity undreamed of only two decades ago. Addiction is a behavior, a state of mind, a way of life—but it is not only these things. It is also a biochemical process. For all their similarities, drugs do have characteristic signatures. They make their own distinctive trails through the reward pathways of the brain.

PART II

FIVE: ALCOHOL AND HEROIN

"To be sure, there are drugs... largely about themselves and the consumption of themselves, whose promise of pleasure comes entirely from the anticipation of their own effects, and that accordingly do not 'expand consciousness' but instead contract it to the point where all other objects are only facets of itself."

—David Lenson

In an ounce-for-ounce comparison of potency, alcohol clearly loses out to heroin. Yet, as any drinker knows, alcohol is a formidable mood-altering substance in its own right. Ethanol, also known as ethyl alcohol—the kind we drink—is composed of a two-carbon backbone with an OH, or hydroxyl group, attached to one of the carbons. This simple arrangement makes ethyl alcohol both water- and lipid-soluble. Water-soluble molecules are known as amphiphilic molecules, and that spells bad news for abusive drinkers. The peculiar dehydration typical of a hangover is a clue to what makes alcohol unique. As a researcher at NIMH put it, "Alcohol replaces water in the cells, so the cells demand it, and when they don't get it, the entire body hurts." The well-known shakes, the intense thirst, the coated tongue, are the results of this process. With alcohol—as with heroin, barbiturates, and benzodiazepines like Valium—abrupt withdrawal can lead to seizures, delirium, and death.

Alcohol's effect does not express itself through a specific receptor site for ethanol. Unlike the endorphins and the specific lock-and-key sites for heroin and morphine activity, there are no booze receptors in the brain. But this does not mean that alcohol has no effect on brain neurochemistry. We know better, from Dr. Li's rats.

When a person drinks an alcoholic beverage, two key enzymes begin breaking it down into byproducts. The first enzyme, alcohol dehydrogenase (ADH), is found in the liver, and its only job appears to be the metabolization of alcohol into acetaldehyde and acetate. Donald Goodwin has speculated that the mammalian liver may have evolved this helpful enzyme millennia ago, as a response to the ingestion of fermenting fruits and grains by horses and other vegetarian mammals—and, eventually, people. The "Al" prefix suggests an Arabic origin for the word, much like "al"gebra and "al"kaline. The "-cohol" may stem from the Arabic root, "Kul," which originally denoted the powder women used to darken their eyelids. Eventually, "al-kul" came to stand for any powder produced in any number of ways, as well as for substances obtained through distillation, according to one line of speculation.

A second enzyme completes the job of transformation, and the major end product of drinking alcohol is acetic acid. Vinegar. "Getting pickled" is a fair approximation of the process. When alcohol is converted into calories, uric acid levels rise, and high concentrations of uric acid lead to gout. The amount of fat in the bloodstream and in the liver increases, too, which can lead to cirrhosis.

Compared to other drug molecules, the alcohol molecule is relatively small. Cell membranes prove to be no barrier to a tiny, water-soluble molecule like alcohol. One school of thought believes that short-term use of alcohol increases membrane fluidity, and long-term use stiffens the membrane. Proper membrane fluidity is crucial to the functioning of receptors and cellular channels on the cell surface. What sets alcohol apart from other drugs, as Eli Lilly's Steve Paul put it, is that "it looks and smells and tastes to the brain like water. Any place water can go, alcohol molecules can go. They wiggle all over the place It's a very scary drug."

Nevertheless, for all its destructive power, alcohol is not a very strong drug in a gram-by-gram comparison of potency. If cocaine were as weak as alcohol, it would take about 50 grams of powder to make a serious night of partying, instead of the customary gram or less. Dr. Steven Paul, who was the director of intramural research programs in the Clinical Neuroscience Branch of NIMH when I spoke with him many years ago, put it this way: "The problem with alcohol is that it's a very weak drug—it doesn't work until you get very high concentrations in the body, and it's rather nonspecific. It produces its effects on many systems in the brain. So it's been hard to tease out what neurotransmitters may be involved."

We are dealing here with perhaps the most organ-toxic drug in the human armamentarium of addictive pharmaceuticals. Since it is also one of the least potent, much of the poisonous effect must be undergone in order to achieve the full fruits of intoxication.

Said Dr. Li: "We believe alcohol works as a reward by utilizing the same pathway that works with amphetamine and cocaine—the so-called dopamine and serotonin pathways. Alcohol appears to cause a release of dopamine, which then goes to the nucleus accumbens, which is the switching station between the limbic system and the cerebral cortex. Our alcohol-preferring rats were deficient in both dopamine and serotonin, and their receptors became upregulated; that is, the nervous system becomes more sensitive to dopamine and serotonin in general. Therefore, when alcohol causes dopamine to come back to normal, there is an enhanced reward effect in the rats."

Alcohol also has a well-documented effect on receptors for benzodiazepine, the class of sedative drugs to which Valium belongs. Alcohol is capable of stimulating the benzodiazepine receptors with the help of the secondary neurotransmitter called GABA. Alcohol causes GABA levels to rise, and higher levels of GABA translate into higher levels of the brain's own form of Valium. The result: feelings of contentment, and a lessening of anxiety.

What other compounds can tickle the GABA receptors? Benzodiazepines, barbiturates, and heroin—which tell us that alcohol's GABA-augmenting effects are probably responsible for its sedative effects at high dosages. It also suggests why people often say they drink when they are anxious. Flooding the brain with GABA results in "disinhibition" and, eventually, unconsciousness. Drinking as a sleep aid, however, is counterproductive. Alcohol disrupts normal sleep architecture, interferes with rapid-eye-movement (REM) sleep, and causes the sleeper to wake more often in the course of the night.

"Alcohol can augment GABA," Dr. Paul said, "like Phenobarbital and minor tranquilizers. It kind of suggests to us that alcohol is a rather bad Valium. Of course, alcohol has been around three thousand years longer than Valium, and people have sort of naturally selected it." This natural affinity between alcohol and Valium is the reason why combining the two drugs can be perilous, and why heroin addicts are more likely to die when they combine heroin with alcohol.

But GABA is not the whole story. Although the mechanism of action isn't clear yet, GABA also affects dopamine and serotonin receptors in the nucleus accumbens. A glass of wine, as we now know, also alters concentrations of dopamine and serotonin in the limbic system. Alcohol makes people feel good, and the bombardment of the limbic system by these two neurotransmitters is a large part of the reason why. "There was always a difference between the preferring and non-preferring rats in the GABA content," Dr. Li noted. "So there are at least three differences involving the nucleus accumbens: The alcohol-preferring animals are low in dopamine, low in serotonin, but high in GABA."

Drugs that lower GABA levels in the brain have the net effect of reducing the stimulation of the Valium-type receptors. "What we've found is that certain drugs that sit on the Valium receptor can prevent alcohol from stimulating the nervous system," said

Dr. Paul, referring to the results of earlier alcohol research at NIMH. "One of these is a drug called Ro15-4513. We showed in animals that Ro15-4513 would block much of the sedation and intoxication produced by alcohol. You can give a rat this drug, and when he drinks, he acts as if he never got the alcohol. These studies suggest to us that if this drug can do this selectively, and it's not just doing it by making animals sick, then such a drug might block some of the reinforcing properties of alcohol. And such a drug would then have therapeutic implications."

Drugs like Ro15-4513 might have a role to play in the case of chronic alcoholics for whom continued drinking might be fatal. But Ro15-4513 itself will not be useful for humans because of a variety of side effects, including liver damage. In addition, drugs that reduce the stimulation of the Valium-type receptors by blocking GABA can actually produce severe anxiety in users.

An antagonist drug that neutralized the intoxicating effects of alcohol, even one without the negative reinforcement properties of Antabuse, would still not address the "drug-seeking behavior" we commonly refer to as craving.

Until quite recently, the only therapeutic medication available to alcoholics was Antabuse, a drug that blocks the final breakdown enzyme that converts acetaldehyde to acetate, carbon dioxide, and water. This causes a surge in acetaldehyde levels, so that when alcoholics on Antabuse take a drink of alcohol, they become violently ill. The process is unsettlingly reminiscent of the deconditioning procedure little Alex undergoes in Anthony Burgess' *A Clockwork Orange*. While this may sound like a good way to keep alcoholics from drinking, it isn't very effective at all. All too often, alcoholics simply "forget" to take their Antabuse.

Japanese drinkers who have a genetic shortage of the enzyme aldehyde dehydrogenase experience the same nausea and heart pounding flush that Antabuse is designed to produce in drinkers. About 50 per cent of the Japanese population "is in a natural Antabuse state," according to David Goldman, an alcoholism researcher with the NIMH. Goldman has researched the alcohol-serotonin connection as well, and spent years doing genetic work with Native American tribes in the Southwest. In some tribes, Goldman believes, more than 80 per cent of male alcoholism is genetically determined. "People are not just making lifestyle choices," Goldman told the Los Angeles Times. "I don't know why people have a problem calling [alcoholism] a disease. Clogged arteries exist because of choices made about eating Twinkies. No one says it isn't heart disease."

Women and Drinking

Despite a clinical bias toward alcoholism as a "male" disorder, recent research has turned up underlying gender differences in alcohol metabolism. MRI scans began documenting more of these differences, and by the late 1990s, it was possible to venture a non-politicized answer to the age-old question of why women tend to get drunk faster, on less alcohol, than men do. Simple body weight is not the whole answer. Levels of alcohol dehydrogenase (ADH) are markedly less active—up to 50 per cent less—in a woman's stomach. A lower concentration of ADH in the stomach lining of women means that less alcohol is broken down on its way to the upper intestine. This results in higher blood alcohol levels in women, when compared to men, after the same number of drinks. In a sense, alcohol is the original date-rape drug. The higher the alcohol intake, the more these metabolic differences manifest themselves. Male alcoholics at autopsy show some degree of brain shrinkage, but when researchers finally got around to taking a look at MRI scans of alcoholic women, they where shocked to discover that the percentage loss of white brain matter in women was significantly greater than that found in men. These gender differences are another reason why the sheer quantity of alcohol consumed is never a reliable indicator for alcoholism. Amount consumed is not even among the criteria for alcohol dependence listed in recent versions of the psychiatric *Diagnostic and Statistical Manual* (DSM). Why didn't this finding about female drinkers surface earlier? Mainly because researchers had not been looking for it. The National Institute on Alcohol Abuse and Alcoholism, among other research centers, has often relied on the Veterans Administration hospitals for clinical test subjects, and VA hospitals are notoriously male bastions. There is reason to believe that there are more women alcoholics than one might think. Studies have shown that doctors are more likely to misdiagnose alcoholism in women than in men. More women than men are treated for secondary depression and anxiety, while their primary alcoholism remains undiagnosed and untreated. Numerous studies have shown that, while there may be fewer female alcoholics, alcoholic women experience more medical complications than their male counterparts, and die more frequently of liver disease and alcohol-related violence. (Remember that we are talking about the disease of alcoholism, a brain chemistry disorder characterized by continued compulsive use of alcohol despite severely adverse consequences. We are not discussing alcohol "abuse", which is the deliberate overuse of alcohol, best typified by college "binge" drinking.)

It is now possible to flesh out the portrait of female alcoholics much more completely. The result of studies undertaken at Columbia University's National Center on Addiction and Substance Abuse, and collectively written up in 2006 by that group, *Women Under the Influence* gathers together a decade's worth of research on gender differences.

Young women with family histories of alcoholism will, like Pavlov's dogs, salivate more intensely at the sight of alcohol than women from families without addiction histories. Studies of female twins also confirm the behavioral link between major depressive disorder and substance abuse. Women who have suffered from major depression are three to six times more likely to suffer from alcoholism than those who have not. Despite these and other commonalities, however, women and men often follow different arcs of addiction on a drug-by-drug basis.

Today, women are no strangers to binge drinking, either. According to the Columbia study, about one out of every four American girls has had one or more alcoholic drinks by the age of 13. In the 1960s, only seven percent of girls reported having consumed alcohol by that age.

In addition to adding much needed information, the study turned a few common assumptions upside down. For example, the more education a woman has had, the more likely she is to be a drinker. White adult women are more likely to be drinkers than African-American, Hispanic, or Asian-American women. And while men traditionally drink more than women, women are fast closing that gender gap. Among high school seniors, the percentage gap between heavy-drinking boys and heavy-drinking girls was 23 percent in 1975. By 2003, the difference was only 12 percent, and among very young teenagers, girls have closed the gender gap completely. In addition, older women have higher rates of late-onset (over age 60) alcohol abuse than men.

Teenage girls whose mothers drank regularly during pregnancy are six times more likely to report alcohol use than girls whose mothers did not drink. Whatever the cause, or most likely causes, no such maternal relationship has been demonstrated for teenage boys of drinking mothers. And—bearing in mind that such estimates are fraught with peril—the Center concludes that genetic factors account for as much as 66 percent of the risk for alcohol dependence in women. As evidence, women who are alcoholics are somewhat more likely that male alcoholics to come from a family with a history of alcohol abuse.

And it is now quite clear that women metabolize alcohol differently than men do. With less water and more fatty tissue in their bodies, blood alcohol levels are higher for women than for men, given the same number of drinks. After two beers, women are more likely than men to exceed legal levels of alcohol in the bloodstream. Women get drunk faster and have heavier hangovers, and the reason may stem from differences in ADH enzyme activity in breaking down alcohol into its byproducts. (More research is needed.)

Female alcoholics also develop liver diseases like cirrhosis more frequently than alcohol-abusing men, and at lower levels of alcohol intake.

Finally, from the sociocultural point of view, women are targeted heavily in alcohol advertising, primarily through promotion of the idea that alcohol will relax sexual inhibitions and improve communication with men. Alcohol advertising has increasingly zeroed in on selling beer to women—"beer's lost drinkers," as one brewery spokesperson put it. Only about 20 per cent of women currently drink beer regularly. Ironically, the alcohol industry's official code of ethics forbade the use of women in alcohol ads until 1958.

All of the foregoing pales in comparison to the potential for damage among pregnant women who drink. The fact that alcohol is dangerous to fetal development is not a recent discovery. Aristotle pointed out that "Foolish drunken or harebrain women for the most part bring forth children like unto themselves." While warning signs on alcohol containers and tavern doors have become a common sight, the study group estimates that about 10 percent of pregnant women still drink. (That number is quite likely higher, given the reluctance of patients to accurately report their alcohol intake). "Drinking during pregnancy," according to the Center, "is the single greatest preventable cause of mental retardation" in America today. Indeed, the number of birth defects caused by alcohol in one year exceeds the total number of recorded thalidomide births.

Tragically, "As many as 60 percent of pregnant women who drink do not discover their condition until after the first trimester," according to the Columbia Center. In addition to the well-known Fetal Alcohol Syndrome (FAS), there is also a range of other neurobehavioral deficits to the fetus associated with drinking during early pregnancy. Pregnant women who drink heavily suffer three times the normal risk of miscarriages and stillbirths. In fact, to this day, no safe level of alcohol intake during pregnancy has been established. The American Academy of Pediatrics continues to advise women who are pregnant or thinking of becoming pregnant to abstain from alcohol completely.

By 1995, so much had changed so quickly in addiction research that Professor George Vaillant of Harvard, author of a 1983 landmark study, *The Natural History of Alcoholism*, felt obliged to bring out a revised version. Vaillant was the motive force behind the Harvard Medical School's Study of Adult Development, which began in 1940 and went on to become the longest formal study of drinking behavior ever undertaken in the United States. The study was divided into three groups: a middle-class "College" sample, a "Core City" sample, and a "Clinic" sample, the latter made up solely of people who had been admitted to a detox clinic, and the only one of the groups to include women.

Vaillant's data verified that the amount of alcohol consumed was not a reliable predictor of alcoholic drinking. "Frequency of intoxication" proved to be a poor indicator as well. Both attributes, Vaillant found, were relatively useless for discriminating between alcoholics and other drinkers. If how much you drink, and how often you drink, are not reliable predictors of alcoholism, then what is? The key item on Vaillant's questionnaires turned out to be: "Admits problem controlling alcohol use." Vaillant had the evidence to prove that alcohol-related problems did not result simply from drinking a lot, but stemmed, instead, "from being unable consistently to control when, where, and how much alcohol is consumed." Alcoholism, Vaillant concluded, is "defined by the number, not by the specificity, of alcohol-related problems." This dovetailed nicely with a definition adopted years ago by the National Council on Alcoholism: "The person with alcoholism cannot consistently predict on any drinking occasion the duration of the episode or the quantity that will be consumed." This behavior is a reasonably reliable predictor of alcoholism.

For George Vaillant and other pioneers of the disease model, the conceptual view had shifted long ago: "As with coronary heart disease, we must learn to regard alcoholism as both disease and behavior disorder." This shift in viewpoint is crucial, since alcohol is so heavily implicated in death by various forms of heart disease and cardiac failure. Genetic loading, says Vaillant, "is an important predictor of whether an individual develops alcoholism," while a difficult childhood environment "is an important predictor of when an individual loses control of alcohol."

Based on his lifelong study of alcoholism, and subsequent follow-ups by other researchers, Vaillant was able to offer strong evidence for the grim fact that very few active alcoholics make it beyond the age of 60. Vaillant's numbers indicated that "roughly 2 percent...become stably abstinent every year and after age 40 roughly 2 percent die every year." That chronic alcoholics are involved in at least half of all vehicle accident deaths comes as no surprise. Half of all emergency room patients with severe multiple fractures are alcoholics, and alcoholics cost six times as much when hospitalized, Vaillant found. Indirectly, alcoholism contributes to death by pneumonia and tuberculosis because of its suppressive effect on immune system functioning. Alcoholics—22 million of them in the U.S. alone, by a recent federal estimate—commit suicide far more often than non-alcoholics do. According to statistics cited by Vaillant, between 10 and 30 per cent of all suicides may be alcoholics. And this does not include estimates of suicides by people addicted to drugs other than alcohol. "Progressive" alcoholics—those who never abstain or go through periods of stable social drinking—were twice as likely to smoke two packs of cigarettes a day, compared to other drinkers. Indeed, alcoholics almost never stop smoking. Vaillant believes that heavy drinking acidifies the urine in a way that increases the excretion of nicotine. Hence, there is a need to smoke more when you are drinking more. Otherwise, blood nicotine levels fall below the comfort range.

Along with cigarettes, Vaillant also found depression: "Like smoking and alcohol abuse, depression is associated with premature mortality; and if alcoholics were three times as likely to be dead, they were also three times as likely to be depressed." This is what we know: Depressed men and women drink more, smoke more, and take more drugs than non-depressed people. This is not to say that all addicts drink, smoke, and take drugs in order to relieve an underlying state of chronic depression, but the tendency toward clinical depression and the urge to abuse addictive drugs both spring from the same biological underpinnings. There is no chicken and there is no egg. The one does not cause the other.

It is not hard to anticipate the chorus of complaint that such reasoning elicits. Everybody has emotional vicissitudes, but not everybody resorts to abusing drugs. Everybody gets the blues, but not everybody drowns them in drink. With courage and discipline, people can resist the easy notion of a whiskey, neat, for every problem.

To combat that complacent notion, Vaillant also documented the dismal record compiled by institutions offering "treatment" for alcoholism: "For short periods, middle-class individuals respond well to treatment in the medical model, but that response may be short-lived and reflect premorbid variables rather than the efficacy of specific treatment." It turns out that if you simply control for two "premorbid" variables—marriage and employment—you can predict with reasonable accuracy how it will go for different people, especially in their first go-round with treatment. People who have solid relationships, and a steady job, fare better in treatment. That accounts for most of the difference. But even the promising cases don't always do so well over time.

By 2000, Dr. Li's findings about dysfunctional brain chemistry in his "alcohol-preferring rats" had been borne out in human and animal laboratories and clinics worldwide. At customary levels, alcohol effects GABA transmission, dopamine release, the activation of endogenous opioids in the hypothalamus, and an alteration in the function of glutamine systems (So far, social drinking does not seem to pose similar problems.)

Neurobiology has taught us that addictive drugs cause long-lasting neural changes in the brain. The problems start when sustained, heavy drinking forces the brain to accept the altered levels of neurotransmission as the normal state of affairs. As the brain struggles to adapt to the artificial surges, it becomes more sensitized to these substances. It may grow more receptors at one site, less at another. It may cut back on the natural production of these neurotransmitters altogether, in an effort to make the best of an abnormal situation. In effect, the brain is forced to treat alcoholic drinking as normal, because that is what the drinking has become.

Take the alcohol away, and the new checks and balances, the new receptor sensitivities the brain has learned to deal with, are thrown back into disarray. In the beginning of the process of abstinence, the brain is stubborn. It has learned to deal with the new chemical state of affairs, and sends signals indicating that the drinking should continue. Add alcohol back into the mix, and the roller-coaster cycle begins anew. "I couldn't get drunk, and I couldn't get sober," is a familiar alcoholic's lament. Dr. Vaillant believes we could be doing more to help bolster "host resistance" to alcoholism. Cultures that encourage the use of low-proof alcohol, like wines, and that sanction the use of alcohol primarily as an adjunct to food—that is, with meals—fare better, Vaillant maintains, when compared with family or cultural habits which tend to separate alcohol from mealtimes—bars, for example—and which emphasis the consumption of high-proof liquors like whiskey and vodka.

The primary problem with the disease model, as many see it, is the public belief "that if alcoholics are taught to regard alcoholism as a disease they will use this label as an excuse to drink or as a reason why they should not be held responsible for their own recovery." That is the counter-argument, and Vaillant insists that it is manifestly false. When alcoholics come to see that they have a disease, "they become more, not less, responsible for self-care," writes Vaillant.

This is why the self-help group Alcoholics Anonymous places such single-minded emphasis on the idea that alcoholism is a disease. For years, alcoholics have labeled themselves wicked, weak, and reprehensible; being offered a medical explanation for their behavior does not lead to irresponsibility—just to hope and improved morale. There is an enormous difference between diagnosis and name-calling.

The likelihood that many alcoholics and other drug addicts have inherited a defect in the production and distribution of serotonin and dopamine is a far-reaching finding, because of serotonin's link with a variety of other behaviors often associated with addiction. While it is difficult to measure neurotransmitter levels directly in brains, there are indirect ways of doing so. One such method is to measure serotonin's principle metabolic breakdown product, a substance called 5-HIAA, in cerebrospinal fluid. From these measurements, scientists can make extrapolations about serotonin levels in the central nervous system as a whole. One of the more extraordinary recent discoveries in behavioral medicine concerns the abnormally low levels of serotonin found in people who have attempted suicide. Moreover, there is some evidence to suggest that a low level of 5-HIAA is an inherited trait. Suicide, like depression and alcoholism, sometimes runs in families. Identical twins tend to have the same levels of 5-HIAA in their cerebrospinal fluid, while fraternal twins have different levels. Low serotonin levels have also been strongly implicated as a factor in two other human behaviors. "Serotonin deficiency is linked with impulsivity and aggression, as well as suicidality," explained Dr. Robert Post of NIMH. "That particular triangle seems to be fairly well replicated and worked out across a number of studies."

A research group at the VA Medical Center in New York City studied a large sample of male alcoholics in 1989 and discovered that those with drinking problems early in life—Cloninger's Type 2 alcoholics—were twice as likely to have done jail time for violent offenses, three times as likely to have suffered from serious depression, and four times as likely to have attempted suicide than other drinkers. The hard-core alcoholics in the VA study also had markedly lower blood levels of tryptophan, serotonin's precursor chemical, shortly after withdrawal from alcohol. While it is far from conclusive, other studies have also demonstrated that Cloninger's

Type 2 alcoholics may have chronically low levels of serotonin, as measured by metabolites in the cerebrospinal fluid.

Another method of indirectly assessing serotonin levels involves measurements of an enzyme called monoamine oxidase, or MAO. The salient fact about MAO is that it helps regulate the availability of brain serotonin. One thought-provoking possibility that evolved out of the Cloninger-Bohman studies is that the victims of Type 2 alcoholism may have inherited a defect in the gene that controls the production of MAO. In a 1988 report published in the *New England Journal of Medicine*, Dr. Boris Tabakoff of NIAAA produced evidence that alcoholics have reduced levels of platelet MAO.

Despite all the promising research on neurotransmission, what can physicians and health professionals do today to identify alcoholics and attempt to help them? For starters, physicians could look beyond liver damage to the many observable "tells" that are characteristic patterns of chronic alcoholism—such manifestations as constant abdominal pain, frequent nausea and vomiting, numbness or tingling in the legs, cigarette burns between the index and middle finger, jerky eye movements, and a chronically flushed or puffy face. Such signs of acute alcoholism are not always present, of course. Many practicing alcoholics are successful in their work, physically healthy, don't smoke, and came from happy homes. Despite the time, labor, and expense that have gone into the search for a better way to diagnose alcoholism, researchers have yet to outdo what may be the simplest, most accurate test for alcoholism yet devised. Developed in 1970 by Dr. John A. Ewing, it is known as the CAGE questionnaire. The questions are brief and relatively noncontroversial. The test takes less than a minute, requires only paper and pencil, and can be graded by the test takers themselves. It goes like this:

1. Have you ever felt the need to (C)ut down on your drinking?
2. Have you ever felt (A)nnoyed by someone criticizing your drinking?
3. Have you ever felt (G)uilty about your drinking?

4. Have you ever felt the need for a drink at the beginning of the day—an "(E)ye opener?

People who answer "yes" to two or more of these questions should consider the possibility of alcoholism or alcohol abuse.

Poppies on the Brain

Alcohol's range of action is diffuse, while opium's effects are concentrated at specific receptor sites. Nonetheless, the two drugs have similar effects along the limbic reward pathway. Morphine comes right from the source, isolated from the crude opium resin found on Papaver somniferum—the opium poppy. Morphine is known as a "pure mu agonist," meaning it locks securely into the "mu" subset of endorphin receptors, and activates them. This alters the transmission of pain messages, and induces a contented, euphoric state of relaxation. Codeine, another natural painkiller, is found in opium in very small concentrations. Most medical codeine is synthesized from morphine.

The body's own opiates are referred to as endogenous opioids. Endorphins and enkephalins are interchangeable terms for these chains of amino acids. An important mechanism of action in this process is morphine's inhibitive effect on GABA. By inhibiting the inhibitor, so to speak, neurotransmitter levels increase down the line, particularly in the nucleus accumbens. Hence, feelings of pleasure.

Alcohol stimulates the mu receptor as well, so we are back to the same basic chain of limbic activation triggered by drinking. GABA is the bridge that connects the alcohol high and the heroin high. Alcohol and heroin both tap into opiate and benzodiazepine receptor systems through the mediation of GABA, dopamine, and serotonin. While morphine and heroin naturally have a more dramatic effect on opioid receptors, alcohol boosts endorphin levels significantly as well. Some of the ill effects of hangovers undoubtedly stem from a temporary shortfall of free-circulating b-endorphin. Alcohol is not just a rather bad Valium; it is a rather bad opioid as well.

Patients take morphine therapeutically for pain in doses that typically fall in the 5 to 10 mg. range. Experienced morphine addicts regularly take several hundred milligrams a day. A gram or more per day is not unheard of. Heroin, as noted, is the semi-synthetic opioid touted as less addictive than morphine. That was not the case, but a long string of other synthetic "near-beer" opioids followed: Dalaudid (commonly used for pain relief in the terminal elderly), Demerol (along with Fentanyl, a prominent designer drug in the opioid family) and Percodan (oxycodone, synthesized from codeine). These effective and fiercely addictive variants are joined by more dilute versions, such as methadone. First produced synthetically by Nazi scientists when morphine supplies became inadequate during World War II, methadone was allegedly named "dolophine" after Adolf Hitler, who used it to ease the pain of withdrawal. Darvon (only mild pain relief), and Talwin (a meager opioid and a poor pain reliever), bring up the bottom of the list.

A recent addition to the pantheon of synthetic painkillers has caused a surge in American opiate addiction. OxyContin, approved by the FDA in 1995, also contains the codeine alkaloid oxycodone, as do Percodan and Percocet. While press reports of an epidemic of "hillbilly heroin" were overblown as usual—Rush Limbaugh notwithstanding—the fact remained that OxyContin was available in doses of 10 to 80 milligrams per day, and 160 mg pills were available for terminal cancer and other forms of intractable pain. Percodan tables contain about five milligrams of oxycodone. Suddenly, pain patients were receiving medication in amounts that were twenty or thirty times higher than Percodan. There were complaints that Purdue Pharma LP, Abbot Labs, and prescribing doctors had done a poor job of explaining to patients that OxyContin was, in fact, an opiate; a swallowable version of morphine. Crushed tablets can be easily mixed with water and injected. OxyContin brought in more than $1 billion in sales during 2000. A recent court case seeks to prove that doctors and pharmacists misrepresented the drug—Purdue Pharma at one point was touting the drug as a first-line treatment for osteoarthritis.

As might be expected, the limbic system contains the highest concentration of opiate receptors in the brain. But there are receptors for endorphin all over the body, including the gastrointestinal tract, where the presence of opiates diminishes "propulsive peristaltic waves" in the lower tract, leading to chronic constipation in opiate addicts. In addition to locking directly into endorphin receptors, opiates make use of the standard limbic reward pathway. One of the first non-opiate drugs to be tried on heroin addicts—clonidine—was chosen because of its actions as a blocker of norepinephrine release in the limbic system.

Unlike alcohol, the opiates rarely present the possibility of a life-threatening withdrawal. Typically, heroin and morphine kill by means of overdose. Endorphin receptors are especially dense in areas of the brainstem that control respiratory reflexes. Hence, when these receptors are flooded with morphine or heroin, breathing is severely depressed, and the user dies by asphyxiation. A quick shot of naloxone will immediately restart respiration by bumping the opiate molecules off the endorphin receptors, if the user ends up in the emergency room quickly enough.

Heroin also kills by means of externalities—the "black market factors." In 1989, the Cato Institute asserted that fully 80 per cent of deaths attributed to heroin were caused by either infections or allergic reactions to common street adulterants used to dilute the drug. And, finally, heroin kills when combined with alcohol. The toxic effects of combining spirits and opiates had been well documented by the end of the 19th Century, and are still being documented today. A blood alcohol level of .10 makes a heroin user 22 times as likely to experience a fatal overdose, according to a study of heroin-related deaths by the Centers for Disease Control.

Rapid cellular tolerance is the hallmark of opiate addiction. Brain cells quickly become less responsive to the same doses of the drug. "The body's natural enkephalins are not addicting because they are destroyed rapidly by peptide-degrading enzymes as soon as they act at opiate receptors," writes Solomon Snyder. "Therefore, they are never in contact with receptors long enough to promote tolerance.... As analgesics, the enkephalin derivatives developed by drug companies have not been superior to morphine, or even as good as morphine." Even the brain's own morphine is not as good as morphine. Nothing is as good as morphine.

Recent evidence for the heritability of opiate addiction looks strong. "Harvard did some really superb studies using a huge cohort of military recruits in the U.S. Army," according to Mary Jeanne Kreek, a specialist in opiate addiction at Rockefeller University in New York. "Heroin addiction has even a larger heritable component than any of the other addictions, so that up to 54% of heroin addictions seem to be on a genetic basis or a heritable basis." Estimates of alcohol's heritability generally run to 40 or 50 per cent.

Kreek's conclusion:

> Of those who self administer heroin, approximately one in three go on to become heroin addicted. Approximately three million in the U.S. have used heroin at some time, for instance, but there are approximately one million that meet the criteria of multiple daily dependence, and a compulsive drug self-administration.

I cannot say whether Kreek's estimates are accurate or not. No matter how generously we extend the margin for error, we are forced to admit that the number of heroin addicts (and the social costs of dealing with them) pale in comparison to the social, financial, and psychological costs levied by the indiscriminate consumption of ethyl alcohol.

When a group of researchers conducted a meta-review of prior clinical studies on the neurotransmitter serotonin for *Alcoholism: Clinical and Experimental Research*, they found that the serotonin hypothesis had held up quite well, despite more than 15 years of scrutiny and skepticism. Yes, the researches reported, serotonin deficiencies were conclusively linked to mood disorders, impulsivity, and other forms of "behavioral dysregulation" that Dr. Begleiter observed in early-onset alcoholics. Furthermore, the lower the serotonin levels, the more alcohol people can drink. And the earlier in life you drink it, the more likely you are to bring forth the dragon of addiction, if you have it within you. In effect, the modern environment in most of the world, including the ready availability and sanctioned use of alcohol, has the effect of selecting out those people with a preexisting genetic propensity for addiction. Perhaps it has always been so.

If you don't eat the fava beans, as Dr. Li put it to me, all those years ago, you don't get the disease.

SIX: NICOTINE AND CAFFEINE

"If alcohol is queen, then tobacco is her consort. It's a fond companion for all occasions, a loyal friend through fair weather and foul. People smoke to celebrate a happy moment, or to hide a bitter regret. Whether you're alone or with friends, it's a joy for all the senses."

—Luis Buñuel

If there is a single, reasonably reliable behavioral marker for alcoholism and substance abuse, it is cigarette smoking.

Nicotine, like alcohol, produces chemical changes throughout the body, and, like all other drugs of abuse, has a focused effect on the reward pathway. Nicotine lights up the usual limbic reward system activated by other drugs of abuse, but does so impressively and almost instantaneously. Dopamine and norepinephrine levels soar, endorphin concentrations increase, and steroid levels rise. Nicotine also has a complex impact on serotonin systems.

"In a lot of ways," said Dr. Neal Benowitz, a leading nicotine researcher at San Francisco General Hospital Medical Center, "nicotine in the brain is doing the same thing cocaine or amphetamine is doing."

In addition, the nicotine molecules quickly bind to receptor sites meant for acetylcholine, a neurotransmitter involved in arousal, heart rate, and sending messages from the brain to the muscles. This direct affinity for acetylcholine receptors is what creates the powerful nicotine rush that frequently accompanies the first cigarette of the day. Nicotine pops into acetylcholine receptors in the brain, the adrenal glands, and the skeletal muscles. "These are not trivial responses," said Professor Ovide Pomerleau of the University of Michigan Medical School. "It's like lighting a match in a gasoline factory."

Acetylcholine is another neurotransmitter we share with other members of the animal kingdom. It is the Achilles' heel of the insect world—insecticides that cause a fatal build-up of acetylcholine are among the most common in our collective chemical arsenal against bugs. While the mechanisms of the toxic effect are not perfectly clear, acetylcholine is involved in diaphragm control, and one of the signs of insecticide poisoning in children is difficulty breathing.

Cigarettes improve task performance and concentration, enhance memory, reduce anxiety and hunger, and increase tolerance to pain. In laboratory tests, people given doses of nicotine perform better on complicated intellectual tasks, compared with their performance in the absence of the drug. The typical methodology for such investigations is to give participants pulls on a cigarette that either contains or does not contain nicotine and then have them perform random word memorization tests. The smokers usually out-perform the nonsmokers. Why? Because smoking activates additional acetylcholine receptors in the part of the brain associated with short-term memory, for one thing. Indeed, if nicotine did not cause cardiovascular disease, pulmonary failure, lung cancer, lip cancer, throat cancer, shortness of breath, and smelly clothing, it might be very nearly the perfect drug.

Experiments at NIDA's Addiction Research Center in Baltimore have confirmed that nicotine withdrawal not only makes people irritable, but also impairs intellectual performance. Logical reasoning and rapid decision-making both suffer during nicotine withdrawal. Acetylcholine appears to enhance memory, which may help explain a common lament voiced by many smokers during early withdrawal. As summarized by one ex-smoker, "I cannot think, cannot remember, cannot concentrate."

Both nicotine and alcohol produce similar patterns of activation at the nucleus accumbens and the prefrontal cortex. Scientists have documented that alcohol has a strong effect on nicotinic receptors, helping to explain the link between heavy drinking and heavy smoking. Alcohol may be making it possible for smokers to smoke more. Researchers have been able to identify common neural substrates linking cocaine and cigarette addiction as well. Nicotine's effect is subtler than most drugs of abuse, and because of these subtleties, smoking's tenacious grip on its victims remains something of a scientific mystery. People who have never shown an inclination toward addiction to any other drug still manage to get into trouble with cigarettes.

One of the difficulties of pinning down the effects of nicotine has to do with its seemingly contradictory strengths. No discussion of smoking would be complete without a reference to the "Nesbitt paradox"—the fact that cigarettes are capable of producing both arousal and relaxation. In the early 1970s, researcher Paul Nesbitt ran a series of tests demonstrating that smokers could withstand an increasingly intense series of electric shocks better than non-smokers could. If nicotine is a stimulant, why, did it have a tranquilizing effect on pain? Nesbitt's personal conclusion was that smoking raises the "arousal baseline." Since smokers are already revved up, operating on "high arousal," they are better able to withstand shocks that might strike a non-stimulated smoker with more impact.

"It's not that it's so intensive," Dr. Benowitz told me, "it's just that it's so reliable, it's available many times per day, and the response is kind of plastic. It arouses you in the morning; it relaxes you in the afternoon. It's a drug that you can dose many times per day for the purpose of modulating your mood, and it becomes highly conditioned, more than any other drug, because it's used every single day, multiple times per day. So even though it's a subtler effect, it is more addictive than any other drug."

Professor Pomerleau once suggested to me that the neurotransmitter changes produced by nicotine might be behind this paradox. At low doses, nicotine stimulates acetylcholine and norepinephrine release, and that translates into arousal. But at high doses, it starts to block out acetylcholine, while increasing endorphin concentrations, and the resulting morphine-like calm might be strong enough to swamp the initial low-dose arousal effect. A review of various studies by Pomerleau and others tends to support the notion that short, quick puffs on a cigarette tend to maximize nicotine's arousing properties, while long, slow drags maximize the sedative aspects of the drug. Smokers may unconsciously learn such mechanisms as a way of matching nicotine's effects to desired moods and behaviors.

It is no secret that smokers smoke more when they are under abnormal stress. We need look no further than the classic crime interrogation scene, where the guilty party furtively chain-smokes through the interview. Routine observation tells us that smokers tend to light up more often at parties or social gatherings. Nervousness and shyness are the usual explanations for this behavior. A closer look suggests that it may have more to do with blood nicotine concentrations: "Both parties and stress acidify the urine," suggests George Vaillant, "and acidified urine leads to a more rapid excretion of nicotine, which significantly lowers blood nicotine levels." In double-blind studies, partygoers who are fed bicarbonate to make their urine alkaline tend to smoke no more under stress than they do under control conditions.

This "plastic" effect also characterizes alcohol to a degree. "Different people take the same substance for different reasons at different times," as Henri Begleiter put it. "That is a very fundamental concept that most people don't accept. An alcoholic may decide he's going out with the boys and they are going to raise hell in town; he wants to feel good, he takes alcohol. Or he may be at home, he is unemployed, he is feeling helpless, he takes alcohol. Totally different reasons."

Legality aside, this may be one reason why alcohol and nicotine have traditionally been more popular through the ages than heroin and cocaine. Because alcohol and nicotine have such a wide range of behavioral consequences, achieved through such a broad cascade of alterations along several different neurotransmitter pathways, users of these two substances may learn to fine-tune their moods with a fair degree of precision. Writes David Lenson: "It is also possible that nicotine, in its ability to punctuate the passage of time, can be used as a kicker to 'officialize' the effects of almost any other drug. A smoker is almost certain to have a cigarette after finishing a joint, snorting a line of cocaine, or taking a shot of heroin." We could easily add a shot of whiskey to this list. Sometimes cigarettes are the punctuation marks in a long sentence composed of other drugs.

Work undertaken by Dr. Alexander Glassman and his associates at the New York State Psychiatric Institute has nailed down an unexpectedly strong relationship between prior depression and cigarette smoking. In a study of heavy smokers who had failed in previous attempts to end their addiction, Glassman documented an unexpectedly high prevalence of prior depressive episodes among the subjects. The findings, which appeared in the *Journal of the American Medical Association*, showed that 61 per cent of the smokers in the study reported histories of major depression. That is a staggeringly high figure, by any yardstick. The sample was admittedly small, but the findings have been confirmed in other work. This sheds important light on the question of why some smokers repeatedly fail to stop smoking, regardless of the method or the motivation. The problem, as Glassman sees it, is "an associated vulnerability between affective [mood] disorders and nicotine." Asking chronically depressed smokers to give up their cigarettes is like asking them to start taking a daily feel-bad pill.

Why is it that the evidence for such a strong link between smoking and depression never showed up before? Ovide Pomerleau had a cogent answer: "Most of us who have worked in the field for some time had missed it, because typically in the studies we conducted, we tended to exclude people with psychiatric histories. So, we didn't see any of these folks. We just screened them out."

Pomerleau was quick to note that an associated vulnerability to depression "isn't going to cover everybody's problem, and it doesn't mean that if you give up smoking, you're automatically going to plunge into a suicidal depression. However, for people who have some problems along those lines, giving up smoking definitely complicates their lives."

If, as associated research suggests, a clear majority of heavy cigarette smokers are also alcoholics, then the pattern becomes clear. Addictive drinking, smoking, and chronic depression share common neural pathways. People who suffer from depression are more likely to smoke and drink than people who do not. Field evidence from hospitals, prisons, and mental institutions further bolster the conclusion that alcoholics, schizophrenics, and depressives are often heavy smokers. A team of investigators led by Mark Zimmerman at the Medical College of Pennsylvania interviewed more than a thousand psychiatric patients and healthy controls, and concluded that cigarette smokers consistently report more depression, anxiety, personality disorders, and substance abuse than non-smokers. There are at least two ways to interpret studies of this nature. Either people with mental disorders tend to smoke because they are more likely to engage in high-risk behaviors in general, or else they smoke because of a biological predisposition toward substance addictions and certain concomitant psychiatric problems and behaviors. In general, smokers take more risks than non-smokers do. Smokers have 50 per cent more traffic accidents and get 46 per cent more speeding tickets. They don't wear seatbelts as often, and they get fewer medical and dental checkups. Female smokers are more likely to experience painful menstrual cramps.

Again, smokers may be smoking because it helps combat depression and anxiety in the short term. They may be self-medicating in the most explicit of ways. What seems to happen with smokers who fail to quit for good is that a relapse into smoking is inevitably preceded by a noticeable worsening of mood. Specifically, nicotine addicts strongly crave cigarettes, cigars, or smokeless tobacco whenever they are bored, or between activities. Boredom, a bad mood, and proximity to social smoking often add up to relapse. The Zimmerman study held true across both genders, and was particularly noteworthy among young adults.

Unlike so many other drug studies, the relationship also held up strongly for women. Other studies tracking women smokers show the same elevated rates of depression, addiction, and suicide. According to The U.S. Centers for Disease Control, nearly one out of every three women of childbearing age was smoking cigarettes in 1991—an appalling statistic, the more so since the combination of oral contraceptives and cigarettes increases the risk of heart attacks among women under 50 by a factor of ten.

In fact, women have lately shown the ability to achieve a grisly parity, or in some cases even outdo men in the damage done by nicotine. About one American woman out of five smokes. While rates of lung cancer in men have been slowly declining since 1980, the number of women with lung cancer has increased 600 percent over the past 70 years. More women now die of lung cancer than the combined fatalities from breast cancer, ovarian cancer, and uterine cancer. As Antonia C. Novella, former U.S. Surgeon General, put it: "The Virginia Slims Woman is Catching up to the Marlboro Man."

80 per cent of female smokers began smoking before the age of 18, and women did not begin smoking in large numbers until the late 1940s, thus producing a delayed epidemic of lung cancer in women. To make matters worse, the Columbia group concluded that "At the same level of exposure to tobacco smoke, women have a greater risk of developing lung cancer than men." Up to three times more likely, according to some studies. Moreover, women who smoke more than 20 cigarettes a day face an 80 per cent greater risk of developing breast cancer, compared to non-smoking women.

Women who smoke heavily have four times as many heart attacks as non-smoking women. Add in oral contraceptives, and the risk of heart attack increases by 1,000 percent. Women who smoke have more respiratory disorders. Wheezing rates are consistently higher for women than for men, at all age levels. Women smokers develop more crow's feet around the eyes than men who smoke. Female pack-a-day smokers suffer a steady accretion of bone density and a concomitant increase in rates of osteoporosis. And the fact that nicotine is an effective appetite suppressant is an open secret, as a couple of generations of chain-smoking supermodels have demonstrated.

Cigarette companies are increasingly placing their bets abroad, among a new generation of young women in countries like China, where authorities estimate that as many as 20 million Chinese women have taken up smoking over the past ten years. Cutting down on female cigarette smoking in developing countries represents a major opportunity for worldwide disease prevention.

The association between smoking and mental disorders, particularly depression, is another of the revolutionary findings beginning to flow from the new biological research. By the late 1990s, there was no longer any doubt about depression being strongly linked to addiction, and to smoking in particular. The National Institute of Mental Health, the National Center for Health Statistics, and researchers like Glassman had demonstrated a convincing link. Moreover, depressed smokers smoked more than "normal" smokers, and had more trouble quitting, even when investigators controlled for variables such as age, weight, cholesterol, exercise, alcohol, and drugs. Epidemiologists have found that lung cancer rates and heart attacks are highest among severely depressed smokers. The relationship held true across age, sex, education, and race variables. Something else was starting to show up in the research, which was that smokers showed better abstinence rates when they were given the newer antidepressant drugs. Intriguingly, this boost seemed to hold even for smokers who had never shown any signs of depression at all. Smoking cigarettes increases brain concentrations of dopamine in particular, and, like serotonin, elevated levels of dopamine reduce reported levels of depression.

Now for the good news: Research going back for several decades shows that cigarettes temporarily relieve the tremors characteristic of Parkinson's disease. Does cigarette smoking protect smokers from Parkinson's disease? There is some evidence that it might. Smoking reduces levels of monoamine oxidase, or MAO. Since the MAO enzyme inhibits dopamine, the net effect is to boost brain levels of dopamine. Smoking also reduces hydrogen peroxide, an MAO by-product thought by some to play a role in the damage to brain cells caused by Parkinson's. Compared to non-smokers, smokers show about half the risk of developing Parkinson's, according to Dr. Glassman. I have not run across any investigators who advocated smoking as a health regimen for older people, but it would not be surprising in the future to see trials of nicotine patches and gum among the elderly.

If a low-level concentration of nicotine in the bloodstream helps older people with memory-related tasks by altering acetylcholine and dopamine levels in the hippocampus, could it also slow the onset of Alzheimer's? It is a tantalizing idea: Nicotine mimics acetylcholine and thereby stimulates these "nicotinic" receptors. Once the hippocampal receptors are switched on by nicotine, they trigger the release of calcium. And that release, in turn, stimulates the release of glutamate. The growth of plaque deposits in Alzheimer's disrupts this chain of events. Nicotine may slow the growth of the offending plaque formation, thereby keeping glutamate, as well as dopamine, at normal levels. Nicotine tablets, patches, and injections have been shown to increase the mental acuity of patient's with Alzheimer's disease—as with Parkinson's, a promising avenue for future studies.

Cigarette addiction has become an important proving ground for medical approaches to treatment. The arrival of nicotine chewing gums and skin patches, while falling short of relieving addiction itself, provided a bridge toward behavior change for many smokers. The use of biological agents like Nicorette as a means of minimizing cravings, during which time an entire roster of behavioral changes can be grappled with, has its parallel in the use of methadone for the treatment of heroin addiction. Too often, the sheer intensity and urgency of the cravings—the drug-seeking behavior—drives addicts back to active drug use before they have become accustomed to the psychology and behavior of abstinence. Like methadone, nicotine gum and patches are not cures, and are not always effective. But these efforts represented a first important step in the direction of pharmacological approaches to the treatment of addiction.

Since dopamine and serotonin are strongly implicated in nicotine detox, we would expect to see the classic drug and alcohol withdrawal syndrome—sweating, shaking, irritability, appetite problems, sleep disruptions, and anxiety. The *Lancet* reported that morphine-addicted rats showed significantly fewer withdrawal symptoms when they were given a dopamine D2 agonist as a booster. A D2 agonist administered to the nucleus accumbens sometimes stopped all visible signs of withdrawal symptoms in the test rats.

The precise mechanisms of nicotine addiction might have fallen together much sooner if papers relating to a little-known animal model developed by scientists at the Philip Morris Research Center had been allowed to see the light of day. Of the various research studies said to have been blocked or suppressed by the tobacco industry, this one would have been of special interest to addiction researchers. In 1983, the science journal *Psychopharmacology* accepted an article by a group of industry researchers from the Phillip Morris Center, only to have the parent company ultimately withdraw the paper. Although the lead author on the study had published elsewhere on nicotine-related research, this particular paper showed that the research group had, for the first time, developed a line of lab rats which would freely self-administer intravenous nicotine by means of the standard bar-press technique. Representative Henry Waxman, the Democrat from California, held a press conference in 1994 to announce that Philip Morris' own research showed that "...without being susceptible to advertisements or peer pressure... rats were willing to go to great lengths to get nicotine." The Addiction Research Foundation (ARF) of Toronto took the opportunity to remind everyone of what we might call human bar-pressing behavior: "People will increase their workload to get nicotine. They will pay more for cigarettes. They will smoke outside in snow storms and rainstorms." Reports at the time confirm the technical difficulty of developing nicotine-addicted rats for research. The Addiction Research Foundation garnered its share of attention several years ago when it independently accomplished the same thing. Everybody wanted a rat model so that one could trace the limbic neural pathways of nicotine desire. Without such a model, researchers had no persuasive way of pinpointing dopamine as the primary culprit. Phillip Morris had developed the necessary animal model years earlier.

Most tobacco industry executives already understood all this, because most of them were addicted to their own product. Quite predictably, they engaged in the kinds of denials and self-justification familiar to any rehab veteran. Tobacco industry executives will one day have to quit smoking, too.

Another crucial finding about the mechanics of nicotine metabolism could potentially save lives and reduce suffering if it were more widely known. Cigarette smoking destroys large amounts of Vitamin C. Much of the work was done with animal models— smoking hamsters, in this case. Vitamin C appears to block at least some of the damage cigarette smoke does to the white blood cells called leukocytes. Vitamin E and other antioxidants have not shown the same protective effect against cigarette smoke. Damaged leukocytes tend to clump together and block blood vessels, causing, among other conditions, emphysema. It appears that daily Vitamin C supplements in the 500 to 1000 milligram range might offer substantial protection against the development of emphysema in long-term smokers. Anyone who smokes should be taking extra Vitamin C daily.

Complicating the picture for neuroscientists is the fact that smokers tend to start very young. For juveniles, cigarettes are usually the first taste of forbidden fruit. (These days, that honor must be shared with the lusty double cappuccino available to minors at any local coffee shop.) The vast majority of smokers have become long-term tobacco industry customers by age 19. Very few adults start smoking for the first time in their late twenties, thirties, or forties.

The presence of a particular gene allele for the production of dopamine receptors appears to correlate highly with vulnerability to nicotine addiction, according to a 1998 report in the *Journal of the National Cancer Institute*. (Given the history of such undertakings, we must approach such gene hunts with the usual skepticism.) The allele reportedly results in the production of a lower than normal number of dopamine receptors. This deficiency of natural receptors thus makes the nicotine high, or the high from any dopamine-boosting drug, considerably more powerful. For chronic nicotine users, as well as chronic cocaine users, the brain's natural ability to produce dopamine is further compromised over time, leading to increasingly intense cravings and a return to abuse, in a spiral of desire that can never be effectively sated. Impulsivity, disinhibition, emotional volatility in the form of anger or aggression, eating disorders or carbohydrate craving, low-mood states, and a general absence of pleasure are all in evidence when smokers are denied nicotine. As an increasing number of researchers and therapists are willing to admit, nicotine, like other addictive drugs, is used by addiction-prone people as self-medication for preexisting neurological deficits that neither doctors nor psychotherapists have been able to treat effectively. Insights from psychopharmacology in particular, and biological psychiatry in general, are making it clear that many cigarette smokers have in fact become "addicted to feeling normal," as David Krogh argues in *Smoking: The Artificial Passion*.

The U.S. military did not stop putting cigarettes in field rations until the late 1980s. Only about a tenth of the nation's corporations had smoking restrictions in place twenty years ago. As a *Science* editorial laid it out: "It remains your choice whether to be more impressed, and heartened, by the massive change in smoking behavior in the United States over the past two or three decades or to be more impressed, and disheartened, by the massive recalcitrance of smoking among 45 million continuing smokers, most of whom have tried unsuccessfully to quit." Two-year abstinence rates, per attempt, seem generally to hover in the 20 per cent range. There is no secret here. Nicotine hits the limbic center of the brain with full power in 5 to 10 seconds, and has an even faster "recycle time" than cocaine. The effect wears off faster, and has to be reinforced sooner with additional quantities of the drug. One pack per day, a common enough dosage among active smokers, adds up to 7,500 cigarettes a year. Hardly anyone, notes the Institute for the Study of Smoking Behavior and Policy, "matures out" of cigarette addiction: "Smokers quit, but not through loss of interest; quitting requires determination."

Given this grim background of addictive potential, it seems a wonder that anyone could ever manage to invoke such massive changes in behavior and quit successfully without medical support. Until quite recently, anyone who attempted to kick the "workplace" drugs, nicotine and caffeine, were on their own. Neither government nor industry offered any help. Now they do. Success rates are marginally higher when there is medical, social, and family support available. Smoking has become a class issue; a question of equal access to treatment.

If certain alleles related to the production of aldehyde de-hydrogenase can protect certain Asian drinkers from active alcoholism, why cannot certain alleles conduce toward this affliction? Perhaps the idea that children emulate their smoking parents is not so much about setting good examples as it is about inherited behavioral tendencies. The panoply of emotions and physical sensations experienced by the addict are very different from the effects experienced by those with only mild addictive propensities. For the severely addicted, drugs are an ongoing obsession. Normal people do not have such anxious reactions to the mere thought of future drug deprivations. (In the same way that normal people do not, generally, have a "hollow leg" and cannot drink everybody under the table, or smoke twenty or thirty cigarettes in an evening.)

As with alcohol, the effect of nicotine shows some ethnic varia-tion. People of Chinese descent clear nicotine more slowly than other ethnic groups. Chinese-American smokers take in less nico-tine per puff than their Anglo-American counterparts, which may help explain a relatively lower rate of lung cancer among Asians. They need fewer cigarettes per day to stave off withdrawal, such research suggests. Suspicion has been cast on an enzyme of metab-olization, CYHP2A6, and its genetic variants. Earlier work done by Neal Benowitz and others also suggests that the opposite effect obtains for African-Americans, who are said to metabolize cigarette smoke more readily—leading, perhaps, to higher blood levels of nicotine and greater risk of lung cancer. Such research is still in its infancy, and is controversial, for all the usual reasons.

Preliminary findings like these are part of what the University of Michigan's Ovide Pomerleau calls "genetic archaeology." The field is still in its infancy, and we will be hearing more from these new medical archaeologists in the future.

Caffeine

Another popular and addictive stimulant found in coffee, tea, soft drinks, and other foods also alters dopamine and norepineph-rine levels along the reward pathway. Without a doubt, the most widely and frequently used psychoactive drug in the world is caf-feine. Millions of adult Americans start their day with it. Millions of young people maintain high blood-caffeine levels throughout the day by consuming soft drinks, candy bars, and other food prod-ucts containing caffeine. We are a caffeinated culture.

Until recently, coffee and tea were rarely thought of as drugs of abuse, even though it is certainly possible to drink too much caffeine. Are the xanthines, the family of compounds that in-cludes caffeine, addictive? The typical dose in a cup of coffee—between 50 and 200 milligrams, with an average of about 115 milligrams—is enough to produce a measurable metabolic effect.

The side effects of overdose—excessive sweating, jittery feelings, and rapid speech—tend to be transient and benign. Withdrawal is another matter: Caffeine causes a surge in limbic dopamine and norepinephrine levels—but not solely at the nucleus accumbens. The prefrontal cortex gets involved as well. At low doses, caffeine sharpens cognitive processes—primarily mathematics, organization, and memory—just as nicotine does. The results of a ten-year study, reported in the *Archives of Internal Medicine*, showed that female nurses between the ages of 34 and 59 who drank coffee were less likely to commit suicide than women who drank no coffee at all. Given the appalling drawbacks of cigarettes, coffee is a much better all-around choice, for young and old alike. It shares many of nicotine's attributes. Caffeine stimulates a structure called the caudate nucleus, which is involved in the regulation of motor activity and sleep cycles, and this is where the physical restlessness and insomnia of caffeine overdose are manufactured. Overall, caffeine affects many of the same dopamine receptor and transporter systems as other stimulants like cocaine or amphetamine. However, its affinity for the cerebral dopaminergic system means that caffeine causes less disorder in the reward pathway, leading to greatly reduced levels of addiction and subsequent drug-seeking behavior.

Of course, coffee and tea are, like nicotine, examples of psychoactive drugs freely and legally marketed in most nations. Without a serious period of prohibition as a test, it will always be hard to know for certain just how strongly caffeinated our nation, and our world, have become. Caffeine's psychoactive power and addictive potential are easily underestimated. The primary receptor site for caffeine is adenosine, which, like GABA, is an inhibitory neurotransmitter. Adenosine normally slows down neural firing. Caffeine blocks out adenosine at its receptors, and higher dopamine and norepinephrine levels are among the results. Taken as a whole, these neurotransmitter alterations result in the bracing lift, the coffee "buzz" that coffee drinkers experience as pleasurable.

Scientists at NIMH have demonstrated that high doses of caffeine result in the growth of additional adenosine receptors in the brains of rats. In order to feel normal, the rats must continue to have caffeine. Take away the caffeine, and the brain, now excessively sensitized to adenosine, becomes sluggish without the artificial stimulation of the newly grown adenosine receptors. Like alcoholics and cocaine addicts, people with an impressive tolerance for coffee and tea may find themselves chasing a caffeine high in a losing battle against fluctuating neuroreceptor growth patterns. Increased tolerance and verifiable withdrawal symptoms, the primary determinants of addiction, are easily demonstrated in victims of caffeinism. Even casual coffee drinkers are susceptible to the familiar caffeine withdrawal headache, which is the result of caffeine's ability to restrict blood vessels and reduce the flow of blood to the head. When caffeine is withdrawn, the arteries in the head dilate, causing a headache. Caffeine's demonstrated talent for reducing headaches is one of the reasons pharmaceutical companies routinely include it in over-the-counter cold and flu remedies. The common habit of drinking coffee in the morning is not only a quick route to wakefulness, but also a means of avoiding the headaches associated with withdrawal from the caffeine of the day before.

Recent studies have documented the existence of severe caffeine addicts who suffer significant depression and lessened cognitive capacity for several weeks or months following termination of coffee drinking. In extreme cases, the primary symptom of hardcore caffeinism is lethargy, rather than nervous jitters, and a primary symptom of withdrawal is often depression. (Balzac, the 19th Century French writer, reportedly died of caffeine poisoning at roughly the 50-cup-per-day level.) Supermarket coffee in a can has considerably more caffeine per brewed cup than gourmet blends. Robusta beans have more caffeine than Arabica varieties. Instant coffee is the most potent coffee of all. The image of truck drivers tanked to the gills on vile black road coffee is a familiar part of American folklore.

Some countries and cultures prefer coffee, and others tea, and the young of all countries prefer caffeinated soda drinks—but caffeine is caffeine. This psychoactive alkaloid is more widely available than alcohol and nicotine, since it is not prohibited below the age of 18. There is scarcely a café or a grocery store anywhere in the world that does not offer caffeine for sale in one form or another. Caffeine scoots through the blood-brain barrier with ease, and blocks adenosine receptors with alacrity. Like nicotine, it can be a sublime and surprisingly powerful drug, which leaves the head clear and does not cause lethargy or markedly alter consciousness.

Balzac notwithstanding, coffee is almost never lethal in overdose. Caffeine clears the body quickly. As with alcohol, the same amount of caffeine affects women more strongly than men. In addition, women on birth control pills metabolize caffeine much more slowly. Pregnant women do, too, and this is one reason they are often advised not to drink it. Coffee and cigarettes go very naturally together. This is probably true for as many different reasons as there are coffee drinkers and cigarette smokers, but as we previously noted in the case of alcohol and tobacco, there is a metabolic synergism at work. The two drugs really do seem to have been made for each other. Rats on caffeine will self-administer nicotine faster and more steadily than decaffeinated control rats. This is because nicotine causes caffeine to clear the body at twice the normal rate, thereby allowing coffee or tea drinkers to imbibe larger amounts than usual, whether consciously aware of it or not. In turn, caffeine has an equivalent reinforcing effect on nicotine. The more you smoke, the more coffee you can drink, and vice versa. At the chemical level, smokers may be drinking caffeine in order to more finely balance the mood-altering effects of nicotine. A moment's reflection brings us to the coffee house, an ancient establishment wherein tobacco and coffee are combined to maximum effect. America is lucky, if that is the word for it: It grows its own tobacco, and it lies relatively near the abundant coffee plantations of Central and Latin America. The U.S. is the leading coffee importer on the planet. Coffee is second only to oil as an export from developing countries, according to studies published in *Science*. In an article entitled "Caffeine and Conservation," the authors note that coffee production employs more than 25 million people in 60 countries around the world.

Coffee and cigarettes, to be sure, are the least psychoactive of the psychoactive drugs—more proof that the sheer intensity of the drug high is not the primary determinant of addiction. Neither drug generally alters perceptual reality, nor causes overdose. The effect of both drugs is plastic, but generally more stimulating than sedating—a chemical fact of life that has helped make both these crucial substances a mainstay of the workplace. Tolerance to caffeine's effects can force users to increase dosage, but in general, the reinforcing functions are muted. Most people tend to steer clear of immoderate, compulsive caffeinism, in the Balzac tradition. Low to medium-sized daily dosages are the norm for most users.

Even though it is chipped by millions of people every day, caffeine is a legitimate drug of addiction, and more troublesome to kick than many people think. Headaches, inability to concentrate, constipation, low-level body aches, depression, drowsiness—the same set of symptoms frequently listed by people withdrawing from any kind of addictive drug are present in caffeine withdrawal. Doctors tend to advise caffeine addicts not to attempt cold turkey detoxification—not because it is life-threatening, but because the severe headaches, persistent depression, and rebound drowsiness that mark rapid caffeine detox can often cause the coffee drinker to abandon his plan of moderation altogether.

Why are we usually able to escape a 50-cup a day habit with this classic reinforcer, a drug that shares some of the same kick as cocaine and amphetamine? While the stimulant effect of caffeine can rev up brain structures, boost energy levels, produce anxiety, and interfere with sleep-wake cycles, caffeine does not hammer the nucleus accumbens with enough extra pleasure chemicals to trigger the same kinds of responses as other stimulants. As with nicotine, older people who drink coffee have a lower rate of Parkinson's disease than their caffeine-free counterparts do. Caffeine appears to prevent the loss of dopamine in key brain areas through its ability to block adenosine receptors, but nobody is entirely sure of the mechanisms involved. Perhaps the day is coming when seniors will be encouraged to brew a strong pot of Joe to go along with that nicotine patch.

What can we say with reasonable certainty about the long-term health effects of coffee? Despite reports of linkages to everything from cardiac arrhythmia to breast cancer, it appears that moderate coffee drinkers are not greatly endangering their health. Coffee is associated with higher cholesterol levels, though it is difficult to rule out the effects of dietary fats in such studies.

It will come as no surprise that people who are clinically depressed drink more coffee than non-depressed people. But the true drugs of choice for those plagued by chronic, debilitating depression are the high-octane stimulants—cocaine and amphetamine.

SEVEN: THE STIMULANTS

"Quite a bit of research has been conducted comparing caffeine with amphetamines.... I'd feel much safer if my pilot on an all-night flight had taken 10mg of methamphetamine before departing... instead of chain-smoking Marlboros and gulping execrable airline coffee all the way."

—Jonathon Ott

If alcohol's impact on brain cells is wide-ranging and diffuse, cocaine's impact is much more straightforward. The same holds true for the other major class of addictive stimulants, the amphetamines. "There is certainly lots of evidence for common neurological mechanisms of reward across a wide variety of drugs," said Dr. Robert Post, chief of the biological psychiatry branch at NIMH. Animals will readily administer cocaine and amphetamine, Dr. Post explained, but when researchers surgically block out areas of the brain that are dense with dopamine receptors, the picture changes dramatically. "The evidence definitely incriminates dopamine in particular," said Dr. Post. "In animal models, if you make selective lesions in the dopamine-rich areas of the brain, particularly the nucleus accumbens in the limbic system, the animals won't self-administer either amphetamine or cocaine."

When you knock out large slices of the nucleus accumbens, animals no longer want the drugs. So, one cure for addiction has been discovered already—but surgically removing chunks of the midbrain just won't do, of course.

We have seen how the amphiphillic alcohol molecule flows into cells, disrupting normal bodily functions and altering the transmission of neurotransmitters involved in reward. The cocaine high is a marvel of biochemical efficiency. Cocaine works primarily by blocking the reuptake of dopamine molecules in the synaptic gap between nerve cells. Dopamine remains stalled in the gap, stimulating the receptors, resulting in higher dopamine concentrations and greater sensitivity to dopamine in general. Since dopamine is involved in moods and activities such as pleasure, alertness and movement, the primary results of using cocaine—euphoria, a sense of well being, physical alertness, and increased energy—are easily understood. Even a layperson can tell when lab rats have been on a cocaine binge. The rapid movements, sniffing, and sudden rearing at minor stimuli are not that much different in principle from the outward signs of cocaine intoxication among higher primates.

Chemically, cocaine and amphetamine are very different compounds. Psychoactively, however, they are very much alike. Of all the addictive drugs, cocaine and speed have the most direct and most devastatingly euphoric effect on the dopamine systems of the brain. Cocaine and amphetamine produce rapid classical conditioning in addicts, demonstrated by the intense cravings touched off by such stimuli as the sight of a building where the user used to buy or sell. Environmental impacts of this nature can produce marked blood flow increases to key limbic structures in abstinent addicts.

In clinical settings, cocaine users have a hard time distinguishing between equal doses of cocaine and Dexedrine, administered intravenously. As we know, it is the shape of the molecule that counts. The amphetamines are shaped like dopamine and norepinephrine, two of the three reward chemicals. In addition, the locus coeruleus is dense with norepinephrine neurons. Speed, then, is well suited to the task of artificially stimulating the limbic reward pathway.

Molecules of amphetamine displace dopamine and norepinephrine in the storage vesicles, squeezing those two neurotransmitters
into the synaptic gap and keeping them there. By mechanisms less
well identified, cocaine accomplishes the same feat. Both drugs also
interfere with the return of dopamine, norepinephrine, and serotonin molecules to their storage sacs, a procedure known as reuptake blocking. Cocaine works its effects primarily by blocking the
reuptake of dopamine.

Amphetamine was once one of the most widely prescribed
drugs in the pharmacological cornucopia. It exists in large part now
as a recreational drug of choice, abuse, and addiction. The same is
true of cocaine. It was replaced as a dental anesthetic long ago, in
favor of non-addictive variants like Novocain. The same tragic list
of statistical side effects that apply to abusers of alcohol, heroin
and nicotine also apply to stimulant abusers: Increased risk of car
accidents, homicides, heart attack, and strokes.

In the late 1990s, scientists at Johns Hopkins and NIDA showed
that opiate receptors play a role in cocaine addiction as well. PET
scans demonstrated that cocaine addicts showed increased binding activity at mu opiate receptors sites in the brain during active
cocaine addiction. Take away the cocaine, and the brain must cope
with too many empty dopamine and endorphin receptors. It is also
easy to understand the typical symptoms of cocaine and amphetamine withdrawal: lethargy, depression, anger, and a heightened
perception of pain. Both the cocaine high and the amphetamine
high are easily augmented with cigarettes or heroin. These combinations result in "nucleus accumbens dopamine overflow," a state
of neurochemical super saturation similar to the results obtained
with the notorious "speedball"—heroin plus cocaine.

In the short run, the use of cocaine or amphetamine causes
increased activity along the dopamine, serotonin, and norepinephrine pathways in the limbic system, as we have come to expect.
"It's a different kind of mechanism compared to alcohol," Dr. Li
explained. "Cocaine also has serotonin effects, but it's not quite
clear how that works."

With the arrival of smokable forms of cocaine and amphetamine, the race to pin down the biology of addiction became even more urgent. "What appear to be the most rapidly addictive stimulants are the smokable forms—crack and ice," maintained Dr. James Halikas, during the speed run-up of the 1990s. "The reason has to do with the hydraulics of the blood supply. High concentrations are achieved with each inhalation, and sent right upstairs to the brain—but not all of the brain simultaneously. The target of the flow of blood is the limbic system, whereas the remainder of the brain is exposed to much milder concentrations." This extraordinarily concentrated jolt to the reward center is the reason why smokable cocaine and speed are able to pack such a wallop. The entire range of stimulative effects hits the limbic system in seconds, and the focused nature of the impact yields an astonishingly pleasurable high.

The long-term result is exactly the opposite. The body's natural stock of these neurotransmitters starts to fall as the brain, striving to compensate for the artificial flooding of the reward center, orders a general cutback in production. At the same time, the receptors for these neurotransmitters become excessively sensitive due to the frequent, often unremitting nature of the stimulation. In the end, says James Halikas, "It's clear that cocaine causes depletion of dopamine, norepinephrine, serotonin—it is a general neurotransmitter depleter. That may account for many of the effects we see after someone has stopped using cocaine. They're tired, they're lethargic, they sleep; they may be depressed, moody, and so on." The continued abuse of addictive drugs only makes the problem worse. One reason why cocaine and amphetamine addicts will continue to use, even in the face of rapidly diminishing returns, is simply to avoid the crushing onset of withdrawal. Even though the drugs may no longer be working as well as they once did, the alternative—the psychological cost of withdrawal—is even worse. In the jargon used by Alcoholics Anonymous, addicts generally have to get worse before they can get better. When addicts talk about "chasing a high," the metaphor can be extended to the losing battle of neurotransmitter levels.

The Nucleus Accumbens

The release of dopamine and serotonin in the nucleus accumbens lies at the root of active drug addiction. It is the chemical essence of what it means to be addicted. The pattern of neural firing that results from this surge of neurotransmitters is the "high." Cocaine increases glutamine transmission as well. Repeated cocaine use alters the glutamine/dopamine interaction, so it would not be surprising to find that addicts are glutamate deficient as well. The hippocampus is an important seat of memory and learning, and glutamate is the mediator in the hippocampus for the release of dopamine. Electrical stimulation of the hippocampus can ignite powerful cocaine cravings in formerly addicted rats.

Dopamine is more than a primary pleasure chemical—a "happy hormone," as it has been called. As we have seen, dopamine is also the key molecule involved in the memory of pleasurable acts. Dopamine is part of the reason why we remember how much we liked getting high yesterday. The nucleus accumbens (also called the ventral striatum) seems to be involved in modulating the emotional strength of the signals originating in the hippocampus. This implicates the hippocampus in relapse, even though this area of the brain does not light up as strongly during actual episodes of craving. The fact that we know this is nothing short of amazing, but it is part of a larger perspective afforded by the insights of contemporary neurobiology. We know, for example, that the emotion of fear arises, in large part, through chemical changes in a peanut-sized limbic organ called the amygdala. Does this information make fear any less, shall we say, fearful? It merely locates the substrate upon which the sensation of fear is built. The building blocks are enzymes and proteins.

Many people have heard of the notorious animal studies in which monkeys preferred cocaine to food, water, and sex. In fact, the famous cocaine monkeys would bar-press for cocaine administered directly into the brain until they died from overdose, in some cases. For human cocaine and speed addicts, drastic psychiatric surgery aimed at knocking out some specific subset of the limbic system is not the answer. Pleasure is there for a purpose.

Amphetamine, first successfully synthesized in Germany in 1887, was, like cocaine, originally intended as a medicine. In the 1920s, scientists with the Lilly Drug Company of Indianapolis, Indiana, were looking for a new asthma treatment. They isolated a substance chemically similar to epinephrine, and named it ephedrine. Epinephrine, better known as adrenaline, is the hormonal neurotransmitter involved in the "fight-or-flight" response. One byproduct of the increased heart rate and oxygenated muscle tissue characteristic of fight-or-flight is the ability to rapidly dilate the bronchial tubes and make breathing easier. Epinephrine itself was poorly absorbed at best, and patients could not take it orally because it was easily destroyed in the stomach and intestines. What asthmatics needed was an inhalable form of adrenaline. Ephedrine and related products were the results. K.K. Chen, a pharmacologist working at Lily, came at the problem through a different door by analyzing the ancient Chinese herb, ma huang. Ma huang worked against asthma, too.

As an asthma treatment, amphetamine straight from the lab was a major improvement over ephedrine and Chinese herbals. Variations on the amphetamine molecule yielded Benzedrine in 1932, followed by Dexedrine in 1935. Burroughs Wellcome, the drug company, added Methedrine to the mix in 1940. By the mid-1930s, the new medications were available to asthmatics in the form of the Benzedrine inhaler, an over-the-counter remedy that remained popular as a non-prescription item in drugstores throughout the 1940s. Inside the vaporizing mechanism was a Benzedrine-soaked strip of paper, and addicts quickly learned to remove and consume the strips.

The American Medical Association approved the sale of amphetamine in tablet form for the treatment of narcolepsy, or "sleeping sickness." However, the *Journal of the American Medical Association* warned in an editorial that students were raiding drugstores and obtaining Benzedrine "for the purpose of avoiding sleep and fatigue when preparing for examinations." (Amphetamine did not become a Schedule II federal drug of abuse until 1969.)

The sense of energy and elation produced by amphetamines made the drugs of obvious interest to depression researchers. At low doses, amphetamines produced an increased sense of well being, a willingness to talk (sometimes for hours on end), and improved performance on simple motor-skill tasks like driving or cleaning the kitchen. There was no doubt about it: Speed was dramatically effective against depression. It was also short-lived, highly addictive, and quickly required people to use more of the drug just to stave off the grinding physical and psychological withdrawal symptoms. One of the amazing things about street speed, biker meth, bathtub crystal, and the free-base form of methamphetamine often called glass, was how rapidly users developed tolerance. When people are using an addictive drug which forces them to ramp up the dosage early and often, the chance of overdose increases correspondingly. Full withdrawal from amphetamine addiction can lead to months of full-blown depression, and an increased risk of suicide. Some researchers believe that prolonged amphetamine abuse can lead to permanent changes in sleep architecture. Nowadays, the medical use of amphetamines is generally confined to low-dose regimens infrequently employed in combination with other drugs for the treatment of adult attention deficit disorder, intractable depression, and narcolepsy. However, there were reports that the use of Dexedrine was still common among aircrews in the U.S. Air Force as recently as the war against Iraq At the typically high dosages used for clinical testing, amphetamine, the stimulant par excellence, was not a reliable antidepressant medication—to put it mildly. In the late 1960s, doctors began to notice that chronic amphetamine addicts exhibited symptoms of what looked very much like schizophrenia.

Speed freaks raved and raged and hallucinated, sometimes injuring themselves when they tried to pull nonexistent creatures off their skin. When the speed wore off, the symptoms went away. Conversely, certain drugs used to quell the symptoms of schizophrenia also relieved amphetamine and cocaine psychosis.

Scientists had learned that large doses of amphetamine were capable of producing major surges of dopamine in the intellectual and perceptual centers of the brain. Massive injections of speed produced an effect that was exactly the opposite of the antipsychotic drugs, triggering a phenomenon known as "amphetamine psychosis." (Prolonged cocaine abuse produces the same symptoms, so it is more accurately described as stimulant psychosis.) It is not surprising that amphetamine is dramatically effective with many unipolar depressives, because it blocks reuptake and floods the neural pathways with an excess of dopamine.

In 1969, amphetamine joined the list of federal Schedule II drugs. But even cocaine and speed, like heroin and nicotine, can be chipped by large numbers of non-addicted users. "Cocaine can be used by a majority of individuals in a way that is not addictive behavior," maintained Dr. Ed Sellers of the Addiction Research Foundation in Toronto. "It's quite clear that that pattern does exist with cocaine, and with alcohol, of course. For them, the drug doesn't have the intrinsic, reinforcing properties that are more important than the other reinforcing properties and constraints under which we all operate. For some people, the properties are not so reinforcing that they push everything else into the background."

Non-addicted users of cocaine, Sellers told me, don't exhibit withdrawal and cravings. "Most of the data which has been collected that relates to the desire to use a given drug are in clear conflict with the popular notion of craving. If you take cocaine users who are not exhibiting any addictive patterns of use, at least half of them have never experienced something that might be called cravings. And of those that have, the vast majority have experienced an intense desire to use cocaine only during the actual time that they're using it."

Ronald Siegel, among others, maintains that most users fit this pattern; an assertion quite consistent with the disease hypothesis as a whole. "The occasional user of narcotics and other drugs is more common than most people realize," writes Siegel in his book, *Intoxication*. "These users are difficult to study because they do not regularly appear in hospitals, clinics, coroners' offices, courts, or other places where abusers surface." In other words, they lead normal lives. Many people experiment with addicting drugs for a period of time and then stop for good, because drugs are simply not that interesting to them.

Despite years of trying, investigators have not been able to show that an understanding of the environmental circumstances under which a drug is used, or a knowledge of the relative potencies involved, moves us any closer to answering the question of how chippers do what they do. Only the biological model of addiction can begin to explain this phenomenon. Chippers can do what they do because they have no underlying biochemical propensities for addiction. They are genetically protected against the likelihood of long-term addiction.

If schizophrenia and amphetamine addiction were marked by too much dopamine, and dopamine was the reward transmitter—one of the chemicals that made eating and drinking enjoyable—then rightly, as one Johns Hopkins psychologist put it, schizophrenics should be "inextinguishably fat and happy." So there is more to schizophrenia then simply dopamine perturbations. Research groups at the National Institute on Drug Abuse and Yale University have turned the spotlight on the specific transporter molecules that ferry dopamine back to its point of origin after firing. These nerve-cell proteins, it turns out, are extremely sensitive to both cocaine and the dopamine-based antidepressants. Cocaine significantly impairs the ability of the transporter proteins to do their job. Serotonin has transporter proteins as well, and the ability of these transporters to take up excess serotonin is degraded in the presence of drugs that block serotonin uptake. Dopamine, dopamine receptors, and the molecules that ferry them about are all controlled by DNA sequences and are therefore a part of our genetic heritage.

Neuroscientists are in the process of identifying individual protein molecules in the brain that react with cocaine and amphetamine in specific ways. For the gene hunters, a glitch in the DNA sequences for making dopamine and serotonin transporter molecules might be partly responsible for addictive responses to dopamine- and serotonin-active drugs of abuse. If this proves to be true, then the gene hunters will have given the drug hunters another avenue of approach to designing medications for addiction.

EIGHT: MARIJUANA

*"We drank bhang and the mystery I AM HE grew plain.
So grand a result, so tiny a sin."*

In J.M. Campbell, "The Religion of Hemp"

In the past few years, as addiction researchers have been busily mapping out the chemical alterations caused by alcohol, cocaine, nicotine, heroin, and tranquilizers, America's most popular illegal drug has remained largely a scientific mystery. It is a drug that millions of Americans have been using regularly for years, and yet it is the least studied drug of all.

The crack scare of the 1980s translated into a flood of research dollars for studying the biochemistry of cocaine. Genetic research throughout the 1990s has led to renewed interest in the biology of alcoholism. Methamphetamine madness is back on the national radar. But marijuana's steady popularity has led to no similar outpouring of funds. For decades, most marijuana research consisted of a hunt for possible adverse effects on the lungs, brain, and sex hormones of heavy pot smokers. Even the results of that effort have been inconclusive.

Marijuana research is at least ten or fifteen years behind the research on every other drug of abuse. Marijuana is still not considered a "sexy" research project, possibly because marijuana abuse does not translate into alarming headlines. The complexity of the drug itself has been another major hurdle. Marijuana has at least sixty active ingredients, called cannabinoids, the most powerful of which is delta-nine-tetrahydrocannabinol. Commonly known as THC, it is the only component of the drug that has been extensively studied.

Historically, the two most popular illicit drugs of modern times have been marijuana and LSD. The irony is that these two drugs have never been thoroughly studied in controlled clinical settings, except for isolated cases. Even so, it is instructive to recall that a presidential commission in the early 1970s recommended the decriminalization of marijuana.

What makes marijuana so popular? Part of the answer has to do with availability and simplicity of preparation. Marijuana, known taxonomically as cannabis sativa, is an easily cultivated weed requiring only a brief drying period before it can be smoked. Several decades of intensive and selective cultivation have resulted in strains of marijuana many times more potent than the common product available thirty years ago. Marijuana is often classed with hallucinogenic drugs like LSD, even though its mind-altering properties are considerably weaker. Overall, marijuana belongs in a class by itself.

Marijuana makes people feel relaxed and contemplative, and it enhances the perceptual pleasures of food, music, humor, and sex. As David Lenson writes, "The demonization of marijuana in America is based on this element of its character: it enables the user to take pleasure from ordinary objects already within the range of perception."

It also triggers odd verbal associations, dislocated trains of thought, and impairment of short-term memory. Another reason for the popularity of pot is that abuse of the drug does not lead to the dramatically adverse effects seen with alcohol, cocaine, and amphetamine—no delirium tremens, no drastic weight loss, no florid psychoses. Researchers who have set out to investigate the neurotransmitter alterations produced by marijuana have learned that common mechanisms of reward in the limbic system play a reduced role in the marijuana story.

The THC molecule was first isolated and identified in the 1960s by Rafael Mechoulam of Hebrew University in Jerusalem. Since cannabis had been used earlier in the century as an over-the-counter nostrum for pain and anxiety, Pfizer, the large U.S. pharmaceutical house, attempted to create marketable pain-killing compounds based on synthetic analogs of the THC molecule. The company dropped the project in the early 1980s.

In 1987, a team of researchers at NIMH was investigating a category of receptors for substances called pain peptides. Through the new methods of DNA sequencing then available, the team discovered a new receptor—but it was not the peptide receptor they had been seeking. The researchers began testing various proteins and other substances to see if the mystery receptor would recognize any of them. Nothing seemed to work.

Meanwhile, in the fall of 1988, pharmacology professor Allyn Howlett and her colleagues at St. Louis University Medical School came up with strong evidence for the specific brain receptor to which the THC molecules were binding. However, the nature of the organic chemical itself—the compound in the brain that was meant to bind to those reported sites—remained unidentified.

Back at NIMH, not too far down the hall from the peptide researchers, neuroanatomist Miles Herkenham was working with some of the superpowered THC analogs Pfizer had come up with. Herkenham was mapping the areas in the brain that lit up with activity under the influence of THC, and the map he was getting looked suspiciously similar to the brain distribution pattern of the mystery receptor down the hall. When the two groups of researchers tested synthetic THC on the new receptors, they had their answer. There was a specific receptor in the brain for THC, the active ingredient in marijuana. Once they went looking for it, the NIMH scientists found the new receptor in all kinds of mammalian brains. Collaborators at the National Institutes of Health were able to make very potent forms of THC radioactive, so that Herkenham could use them as tracers. "I've looked at rats, monkeys and humans," Herkenham told me at the time. "As far as receptor distribution, if you've seen one animal, you've kind of seen them all. No other drug we tried will recognize that receptor. Opiates won't recognize it, nor will amphetamine, or cocaine, PCP, LSD—it's a very unique receptor, and it's been conserved in evolution."

Marijuana was another drug for which the human brain seemed to be prewired. Archaeologists have discovered the remains of a 1600-year-old girl who had evidently died during childbirth, and among the remains were ashes containing THC. Scientists speculate that a midwife might have administered the drug in an attempt to ease the pain of a difficult delivery.

The NIMH researchers were struck by the relative density of cannabinoid receptors in the cerebral cortex, and the relative lack of the same receptors in the limbic system. Marijuana use, of itself, very rarely causes the kind of violent limbic explosions associated with abuse of alcohol, cocaine, and amphetamine. In a sense, marijuana is a thinking drug. The receptor for THC is "a very unique receptor," as Herkenham described it. "Sort of a high-brow receptor."

Nonetheless, even fruit flies appear to have a few cannabinoid receptors. The same THC receptor has been discovered in fish and sea urchins as well, leaving researchers to puzzle over the evolutionary role played by this ancient psychoactive substance. Of what use is a THC receptor to a chicken or a trout? "This phylogenetic distribution suggests that the gene must have been present early in evolution," a paper from Toronto's Addiction Research Foundation attests, "and its conservation implies that the receptor serves an important biological function." Or, as a researcher at the University of California, San Francisco summed it up: "Why would we express the receptor at high levels if it just made us stupid?"

The Bliss Molecule

The surprising abundance of THC receptors in the higher brain told researchers that the unknown chemical was an important one for humans. Herkenham and others believed that the receptor had something to do with combating anxiety. "It's a little like the alcohol-Valium system," he said. "You see something similar with the benzodiazepines like Valium, when you look at their receptor distribution—they're relatively dense in the cerebellum and the cortex. The high cannabinoid receptor densities are on neurons whose primary transmitter is GABA."

What about THC receptors along the reward pathways in the limbic system?

"The areas of highest density are not reward systems at all," said Herkenham. "THC does not select out limbic targets the way other drugs of abuse do. It's been proposed that if a drug is going to have abuse potential, it's going to be localized on dopamine neurons where it can affect dopamine release. So, we did a specific study in which we made lesions in the dopamine system of animals to see if it would affect the distribution of cannabinoid receptors, and it did not. The bottom line is that cannabinoid receptors are dense in brain structures serving movement and cognition."

This density of cannabinoid receptors is particularly noticeable in the hippocampus, the area of the brain involved in learning and memory. This accounts for a number of marijuana's well-known effects, according to Herkenham. "These are the sites where the cognitive effects on attention and short-term memory occur. Impaired estimation of temporal events, distractions, memory intrusions, free-association types of things—they're all cortical, and especially hippocampal, phenomena."

Another finding about the distribution of cannabinoid receptors is of indisputable interest to users. There are no receptors of this type in the brain stem. "Our research shows that the cannabinoid receptors are sparse throughout the brainstem, the medulla oblongata and the spinal cord," said Herkenham. "These are the areas of the brain that control crucial life functions, like respiration and cardiovascular function. This is critically important, because it means cannabinoids are not life-threatening drugs. There's no such thing as a fatal overdose of marijuana."

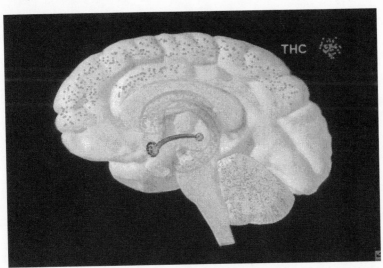

Localization of THC binding sites

And yet, there have been reports of monkeys dying after repeated doses of THC, just as monkeys have been known to die after chronically high doses of cocaine.

"Animals given chronic high levels of THC eventually become sick, and die," Herkenham explained. "They just don't like it. The THC is aversive to them, so it raises their stress levels, and compromises their immune systems. It's just like chronic stress. Even the reports of animal brain damage seem to be mediated by this phenomenon—the parts of the brain that are damaged are the parts affected by chronic stress."

Molecular biologists quickly identified the elusive THC receptor, but what was it for? Apparently, for something that might be called the opposite of anxiety. Bliss, perhaps. That, at least, was the line of thinking followed by William A. Devane, one of the researchers at Hebrew University in Jerusalem who, along with Rafael Mechoulam and others, identified the body's own form of THC in pulverized pig brains in 1992. The substance that stuck to the THC receptors was known as arachidonyl ethanolamide. Devane christened the substance "anandamide," after the Sanskrit ananda, or bliss.

The "bliss molecule" fit the THC receptors Howlett, Herkenham, and the others had been working with. Anandamide had a streamlined three-dimensional structure that THC mimicked, and both molecules slipped easily across the blood-brain barrier. "Not only did anandamide fit the same lock as THC," as the New Scientist reported, "but it appeared to open similar doors in the brain." Recently, researchers at the Keck Center for Integrative Neuroscience at the University of California-San Francisco have found evidence that THC may perform some manner of signaling function in systems of neurons containing GABA and glutamate. Anandamide is a short-lived, fragile molecule, and does not produce a dramatic natural high, unlike a surge of endorphins, or dopamine—or the THC in a joint. However, anandamide has a number of subtle effects on movement and cognition. Because of this, the "bliss molecule" moniker is a bit misleading. THC and its organic cousin make an impressive triple play in the brain: They effect movement through receptors in the basal ganglia, they alter sensory perception through receptors in the cerebral cortex, and they impact memory by means of receptors in the hippocampus.

It was left for animal physiologist Gary Weesner of the U.S. Department of Agriculture (USDA) to ask the burning question: "How do pigs use their anandamide?" In a study of the possibility of using anandamide as a safe sedative for animals, Dr. Weesner discovered that pigs treated with anandamide tended to show lower body temperature, slower respiration, and less movement—all indicative of a calmer porcine state of mind.

Not only does the brain manufacture its own heroin, it also makes its own marijuana. As for why it does so, we can look toward those controversial indications for which marijuana is already being prescribed: anxiety relief, appetite enhancement (compounds similar to anandamide have been discovered in dark chocolate), suppression of nausea, relief from the symptoms of glaucoma, and amelioration of certain kinds of pain. Recall that U.S. pharmaceutical houses, Pfizer in particular, worked on THC for years, without any successes leading to profitable patents. Pfizer never succeeded in separating out the various pharmacological effects of marijuana, and in the end, their efforts were limited to the manufacture of synthetic THC.

The discovery of anandamide has changed the research picture considerably. Marijuana research can now be pitched to funding agencies on the strength of a wholly novel and purely natural neurotransmitter system in the brain. Research at the University of Buffalo suggests that anandamide and THC are involved in some way in the timing of reproductive functions as well. In 1998, scientists at NIMH uncovered preliminary evidence that cannabis may afford a measure of protection from brain cell damage due to stroke or trauma. Marijuana is being investigated by the National Institutes of Health as a chemical that could fight strokes, due to a particular antioxidant effect of THC. An Israeli pharmaceutical company announced plans to test a synthetic marijuana derivative for the treatment of strokes and brain injury. There are few effective treatments for stroke, the third leading killer in the United States.

The question of short-term memory loss under the influence of pot appears to have been answered as well. Findings from the Neurosciences Institute in San Diego show that cannabinoids are capable of blocking new memory formation in animal brain tissue. If anandamide receptors trigger a form of forgetfulness, this may be part of the brain's system of filtering out unimportant or unpleasant memories—a vital function, without which we would all be overwhelmed by irrelevant and unprovoked memories at every turn. For example, the brain's own cannabis may help women "forget" the pain and stress of childbearing, allowing them to concentrate on the immediate needs of the newborn. Other animal research suggests that the uterus grows anandamide receptors in heavy concentrations before embryo implantation. Still other studies show that newborn kittens and monkeys have more marijuana receptors in the cortex than adults do, so it is possible that anandamide may play some role in setting up the development of cortical function in infants.

There is little doubt among responsible researchers that marijuana is sometimes a clinically useful drug for glaucoma. As for the relief of nausea caused by chemotherapy, the precise "antiemetic" mechanism has not yet been identified, but vomiting is known to be a serotonin-mediated reflex. Several studies show that marijuana works at least as well as the popular remedy Compazine for controlling nausea. Moreover, Compazine can cause a variety of unpleasant neuromuscular side effects. Cancer patients have used marijuana successfully to increase appetite and combat severe weight loss. Yet another intriguing possibility centers on Huntington's chorea, the single-gene disease researchers spent years chasing down. Early data from Miles Herkenham showed a loss of THC receptors in the brains of Huntington's sufferers. Cannabis augments the effects of morphine in animal studies, thus allowing for a lower dose of opiates. Queen Elizabeth believed that marijuana tamed her menstrual cramps back in the 16th Century, but there is no clinical and little anecdotal evidence to support this notion. Perhaps the anti-anxiety and mood elevating effects associated with marijuana are useful for menstrual irritation and mood swings, just as they are sometimes perceived to be useful by those suffering from depression. Certainly there is little incentive for pharmaceutical houses to pursue research on the cannabis plant itself, since they cannot patent it.

The typical joint rolled in paper contains roughly 0.5 grams of plant matter, of which anywhere from 1 to 15 per cent is THC. THC content varies widely because some genetic strains of Cannabis sativa are more potent than others. The half-life of marijuana is fairly short—about 50 hours for inexperienced users, and about half that for experienced users. However, THC and its metabolites are fat soluble, and are therefore easily stored in fatty tissue. Other drugs clear the system much more efficiently. The marijuana high may be history, but the metabolites live on—for up to 30 days. This is one reason why standard drug testing by urine sample is grossly misleading. Cocaine metabolites clear completely in a matter of hours, and if a cocaine abuser hasn't done any coke in a day or two, the odds of passing a urine test are high. However, a person could fail a drug test for simply having been in the same room where marijuana was smoked a few weeks before the test.

Blood tests can confirm THC in the body, but cannot reliably determine how recently the marijuana was smoked. There is no marijuana analysis kit comparable to the breathalyzer test for alcohol. Drivers under the influence of cannabis may suffer some perceptual impairment. They tend to drive more slowly and take fewer risks, compared to drivers under the influence of alcohol. Possibly, cannabis smokers are hyperaware of the modest motor impairments they exhibit under the influence. Heavy drinkers are often unaware that there is anything wrong with their driving at all, as their sometimes vociferous arguments with police officers and state troopers can attest.

Does cannabis, as some researchers have alleged, impair the immune system? This is unlikely, given the massive field experiment among Americans of all ages over the past 35 years or so. For one thing, no major outbreaks of infectious diseases have accompanied the rise of marijuana smoking in the United States between roughly 1965 and the present. As with cigarettes, chronic pot smoking can lead to chronic bronchitis. We don't know whether heavy marijuana use can cause lung cancer, but it seems safe to assume that smoking vegetable matter in any form is not compatible with the long-term health of lung tissue. Patients with risk factors for cardiovascular disease are well advised not to smoke anything. Marijuana smoking can raise the resting heart rate as much as 30 per cent in a matter of minutes, and while there is no present evidence of harmful effects from this, we will have to monitor the situation more closely as pot-smoking and former pot-smoking Baby Boomers enter their cardiovascular disease years. Other patients for whom marijuana is definitely not indicated include those suffering from respiratory disorders—asthma, emphysema, or bronchitis. In addition, schizo-phrenics or anyone at genetic risk for schizophrenia should shun pot, as it has been known to exacerbate or precipitate schizophrenic episodes.

The evidence for significant impairment of cognitive function is equally slim—heavy marijuana use does not, like alcohol, result in gross structural brain damage. Numerous studies have addressed the possibility of subtler impairments in memory, attention, and the retention of new information. What people get out of such studies is generally what they bring to them—their own precon-ceived notions about these issues. If marijuana turns out to be both therapeutic (glaucoma, nausea, chemotherapy, convulsions) and ad-dictive, it would certainly not be the first such drug.

Pain relief may be a primary attribute of anandamide itself. When gradual pressure or minor heat is applied to a lab rat's paw, the rodent removes its paw from the source of discomfort faster than control animals. This humane test—the animals can remove their paw from the pain source voluntarily at any time—demonstrated the efficacy of a drug which stimulated cannabinoid receptors in the immune system. Rats given the drug were less sen-sitive to pain than their non-drugged counterparts, as detailed in a report in the Proceedings of the National Academy of Sciences.

Pfizer may have closed the book on marijuana spin-offs too early. It would not be surprising if pills to selectively block the reuptake of anandamide will one day augment or offer an alterna-tive to existing anti-anxiety medications or pain relievers. On the other hand, a substance that blocks anandamide might find use as an agent to help combat memory loss.

Is Marijuana Addictive?

Marijuana may not be a life-threatening drug, but is it an ad-dictive one?

"It depends on what evidence you tap into," according to Miles Herkenham. "The scientific literature on marijuana is fraught with problems, because for every reported effect, someone else is reporting the opposite effect. If you compare all the literature from the human realm and the animal realm, a lot of what's found in humans is not found in animals. It's clearly not an addictive drug in animal research models. It's not even reinforcing. In animals there's a much more profound motor impairment, so that a rat given a fairly high dose of THC the first time will basically just get knocked down by it. What we don't understand is why humans are more susceptible to the psychological and cognitive aspects of it, whereas animals are more susceptible to the motor aspects of it." This is curious, because the receptor distribution is roughly the same in all mammals, including humans. Nonetheless, THC produces very different behavioral responses in people than it does in animals. Until researchers solve this puzzle, our understanding of marijuana's effects on the human brain will remain incomplete.

There is little evidence in animal models for tolerance and withdrawal, the classic determinants of addiction. For at least four decades, million of Americans have used marijuana without clear evidence of a withdrawal syndrome. Most recreational marijuana users find that too much pot in one day makes them lethargic and uncomfortable. Self-proclaimed marijuana addicts, on the other hand, report that pot energizes them, calms them down when they are nervous, or otherwise allows them to function normally. They feel lethargic and uncomfortable without it. Heavy marijuana users claim that tolerance does build. And when they withdraw from use, they report strong cravings.

People claiming to be addicted to marijuana—and why should we doubt them?—have been turning up in Alcoholics Anonymous and chemical dependency programs over the past twenty years or so. Aging Baby Boomers who have become addicted to marijuana may finally be realizing that they have a problem; a recognition all the more belated because of the widespread belief that the substance they are addicted to is not addictive at all.

While the scientific evidence weighed in against the contention that marijuana is addictive, there were a few researchers in the 1990s who were willing to concede the possibility. "Probably not, for most people," said Dr. James Halikas, then with the University of Minnesota's Chemical Dependency Program. "But there may be some small percentage of people who are on the same wavelength with it chemically, and who end up in some way hooked to it physically. It's a complicated molecule."

In Herkenham's lab, they had used a Pfizer THC analog approximately one thousand times more potent than regular marijuana.

THC isn't the same thing as marijuana. Different strains of grass have different effects, and there are dozens of active ingredients in addition to THC. Self-confessed marijuana addicts have tried THC pills, such as Marinol, which are sometimes prescribed for certain kinds of intractable cancer pain. Experienced users report that the effect of synthesized THC is more like a 5mg. Valium than a joint of marijuana. Like Herkenham's monkeys, regular marijuana users don't much care for strong synthetic THC, either. They basically just get knocked down by it.

"I think it's the difference between smoking and oral administration," Herkenham told me.

But daily marijuana users who occasionally eat marijuana in brownies or other concoctions report that the effect is still not the same as pure THC pills. The difference between animal models and humans may be the difference between pure THC and naturally grown marijuana. Despite the fact that rats and monkeys find whopping doses of synthesized THC aversive in the lab, psychopharmacologist Ronald Siegel has documented numerous instances of rodents feeding happily on wild marijuana plants in the field. There are apparently other components in the psychoactive mix that makes marijuana what it is. When the lab version of THC is hundreds of times more potent that the genuine article, it is hard to know exactly what the research is telling us.

Marijuana is the odd drug out. To the early researchers, it did not look like it should be addictive. Nevertheless, for some people, it is. Recently, a group of Italian researchers succeeded in demonstrating that THC releases dopamine along the reward pathway, like all other drugs of abuse. Some of the mystery of cannabis had been resolved by the end of the 1990s, after researchers had demonstrated that marijuana definitely increased dopamine activity in the ventral tegmental area. Some of the effects of pot are produced the old-fashioned way after all—through alterations along the limbic reward pathway.

By the year 2000, more than 100,000 Americans a year were seeking treatment for marijuana dependency, by some estimates. A report prepared for Australia's National Task Force on Cannabis put the matter straightforwardly.

There is good experimental evidence that chronic heavy cannabis users can develop tolerance to its subjective and cardiovascular effects, and there is suggestive evidence that some users may experience a withdrawal syndrome on the abrupt cessation of cannabis use. There is clinical and epidemiological evidence that some heavy cannabis users experience problems in controlling their cannabis use, and continue to use the drug despite experiencing adverse personal consequences of use. There is limited evidence in favour of a cannabis dependence syndrome analogous to the alcohol dependence syndrome. If the estimates of the community prevalence of drug dependence provided by the Epidemiologic Catchment Area Study are correct, then cannabis dependence is the most common form of dependence on illicit drugs.

While everyone was busy arguing over whether marijuana produced a classic withdrawal profile, a minority of users, commonly
estimated at 10 per cent, found themselves unable to control their
use of pot. Addiction to marijuana had been submerged in the wel-
ter of polyaddictions common to active addicts. The withdrawal
rigors of, say, alcohol or heroin would drown out the subtler, more
psychological manifestations of marijuana withdrawal.

What has emerged is a profile of marijuana withdrawal, where
none existed before. The syndrome is marked by irritability, restlessness, generalized anxiety, hostility, depression, difficulty sleeping, excessive sweating, loose stools, loss of appetite, and a general
"blah" feeling. Many patients complain of feeling like they have a
low-grade flu, and they describe a psychological state of existential
uncertainty—"inner unrest," as one researcher calls it.

The most common marijuana withdrawal symptom is low-
grade anxiety. Anxiety of this sort has a firm biochemical substrate,
produced by withdrawal, craving, and detoxification from almost all
drugs of abuse. It is not the kind of anxiety that can be deflected by
forcibly thinking "happy thoughts," or staying busy all the time.

A peptide known as corticotrophin-releasing factor (CRF) is
linked to this kind of anxiety. Neurologists at the Scripps Research
Institute in La Jolla, California, noting that anxiety is the universal
keynote symptom of drug and alcohol withdrawal, started looking
at the release of CRF in the amygdala. After documenting elevated
CRF levels in rat brains during alcohol, heroin, and cocaine withdrawal, the researchers injected synthetic THC into 50 rats once
a day for two weeks. (For better or worse, this is how many of
the animal models simulate heavy, long-term pot use in humans).
Then they gave the rats a THC agonist that bound to the THC
receptors without activating them. The result: The rats exhibited
withdrawal symptoms such as compulsive grooming and teeth
chattering—the kinds of stress behaviors rats engage in when they
are kicking the habit. In the end, when the scientists measured CRF
levels in the amygdalas of the animals, they found three times as
much CRF, compared to animal control groups.

While subtler and more drawn out, the process of kicking marijuana can now be demonstrated as a neurochemical fact. It appears that marijuana increases dopamine and serotonin levels through the intermediary activation of opiate and GABA receptors. Drugs like naloxone, which block heroin, might have a role to play in marijuana detoxification.

As Dr. DeChiara of the Italian research team suggested in *Science*, "this overlap in the effects of THC and opiates on the reward pathway may provide a biological basis for the controversial 'gateway hypothesis,' in which smoking marijuana is thought to cause some people to abuse harder drugs." Marijuana, De Chiara suggests, may prime the brain to seek substances like heroin. Pot advocates don't like hearing this kind of news about American's second favorite drug. In rebuttal, marijuana experts Lester Grinspoon and James Bakalar of Harvard Medical school have protested this resumed interest in the gateway theory, pointing out that if substances that boost dopamine in the reward pathways are gateways to heroin use, than we had better add chocolate, sex, and alcohol to the list.

In the end, what surprised many observers was simply that the idea of treatment for marijuana dependence seemed to appeal to such a large number of people. The Addiction Research Foundation in Toronto has reported that even brief interventions, in the form of support group sessions, can be useful for addicted pot smokers.

If you cannot stop when you want to, does it really make a difference which drug you are using? (We will take up the subject of marijuana withdrawal again in Chapter 11.)

NINE: CARBOHYDRATES

"Food, like money, is a good servant but a poor master."

—Tuchy Palmieri

Amino acids in the foods we eat serve as the raw materials for the production of neurotransmitters. What we eat alters the chemistry of the central nervous system. Diet affects neurotransmission. "Food consumption," wrote Dr. Neil Grunberg, one of the scientific editors of the Surgeon General's 20th Report on Tobacco and Health, "may be considered as self-administration of a psychopharmacologic agent."

The proper functioning of the brain depends critically upon proper nutrition. Tryptophan, an amino acid present in milk and many other foods, is a "precursor" for serotonin, meaning that tryptophan is used by certain cells in the body as the raw material for the manufacture of serotonin. Since two of serotonin's functions are the regulation of sleep and the production of feelings of contentment, the idea of drinking a glass of milk in order to relax before bedtime is not just an unsupported folk remedy for insomnia. Other substances found in foods have similar effects on neurotransmission. Certain meats like pork and duck, for example, have high concentrations of tyrosine, an amino acid that serves as a precursor for dopamine. And chocolate, that perennial snack favorite, not only boosts serotonin levels, but also contains small amounts of phenylethylamine, a chemical substance which turns out to be a distant cousin of the amphetamines. Researchers in France have managed to get rats addicted to phenylethylamine. One French newspaper, in reporting the findings, referred to chocolate as "le speed nouveau."

Since serotonin pathways in particular are involved in the control of appetite, individuals who are prone to drug addiction and depression might be prone to certain eating disorders as well. Or, to put it another way, what do alcoholism, drug abuse, depression, suicide, impulsivity, bulimia, and an excessive appetite for carbohydrate foods have in common? "It can't be coincidence that we've had this tremendous increase in illicit drug use among adolescents almost coinciding with the epidemic in eating and sexual disorders, at the same time neuroscientists are saying drugs of abuse access brain sites normally used for species survival reward," according to Dr. Mark Gold, professor of neuroscience at the University of Florida College of Medicine.

The primary architects of the theory of carbohydrate craving are Dr. Richard Wurtman, a neuorendocrinologist at the Massachusetts Institute of Technology's Department of Applied Biological Sciences, and his wife, Judith, a biochemist at MIT. The two had been investigating eating disorders at MIT's Clinical Research Center as a team, and by the early 1990s, the ongoing results of the Wurtman's work had already cast doubt on a number of obesity myths. The Wurtmans believed that the intense craving some people manifested for sugar and other carbohydrates meant that certain forms of overeating were on the same biological footing as addiction. The Wurtmans soon experienced both the good news and the bad news that came with being right.

Richard and Judith Wurtman verified that all obese people do not simply overeat any food that tastes good, any time it is available. The Wurtmans provided compelling evidence for the involvement of serotonin as a regulator of the appetite for carbohydrate-rich foods, and they documented a fascinating connection between depression and carbohydrate craving that was to have important—and disturbing—ramifications for the treatment of obesity.

Richard Wurtman had made his reputation with some pioneering research on melatonin, a hormone derived from serotonin. A good deal of what is known about circadian rhythms can be traced back to Wurtman's work at the MIT Sleep Lab. When his findings about melatonin were widely publicized, consumers flocked to health food stores to try melatonin as an "organic" sleep aid, and as a treatment for jet lag. (In the pharmaceutical world, common, unpatentable, or cheaply manufactured compounds incite little interest. "Organic" usually equals "low profit margin.").

How does a brain scientist like Richard Wurtman go from investigating the release of melatonin in circadian sleep cycles to researching the dietary habits of college students? The connection was serotonin. Every night, the central nervous system signals the pineal gland to produce melatonin from serotonin, and it is this nightly release of melatonin that governs the sleep-wake cycle. The body converts dietary tryptophan to serotonin, and the pineal gland converts serotonin into melatonin.

Richard and Judith Wurtman showed that overweight people fall into distinct categories, one of which they named carbohydrate-craving obesity. In the MIT studies, the Wurtmans monitored the eating habits of student volunteers with the aid of computer-operated vending machines. Regular meals and between-meal snacks—everything from carbohydrate-packed cookies to protein-rich sardines—were available to the participants 24 hours a day. Everything everybody ate was meticulously recorded. Over time, the Wurtmans observed that a particular category of eater would eat normally at regular mealtimes, but would begin to snack heavily in the late afternoon and evening. People in this category willingly ate protein-rich food during normal meals, but the snacks they chose later in the day were almost exclusively high-carbohydrate foods. More than half of the carbohydrate cravers never selected a protein food as a snack. Other obese people in the study did not show the same marked preference for carbohydrates, and often ate heavily only at mealtimes, snacking rarely, if at all, between meals.

When the participants in the study were given standard psychiatric tests, a propensity for clinical depression stood out markedly among the carbohydrate-craving group. Indeed, carbohydrate cravers reported that they succumbed to carbohydrate foods not because of the taste, but because such foods made them feel calmer, more clear-headed, more energetic, and less tense. Carbohydrate foods made them feel more normal. This was especially true later in the day, perhaps due to diurnal cycles of serotonin production.

As the Wurtmans reported in *Scientific American*:

> We wondered whether the consumption of excessive amounts of snack carbohydrates leading to severe obesity might not represent a kind of substance abuse, in which the decision to consume carbohydrates for their calming and anti-depressant effects is carried to an extreme—at substantial cost to the abuser's health and appearance.

In the case of certain carbohydrate cravers, the Wurtmans found, dietary tryptophan was being converted into serotonin, like always—but this concentrated serotonin surge was also a powerful mood-booster. It was medicine.

The Wurtmans had hit on something big. People who tended to binge late in the day on carbohydrate foods, particularly simple sugars, got a drug-like "buzz" that was highly reinforcing. In the experiments, these people quite specifically, if unconsciously, selected the kinds of foods richest in serotonin-building compounds.

The serotonin-boosting effects of carbohydrates may explain why addicts in recovery, as well as carbohydrate cravers and PMS sufferers, show a tendency to binge on sugar foods. Abstaining addicts apparently turned to the overconsumption of carbohydrates as a means of attempting to redress the neurotransmitter imbalances at the heart of their disorder. Perhaps some addicts discover early in life that carbohydrate-rich foods are their drug of choice.

None of this should be taken to mean that large doses of supplemental tryptophan constitutes some sort of easy remedy for serotonin-mediated disorders. It isn't that simple. However, many drug treatment experts are convinced that dietary alterations, vitamin therapy, and nutritional supplements—as well as strenuous exercise, which also has a marked effect on neurotransmission—play vital roles in addiction treatment programs.

Dopamine is involved with eating behaviors, too. A Princeton University animal study compared dopamine levels while rats were experiencing stimulant drugs, and while they were eating preferred foods. The researchers found that "amphetamine and cocaine increase dopamine in a behavior reinforcement system which is normally activated by eating. Conversely, the release of dopamine by eating could be a factor in addiction to food."

Bulimia

Bulimia, the binge-and-purge disorder that tends to afflict young women, seems especially linked to serotonin abnormalities. Bulimics gorge themselves and then induce vomiting—a debilitating cycle that often leads to severe health consequences. Richard and Judith Wurtman identified a subset of bulimics who binge severely on carbohydrate foods. These bulimics tended to be mildly obese, severely depressed, and came from families with a strong history of alcohol abuse. Other researchers have reported that a significant number of bulimics are themselves abusers of alcohol and other drugs. What is being suggested is that carbohydrate-craving obesity and bulimia may turn out to be two additional forms of drug addiction. They may be variations on the addictive theme, and the underlying cause may be the same—irregularities in the reward system neurotransmitters. If this proves true, traditional diet-based approaches to weight loss are likely to prove ineffective for obese carbohydrate cravers and bulimics. Such people cannot "just say no" to carbohydrates, because the underlying biochemical irregularities that lead to the overeating are not addressed by the moral exhortation to "just eat less." Like biological alcoholics, they must struggle against a physiology that is telling them otherwise. A chronic deficiency of brain serotonin might be the underlying cause of carbohydrate craving, the Wurtmans have theorized. For those who may be suffering from carbohydrate-craving obesity, dieting—that is, carbohydrate withdrawal— produces the same symptoms as withdrawal from addictive drugs: depression, anxiety, irritability, and an uncontrollable obsession with the substance in question.

Whether or not Judith and Richard Wurtman have worked out all the particulars of bulimia, it is clear that the disorder is not caused solely by an obsessive desire to remain thin. Bulimia may turn out to be a particularly virulent form of late-day carbohydrate craving. For women whose bodies do not regulate the production of serotonin and dopamine successfully, bulimia is one of the possible symptoms of a disordered reward pathway. Unlike anorexia, its "partner" disorder, bulimia resembles addiction in several ways. There is a definite high, which comes with the purging, and which has no analogue in anorexia. Recall that serotonin is involved in smooth muscle functions, like vomiting and bowel movements. Bulimia's impact on the brain's reward center also seems to be quite direct, judging by the high relapse rates of bulimics. As further evidence, studies were performed by Walter Kaye and colleagues at the University of Pittsburgh Medical Center, where PET scans were taken of women who were former bulimics, and compared to a set of PET scans from healthy, age-matched women. The ex-bulimics showed a marked decrease in serotonin binding at the 5HT receptors. Although it cannot be known for certain whether the abnormalities preceded, or were caused by, the bulimic behavior, the idea that serotonin disturbances were at the root of bulimia was beginning to make sense. Preliminary twins studies were bolstering the hypothesis by showing evidence of genetic predispositions toward bulimia.

The innate drive among the addiction-prone for simple sugar carbohydrate foods might reasonably be called "carboholism." In the Democratic Republic of Congo (Zaire), there is a tribe of pygmies whose natural diet is marked by the virtual absence of sugar foods. Each year, the tribe gathers for an intoxicating group celebration—and the substance they ingest is honey. "The sugar seems to affect them like a powerful drug," an anthropologist reported in the *San Francisco Chronicle*. "They drop everything to get the honey, and it sure looks like a binge."

The Hidden Addiction?

The carbohydrate connection also turns up in studies of the mood disorder known as Premenstrual Syndrome, or PMS. Common symptoms of PMS begin several days before a woman's menstrual period and include depression, anger, anxiety, irritability—plus cravings for carbohydrates. Women who suffer from severe PMS and its accompanying depression tend to markedly increase their intake of carbohydrates during these monthly bouts, and they may be doing it for the same reason that drug addicts in withdrawal do so: because serotonin synthesis increases after carbohydrate intake, causing increased feelings of reward and well being.

The thinking about gateway drugs may need to be rerigged yet again, according to the alternative view shared by Janice Keller Phelps and other nutrition-oriented practitioners. In their view, the gateway drug is, and always has been, refined sugar. The idea of a link between addiction and appetite control is not new, and the controversy over the addictive properties of sugar foods is an old one. Heroin addicts, alcoholics, and cigarette smokers, when deprived of their drug of choice, will sometimes binge on sugar foods in a pattern highly suggestive of cross-addiction or substitute addiction. Old-time alcoholics tell stories of pouring bottles of pancake syrup down the gullets of colleagues in dire need of sobering up. (Fructose does indeed speed the elimination of alcohol.) The practice of referring to drug cravings as "drug hunger" may be closer to the mark than we realize. Intense physical hunger may be as close as any non-addict ever comes to experiencing the mind/body sensations of drug craving.

As Dr. Phelps wrote in *The Hidden Addiction*:

> Their addiction to sugar is a real, harmful, highly damaging health problem, just as debilitating as addiction to any other substance. Like any addiction, when their chemical isn't supplied, they suffer identifiable withdrawal symptoms; like any addiction, the process of feeding their physiological hunger with a chemical is destructive to the body; and like any addiction, the point may be reached when supplying the chemical becomes as painful as withdrawing from it.

This considerably widens the field when it comes to cross-addiction and pan-addiction. Take away an alcoholic's liquor, and he or she is likely to become addicted to some other drug. Take the heroin away from a heroin addict, and he or she is at high risk for becoming an alcoholic. Many addicts with alcoholic relatives report that they have experienced substitute addictions and multiple addictions repeatedly—and sometimes, these substitutions and additions center on food.

The case of nicotine is also instructive. Under the dictates of earlier, predominately psychological models of addiction, food binges by abstaining smokers were commonly considered to be a case of substituting one classic oral fixation for another. As we have seen, though, one of the reasons smoking induces a sense of well being in smokers is because it raises serotonin and dopamine levels.

The concentrations of serotonin, dopamine, insulin, and other neurotransmitters involved in both drug addiction and appetite control begin to change, as the brain readjusts during withdrawal from nicotine. And the result, for many people, is a raging sweet tooth. Carbohydrates also increase the secretion of insulin, which in turn increases the rate at which most amino acids are taken up from the bloodstream. Tryptophan, the serotonin precursor found in foods, is unaffected by this insulin-aided uptake, and thus the proportion of tryptophan in the blood stream increases when carbohydrates are eaten. Under these conditions, tryptophan has less competition from other amino acids for transport from the blood to the brain. The result is an increase in circulating brain serotonin.

As usual, some of the best hard evidence comes from rats. In an early study by Dr. Neil Grunberg at the Uniformed Services University of the Health Sciences in Bethesda, Maryland, rats were regularly injected with nicotine over long periods. When the injections were suddenly withdrawn, the rats chose sweetened food over regular food—a complete reversal of the food preference they had previously shown.

The brain's ability to sniff out calories in the form of sugar depends upon sugar's drug-like effect on the dopamine-rich reward center known as the nucleus accumbens, according to research at Duke University and the Universidade do Porto in Portugal. As we have seen, this tiny structure in the mid-brain is also the locus of reward activity for all addictive drugs.

The study demonstrated that lab mice lacking the ability to taste sweet foods still preferred sugary water to regular water. The genetically altered mice, lacking functional taste receptor cells for bitter and sweet, consistently chose to consume sugar water—even though they could not sense the sugar. (The lab animals were also prevented from smelling or sensing textural differences in the offerings.)

The findings bolstered the contention that simple carbohydrate foods—because of their effect on reward pathways in the brain—can be addictive for certain people. As Tamas Horvath of

Yale University's School of Medicine told *Science News*: "This is a very exciting new element in how you get addicted to food. It doesn't even matter how it tastes."

The "sweet-blind" animals did not go for the low-cal alternative, when they were offered water mixed with sucralose, otherwise known as Splenda. Low-cal sweeteners did not result in a similar dopamine boost along the reward pathways of the brain.

The brain's ability to "sense" calories may help explain why diet foods are often ignored in favor of sweets. As Ewan Callaway of *New Scientist* wrote: "Anyone who has devoured a tub of ice cream in one sitting knows that delicious foods can override our body's pleas of 'enough.'" We have increased levels of dopamine in the nucleus accumbens to thank for that.

As one of the researchers explained to *New Scientist*, "even when you do not stimulate the sensory pathways in the mouth you still have this reward signal in the brain."

In *Neuron*, the authors speculate that "fructose produces stronger activation of the reward system and that removing high-fructose corn syrup as a sweetener will curb some desire for these products."

And finally, when Yale University hosted the first-ever conference on food and addiction in 2007, Dr. Nora Volkow of the National Institute on Drug Abuse told the collection of experts on nutrition, obesity and drug addiction that "commonalities in the brain's reward mechanisms" linked compulsive eating with addictive drug use. "Impaired function of the brain dopamine system," Volkow told the group, "could make some people more vulnerable to compulsive eating."

Conference organizer Kelly Brownell, director of the Rudd Center for Food Policy and Obesity at Yale, conceded that "it wasn't obesity experts who got interested in addiction, it was the addiction scientists who got interested in food." Brownell suggested that psychologists have been slower to grasp the import of food addiction "in part because of a bias that obesity is all about failure and personal responsibility, so why look at biology?"

Moreover, animal studies and brain imaging research in humans strongly support the notion of food addiction, especially in the case of binge eating. As summed up by Dr. Mark Gold, chief of addiction studies at the McKnight Institute at the University of Florida and a well-known authority on cocaine abuse: "It turns out that food and drugs compete for the same reward system in the brain."

Not all overeaters are abstaining drug addicts, of course. Obesity, like drug addiction, comes in a variety of forms, and is influenced both genetically and environmentally. But the spotlight is now on a subset of obese people in which obesity does not seem to be a behavior learned from obese parents, any more than alcoholism is inevitably a learned behavior picked up from alcoholic parents.

Richard and Judith Wurtman provided strong evidence that depression is intimately linked with carbohydrate craving. Drug addicts themselves have provided evidence that depression is a common feature of drug addiction and withdrawal. A substantial number of addicts report prior episodes of depression before their active addictions began.

"Many addicted people I have treated recall being depressed as children or adolescents," maintained Dr. Janice Keller Phelps, "but simply assumed at the time that that was the normal way to feel. Then when they experimented as teenagers with alcohol or various other addicting drugs, they experienced sudden, temporary relief from a depression they didn't even know they had."

Perhaps, then, it is not so surprising to discover that one of the first things researchers discovered about Prozac, the new antidepressant, was that it made alcohol-preferring rats drink less alcohol.

PART III

TEN: FIGHTING FIRE WITH FIRE

"The most complicated, multicellular, multitissue, and multi-organ diseases I know of are tertiary syphilis, chronic tuberculosis, and pernicious anemia.... Before they came under scientific appraisal each was thought to be what we now call a 'multifactorial' disease, far too complex to allow for any single causative mechanism. And yet, when all the necessary facts were in, it was clear that by simply switching off one thing—the spirochete, the tubercle bacillus, or a single vitamin deficiency—the whole array of disordered and seemingly unrelated pathologic mechanisms could be switched off, at once...."

—Lewis Thomas

Addictions are chronic diseases. They may require a lifetime of treatment. After a number of severe episodes of alcohol or drug abuse, the brain may be organically primed for more of the same. Long-term treatment may be the only effective way out of this dilemma. This is true of unipolar depression as well.

Thus far, we have explored the best current thinking about the biochemical mechanisms that govern addiction. In other words (with apologies to David Byrne), "How did we get here?"

The rest of the book is concerned with the obvious corollary: How do we get *out* of here?

In order to survive in the present millennium, we will need to learn a lot more about chemicals—the ones we ingest, and the ones that are produced and stored naturally in our bodies. What we have learned about the nature of pleasure and reward is a strong start. The guiding insight behind most of the work is that addiction to different drugs involves reward and pleasure mechanisms common to them all. The effects of the drug—whether it makes you sleepy, stimulated, happy, talkative, or delusional—constitute a secondary phenomenon. What these powerful engines of reward do to the dopamine and serotonin systems is what counts. Much of the earlier research had been directed at teasing out the customized peculiarities of one drug of abuse compared to another. Now what mattered was the re-regulation of limbic receptor arrays in response to the flood of artificial stimulation produced by the drugs. An addict beats addiction by desensitizing abnormally stimulated receptors, allowing the brain to retrain itself.

But in order to do that, you have to stop taking the drugs.

Comparing our reservoir of pleasure chemicals to money in the bank, Dr. George Koob, neuropharmacology professor at The Scripps Research Institute in La Jolla, California, draws the following analogy:

> We can expend that money over the course of
> a single weekend's binge on cocaine or we can
> expend it over a two-week period in the normal
> pleasures of everyday life. If you spend these
> pleasure neurochemicals in one lump sum such as
> a crack binge, you use up your supply of pleasure
> for a certain period, and so you pay for it later.

There really is no cheating in this game. The system has to self-regulate. Craving and drug-seeking behavior, once set in motion, disrupt an individual's normal "motivational hierarchy." The need to seek out and maintain a steady supply of the drug becomes as important as fighting, fleeing, feeding, and, yes, fucking. These alterations of desire have been documented in animal studies. Once rats learn to bar-press for an injection of an addicting drug, experimenters can progressively increase the number of bar presses necessary to produce a single injection, and the rats will perform the extra labor. This "work output" is used as one measure of a drug's motivational strength. How does this motivational express train come about? It happens at the point where casual experimentation is replaced by the pharmacological dictates of active addiction. It happens when the impulse to try it with your friends transforms itself into the drug-hungry monkey on your back.

Addicts vividly demonstrate a compulsive need to use alcohol and other drugs despite the worst kinds of consequences—arrest, illness, injury, overdose. What kind of euphoria could be *worth* such psychic pain? What makes these people eat their words, shred their best intentions, break their promises, and starting using or drinking again?

Participation in a treatment program—any treatment program, whether mandatory or voluntary—seems not to have any demonstrable effect on abstinence success rates. Admittedly, this is a generalization, and one that assumes a treatment timeline longer than the standard thirty days of rehab. Formal medical treatment and intervention *can* work, but they do not seem to work any better than no formal treatment at all. Most alcoholics and smokers and other drug addicts, it is frequently asserted, become abstinent on their own, going through detoxification, withdrawal, and subsequent cravings without benefit of any formal programs. Our health policy should not only encourage addicts to heal themselves, but must also help equip them with the medical tools they need. After all, behavioral habits as relatively harmless as nail biting can be all but impossible to break.

Consider how strong such habitual attachments can grow if they happened to trigger significant changes in the function of major neurotransmitters in areas of the brain involved in reward, pleasure, learning, and memory. It takes time to become addicted. It doesn't happen overnight. Neither does recovery. People sometimes speak of being hooked on a certain drug from the very first time they used it, but that is not strictly true. It doesn't happen with a single dose, or a single evening's misadventures. Until the drug itself begins to motivate behavior, true addiction has not occurred. Until the anticipation of reward in the limbic takes precedence over other actions, serious addiction has not taken hold.

As detailed by Dr. Mary Jeanne Kreek, a Rockefeller University professor and head of the Laboratory of Biology of Addictive Diseases:

> Toxicity, destruction of previously formed synapses, formation of new synapses, enhancement or reduction of cognition and the development of specific memories of the drug of abuse, which are coupled with the conditioned cues for enhancing relapse to drug use, all have a role in addiction. And each of these provides numerous potential targets for pharmacotherapies for the future.

For any addiction, once it has been active for a sustained period, the first-line treatment of the future is likely to be biological. New addiction treatments will come—and in many cases already do come—in the form of drugs to treat drug addiction. Every day, addicts are quitting drugs and alcohol by availing themselves of drug treatments that did not exist fifteen years ago. As more of the biological substrate is teased out, the search for effective approaches narrows along more fruitful avenues. This is the most promising, and, without doubt, the most controversial development in the history of addiction treatment.

Fighting fire with fire is not without risk, of course. However, consider the risks involved in *not* finding effective medical treatments. In 1996 alone, about $5 billion a year was required for the medical care of untreated heroin addicts; about another $5 billion in criminal activity was associated with heroin addiction; and as much as $10 billion was attributed to lost productivity, wages, etc. Addiction treatment, by almost any measure, is a cost-effective proposition.

Addiction researchers and pharmacologists had speculated for years about developing drugs that went to work specifically on an alcoholic's *desire* to drink, or a crack addict's *craving* for the next rock. Scientists were learning how to shut off or dampen a drug's addictive effect by means of antagonists. If you could tie up the receptor and block other molecules from binding at that site, without activating the receptors and triggering the chemical chain of events that leads to a high, then you could conceivably blunt the limbic demands of withdrawal and detox.

Naltrexone and naloxone, two virtually identical opiate antagonists, blocked the heroin high in a relatively neutral manner. Naloxone (sold as Narcan) and Naltrexone (sold as Revia), stopped heroin cold by knocking it off its receptors and replacing it with "dead weight," so to speak. Naltrexone would seem to be the perfect drug for heroin addicts—but it is not. It does nothing to reduce cravings, and hence suffers the same limitations as Antabuse in that application. While some physicians use naloxone to treat heroin addiction, the record of accomplishment is mixed, and the dropout rate is high. There is not even a mild high or drug like effect to provide cross-tolerance and dampen the effects of withdrawal, as with methadone. Recently, naltrexone for heroin addiction has been offered by a few doctors in the highly controversial form of "rapid detox." The addict is anesthetized and placed on a respirator, then injected with naltrexone. The result: complete detoxification in about four hours, as the Narcan molecules knock the opium molecules off their receptors. It can be lethal if not carefully controlled and supervised. The problem, as always, is that the detoxified addict is just as vulnerable to heroin addiction as before. Rapid detox does nothing to combat subsequent cravings, and relapse is frequent.

Disulfiram, or Antabuse, relies on negative reinforcement to do the job with alcoholics. By blocking a key enzyme of metabolization, Antabuse produces significant physical discomfort when combined with alcohol. Like Narcan, it can be fatal. Antabuse was one of those serendipitous discoveries—two Danish pharmacologists, looking for a new drug treatment for people with parasitic worms, tested one of the drugs on themselves, whereupon they adjourned to a cocktail party and became seriously ill after a drink or two. Antabuse is a perfect example of the antagonist theory of addiction treatment—and the best example of why antagonist drugs are not necessarily the answer to treating addiction pharmacologically. With Antabuse, the craving to drink is not affected. Patient compliance, then, is an obvious problem. An alcoholic can solve all of his immediate biochemical distress by discontinuing Antabuse and taking a drink. Since his craving remains undiminished, the reward motivation runs high.

Antagonist drugs rarely lead to successful long-term cessation of drug use in clinically addicted users. It is not hard to see why. For addicts, Antabuse and Narcan effectively enforce the necessity for "white knuckle" sobriety. The addict isn't drinking or taking drugs right now, but very much wishes to, and hasn't given up hope of seizing an opportunity to do so. If, in body and mind, addicts want the alcohol or the heroin just as badly as ever, then sooner or later—usually sooner—they will "forget."

Detoxification and short-term withdrawal are the primary concerns of the medical community. The maintenance of long-term abstinence is another matter entirely. Doctors are sometimes able to put compliant white-collar opiate addicts—fellow doctors are a good example—on a course of naltrexone, and if sufficiently motivated by courts or family, addicts can get straight this way. The same is true of Antabuse: With a sufficient social support system in place (and medical insurance), highly motivated alcoholics can sometimes use Antabuse to learn sobriety and prevent relapse. But for the majority of opiate addicts, daily naltrexone is not enough. For most alcoholics, Antabuse won't solve the problem. They represent crude, early attempts at treating addiction pharmacologically.

Was there a way to "design out" the craving experienced by an addict? Mitigate its intensity, at least? "The proneness to relapse is based on changes in brain function that continue for months or years after the last use of the drug," writes Charles O'Brien of the University of Pennsylvania VA Medical Center. Well-known for his work on craving and relapse, O'Brien has published widely on external cocaine "cues"—the sight of a crack pipe, or the neighborhood where an addict used to use. What was once a voluntary decision becomes an iron-tight compulsion, despite a heartfelt desire to abstain. These reflexive patterns defeat the most dedicated of patients, causing a cycle of treatment, release, relapse, and treatment—as the problems and complications brought on by addiction continue to multiply. Like NIDA's Leshner, O'Brien believes that "treatment should be based on a chronic disease model such as that used for diabetes or asthma rather than modeled on treatment for an acute disease such as pneumonia. The shift from acute or short-term treatment to a chronic model is still in process, and there is resistance to this change."

Methadone for Heroin

In contrast to antagonist drugs, the agonist theory is based on drugs that bind to specific sites and which *do* mimic some of the addictive drug's typical range of effects. For obvious reasons, this greatly reduces craving. But is it simply a replay of the historical tactic of substituting one addictive drug for another? The most successful use of the agonist theory remains heroin's most controversial and stigmatized treatment—methadone therapy. Back in the 1960s, researchers at Rockefeller Hospital and The Rockefeller Institute, led by Professor Vincent Dole of Rockefeller University, began a series of studies that led to the development of methadone treatment. They did it on the strength of their belief in the un-folding biological model. "Heroin addiction is a disease of the brain, with diverse physical and behavioral ramifications, and not simply due to criminal behavior, a personality disorder, or 'weak will,'" wrote Dr. Kreek, one of the principle methadone research-ers at Rockefeller. Methadone was approved by the FDA in 1973 for medical use against heroin addiction. It is a slow-acting opi-ate receptor agonist, meaning that it has some of the properties of heroin and morphine. However, the buzz it provides is no real substitute for heroin or morphine, from an addict's point of view. It was nobody's idea of a sweet drug holiday. But why give agonist drugs to addicts at all? Isn't that just like giving them watered-down heroin? Writing in the September 2002 issue of *Nature Reviews*, Dr. Kreek summed up what doctors face when dealing with long-term addiction:

> Repeated 'on-off' exposure to a drug of abuse progressively leads to stable molecular and cel-lular changes in neurons, which alter the activity of neural networks that contain these neurons. This eventually results in complex physiological changes and related behaviors that characterize addiction, such as tolerance, sensitization, de-pendence, withdrawal, craving and stress-induced relapse. These drug-induced changes are, in part, counteradaptive, and they contribute to dysphoria and dysfunction, which promotes continued drug use through negative-reinforcement mechanisms.

Daily methadone doses of 80mg or more exert a definite blocking effect on heroin craving. Patients who use it do not suffer the lassitude and cognitive distortions of the heroin addict. Meth-adone's other strength is that it doesn't mix well with heroin or alcohol. More recently, Kreek and her colleagues, in collaboration with the NIH, used PET scans to watch opioid-receptor binding occur in the living brains of methadone-maintained patients. The brain scans confirmed that methadone leaves a significant number of opioid receptors unoccupied, allowing those regions of the brain to carry out normal physiological roles. "In methadone-maintained patients there is modest occupancy of the receptors but still a lot of available receptors for normal cognition, normal reproductive function and normal stress responsivity," Kreek reports. Another underreported advantage of methadone is its oral administration, thus eliminating the need for hypodermics and reducing the risk of AIDS and hepatitis from contaminated needles. Provided the dosage is right, patients can be maintained for years on methadone. One reason methadone therapy fails, say researchers, is because of inadequate dosages—but higher dosages are much harder to withdraw from.

SSRIs and Alcoholism

In order to gain perspective on new drugs for the treatment of addictive disease, we need to briefly trace the underpinnings of drug therapy for common mental illnesses.

In the 1950s, an Australian psychiatrist discovered that a common mineral salt called lithium carbonate, when administered to manic-depressive patients, dramatically dampened their mood swings. The discovery was not put to use in America until the 1960s, when the FDA approved lithium as a prescription drug for the manic phase of manic depression. Curiously, lithium also diminished the euphoric effects of cocaine. Since depressed people often resort to stimulant drugs like cocaine and amphetamine to lift their mood, it was here that the first hints of a possible neuronal connection between addiction and depression began to surface.

Psychiatrists also discovered that a certain tranquilizer, trade name Thorazine, did more than just calm schizophrenic patients.

In many cases, it made schizophrenic hallucinations disappear like magic. No one knew how or why it worked. Thorazine was psychiatry's first true "wonder drug," but in addition to the wonders, mental health facilities tended to overuse Thorazine and the other "antipsychotic" drugs as chemical billy clubs with which to sedate their patients into a haze. Moreover, the side effects could be truly terrible. Tardive dyskinesia, a condition marked by twitching, drooling, and involuntary movements similar to the symptoms of Parkinson's disease, was a permanently debilitating effect seen in some schizophrenics who had been on these medications for years. It was a classic case of a treatment creating symptoms every bit as unfortunate as those it was designed to prevent.

By analyzing the effect of the antipsychotic drugs on the neurotransmitter systems of rats, scientists showed that the drugs capable of dampening the symptoms of schizophrenia did so by means of receptors meant for dopamine. Scientists came up with other medications that made schizophrenics act less crazy, and there was one thing almost all of them had in common: By various mechanisms, they all seemed to block the action of dopamine.

Evidence of abnormally low levels of dopamine in patients suffering from Parkinson's disease led researchers to an effective treatment for that disorder. L-Dopa, a drug that the neurons can make into dopamine, helped control Parkinsonian seizures, although it too has adverse side effects.

Clearly there was a link between schizophrenia and Parkinson's disease: Dopamine imbalances were implicated in both disorders.

As scientists mapped out the different dopamine pathways in the brain, it became evident that there was a dopamine pathway involving motor control, and a separate pathway involving the higher intellectual centers. This explained why the symptoms of tardive dyskinesia caused by constant use of the antipsychotic drugs looked for all the world like Parkinson's. When schizophrenics took the antipsychotic drugs, dopamine levels dropped in the intellectual center, which muted their symptoms. But the drugs also lowered dopamine levels in the motor control center, where everything had been working fine before.

The dopamine connection was not a cure, but it was a giant step forward in the understanding of two major—and incurable—mental illnesses. Dr. Arvid Carlsson, the Swedish pharmacologist who pioneered our understanding of dopamine as a neurotransmitter, was confident from the beginning that his discovery would garner him the Nobel Prize. It was the key to the effective treatment of Parkinson's disease, and it led Dr. Carlsson to arrive at the "dopamine hypothesis of schizophrenia," which held sway in the field for decades. Dr. Carlsson was right about the Nobel Prize, but it took the Nobel Committee almost 40 years to agree with him. In 2000, Carlsson won the Nobel Prize in Physiology or Medicine for his discovery of dopamine's key role as a brain chemical.

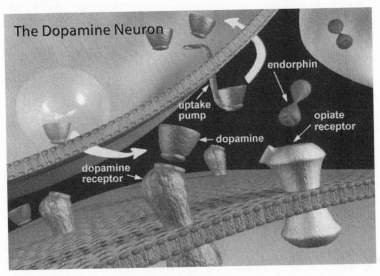

The Dopamine Neuron

Back then, one of the hotbeds of research on drugs and the brain (a discipline soon to be known as neuropsychopharmacology) was the Chemical Pharmacology Lab at the National Heart Institute in Bethesda, MD. Under the direction of

Dr. Bernard B. Brodie, Arvid Carlsson and his colleagues there had been looking into reserpine, a strange compound already in use as an herbal remedy in India. The group intended to investigate reserpine as a blood pressure drug, but reserpine unexpectedly caused serious episodes of depression in about one-fifth of the patients who took it. Further studies confirmed that reserpine caused an enormous depletion of serotonin from blood platelets. Again, the connection between mental illnesses and psychoactive drugs showed itself. Reserpine also blocked the action of LSD.

Carlsson later returned to Sweden, where he assembled a research team for the purpose of investigating dopamine and serotonin in more detail. The group came up with an eye-catching demonstration of what dopamine could do. The "reserpine rabbits" achieved a level of fame not unlike Dr. Li's rats. A 5mg per kilogram intravenous dose of reserpine would cause the rabbits to drop to the floor of their cages in seconds, deeply sedated, all but immobile, like an attack of sleeping sickness, or... severe Parkinson's Disease. Reserpine was a serious dopamine depleter. The reserpine rabbits were undeniable evidence of the effects of too little dopamine.

Carlsson and his researchers had hit upon the animal equivalent of the patients described years later by Oliver Sacks in his book, *Awakenings*. If massive dopamine depletion due to reserpine caused Parkinson's-like symptoms, would a dopamine agonist—a dopamine booster shot, in effect—reverse these symptoms? It would. Injections of L-Dopa, an agonist, dramatically brought the reserpine rabbits back to life. The fact that the animals could "instantaneously be restored to full motion and wakefulness by repletion of dopamine through treatment with its precursor L-DOPA, was one of the most astounding experiences in my scientific career," Carlsson later wrote in *Science*. It also helped shift the direction of brain research from electrical action potentials to chemical neurotransmission. Such discoveries led to the knowledge that Parkinsonism involved the death of dopamine-producing neurons in the brain.

Reserpine's action, it turned out, depleted serotonin, dopamine, *and* norepinephrine. Reserpine lowered levels of all three neurotransmitters, known collectively as monoamines, and this is what caused people to feel depressed, according to the monoamine hypothesis of mental illness.

In the year of the reserpine rabbits, pharmacologist Julius Axelrod was also studying new psychoactive drugs for mental illness. Like Carlsson, Axelrod had done serious research on LSD-25. The only known drugs that operated as serotonin-specific compounds were the "mind-altering" psychedelics—LSD, DMT, psilocybin, and Ibogaine.

At the University of Saskatchewan, Humphrey Osmond and Abraham Hoffer, two pioneers in the small world of clinical research on LSD, began working on their theory that niacin (B-3) could relieve the symptoms of schizophrenia. Axelrod had attended an NIMH seminar at which Seymour Kety, then with the NIMH, had presented the work by Osmond and Hoffer. Kety was doing his own work on the distribution of neurons for norepinephrine, and Axelrod was looking for enzymes released from these same norepinephrine-producing neurons. One of the enzymes was monoamine oxidase, or MAO. Scientists knew that the job of MAO was to degrade neurotransmitters. Drugs that inhibited MAO release buoyed mood by allowing more dopamine, serotonin, and norepinephrine to remain active in the brain. This was the basis of action for the MAO-inhibitors used against depression.

The idea that some people naturally suffered from depression because of chemical deficiencies or abnormalities fit perfectly with the genetic theory of depression. Stop MAO from doing its job, and more norepinephrine and other neurotransmitters became available. Catecholamines, the category of neurotransmitters that includes norepinephrine, were once thought to be the primary culprits, but the catecholamine theory had to be broadened when researchers began to understand the essential roles of serotonin and dopamine. "I'd be very surprised if anything about addiction turns out to be a one neuroregulator story," said Ovide Pomerleau at the University of Michigan. "These brain chemicals all interact, and I think they're just going to be different flavors in the soup, under different circumstances and conditions."

Working with a series of postdoctoral researchers, Julius Axelrod demonstrated that norepinephrine and other neurotransmitters underwent the process of reuptake and storage. This work eventually netted Axelrod a Nobel Prize of his own. When the director of the NIMH asked the newly minted Nobel recipient if he needed anything, Axelrod famously replied that a parking space would be nice.

Normally, the neurotransmitter systems in the human body are in complicated and exquisite balance. The reward pathway chemicals are stored and ready to be used when needed. The amphetamines, to take one example, prevent norepinephrine, dopamine, and serotonin from being reabsorbed. The "bonus" joy molecules, having done their job of stimulating the dopamine receptors, are now stalled in the gap between neurons, bombarding the receptors repeatedly. The human nervous system, ever striving to maintain the proper balances, adapts to the artificial surge by cutting back on production, while the brain alters the distribution of receptor sites in an effort to keep the system functioning normally. Postmortem investigations of the brains of deceased depressives show unusually dense receptor arrays for norepinephrine—the brain's attempt to compensate for lower neurotransmitter levels through a process known as "up-regulation." By increasing the number of receptors for a neurotransmitter in short supply, the brain's strategy is to snag as much of the scarce chemical as possible by way of compensation. Correspondingly, the brain "down-regulates" by growing fewer receptors in times of abundance—such as active drug addiction—and by releasing less of the transmitter when stimulated. These are strategies the brain uses to regulate neuropeptide levels, but it works out differently for different people. Since the number of receptors is determined by genetic mechanisms, writes Michael Gazzaniga in Nature's Mind, "[I] t would follow that there should be variation in the number of these receptors and in the efficiency of their mechanism of action." As tolerance builds, it takes more and more drug to produce the desired effect, and the body becomes progressively less efficient at "organically" producing sufficient amounts of neurotransmitters. The same drug that makes people feel good will make them feel worse after chronic, heavy use—the central paradox at the heart of addiction. The body's natural supply of these neurotransmitters, now curtailed as compensation for the overabundance produced during addiction, is no longer enough to fulfill the artificial demand. When the speed freak goes cold turkey, everything in the neurotransmitter universe is instantly out of balance again, and all hell breaks loose.

Since the reward pathways are major reinforcers of survival drives, the basic message of neurotransmitter depletion caused by overuse of addictive drugs is: Get more dopamine, get more serotonin, get more norepinephrine—or else. In extreme cases of addiction, the message is: Get more drugs, or die.

Other research led to even more surprising drug discoveries. Among the huge stores of wartime chemicals the Nazis turned over to Allied forces at the end of World War II, none found a stranger application than hydrazine. A toxic compound used by the Germans as fuel for the V-2 rockets that rained down on London, hydrazine was snatched up by U.S. drug companies at bargain prices. Researchers tweaked up a series of non-lethal hydrazine derivatives, some of which showed promise as tuberculosis treatments. One such compound used in tuberculosis wards—Iproniazid—dramatically boosted the mood of severely depressed patients. By the late 1950s, the first of a new class of antidepressants—the tricyclics—was available as imipramine, trade name Tofranil.

The early antidepressant drugs came in two classes, then—the tricyclics and the MAO inhibitors. The mechanics of action were different in each case, but the results were the same. Both types of drugs increased the concentrations of serotonin and norepinephrine in the limbic system, and sometimes seemed to counteract depression in hospitalized subjects. The early tricyclics and MAOI antidepressants were "dirty" drugs: They affected the holy trinity of brain amines—norepinephrine, dopamine, and serotonin—in non-selective, shotgun fashion. Some researchers believed that one of the limitations of these drugs, in addition to side effects, was that they didn't sufficiently boost serotonin levels in the brain. If the serotonin hypothesis of depression had validity, then the older drugs weren't selective enough.

As chairperson of the Department of Pharmacology at the University of Gothenburg, the intrepid Arvid Carlsson and co-workers went on to develop the first drug in a new class of antidepressant compounds that would become the most profitable, the most famous, and the most controversial class of drugs in recent history—the so-called selective serotonin reuptake inhibitors, or SSRIs. In 1968, Carlsson later wrote, the group began to discover drugs that "could block the reuptake of serotonin, and this led us to develop a compound that selectively blocked the reuptake of serotonin without acting on noradrenaline [as the older tricyclics did]." This meant that SSRI compounds had the net effect of boosting serotonin levels, because more serotonin molecules became stalled in the synaptic gap, and remained available for stimulating serotonin receptors. This helped with depression, while avoiding the weight gain, drowsiness, and dry mouth associated with drugs that also boosted norepinephrine. The first such drug developed under Carlsson's direction was called zimelidine. Zimelidine looked good in pre-clinical studies against depression as early as 1972, almost twenty years before Prozac, the most famous selective serotonin uptake blocker of them all, became a blockbuster drug. Nevertheless, zimelidine ultimately had to be discontinued due to potentially lethal side effects.

What led Carlsson and others to this new class of serotonin-active drugs, known as SSRIs? It was the fact that some antihistamines had shown serotonin-boosting properties, though not selective enough for use as reliable antidepressants. The pheniramines and diphenhydramine, common agents in over-the-counter cold and allergy remedies like Triaminic and Benedryl, respectively, were particularly strong in this respect. They were, in fact, the direct antecedents to drugs like Prozac and Zoloft. "We started from the pheniramines to develop zimelidine," Carlsson recalled. "The Lilly scientists started out from diphenhydramine and developed Prozac."

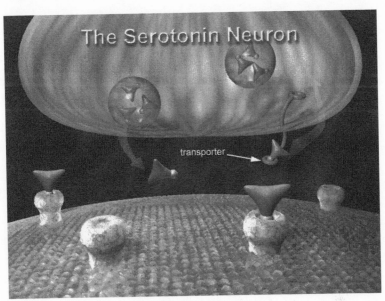

The Serotonin Neuron

Psychoactive drugs, the mind-altering drugs, and the addictive drugs all played a crucial but largely unheralded role in the development of neuropharmacology. Discoveries about psychoactive drugs, mental illness, and addictive disorders all went hand in hand. In his book, *Drugs and the Brain*, Solomon Snyder writes:

> Within the past twenty years, neuroscientists, the
> scientists whose primary interest is brain func-
> tion, have come to realize that psychoactive drugs
> are powerful tools for unraveling the intricacies
> of information processing in the brain. The

use of these drugs in brain research has already brought about some of the most important recent advances in the neurosciences; and once researchers have discovered, at a molecular level, how these drugs act in the brain to bring about such striking changes in mental processes, they might find it possible to design new therapeutic agents that are far more potent, more efficient, and safer than the ones available now. This reciprocal interaction between drug development for therapeutic purposes and the use of drugs to understand the brain has been largely responsible for an explosion in brain research that began in the 1950s and continues today.

Meanwhile, at Eli Lilly and Co., several organic chemists had been working on identifying new compounds that showed activity at serotonin receptor sites. Since the same broad family of compounds that relieved allergy symptoms often proved promising for the treatment of depression, one common starting point was over-the-counter allergy pills. A group of researchers including Bryan B. Molloy, David T. Wong, Ray W. Fuller, and Klaus Schmiegel were playing around with variations on the diphenhydramine molecule (Benadryl) in search of promising new antidepressants that did not tweak norepinephrine systems, or histamine, or acetylcholine, or dopamine. They were on the hunt for a drug specifically targeted at serotonin receptors. If they could avoid stimulating nerve cells that used acetylcholine, the researchers believed they could avoid the worst side effects of the tricyclics, such as dry mouth, rapid heartbeat, and extreme fatigue. These were exactly the side effects that often plagued users of over-the-counter antihistamines for seasonal allergy relief.

The standard testing procedure, "binding and grinding," involved giving the test drugs to rats, putting the rats to sleep, removing the brains, and grinding them up in high-tech blenders. Then scientists spun the resultant goo in a centrifuge, extracting material rich in nerve endings, and, by exposing the extract to a given neurotransmitter, they could measure how much of that neurotransmitter the extract absorbed or blocked.

In 1972, the Lilly researchers came across Compound 82816, another in a long series of new chemicals being tested. Compound 82816 very cleanly and very selectively blocked the reuptake of serotonin, and it did so without effecting any other neurotransmitter system at all. Clinical trials of compound 82816, chemically known as fluoxetine, continued into the early 1980s. At the same time, compounds with profiles similar to fluoxetine were being tested at various universities and drug firms.

The new drugs—with names like citalopram, zimelidine, fluoxetine, and fluvoxamine—were extensively investigated in animal models, and along the way, investigators made some unexpected discoveries. European investigators had shown that one serotonin uptake blocker in particular—zimelidine—seemed to reduce the self-administration of morphine and alcohol in addicted rats. A good part of the research began to center on three serotonin-enhancing compounds—zimelidine, citalopram, and fluoxetine.

Since rats decreased their administration of both alcohol and morphine when given zimelidine, and since low serotonin is a strong potential marker for human alcoholics and other addicts, Dr. Claudio Naranjo and Dr. Ed Sellers, along with their colleagues at Toronto's Addiction Research Foundation, began testing zimelidine on heavy drinkers. In order to distinguish between zimelidine's possible effects on drinking behavior, and its effects as an antidepressant, the researchers selected 16 male test subjects who consumed an average of more than six drinks a day, but who were not clinically depressed.

Characterized as "early stage problem drinkers," the test subjects showed a slight but noticeable decrease in the number of drinks consumed per day when they took zimelidine. There was also a consistent increase in the number of days the drinkers were completely abstinent. Zimelidine was later withdrawn from use worldwide because it sometimes caused problems related to the immune system.

The Toronto group found much the same result when they tried citalopram, another serotonin reuptake inhibitor. Again, citalopram decreased the number of drinks consumed, and increased the number of abstinent days in nondepressed heavy drinkers. Citalopram also seemed to be responsible for a slight but noticeable weight loss in most of the test subjects.

The small number of subjects, the relatively high dropout rates, and the fact that the subjects were not necessarily alcoholics all combined to create uncertainty about the striking results. Nonetheless, when rats were given other serotonin reuptake inhibitors in routine testing for adverse side effects, two notable changes in their behavior became evident: They reduced their consumption of alcohol, and they lost weight.

As research continued across North America, it became consistently evident that drugs capable of increasing concentrations of brain serotonin tended to cause large numbers of animals and human test subjects to drink less alcohol. Dr. Louis Lemberger of the Lilly Laboratory for Clinical Research published a study showing that fluoxetine had no direct effect on alcohol metabolism in human subjects. The Lilly study concluded that alcohol and fluoxetine were not likely to cause a fatal reaction in combination. But it wasn't simply an aversive reaction at work, as in the case of Antabuse. People in the clinical trials still drank, but in many cases, the urge to drink seemed to diminish, and while the decrease was modest, it was measurable.

Dr. Ting-Kai Li, noting that "depression, eating disorders, and carbohydrate craving are frequently seen in alcoholics or recovering alcoholics," undertook an investigation of the effects of fluoxetine on his alcoholic rats at the University of Indiana. Sure enough, fluoxetine modestly curbed the alcohol-seeking behavior of the P-line rats. Moreover, Dr. Richard Wurtman of MIT produced evidence to show that serotonin-enhancing drugs such as fluoxetine and fenfluramine did not just curb appetite in general, but *specifically* reduced the intake of carbohydrates in animal studies. Rats given serotonin-enhancing drugs selectively cut back on carbohydrates, and that was why they lost weight. (Conversely, drugs that lower brain concentrations of serotonin can cause carbohydrate craving and weight gain.) Another drug, D-fenfluramine, began to show promise as an appetite suppressant in human trials.

In late 1987, *Fortune* magazine's article on fluoxetine reported that "the prospect of making people both happy and thin has helped Lilly stock rise 28 per cent this year."

The prospect of making alcoholics drink less, or stop drinking altogether, was a less publicized but equally attractive notion.

Lilly already had a trade name picked out for fluoxetine. They were calling it Prozac.

A year after its introduction as an antidepressant, Prozac was a runaway success. Prozac quickly proved the existence of a huge potential market for serotonin reuptake inhibitors. Research continued on the diminished craving response that the serotonin uptake blockers seemed to produce in certain drinkers. The drug's allure as an anti-craving medication for alcoholism and other possible addictions remained an open secret among researchers. Lilly wasn't saying much in public about it, and with sales booming for fluoxetine as an antidepressant, the company could afford to concentrate on that indication.

"All drugs have a range of pharmacologic action," Dr. Ed Sellers of the Addiction Research Foundation explained, "and from a regulatory point of view, when new drugs come along, companies don't try to develop them for forty-three different things. But these drugs still carry with them many other pharmacologic actions. The history of virtually every drug that comes to market is that all these other secondary applications start to manifest themselves."

As time went by, Sellers professed not to be surprised by Lilly's reluctance to pursue the SSRIs as medications for alcoholism. "The treatment of alcohol and substance abuse is not an area that historically the pharmaceutical industry has been terribly concerned about," he said. "In fact, it seems to have had some liabilities, from their point of view." Some addiction researchers were not particularly pleased with Lilly's early work on Prozac as an anti-craving drug. "The first trial Lilly did was flubbed," the director of a major chemical dependency program complained to me. "That's the basic problem. Marketing drives a lot of their research, and that's a problem, too, of course. But scientifically there's something there. For Lilly, it's a question of whether it's a robust enough effect to justify the investment." Nonetheless, sometimes when people take Prozac, they lose weight. And sometimes they drink less.

For a company like Eli Lilly, contemplating whether to seek FDA approval for a drug that *may* cut down on alcohol consumption in alcoholics, many of the liabilities have to do with lawsuits and related entanglements. In addition to the medical and legal liabilities, there remains a social stigma attached to addictive diseases. Regulation and review of such drugs in trials on human subjects is fraught with potential problems, due to the complex psychobiology of addiction.

By 1994, Sellers, Naranjo, and others had shown quite consistently that serotonin-boosting drugs had an effect on alcohol consumption. Dr. Li and the others had been right about their alcoholic rats: If you increase serotonin levels, alcohol consumption goes down. In certain randomized, double blind, placebo-controlled trials, fluoxetine and other SSRIs lowered alcohol consumption by about 20 per cent among non-depressed alcoholics. Sometimes the drop was as high as 60 per cent. This wasn't abstinence, but the numbers were far better than the numbers for any other medication ever tried on alcohol abusers. That same year, Dr. Steve Paul left his job as director of intramural research at the National Institute of Mental Health. Dr. Paul took a job, instead, with Eli Lilly Co., as vice president of CNS research. The move was seen by some as the typical lucrative shift from federal to private industry, for the usual financial reasons. Steve Paul offered an alternative view. "I am leaving government because of the real—even likely—possibility that in the private sector I will make a direct contribution to discovering and developing drugs to treat some of the world's most devastating brain disorders," Dr. Paul told the *Wall Street Journal*. Noting that the industry he was joining had been charged with pursuing "profits at the expense of our children," Dr. Paul said that "Government cannot produce these new medicines...But Eli Lilly, just one such company, spends almost $1 billion a year on high-quality research, as much as NIH spends on all its intramural research programs together. Thus the medicines we need can be found and developed only through private entrepreneurship."

Prozac garnered the kind of press attention and public controversy that LSD-25 had attracted some 30 years earlier. Once again, a serotonin-active drug had grabbed the headlines. (The serotonin-active drug Ecstasy was soon to follow.) Unlike LSD, Prozac was very "transparent." It did not cause hallucinations or grandiose thoughts, nor did it make colors brighter or music more mysterious. In fact, Prozac *did* alter perception and feeling, but it did so much more subtly and consistently over longer periods. The more Prozac was seen to do just that—to alter consciousness and change people's behavior in discernable ways—the more a Prozac backlash flourished.

It was hard to explain exactly what Prozac did, when it did anything at all. For positive responders, as they were called, trying to explain exactly how Prozac lifted their depression was very much like trying to describe the specific contents of consciousness. It was hard to describe a slow but steady elevation of mood over time. Like LSD, Prozac altered serotonin levels, and little else. But Prozac didn't disorder the senses, didn't have LSD's fireworks, didn't trip you out. Bolting two cups of strong coffee generally afforded more direct sensory stimulation than Prozac. It was a powerful and elusive drug, nonetheless.

Peter Kramer, in his book *Listening to Prozac*, did a fine job of highlighting the descriptions given by patients who had benefited dramatically from the drug. It made lifelong depressives feel brighter, more energetic, more assertive—more "upful" in the memorable phrase of one patient—but it didn't do this for everybody. Unlike LSD, Prozac didn't do anything for most people. When it worked, Prozac did not provide mood benefits primarily through the classic reward pathway stimulations induced by heroin, amphetamine, alcohol, and the rest of the usual suspects.

Kramer writes, "I like the model of serotonin-as-police. Yes, serotonin is known to affect sleep, appetite, and the like. But, most dramatically, raising the level of serotonin seems to enhance security, courage, assertiveness, self-worth, calm, flexibility, resilience. Serotonin sets tone."

Consider this description of a serotonin-active drug: "The unique behavioral properties... do not involve profound sensory disruption, but instead produce powerful enhancement of emotions, empathy, and affiliative bonds with other persons." The description seems to fit the SSRIs. Nevertheless, the authors of the paper from which it is taken were referring, instead, to MDMA, also known as Ecstasy.

It has to be admitted that the early LSD theoreticians did score some successes using these wildly unpredictable substances for the treatment of alcoholism, drug addiction, and depression. Their work helped focus the spotlight on the various functions of serotonin in the human brain. Both Prozac and LSD testify to the power of receptor-active drugs. They were key breakthroughs in our understanding of receptors and ligands (neurotransmitters, hormones and peptides). They are non-addictive, neither is right for everybody, and users of both have at times been vilified and stigmatized. Both drugs, in their turn, have sparked resistance to the notion that psychological wellness, spiritual awareness, and addiction recovery are conditions that can be positively influenced by drugs. Both drugs, in their turn, have been over prescribed and over extolled as panaceas for every ill, and have frequently been put to trivial uses. They have both been the subject of urban folklore and disturbing press coverage.

Both drugs have been blamed for numerous suicides—from TV personality Art Linkletter's daughter, whose suicide in the

1960s was blamed on LSD, to the "Prozac Kills" campaign waged by the Church of Scientology in the 1990s, to the recent concern over suicidal ideation in teenagers on SSRIs. But for all of this, LSD and Prozac are curiously benign compounds. Few fatal overdoses have ever been recorded for either drug. LSD and Prozac, for all that they are capable of, do not addict or kill their users.

Enthusiasts within the medical community, as well as positive responders, were not suggesting that Prozac created joy, or bliss, or spiritual insight, as proponents of LSD and MDMA (Ecstasy) therapy were inclined to do. The FDA had approved Prozac and similar drugs that followed for use in cases of clinical unipolar depression only. Nonetheless, scientists were excited about the new SSRIs. In addition to unipolar depression, there was a substantial list of conditions involving serotonergic and dopaminergic dysfunctions—alcohol consumption, drug use, weight loss, obsessions, compulsions, phobias, bulimia, premenstrual syndrome, and Tourette's syndrome—that might also be attacked pharmaceutically by means of these medications. The problem was that none of these other conditions was a legal reason to prescribe the drug.

"In an era when personality was understood to be the summation of psychological defenses, and the defenses were understood as responses to trauma during development, it was threatening to see personality as responding to medication," writes Kramer. "Prozac has allowed us to see an effect of medications that we should have attended to long ago."

Opiates, amphetamines, and all other addictive drugs shortcut the "hedonic process," according to Kramer. Such drugs allow "pleasure without the pleasurable acts, and thereby cut us off from the realities of the world." Prozac does what it does "without being experienced as pleasurable in itself and without inducing distortions of perception. Prozac simply gives anhedonic people access to pleasures identical to those enjoyed by other normal people in their ordinary social pursuits." We can borrow and adapt this statement so that it represents the central paradox of addiction: Freedom from drugs, coupled with treatment for depression when necessary, eventually gives former addicts and alcoholics access to the ordinary social pleasures enjoyed by non-addicts.

Prozac and other drugs that work on serotonin and dopamine systems have sparked an ideological war in the medical community. In one corner stand those who believe that taking drugs to treat an addiction or a mental disorder is always wrong. In the opposite corner are the brash biological psychiatrists, and to hear them tell it, decades of pointless therapeutic intervention is about to end. To non-scientists, this sometimes sounded a bit too much like *Brave New World*. But it was gaining a foothold with many doctors, especially G.P.s, who well knew that alcoholism, drug addiction, and depression were all notoriously resistant to treatment. Medical responsibilities often ended when one of these three diagnoses was pronounced. In the past, doctors had always felt largely free of any pressure to probe their patients about diet, drink, and drug habits. If you ate too much, or drank too much, or took addictive drugs too often, you would, if pushed into treatment, inevitably find yourself in the hands of doctors who didn't believe there was much they could do for you except assist in the detoxifying process and counsel you not to do it again. It fell to psychiatrists and psychologists, almost by default, to attempt to devise treatments for these relentlessly biological disorders. Even though addiction science was only emerging from infancy in the mid-1990s, an inordinate number of psychiatric practices were dedicated to the treatment of addiction.

Ovide Pomerleau and so many other researchers had come to the conclusion that the biological substrate unifying alcoholism, addiction, depression, and certain eating disorders was simply "one of those things that must be so." By 2000, the connection had become irrefutable. Population surveys had shown that nearly half of alcoholic patients had a long history of coexisting depression and/or anxiety disorders. Overall, about a third of patients with depression or panic disorder have had lifelong problems with drug abuse. These are estimates, best clinical guesses, but associating depression and addiction is no longer a speculative venture.

As with more familiar forms of addiction, bulimia was coming to be seen as another serotonin/dopamine-mediated medical condition. As noted, serotonin is involved in both the binge and the purge. Once researchers began performing the necessary double blind, placebo-controlled studies, it became clear that serotonin-boosting drugs dramatically lessened bulimic behavior in general, and associated carbohydrate binging in particular, in a large number of diagnosed bulimics. (Anorexia nervosa, another eating disorder, does not show the same serotonin affinities in action.) Bulimics often maintain a normal weight, but can suffer serious physical consequence—heart rhythm irregularities, electrolyte imbalances, low blood pressure, and damage to the esophagus. Once the binge-purge cycle has been established, some researchers believe, drug-like changes in serotonin 5HT receptor distributions help reinforce the pattern. It is not surprising to learn that Prozac and other serotonin reuptake inhibitors such as dexfenfluramine were prominent among the drugs being tested against bulimia in the 1990s. By 1995, a paper presented at the National Social Science Association Conference in San Diego stated: "The serotonin hypothesis of bulimia nervosa suggests that bulimia is the behavioral manifestation of functional underactivity of serotonin in the central nervous system."

In 1997, Prozac became the first drug ever licensed by the FDA for the treatment of bulimia nervosa, as this chronic disorder is officially known. The drug's formal approval was based on three clinical studies showing median reductions in binging of as much as 67 per cent for Prozac, compared with 33 per cent for placebo. Vomiting was reduced by 56 per cent, compared to 5 per cent for female placebo users. (About 10 per cent of diagnosed bulimics are males.) There is often a family history of alcoholism and/or eating disorders. The locus of "serotonergic dysfunction" appears to be the hypothalamus. Low levels of serotonin and dopamine metabolites have been documented in the cerebrospinal fluid of bulimic patients. Evidence exists for the involvement of norepinephrine as well. Bulimia, like alcoholism and addiction, has its psychosocial side, but twins studies show that there is very probably a genetics of bulimia to be pursued. In one influential study, an identical twin stood a one-in-four chance of developing bulimia, if the other twin was diagnosed with the disorder. A combination of SSRI drugs and some form of structured cognitive therapy is the recommended approach.

Under the umbrella of possible serotonin-driven disorders, perhaps none is stranger than the ailment clinicians have dubbed "body dysmorphic disorder" or BDD. People with this disorder feel deeply unattractive because of a perceived flaw in skin, hair, or facial features—minor flaws at best, or defects which demonstrably are not there—and cannot be reasoned out of this core belief. What they see in the mirror is simply different from what others objectively see about them—a symptom shared with anorexia and sometimes bulimia. People with body dysmorphic disorder, however, believe they are disfigured, and often refuse to go out in public. A woman with a perfectly ordinary nose insists it is repugnantly small. A young man with no observable skin conditions believes he has repulsive freckles and picks at them constantly. These and other clinical reports prompted doctors to try Prozac, with excellent results. Obsessive-compulsive sufferers who try SSRIs sometimes find relief as well, but here the drug manufacturers jumped the gun. Pfizer got in trouble with the FDA for marketing Zoloft for off-prescription uses such as obsessive-compulsive disorder, postpartum depression, and severe premenstrual syndrome. (SSRIs were eventually approved for severe PMS.) Over-prescribing Prozac was the dirty little secret of the SSRI revolution. Doctors, patients, therapists, all knew that the drug was being used far afield of its indications in the accompanying literature. Rumors of Prozac prescriptions for weight loss became commonplace. The huge success of lower-dose Prozac for depression and bulimia may have put Lilly off the idea of pursuing approval for a high-dose version of the drug for weight loss. Lilly backed off on efforts to secure approval for Lovan, a very high-dose version of Prozac, as an anti-obesity drug. As we will see, those who did pursue serotonin boosters for weight loss did not fare so well.

It was also being used for situational depression—the death of a loved one, for example—where tranquilizers or sedatives might have been previously employed. And it was being used in cases just short of clinical depression, a conditioned termed "dysthymia." It was being tried against eating disorders, shyness, lack of energy, fear of failure, anxiety, codependency, menstrual cramps—the list is long and troubling.

Due to the modulating role serotonin plays in the release of other neurotransmitters, serotonin reuptake inhibitors have a secondary effect on dopamine release. However, SSRI medications have not proven useful against the more dopamine-driven disorders like amphetamine and cocaine addiction.

Serotonin was eventually hailed in the popular press as the Neurotransmitter of the 1990s, and Prozac made it to the cover of *Time Magazine*. (Soon to come was Zyban for nicotine addiction, with its gently hectoring tagline, "Now you have no more excuses.") Drs. Li, Cloninger, Begleiter, Pomerleau, Sellers, Naranjo, and scores of others had correctly seen that addiction and depression arose biologically, out of an overlapping physiological substrate composed of the primary reward neurotransmitters. The addictive process for many drugs also impinges on systems for endorphins, glutamate, and GABA. These researchers had deduced that the two afflictions had more affinities and connections than anyone previously had realized, however environmentally-mediated these maladies might be.

By 2000, receptor-active drugs were already big business in other arenas of medicine. A foreshadowing of things to come were the so-called beta-blockers; top-selling cardiac care drugs which "sit" on beta-adrenergic receptors meant for adrenaline, thereby reducing heart rate and lowering blood pressure. Another designer drug success story, and a serious blockbuster all its own, was cimetidine for ulcers. Histamine receptors come in at least two forms—the well-known receptors in the lungs and upper respiratory tract, and a second type of histamine receptor in the gut. Histamine release in the stomach contributes to the symptoms of peptic ulcer. Therefore, scientists designed an antagonist for H2 receptor sites in the stomach, which drastically reduced many ulcer symptoms. Marketed as Tagamet, the drug was a billion-dollar baby for Smith, Kline. Soon after, Glaxo hit the same jackpot with its own variant, Zantac. The drugs were not cures, and for better or worse, all they did was temporarily relieve symptoms. They became two of the most successful drugs in the history of medicine.

Addicts who face the most difficult struggle, and the toughest odds, are the cases of "dual diagnosis," such as chain smokers diagnosed with unipolar depression, or alcoholics suffering from debilitating anxiety attacks. It is easy to see why the SSRIs have become a popular treatment modality in such "co-morbid" patients. It was well known in treatment centers that patients who scored high on the Beck Depression Inventory and other common diagnostic depression screens were at the highest risk for relapse. The challenge lies in developing drugs that wipe out cravings without radically altering reward pathways and diminishing the ability to experience other forms of pleasure. "My own bias is that the selective anti-craving drugs are going to be very hard to come by," Dr. Post at NIMH predicted. "Inhibiting the reward areas of the brain to effect craving may have more general side effects on mood and other essential components of physiological functioning."

Can we find safe and reliable ways to turn off, or alter, or otherwise fine-tune selected portions of the human reward pathways? We had better hope so. Drug abusers of all stripes have found safe and unreliable methods for doing so. Addiction science is about arresting and reversing the brain changes that result.

Craving and relapse are biological imperatives, not failures of will. Anticipating the rewards of a drug experience, which lies at the heart of what we call craving, has firm physical underpinnings. Simply detoxifying addicts will not arm them against repeated episodes of craving and assorted drug-seeking urges. Physiological changes in the brain caused by long-term drug abuse occur, says Dr. Kreek, "due to the intrinsic neuroplasticity of the brain." These changes, she writes, are "persistent and, at best, slowly reversible. Unfortunately, after any type of detoxification, relapse rates in individuals who do not receive targeted medications... have been shown to be more than 80% (within one year and usually much sooner)."

It is, however, this "intrinsic neuroplasticity" of the brain that is its redeeming feature. It is the way out of the cycle of addiction.

Beyond matters of scientific research, what stands between many addicts and the new forms of treatment is "pharmacological Calvinism." I would love to claim this term as my own, but it was coined by Cornell University researcher Gerald Klerman. Pharmacological Calvinism may be defined as the belief that treating any psychological symptoms with a pill is tantamount to ethical surrender, or, at the very least, a serious failure of will. If a drug makes you feel good, "It not only represents a secondary form of salvation but somehow it is morally wrong and the user is likely to suffer retribution with either dependence, liver damage, or chromosomal change, or some other form of medical-theological damnation." (Klerman labeled the other, more drug-indulgent, equally wrong-headed end of the behavioral spectrum "psychotropic hedonism".)

Eli Lilly and other drug companies have always been reluctant to discuss the anti-craving aspects of serotonin and dopamine research, but not only is the anti-craving approach the treatment most likely to work, it is also the treatment most likely to win approval from addicts themselves. The effect of current SSRIs is too weak and too transient to be of major assistance to alcoholics who do not show a lifetime of major depressive symptoms as well. But the fact that these drugs can influence drinking behavior, however modestly, pointed the research squarely in the direction of the receptor-active drugs discussed in the next chapter.

ELEVEN: THE ANTI-CRAVING DRUGS

"Alcoholism, by definition, is a chronic relapsing condition, although relapses are not inevitable. It resembles manic-depressive disease in this regard and also has similarities to such chronic medical illnesses as diabetes and multiple sclerosis. When the alcoholic has a relapse, his physician often feels resentful. When his diabetic patient has a relapse because he failed to take insulin, the doctor tends to be more understanding. The reason for this inconsistency is not clear."

—Donald Goodwin

"In terms of treatment, you can't just attack the rewarding features of the drug," according to Dr. Li. "In the case of alcohol, we already have a perfect drug to make alcohol aversive—and that's Antabuse. But people don't take it. Why don't they take it? Because they still crave. And so they stop taking it. You have to attack the other side, and hit the craving."

That is precisely what has happened, because scientists have gained a much deeper understanding of how and why addicts crave. For years, craving was represented by the tortured tremors and sweaty nightmares of extreme heroin and alcohol withdrawal. Significantly, however, the symptom common to all forms of withdrawal and craving is anxiety. This prominent manifestation of craving plays out along a common set of axes: depression/dysphoria, anger/irritability, and anxiety/panic. These biochemical states are the result of the "spiraling distress" (George Koob's term) and "incomprehensible demoralization" (AA's term) produced by the addictive cycle. The mechanism driving this distress and demoralization is the progressive dysregulation of brain reward systems, leading to biologically based craving. The chemistry of excess drives the engine of addiction, which in turn drives the body and the brain to seek more of the drug.

Whatever the neuroscientists wanted to call it, addicts knew it as "jonesing," from the verb "to jones," meaning to go without, to crave, to suffer the rigors of withdrawal. Spiraling distress, to say the least—a spiraling rollercoaster to hell, sometimes. Most doctors didn't get it, and neither did the therapists, and least of all the public policy makers. Drug craving is ineffable to the outsider.

As most people know, behavior can be conditioned. From maze-running rats to the "brain-washed" prisoners of the Korean War, from hypnotism to trance states and beyond, psychologists have produced a large body of evidence about behavior change—how it is accomplished, how it can be reinforced, and how it is linked to the matter of reward.

It is pointless to maintain that drug craving is "all in the mind," as if it were some novel form of hypochondria. Hard-core addicts display all the earmarks of the classical behavioral conditioning first highlighted almost a century ago by Ivan Pavlov, the Russian physiologist. Pavlov demonstrated that animals respond in measurable and repeatable ways to the anticipation of stimuli, once they have been conditioned by the stimuli. In his famous experiment, Pavlov rang a bell before feeding a group of dogs. After sufficient conditioning, the dogs would salivate in anticipation of the food whenever Pavlov rang the bell. This conditioned response extended to drugs, as Pavlov showed. When Pavlov sounded a tone before injecting the dogs with morphine, for example, the animals began to exhibit strong physiological signs associated with morphine use at the sound of the tone alone. Over time, if the bell continued to sound, but no food was presented, or no drugs were injected, the conditioned response gradually lost its force. This process is called extinction.

Physical cravings are easy to demonstrate. Abstinent heroin addicts, exposed to pictures of syringes, needles, or spoons, sometimes exhibit withdrawal symptoms such as runny noses, tears, and body aches. Cravings can suddenly assail a person months—or even years—after discontinuing abusive drug use. Drug-seeking behavior is a sobering lesson in the degree to which the human mind can be manipulated by itself. The remarkable tenacity of behavioral conditioning has been demonstrated in recent animal studies as well. When monkeys are injected with morphine while recorded music is played, the music alone will bring on withdrawal symptoms months after the discontinuation of the injections. When alcoholics get the shakes, when benzodiazepine addicts go into convulsions, when heroin addicts start to sweat and twitch, the body is craving the drug, and there is not much doubt about it. But that is not the end of the matter.

"Craving is a very misunderstood word," said Dr. Ed Sellers, now with the Centre for Addiction and Mental Health in Toronto. "It's a shorthand for describing a behavior, but the behavior is more complicated and interesting than that. It's thought to be some intrinsic property of the individual that drives them in an almost compulsive, mad way. But in fact when you try to pin it down— when you ask people in a general context when they're exposed to drugs about their desire to use drugs, they generally give rather low assessments of how important it really is."

While cravings can sometimes drive addicts in an almost autonomic way, drug-seeking urges are often closely related to context, setting, and the expectancy effect. It has become commonplace to hear recovering addicts report that they were sailing through abstinence without major problems, until one day, confronted with a beer commercial on television, or a photograph of a crack pipe, or a pack of rolling papers—or, in one memorable case of cocaine addiction, a small mound of baking powder left on a shelf—they were suddenly overpowered by an onrush of cravings which they could not successfully combat. "If you put them in a setting where the drug is not available, but the cues are," said Sellers, "it will evoke a conditioned response, and you can show that the desire to use goes up." Most people have experienced a mild approximation of this phenomenon with regard to appetite. When people are hungry, a picture of a cherry pie, or even the internal picture of food in the mind's eye, is enough to cause salivation and stomach rumblings. Given the chemical grip which addiction can exert, imagine the inner turmoil that the sight of a beer commercial on television can sometimes elicit in a newly abstinent alcoholic.

When addicts start to use drugs again after a period of going without, they are able to regain their former level of abuse within a matter of days, or even hours. Some sort of metabolic template in the body, once activated, seems to remain dormant during abstinence, and springs back to life during relapse, allowing addicts to escalate to their former levels of abuse with astonishing speed. Hard-core addicts sometimes seem to have two brains, or, more precisely, two specific chemical conditions under which their brain can operate—abstinence and intoxication. State-dependent memory, says Professor Pomerleau at the University of Michigan, is capable of interfering with the effectiveness of anti-craving efforts. Insights gained while sober may be lost to addicts in a state of intoxication, and vice versa. In Pomerleau's clinic, nicotine-dependent patients will be asked during the early days of treatment to delay the first cigarette of the morning as long as possible, in an effort to break down the conditioned response to the memory of "wake up-get up-light a cigarette."

External cues—the conditioned cravings brought about by environmental triggers—can be attacked through more classical approaches to behavioral deconditioning. The typical treatment, as devised by Dr. O'Brien, Dr. Anna Rose Childress, and others, consists of repeatedly exposing recovering cocaine addicts to the sights, sounds and smells of their former habit. Patients handle crack pipes, load pipes with crack, and do everything they used to do, except light up. Eventually, abstinent addicts become less sensitized to these cues, and less responsive to externally motivated cravings. This approach to deconditioning is also quite different from early, cruder forms of "aversive" therapy, in which, for example, electric shocks were given to alcoholics as they smelled or tasted their favorite drink. Happily, such gruesome approaches have fallen out of favor, because they aren't very effective. The strategy employed in the case of the recalcitrant hoodlum in Anthony Burgess' *A Clockwork Orange* simply isn't reliable. The aversion wears off. The behavior of drinking is rarely successfully extinguished in this manner.

It is not clear whether external cravings can be completely extinguished in the Childress-O'Brien program, or whether they are only rendered dormant for some undetermined period. Nonetheless, the program is a promising way of dealing with the most obvious kinds of external cues, which can quickly lead an addict to relapse.

Often, the cues that lead to episodes of craving occur in what appears to be the complete absence of external stimuli. This is where anti-cravings drugs will be an extremely effective approach. "The important thing is that patients tell us there are internal cues as well as external triggers," said Dr. Halikas at the University of Minnesota. "If they're bored, for example—that stimulates craving. If they're in a lousy mood, if they're dysphoric, that stimulates craving." Even if it were possible to identify and extinguish every form of external cue, many addicts would still report strong cravings. The association between internal mood disorders and craving is not as amenable to classical deconditioning.

Relapse sometimes seems to happen even before addicts have had a chance to consciously consider the ramifications of what they are about to do. In A.A., this is often referred to as forgetting why you can't drink. It sounds absurd, but it is a relatively accurate way of viewing relapse. Addiction, as one addict explained, "is the only disease that tells you you ain't got it."

From the public health point of view, most of our money has gone for drug prevention programs, rather than treatment programs, and certainly not for relapse prevention programs. U.S. health care typically pays for drug and alcohol detoxification over a 30-day period, but after that, there are rarely mechanisms and money available for relapse prevention. This virtually guarantees a revolving door at treatment centers. Spending public and private money to detox the same addict repeatedly is not money well spent. Relapse is expensive. In fairness, until quite recently, there was little that the medical community could offer by way of long-term craving prevention, even if the funding bodies had been interested. But that has changed.

Testing anti-craving drugs, from animal models to double blind, placebo-controlled trials in humans, is an expensive proposition in its own right. There are dozens of complications that bedevil this brand of neuropharmacological research. It cannot be otherwise, given the remarkable overlap in the way the central nervous system processes both natural and chemical rewards. Several centuries of external chemical pleasures have mislead our brains. As psychologist Mihaly Csikszentmihalyi writes, "The brain won't tell us when enough is enough."

What would the ideal drug therapy for drug addiction look like? To begin with, the drug obviously must be capable of attenuating episodes of acute craving. It must be tailored for a specific addiction. It must also be able to efficiently cross the blood-brain barrier. It would be available in time-release oral dosages that last for two or three days, obtainable at the local doctor's office, rather than limited to special addiction treatment facilities (as is the case with methadone). Ideally, it would have a slow rate of onset, and a long duration of action. It would be weakly addictive, or else free of abuse potential entirely, and if it decreases the pleasurable effects of the drug in question, so much the better. It must have a minimum of deleterious side effects, and it must be covered by most medical insurance programs. Furthermore, it must be relatively cheap. And, finally, addicts and alcoholics must hear about it. Doctors, too. Addiction science is still poorly covered in most medical schools.

The use of anti-craving medications is complicated by the existence of several types of craving—drug hunger from abstinence, drug craving primed by drug use itself, and cue-induced cravings, for starters. The fact that such first-generation compounds have been identified, and in some cases effectively employed, marks a turning point in the history of drug addiction. To date, the sad fact is that most of the people who might benefit from these drugs have never heard of them. There has never been a better time in history to be an addict seeking to recover.

While the trio of primary reward chemicals governs the process of addiction and its reinforcement potential, it is almost never just one drug, or one gene, or one family of neurotransmitters, despite the articulate optimism of Lewis Thomas. Drug craving itself is also mediated by glutamate receptor activity in the hippocampus—the seat of learning and memory. A fundamental branch of what we might dub the "relapse pathway" runs through the glutamate-rich areas of the hippocampus. The puzzling matter of craving and relapse began to come into focus only when certain researchers began to rethink the matter of memory and learning as it applies to the addictive process. This led back to the role of glutamate, and it gradually became clear that the drug *high* and the drug *craving* were, in a manner of speaking, stored in separate places in the brain. The sustained release of reward neurotransmitters in the limbic structures is part of withdrawal and craving as well as reward. But recent research at NIDA suggests that drug memories induced by environmental triggers originate primarily in the hippocampus.

As a precursor for the synthesis of GABA, glutamate has lately become a tempting new target for drug research. Eli Lilly is working on new glutamate-modulating antianxiety drugs. Glutamate may be the substance out of which the brain fashions "trigger" memories that lead certain addicts down the road to relapse. Roger

Williams, that contrary old Texan, was definitely on to something when he stressed the importance of glutamine in the process of withdrawal and abstinence. Glutamate is the most common neurotransmitter in the brain. (In sodium salt form, as monosodium glutamate, it is a potent food additive.) About half of the brain's neurons are glutamate-generating neurons. Glutamate receptors are dense in the prefrontal cortex, indicating an involvement with higher thought processes like reasoning and risk assessment. High levels of glutamate are toxic, and drugs that boost glutamate levels in the brain can cause seizures. Glutamate does most of the damage when people have strokes. The receptor for glutamate is called the N-methyl-D-aspartate (NMDA) receptor. And unfortunately, as the gifted science writer Constance Holden related in *Science*, NMDA antagonists, which might have proven to be potent anti-craving drugs, cannot be used because they induce psychosis. Dissociative drugs like PCP and ketamine are glutamate antagonists. Dextromethorphan, the compound found in cough medicines like Robitussin and Romilar, is also a weak glutamate inhibitor. In overdose, it can induce psychotic states similar to those produced by PCP and ketamine.

The symptoms common to those drugs in overdose have led to the construction of a glutamate theory for schizophrenia. Some researchers have claimed that schizophrenics cannot distinguish between a dose of ketamine and a full-blown relapse into psychosis.

Research at the National Institute for Drug Abuse strongly supports the hypothesis that drug memories induced by environmental triggers originate primarily in the hippocampus.

Drugs that play off receptors for glutamate are already available, and more are in the pipeline. As a precursor for the synthesis of GABA, glutamate has lately become a tempting new target for drug research. Ely Lilly and others have been looking into glutamate-modulating antianxiety drugs, which might also serve as effective anti-craving medications for abstinent drug and alcohol addicts.

What follows is a survey of currently available anti-craving drugs for the most common drugs of abuse:

Heroin

A quiet revolution is taking place in the treatment of heroin addiction. Buprenorphine, a partial opiate agonist sometimes used in hospitals as a pain medication, offers addicts a different approach to abstinence. Approved for heroin treatment by the FDA in 2002, "bupe" targets opiate receptors and is itself addictive, like methadone. But it has several advantages over methadone.

As of this writing, there are three government-approved drug therapies available for heroin addiction: methadone, LAAM (a methadone analogue), and buprenorphine, sometimes combined with naltrexone. NIDA-sponsored research at Johns Hopkins University, under the direction of Dr. Rolley Johnson, compared the results of four treatment groups—buprenorphine, LAAM, high-dose methadone, and low dose-methadone. In the 17-week study, reported in the November 2, 2000 issue of the *New England Journal of Medicine*, buprenorphine administered once every three days showed itself to be at least as effective a deterrent to heroin use, judged by negative urine specimens, as either LAAM or high-dose methadone.

Low-dose methadone did not fare as well. According to Dr. Johnson, there are several advantages to buprenorphine: "Less-than-daily dosing reduces the need for take-home medication, requires fewer clinic visits, and allows a more normal lifestyle." Equally significant is the unprecedented circumstances for the dispensing of bupe: It can be prescribed by an M.D., and obtained at a local pharmacy. Methadone is dispensed daily at special government clinics. NIDA has estimated that at least half of the heroin addicts offered methadone treatment turn it down, often due to the atmosphere of bureaucratic overregulation at methadone clinics. Buprenorphine became the first medical treatment for heroin addiction that could be obtained at a local doctor's office. Some European countries have been using the drug for several years. Buprenorphine is marketed as Subutex, or, in combination with naltrexone, as Suboxone. Buprenorphine has proven relatively easy to withdraw from, compared to methadone, and it frees people from the daily methadone regimen. It also presents less danger of overdose than methadone—always an important consideration. Buprenorphine is less sedating, with less of a traditional opiate buzz than methadone. Finally, and perhaps most significantly of all, buprenorphine has a definite "ceiling effect." Beyond a certain dosage, taking more of the drug will not increase the intensity of its effect. A user cannot get higher on bupe simply by taking more and more. The buprenorphine molecules fit the opiate receptors tightly enough that opiate molecules cannot knock them off, so taking a shot of heroin while on bupe won't work, either. In fact, it won't work for three full days, as buprenorphine remains tenaciously locked to the heroin receptors. All of this combines to make withdrawal from buprenorphine less rigorous than going off methadone or heroin itself.

"I'm more clear-headed than I've been in years," one recovering addict, who previously had been on methadone for five years before switching to buprenorphine, told the *New York Times*. "I feel better physically. For the first time in a long time, I can see myself getting off everything..." The idea with both medications is to stabilize and ultimately to come off them entirely. Bupe causes a reduction in heroin craving and heroin-seeking behaviors. Less crime, less drug dealing, and less jail time are the results. Drug experts are hoping to double or triple the number of heroin addicts currently in treatment. "Buprenorphine is the most important advance certainly in heroin and opiate treatment if not all addiction treatments in the last 30 years," declared NIDA's former director, Dr. Alan Leshner. Dr. Rolley Johnson believes that "expanding the numbers and types of potential treatment medications should help bring the treatment of opiate addiction into mainstream medical practice." In 2003, radio host Rush Limbaugh's addiction to OxyContin served as a reminder of the nation's problem with addictions to various forms of prescription opiates, including hydrocodone and codeine. Buprenorphine should be of use in these cases as well.

In time, buprenorphine will quite likely replace methadone as the drug treatment of choice for opiate addiction. It is a more targeted, receptor-active drug that fulfills many of the criteria for a successful anti-craving medication. Bupe stands a very good chance of being much more effective for addicts than methadone. Indeed, we may be seeing the last days of methadone as a front line treatment for heroin addiction.

Starting at Fair Oaks Hospital in New Jersey in the late 1970s, Dr. Mark Gold has been conducting experiments involving clonidine, a drug prescribed for the reduction of high blood pressure. His clinical trials involving clonidine were hard to ignore. Clonidine is not an antagonist for heroin, like naloxone, or a partial agonist, like buprenorphine. Clonidine works on the norepinephrine pathways. Since the opiates calm the nervous system, they also inhibit the release of norepinephrine, the body's "go" signal, the fight-or-flight chemical. The use of opiates decreases firing along the norepinephrine pathways, meaning that part of the anxiety reaction heroin addicts experience during withdrawal can be traced to a corresponding increase in norepinephrine activity—a rebound effect.

Panic sets in when the natural stores of endorphin, now seriously depleted by chronic heroin addiction, are not sufficient to properly regulate the release of the fight-or-flight neurotransmitter. Gold has postulated that norepinephrine is the neurotransmitter primarily responsible for the generation of withdrawal symptoms in heroin addicts. Some of the panic and paranoia experienced by heavy cocaine users also might be due to excess activity along norepinephrine pathways.

In brief, clonidine decreases norepinephrine levels by activating certain inhibitory receptors along the reward pathways. As Dr. Robert Post of NIMH explained, "It is tickling those receptors and saying there is plenty of norepinephrine out here, we don't need to fire any more. That's how clonidine shuts off norepineph-rine firing."

Dr. Gold has used clonidine successfully on heroin addicts to suppress the panic and craving associated with opiate withdrawal. Clonidine is not a tranquilizer, and while it does have some seda-tive effects, its impact on heroin addicts during withdrawal is not simply a matter of sedation. Sedation is not a very effective form of treatment for long-term withdrawal, including the case of alcohol-ism. (Clonidine doesn't work for alcoholism.)

Clonidine is also being investigated as an anti-craving drug for nicotine. This makes sense, since clonidine exerts its effect on norepinephrine, and norepinephrine has been strong implicated in cigarette smoking. Since panic and anxiety are also prominent symptoms of nicotine withdrawal, investigators have tried cloni-dine on intractable cigarette smokers, with promising results. In a major study under the direction of nicotine researcher Alexan-der Glassman, hard-core smokers given clonidine were consistently more successful at quitting than test subjects given a placebo.

Clonidine has generated considerable excitement, but like some of the other first-generation anti-craving compounds, it has signifi-cant drawbacks. Clonidine is a medication for high blood pressure, and the side effects of this powerful drug can include fatigue, head-aches, and extreme dizziness, for starters. Dropout rates as high as 40 percent have occurred in some clonidine studies. There is also debate over the question of whether clonidine itself can be addic-tive. Clonidine is a very potent drug, and abrupt withdrawal from this medication can be lethal.

Alcohol

According to estimates from a variety of sources, including the *Journal of the American Medical Association*, at least 10 per cent of Americans will suffer from alcoholism at some point in their lives. Alcoholic relapse, according to many experts, is at least as high as

60 per cent in the first year of abstinence, and anecdotal evidence suggests that it is even higher than that. While naltrexone, the opioid-receptor antagonist, is essentially a "feel bad" pill for abstinent junkies, it sometimes has a quite different effect on alcoholics. Naltrexone, a drug once considered a possible answer to the riddle of heroin addiction, became the first new treatment for alcoholism since Antabuse.

Given the chemical affinities between heroin and alcohol, it will not come as a surprise to learn that naltrexone, naloxone and a third version, nalmefene, have been extensively studied in animals as pharmacological treatments for alcoholism. "How an opiate receptor antagonist came to be found useful in the treatment of alcoholism is a tribute to the utility of animal models in the search for medications to treat addictive disorders," writes Charles O'Brien. In the 1990s, O'Brien and others discovered that published studies from a decade earlier, mostly ignored at the time, strongly suggested that alcohol consumption in alcoholic rats, mice, and monkeys could be reduced by blocking opiate receptors. Remember that alcohol, through some cascading neuromechanism, has a strong effect on opiate receptors. Alcohol is dramatically less rewarding when opiate receptors are blocked. We already know there is a demonstrated connection between alcohol and the excitation of opioid receptors in the nucleus accumbens and locus ceruleus. This has led to the opioid compensation hypothesis, which says that in addition to whatever serotonin and dopamine disturbances may occur along the limbic reward pathway, a biologically based deficiency in brain opioids is also part of the problem. Furthermore, like most drugs of abuse, alcohol is a chronic dopamine-depleter, particularly in the nucleus accumbens.

In 1994, Dupont's Revia (naltrexone) became the first drug to be medically approved by the FDA for use against alcohol dependency since Antabuse 50 years earlier. Unlike Antabuse, it does not interfere with alcohol metabolism. Numerous studies demonstrated that naltrexone patients had fewer drinking days and a lower rate of relapse drinking, compared to placebo users.

Naltrexone also decreased some of the positive effects of alcohol. In addition to its well-known blockade of the mu receptor sites for opiates, naltrexone exerted a blocking effect on one of the crucial chemical elements in the microbiology of the "rush"—the release of dopamine in the nucleus accumbens. Naltrexone even increases the frequency of vomiting after one too many. Naltrexone decreased sensitivity to craving—including craving triggered by environmental cues. In one test, subjects who reported the highest levels of craving at the beginning of the naltrexone trial proved the most likely to decrease their drinking during the course of the study.

Does this particular pharmacotherapy for alcohol addiction really work well enough to merit such enthusiasm? The studies leading to naltrexone's approval had shown that alcoholics were less prone to relapse than control groups during the first 90 days of sobriety, a period when the dangers of relapse are all too evident, but not all clinical trials of naltrexone have been so positive, and many of the trials involved patients simultaneously involved in cognitive and behavioral therapy. Revia is not foolproof, but it helps many alcoholics ease their way through the pain and difficulty of the "protracted abstinence syndrome," as Mark Gold has called it. "Naltrexone-related decreases in dropouts and relapse would be a welcomed addition to the treatment armamentarium and further support a common neurobiology of addiction and relapse," Gold told *Psychiatric Times*.

Using an opiate antagonist as an aid to the prevention of alcoholic relapse would have been unthinkable without the underpinnings of a neurophysiological model of addiction. It is an ironic reversal of how things stood in the early 1900s, when catalogs advertised opium for alcohol addiction, and alcohol for opiate addiction.

While naltrexone has yet to become the huge treatment breakthrough for alcoholism addiction that researchers hope for it, naltrexone did, in the end, prove to be the first anti-craving medication widely available for alcoholics. It is a fact that naltrexone is now used more commonly for alcoholism than for its original indication, heroin addiction.

There are four medications now legally available by prescription for alcoholism: disulfiram (Antabuse), SSRIs (informally), naltrexone (Revia), and acamprosate, the newest entry. Acamprosate binds to both GABA and glutamate receptors. Acamprosate, marketed in the U.S. as Campral, has been widely used in Europe on problem drinkers.

For all the knowledge gained about the workings of dopamine and serotonin, it was a secondary transmitter—GABA—that proved to be one of the most encouraging initial avenues of approach for alcoholism. American researchers came late to this one. An earlier thread of the research had pointed toward GABA all along. For years, doctors and clinicians had frequently resorted to the use of benzodiazepines like Valium, Xanax, and other GABA-active drugs for alcohol withdrawal. Indeed, it was often a life-saving tactic, in cases of extreme alcohol detoxification. (Since benzodiazepines are also addictive drugs, care must be exercised, and patient monitoring is a must.) The benzo treatment is better than nothing, in some cases, but it is nobody's idea of a good answer.

Alcohol and benzodiazepines like Valium can cause short-term memory problems due to an abundance of GABA receptors in the hippocampus. Acamprosate attacks the craving and relapse dilemma by stimulating GABA, the inhibitory transmitter that is the target of drugs like Valium, Xanax and Klonopin. However, Campral, or calcium acetyl-homotaurinate, is not sedating. It doesn't do anything for anxiety, like benzodiazepines, barbiturates, and alcohol. It is not a hypnotic, or a sedative, or an antidepressant, or a muscle relaxant. Scientists aren't entirely sure what it is. But there is no buzz, no psychoactive effect, and no evidence of abuse potential whatsoever. Major side effects are at this point limited to gastrointestinal cramps and diarrhea. In addition, Campral may also "restore receptor tone" in the hyperactivated glutamate system of the alcoholic, specifically in the nucleus accumbens.

While acamprosate enhances the GABA mechanism, it inhibits the glutaminergic system by occupying sites on the glutamate (NMDA) receptors. Acamprosate, then, can find binding sites on receptors for both GABA and NMDA receptors. In a dozen clinical trials conducted in Europe, involving thousands of alcohol abusers, 50 per cent of acamprosate users maintained sobriety for three months without relapse, compared to 39 per cent of the placebo group. (The distressingly low numbers are testimony to the fierce mechanism of relapse.)

The long-standing, often bitter debate about the ethics of treating addiction with prescription medications came to a head when German drug maker Merck KgaA (no relation to Merck, the American company) decided to market Campral in the U.S., as it had been doing with some success in Europe. In the U.S., fierce advocates for drug-free addiction therapy came out in force to oppose its adoption here. Determined to prevail, Lipha S.A., a French subsidiary of Merck KgaA, found a U.S. partner, Forest Laboratories, and awarded that firm the U.S. marketing rights to Campral—even though Forest Labs could not then legally exercise those rights. Due in no small part to differences in methodology between American and European drug studies (acamprosate was already in use in 28 other countries), the FDA, in a rare action that went against the recommendations of its own advisory committee, turned down the first attempt at certification in 2001. At this writing, Forest Labs and Merck KgaA have submitted additional data, and the FDA is expected to approve the drug for use in the treatment of alcoholism. Campral does not appear to have any direct effect on opiate receptors. This opens the possibility of combining it with naltrexone, and clinical trials of that combination are underway. Studies submitted to the FDA showed lower relapse rates over a 12-week period, compared to naltrexone (23 per cent, compared with 19 per cent.). Dozens of high-quality European studies of the drug's usefulness in alcoholism treatment were already available in France. Several double-blind studies documented an increase in abstinence days in alcoholic subjects. Patients reported reductions in anxiety, irritability, and insomnia. "Once patients give up alcohol and go on with their lives, they see it, smell it, dream about it," Dr. Karl Mann of the University of Tubingen in Germany told the *New York Times*. "Acamprosate helps them get through all that." Acamprosate superbly fulfills several of the criteria for a successful anti-craving drug. To start with, about 90 per cent of acamprosate is excreted in the urine without being metabolized by the liver. This eliminates both potential liver toxicity, and potentially lethal drug interactions. Low liver toxicity is essential, if a new drug is to be widely adopted. Campral appears to have no abuse potential, and it is reasonably cheap (at least the European version). It works directly on the desire to drink by reducing alcohol cravings and the initial distress of sobriety.

Acamprosate is intended to be used during abstinence, not during an active drinking phase. Another drug, however, can be taken by active drinkers, and stands a good chance of becoming another alcoholism drug approved by the FDA.

One serious drawback to the anti-alcoholism drugs discussed thus far is that they are intended for use with alcoholics who have already been detoxified. Drinkers must be abstinent already in order to use Revia and Campral. Obviously, a drug that could be used on active drinkers would have certain advantages. Topamax, the trade name for topiramate, is a dopamine-active epilepsy drug. Like Campral, topiramate causes changes in the GABA and glutamate systems, which in turn affect dopamine and serotonin function.

Researchers from the University of Texas conducted topiramate studies at the South Texas Addiction Research and Technology Center, later published in *Lancet*. The researchers checked blood levels of gamma-glutamyl tranferase (GGT), a liver enzyme that increases with heavy drinking, for the twelve-week trial. Alcoholic patients achieved a rate of continuous abstinence six times higher than those in a placebo group did, as measured by GGT levels. They also reported fewer cravings, compared to a placebo group.

The NIAAA's Ray Litten, chief of treatment research, believes that the drug may ultimately be a strong player. "On the other hand," he cautions, "Topiramate appears to have more severe side-effects than naltrexone and acamprosate." Litten argues that greater efforts at testing are needed. "We also need to test medications in special, understudied populations such as those suffering from psychiatric and/or substance abuse comorbidity, adolescents, and minorities. Because alcoholism is a heterogeneous disease, we most likely need medications that act on multiple sites."

At this writing, Topamax is only approved by the FDA for use against seizures and migraine. The controversial practice of "off-label" prescribing—using a drug for indications that are not formally approved by the FDA—has become so common that Johnson & Johnson said it had no plans to seek formal approval for the use of Topamax as a medicine for addiction.

The Journal of the American Medical Association (JAMA) reported that in a study of 371 male and female alcoholics receiving topiramate for 14 weeks, patients taking topiramate showed a significantly higher rate of abstinence, compared to a placebo group.

In an editorial accompanying the 2007 study, Mark Willenbring of the National Institute on Alcohol Abuse and Alcoholism (NIAAA) wrote: "We now have very high-quality evidence that shows efficacy. The medical world doesn't wait for the indication. Topamax is a drug that many physicians have used and many patients have had an experience with because of its use in migraines."

Dr. Bankole Johnson, chairman of Psychiatry and Neurobehavioral Sciences at the University of Virginia, said that Topamax does everything researchers want to see in a pharmaceutical treatment for alcoholism: "First, it reduces your craving for alcohol; second, it reduces the amount of withdrawal symptoms you get when you start reducing alcohol; and third, it reduces the potential for you to relapse after you go down to a low level of drinking or zero drinking."

Topiramate is not without serious side effects for some users, including vision problems, difficulty remembering words, and a tingling in the arms and legs known as parasthesia.

Moreover, some of the studies were funded by Ortho-McNeil-Janssen, the subsidiary of Johnson & Johnson that produces and markets Topamax. Citing this and other alleged irregularities, Public Citizen's Sidney Wolfe, Director of the Health Research Group, sent a stinging letter to the FDA demanding that the agency "stop the illegal and dangerous promotional campaign by Ortho-McNeil-Janssen-funded researchers for the unapproved use of Topamax (topiramate) for treating alcoholics."

An old European tree may yield another alcoholism treatment. Varenicline, a drug currently marketed by Pfizer for smoking cessation under the trade name Chantix (discussed in the nicotine section below), has also shown promise for use against alcoholism

Varenicline dramatically curbed drinking in alcohol-preferring rats in recent studies. The synthetic drug is modeled after a cytosine compound from the European Labumum tree, combined with an alkaloid from the poppy plant.

Since an estimated 85 per cent of alcoholics are also cigarette smokers, varenicline could have an immediate effect on this common dual addiction. Selena Bartlett of the UCSF-affiliated Gallo Clinic and Research Center said that the drug works by binding to acetylcholine receptors. Through a cascade effect, stimulating these receptors causes a release of dopamine. Varenicline prevents alcohol and nicotine from causing a major release of dopamine at those sites.

"Treatments for alcoholism today are like those for schizophrenia in the '60s," Bartlett said. "People don't talk about it. There are very few treatments, and most drug companies are not interested in it."

And finally, researchers at the National Institute of Alcohol Abuse and Alcoholism (NIAAA), working with colleagues at

Lilly Research Laboratories and University College in London, announced that a drug that blocks the so-called NK1 receptor (NKIR) reduced alcohol cravings in a study of 25 detoxified alcoholic inpatients. The NIAAA researchers were making effective use of recent findings about the role played by corticotropin-releasing hormone (CRH) in the addictive process. CRH is crucial to the neural signaling pathways for both drug reward and stress.

Another neurotransmitter of this type is substance P, together with its preferred receptor, NKIR. As it happens, NKIR sites are densely concentrated in limbic structures of the mid-brain, such as the amygdala, or so-called "fear center." The experimental drug, known as LY686017, blocks NKIR receptors, shutting off substance P, which in turn diminishes anxiety-related drug cravings.

Other researchers had previously demonstrated that deletion of NKIR sites eliminated opiate use in animal studies. And in humans, at least one earlier study showed decreased stress and anxiety reactions in human subjects taking a drug that blocked the Neurokinin I receptors.

The authors of the study suggest that "blockade of NKIRs might modulate stress- and reward-related processes of importance for excessive alcohol use and relapse."

The National Institutes of Health (NIH) recently estimated that it would be sponsoring more than 30 new clinical trials of drugs for alcoholism in the next few years.

Nicotine

The first medication to genuinely realize the promise of a widely effective anti-craving drug was not a serotonin uptake blocker, or a tricyclic, but rather a mid-range, broad-spectrum antidepressant known as bupropion. Marketed as Wellbutrin, bupropion did not fall into any of the existing chemical classes of antidepressants. Glaxo's repackaging of the antidepressant drug Wellbutrin as the

245

anti-smoking medication Zyban in 1998 was the beginning of true pharmacological treatment for nicotine addiction.

Zyban had no detectable effect on serotonin uptake, and did not inhibit MAO. Rather, it exhibited a weak affinity for dopamine and norepinephrine receptors. After more than twenty years of study, scientists still don't understand exactly how it works. But it arrived at a propitious time. As Ovide Pomerleau said: "We are seeing more and more heavily dependent smokers, over the years. The easy ones quit first, and increasingly we're left with the ones who are more nicotine-dependent."

It is ironic that the addiction affording neuroscientists their first big splash of publicity was generally considered, in a sort of loose tie with heroin, to be the toughest of them all: nicotine addiction. Few scientists had expected cigarettes to be among the early success stories.

As often happens in the sciences, the use of bupropion for nicotine cravings was discovered by accident, after patients using the drug as an antidepressant reported a marked decrease in their craving for cigarettes. Since we know that dopamine and norepinephrine are strongly implicated in nicotine addiction, this finding makes sense. The two main side effects of Wellbutrin/Zyban are tremors (commonly caused by dopamine agonists) and sweating (associated with norepinephrine agonists). Zyban also shares with the SSRIs the tendency to cause some slight, early weight loss.

GlaxoSmithKline, then known as Burroughs-Wellcome, had invested millions in Wellbutrin as the company's entry into the lucrative market for new antidepressants with milder side-effect profiles. It was approved for release before Prozac, and would have beaten Prozac to the market if not for a major study demonstrating that Wellbutrin was two to four times more likely to cause seizures than Prozac. Dr. Sheldon H. Preskorn, a member of the FDA's neuropsychopharmacology advisory committee that reviewed and recommended bupropion for approval, remembers that the finding "caused Burroughs-Wellcome to literally recall the trucks that were delivering the drug to pharmacy shelves." The seizures caused by Wellbutrin were dose-related. At the level of 300 milligrams per day, the recommended dosage for smoking cessation, the frequency of seizures fell to within normal ranges associated with other antidepressants—about two per 1,000. A revised low-dose, slow-release version of Wellbutrin was subsequently approved for use. But the widely publicized association with seizures remained, and Wellbutrin was never a hit with prescribing physicians and their patients. This changed in 1997 and 1998, when the company began touting a flurry of findings showing that Wellbutrin caused far fewer sexual side effects than the SSRIs (see Ch. 12). Thus it was that a new antidepressant that could have beaten Prozac to the market became an also-ran—until the discovery of its ability to diminish nicotine cravings and to combat the "erectile dysfunction" often associated with Prozac, Zoloft, and the others. Serendipity is always spoken of highly in the world of clinical science. Wellbutrin is a good case in point.

Prozac and the other SSRIs did not seem to help people quit or cut down on cigarettes. With cigarettes, serotonin interactions seemed to be secondary to dopamine, norepinephrine, and acetylcholine enhancement. In the early studies on Zyban, more than a third of the patients taking the drug kicked cigarettes for extended periods, compared with smokers in control groups. *In vitro* studies showed that bupropion increased dopamine levels in the nucleus accumbens, while reducing the firing rates of norepinephrine-rich cells in the locus ceruleus. By now, readers can deduce the likely effect of these changes: less anxiety and discomfort for smokers withdrawing from nicotine. In 1998, the FDA approved the use of bupropion in smoking cessation programs. (Unfortunately, bupropion has not shown the same success against cocaine cravings.)

Zyban works amazingly well for many intransigent smokers. It works even better when combined with counseling and some initial form of nicotine replacement therapy, such as patches, gums, or nasal sprays.

Zyban was tried at a variety of clinics, and with a cross-section of patients, and the percentage of users who remained smoke-free for 3 to 12 months or more averaged 25 to 60 per cent. The numbers were best when Zyban was combined with nicotine patches over a period of ten weeks or more. In fact, they were the best numbers anybody had ever seen in trials of an anti-craving medication. Every struggling smoker who was tested did better on the Zyban-patch combination than on any other mix of therapies—better at six months, at 12, at 18. The combination approach was pioneered by Dr. Linda Ferry at the VA Medical Center in Loma Linda, California, along with Dr. Neal Benowitz of UC-San Francisco, and Dr. Alex Glassman of Columbia University. No one can say with certainty that Zyban's action on dopamine and norepinephrine receptors is the whole answer. Even though SSRI antidepressants do not inhibit craving for cigarettes, it is still conceivable that Zyban works in some cases by addressing the underlying clinical depression suffered by a disproportionately large number of smokers (a sort of sneaky end-run around any recalcitrance the smoker might have felt about taking an antidepressant drug.)

Whatever the precise mechanisms involved, there was no doubt about Zyban's ability to help quell cravings in a large number of nicotine users trying to quit. Before Zyban, no medication that claimed to block cravings for tobacco had ever been approved by the FDA. Within three years, Zyban had become the most striking success story in the short history of anti-craving drugs.

A few years later, Zyban was followed by a potentially more effective drug: Chantix. In 2007, the FDA okayed the drug as a second medication for the treatment of nicotine addiction. Chantix, the trade name for varenicline tartrate, works on the dopamine system to reduce withdrawal and craving symptoms, as does Zyban. In randomized, placebo-controlled clinical studies involving more than 3,500 smokers, Chantix outperformed both placebos and Zyban.

The euphoria over Chantix, and its many early successes, were overtaken by developments at the FDA, which issued a formal alert on Chantix roughly a year later.

The FDA fired both barrels, announcing that a variety of anti-seizure medications—including the anti-smoking pill, Chantix—may increase the risk of suicidal thoughts in patients who take them. The FDA demanded new label warnings for a total of 11 drugs used for epilepsy.

The FDA reviewed clinical data on anti-epileptic medications, including Pfizer's Neurontin and Ortho-MacNeil's Topamax, and concluded that "patients who are currently taking or starting on any anti-epileptic drug should be closely monitored for notable changes in behavior that could indicate the emergence or worsening of suicidal thoughts or behavior or depression." (As we have seen, both Chantix and Topamax have shown promise as anti-craving medications for alcoholism.)

Discussions about a possible link between Chantix and suicide were fueled by the death of New Bohemians lead singer Carter Albrecht, who was shot while attempting to break into a house in Dallas. His girlfriend told authorities that his behavior had been erratic since he began taking Chantix in an effort to stop smoking. This followed on the heels of earlier warnings about increased suicide risk in adolescents taking SSRI antidepressants.

In the case of Chantix, the FDA's Bob Rappaport, in a conference call with reporters, said the agency had "no definitive evidence there is a causal relationship here, they are just strongly appearing to be related."

Rappaport also said that "Chantix has proven to be effective in smokers motivated to quit," and that the new warnings would help doctors and patients "make an informed decision regarding whether or not to use this product."

In no case are the numbers of suicides linked to any of the drugs alarmingly high. The FDA study of epilepsy medications appears to demonstrate, as summed up by the *San Francisco Chronicle*: "2.1 more people for every 1,000 on the medications exhibited suicidal thoughts or behavior, compared with every 1,000 on placebo."

Note that the FDA is not discussing an increased risk of suicide, but rather an increased risk of suicidal thoughts or feelings.

This is called "suicidal ideation." The FDA usually refers to it as "suicidality." Unlike an actual suicide attempt, suicidal ideation is the act of contemplating the act—a sort of "what if." It is the difference, as a mental patient once put it, between buying the rope, and contemplating buying the rope

Persistent suicidal ideation is obviously not a desirable state of mind. But it does not downplay this behavior to note that it is, by nature, often fleeting and difficult to quantify. Moreover, the act of going cold turkey itself can cause heavily addicted people to feel temporarily suicidal—to ideate about killing themselves without killing themselves. These and other factors make it difficult to reach firm statistical conclusions about such risks.

There is literally no time to lose, as recent medical findings continue to make clear. A variation on chromosome 15 among the genes that code for nicotine receptors has been linked with both cigarette smoking *and* a heightened risk for lung cancer, according to recent studies published in *Nature*.

The collection of studies demonstrated that people who inherited the genetic variation, or allele, from one parent—roughly 50 percent of the population—had a 30 percent higher risk of developing lung cancer. More than 35,000 Caucasian smokers in Europe and North America took part in the government-funded research. It was the strongest evidence to date of a firm link between genetics and lung cancer.

Earlier studies had demonstrated that having a parent or sibling with lung cancer could triple the odds of developing the disease. But teasing out the precise genes responsible has been, as always, a frustrating hunt.

Christopher Amos of the University of Texas, author of one of the studies, characterized the variant as "kind of a double whammy gene."

Psychiatry professor Dr. Laura Bierut of Washington University in St. Louis told the Associated Press that the three studies are "really telling us that the vulnerability to smoking and how much you smoke is clearly biologically based."

It is not clear whether non-smokers with the mutation suffer an increased risk of lung cancer as well. (However, even smokers who lack the gene variant are still ten times as likely to develop lung cancer than nonsmokers).

About one million people die annually from lung cancer. According to the World Health Organization, smoking remains the leading cause of preventable death worldwide.

Cocaine

For addiction to cocaine, amphetamine, and other stimulants, the picture is currently much less promising. Anna Rose Childress and Charles O'Brien, in a 2000 article for *Trends in Pharmacological Sciences*, spelled out the bleak facts: "Despite an intensive search for specific drug therapies since the mid 1980s, there is still no uniformly effective medication for human cocaine craving and there are no medications that are able to prevent cocaine relapse." We simply do not have any anti-craving drugs that work reliably for cocaine and speed—but new drug trials are continuing. The problematic nature of dopamine-receptor antagonists complicates the picture. Drugs that block the dopamine D2 receptor—antipsychotics like haloperidol—do not always block the stimulant rush. Their previously discussed side effects, such as lethargy, emotional blunting, and tardive dyskinesia, make them unsuitable for ongoing addiction therapy. Conversely, some drugs that act as dopamine agonists turn out to be addictive in their own right. Many designer drugs are like that. Other avenues of attack will have to be exploited, such as partial agonists. But here again, drugs that fill the bill tend to have unacceptable side effects.

Dopamine reuptake inhibitors, operating on the same principle as the SSRIs, are another avenue of approach. Methylphenidate, trade name Ritalin, stalls dopamine in the synaptic gap, but it is still a highly reinforcing chemical—the user feels a muted stimulus, like methadone. However, just as methadone is considered to produce a qualitative life improvement compared to continued heroin use, the longer duration of action and the lower level of reinforcement of Ritalin, or some other drug like it, may constitute a reasonable tradeoff for crack or speed addiction.

No antidepressants have shown themselves to be reliably useful in clinical trials on cocaine or amphetamine addiction. Serotonin-boosting drugs do not seem to help, any more than they help with nicotine addiction. The direct ride to the pleasure pathway provided by stimulants makes it difficult to tamper selectively with their effects.

Because of all this, different approaches may be needed. An antibody that would reduce cocaine consumption and sop up cocaine molecules in the brain, a kind of vaccine against cocaine, is one approach being pursued. It is unclear whether future vaccines of this kind will be able to address the anti-craving question. Can a cocaine analog, or a vaccine molecule that soaks up cocaine molecules as fast as they enter the blood stream, dampen desire for the drug, or will they be overwhelmed by a high dose of cocaine, or a different sort of stimulant?

Developing a pill or a vaccine for a specific drug addiction has long been one of the tantalizing potential rewards of addiction research. A company in Florida has garnered national attention, a spate of clinical trails, and a positive response from NIDA with a compound called NicVAX, aimed at nicotine addiction. In addition, Celtic Pharma in Bermuda is working on a similar product for cocaine addiction.

The idea of vaccinating for addictions is not new. If you want the body to recognize a heroin molecule as a foe rather than a friend, one strategy is to attach heroin molecules to a foreign body—commonly a protein that the body ordinarily rejects—in order to switch on the body's immune responses against the invader. The strategy behind a vaccine for cocaine, for example, is that the body's immune system will crank out antibodies to the cocaine vaccination, preventing the user from getting high. A strong advantage to this approach, say NIDA researchers, is that the vaccinated compound does not enter the brain and therefore is free of neurological side effects.

Preliminary research at the University of Minnesota showed that a dose of vaccine plus booster shots markedly reduce the amount of nicotine that reaches the brain. Animal studies have shown the same effect. NicVAX, from Nabi Biopharmaceuticals, consists of nicotine molecules attached to a protein found in a species of infectious bacteria. When smokers light up, the antibodies piggyback onto the protein-laden nicotine molecules, making them too big to fit through the blood-brain barrier and allow users to enjoy their smokes.

That, at least, is the idea. It is a difficult and expensive proposition, the closest thing to a miracle drug for addiction. A vaccine like NicVax, however, does not attack the craving for nicotine. It contains no nicotine and is non-addictive. Rather, the vaccine makes the attempt to assuage nicotine cravings an impossible task. And in this respect, NicVax resembles Antabuse for alcoholism—except that the vaccine does not cause the smoker to become seriously ill when he or she takes a puff.(The company reported that side effects were "well tolerated.") It simply (or not so simply) cancels out the nicotine high altogether, or at least that is the idea. It is unclear to what extent the antibody reaction prevents nicotine binding in other areas of the body where nicotine-type receptors are found, such as acetylcholine receptors in muscle tissue. It does not specifically attack drug craving in addicted users. The idea of vaccination is that, once a drug user cannot get high on his or her drug of choice, the user will lose interest in the drug.

This assertion is somewhat speculative, in that users of the classic negative reinforcer, Antabuse, have found ways to circumvent its effects—primarily by not taking it. There remain a wealth of questions related to the effects of long-lasting antibodies. And it is sometimes possible to "swamp" the vaccine by ingesting four or five times as much cocaine or nicotine as usual. In addition, NicVax must be injected, while Chantix and Zyban or taken orally.

Another approach to crack addiction that excited researchers in the early 1990s was the "kindling" theory of cocaine use, which led to experiments with an existing anticonvulsant drug called carbamazepine, trade name Tegretol. The dopamine depletion hypothesis generally explains addiction to cocaine and subsequent cravings. The cellular phenomenon of "kindling," so called because the theory posits that an episode of cocaine use prepares the brain for the next bout, may be associated with a long-standing mystery about the use of cocaine. Cocaine users are plagued by the occasional incidence of life-threatening seizures, which are generally assumed to be the result of an overdose. This is how it works with the dopamine-booster Wellbutrin—take too much, and the odds of seizure shoot up dramatically. But that isn't necessarily the way it works with cocaine. Fatal seizures have sometimes been triggered by quite modest doses of cocaine, in naïve and experienced users alike.

"Kindling has been known for sixty years in animal studies," said James Halikas. "If you give a rat an injection of cocaine, and give him the same amount every day for a month or more, the same dose that made the rat jolly, euphoric, and high in the beginning will be causing seizures by the end of the month. And when you examine his brain, there's no evidence of any brain damage from the drug."

So, the seizures seem to come unexpectedly, and they are not necessarily related to an escalating pattern of use. Seizures are sometimes seen in chronic alcoholics, and something similar occurs on rare occasions under the influence of the general anesthetics used in surgery. Doctors have learned to their chagrin that, on rare occasions, a normal amount of surgical anesthetic will cause a patient to have a seizure on the operating table—one of the many reasons why general anesthesia is so carefully monitored.

At the National Institute of Mental Health, Dr. Robert Post studied the kindling phenomenon for years. He had determined that the same kindling effect was involved in epileptic seizure, and carbamazepine dampened the occurrence of the wild, out-of-control firing of neurons that characterized epilepsy. A colleague,

Dr. Susan Weiss, discovered that carbamazepine also blocked co-caine-related seizures in animals.

At the time, Dr. Post told me there was also "a kindling theory for alcohol withdrawal, which says that repeated bouts of alcohol withdrawal can lead to increased severity of withdrawals, and finally you get withdrawal seizures and D.T.s. Some people are trying it for alcoholics, but it is an open question as to whether it is actually going to help with craving or not."

In the initial study by Dr. Halikas at the University of Minnesota Medical School, 21 addicts who had been using cocaine for more than six years were given carbamazepine. Six of the addicts virtually stopped using altogether, seven reduced their cocaine use by two-thirds, and eight dropped out because of side effects.

Robert Post remained cautious. "Cocaine is two drugs in one—a local anesthetic and a psychomotor stimulant. So, it's essentially Novocain and an amphetamine thrown into one compound. It turns out that carbamazepine doesn't do very well on cocaine hyperactivity, so it doesn't look like the typical stimulant or dopamine-related effects are impacted in a primary way. It's a question of whether the kindling mechanism is relevant to the anti-craving potential of carbamazepine."

In the years since, carbamazepine studies have often been plagued by high dropout rates and adverse side effects. It is difficult, at this writing, to say how well carbamazepine will ultimately pan out.

Cocaine addicts may not in fact suffer an excess of dopamine receptors that need filling artificially, but rather an innate shortage of D2 receptors. This might mean that the person has trouble getting sufficient kicks from the normal satisfactions of daily life. The normal rewards available in society, in recreation, sex, sports—are simply not enough to bring pleasure. Something is askew in the dopamine and serotonin accounting systems. The powerful, abnormal, supercharged pleasure zone achievable with psychoactive drugs is experienced by addicts as a sense of finally feeling good. Finally feeling normal. Not too hot, not too cold—just right.

Another GABA receptor agonist that boosts dopamine levels is under study for cocaine addiction. Baclofen, trade name Lioresal, is an antispastic muscle relaxant commonly used in the treatment of multiple sclerosis. After looking into the use of baclofen for opium and alcohol withdrawal, research centered on its ability to reduce cocaine administration in rats. In late 2003, researchers at UCLA showed that baclofen can reduce cocaine use in human addicts as well.

The evidence thus far suggests that baclofen reduces "withdrawal symptom intensity," but we do not yet know the extent to which the drug attenuates craving itself. Associated preclinical studies on rats support the idea of trying baclofen for methamphetamine and nicotine as well. The interaction between GABA receptors and dopamine release in the nucleus accumbens seems to be the common factor. Baclofen appears to show promise for use with many drugs of abuse, and has a chance of becoming the first drug to be approved for the treatment of cocaine addiction.

Research on baclofen at the University of Minnesota again pointed up the perennial problem of gender differences in drug studies. In animal trials, baclofen suppressed cocaine more robustly in female rats than in males. "These studies highlight the importance of paying attention to sex differences in the development of pharmacotherapies and in other drug abuse research," said Dr. Cora Lee Wetherington, NIDA's women and gender research coordinator.

There is also some research in the making—the sexiest drug in this class is called BP897. BP897 is a partial agonist at D3 receptors, which are yet another dopamine receptor subtype. The drug has been shown to curtail drug-seeking behavior in cocaine-addicted rats. BP897 works around what Anna Rose Childress and Charles O'Brien call the "medications quandary"—finding a drug that is neither wholly an antagonist, nor wholly an agonist. BP897 is a little bit of both.

Under conditions of dopamine depletion, such as drug withdrawal, BP897 acts as an agonist and occupies empty D3 sites. When cravings go up in the presence of strong drug cues, BP897 acts as a weak D3 receptor antagonist and blunts drug-seeking behavior. Partial agonists of dopamine circuitry in the limbic system might be of use for other addictive drugs as well. Amazingly, the drug does not seem to be reinforcing on its own. It isn't addictive. But it isn't perfect, either. BP897 does nothing directly to alter the reinforcing properties of cocaine itself. If a recovering addict slipped and took a lot of cocaine, the effect of BP897 would wash out. Even pure antagonist drugs that bind snugly to dopamine receptors do not always confer complete protection against a cocaine binge. As we have noted, single-receptor theories are unlikely to provide a complete solution. Some manner of pharmacological cocktail will probably be necessary.

Neuroscientists are aggressively studying several other drugs for cocaine addiction. Propranolol, originally developed to treat hypertension and cardiac arrhythmia, blocks a form of norepinephrine receptor. Early reports suggest that it lessens cocaine withdrawal symptoms. Another drug under investigation is the GABA-active drug gabapentine, sold as Neurontin and currently available as a prescription drug for nerve pain. There are several other possibilities being studied for use against cocaine addiction. Dr. Mark Gold and others have used bromocriptine, a drug prescribed to treat Parkinson's disease, to help patients overcome cocaine cravings in clinical trials. Bromocriptine stimulates dopamine receptors and serves to decrease the "get dopamine" message of cocaine withdrawal, but it doesn't cause a cocaine-style high. It is also being investigated for alcoholism.

A series of tests under the direction of Dr. Frank Gawin of UCLA's Department of Psychiatry has demonstrated that the antidepressant desipramine may help cocaine addicts abstain. Another antidepressant, imipramine, seems to ease cocaine cravings as well, particularly in the first few months of treatment.

Antabuse, the original pharmacological treatment for alcoholism, is being given a second look as a possible treatment for cocaine dependence due to its secondary effect on dopamine transmission. Also in the works is Modafinil, a drug that is used to treat narcolepsy, and which activates glutamate receptors without inducing seizures. In addition, Ritalin has been proposed as a controversial methadone-style treatment for cocaine addiction.

Methamphetamine

Amphetamine, whether in the form of prescription Dexedrine or street meth, is perhaps the "stickiest" addiction of all, from the standpoint of receptor science. Speed's impact on the reward system is direct, profound, and long lasting. Addiction science simply has not caught up with this one—which makes meth a very scary proposition.

Despite promising trials of several compounds, methamphetamine addiction remains largely impervious to anti-craving pills and other forms of drug treatment. No medications are approved by the FDA for the treatment of stimulant dependence. And this despite the fact that treatment for amphetamine addiction increased eight-fold from 1992 to 2005. However, researchers have identified several promising candidates for further study.

One of the leading candidates does not act directly on dopamine transmission. Interestingly, it is a serotonin booster, but of a different kind. Unlike SSRI drugs, which have not been very successful with amphetamine addiction, ondansetron is an antagonist at serotonin 5-HT3 receptors. Rats on amphetamine reduce their amphetamine-induced hyperactivity under the influence of ondansetron, so there was already evidence that this serotonin-active drug had a secondary effect on dopamine. Currently in the FDA approval pipeline, ondansetron may become the first anti-craving drug approved for use against amphetamine addiction. Ondansetron is already in use as a medication for nausea and vomiting in chemotherapy patients. It has also been tried against alcohol addiction, but the clinical record is mixed. There is some thinking that ondansetron might be effective with early-onset alcoholics, like Cloninger's Type 2s.

In 2008, the FDA gave Fast Track designation to vigabatrin, sold as Sabril by Ovation Pharmaceuticals. Ovation is collaborating with the NIDA on Phase II studies to evaluate the safety of Sabril, with Phase III trials scheduled for the end of this year.

Vigabatrin, an anti-epilepsy drug called Gamma-vinyl-GABA, or GVG for short, showed early promise for use with cocaine addicts in a 60-day study and appears to increase GABA transmission.

Another entry in the vigabatrin sweepstakes, Catalyst Pharmaceuticals, is also testing its version of the drug, dubbed CPP-109, for the treatment of methamphetamine addiction in Phase II double-blind, placebo-controlled studies.

However, questions remain about the safety of vigabatrin. Although available abroad, it is not approved for use in the U.S., due to an association with serious visual effects after long-term use. The use of vigabatrin for stimulant addiction, if approved, might require associated eye examinations.

Buproprion, a drug that has shown some promise in the treatment of cocaine addiction, is also a candidate for meth addiction. The drug inhibits the reuptake of dopamine, thus allowing more dopamine to circulate in the brain. In addition, there are plans to test other drugs being investigated for cocaine craving, such as topiramate and modafinil.

Marijuana

Perhaps it is marijuana's more diffuse manner of playing on the brain's reward pathways that has made pot another difficult target for drug therapies. The U.S. government's essentially unchanged opposition to marijuana research has meant that, until quite recently, precious few dollars were available for pot research. This official recalcitrance is one of the primary reasons for the belated recognition and characterization of marijuana's distinct withdrawal syndrome. To pluck one statistic out of many, representing estimates in one decade out of many, more than 11 million Americans smoked marijuana in the month under study in 1997's NIDA-sponsored "National Household Survey on Drug Abuse." What NIDA learned about cannabis addiction, according to the principal investigator of a recent NIDA study, was that "we had no difficulty recruiting dozens of people between the ages of 30 and 55 who have smoked marijuana at least 5,000 times. A simple ad in the paper generated hundreds of phone calls from such people" (roughly equivalent to 14 years of daily pot smoking).

According to research undertaken as part of the Collaborative Study of the Genetics of Alcoholism, 16% of people with a lifetime history of regular marijuana use reported a history of cannabis withdrawal symptoms In earlier research, it was discovered that those seeking treatment for cannabis addiction tended to cluster in two age groups—college age and mid-50s. We don't really need animal models to study many aspects of this most popular of all illegal drugs, but there now exists a nice body of clinical trials showing that mice and dogs also show evidence of cannabis withdrawal. (For THC-addicted dogs, it is the abnormal number of wet-dog shakes that give them away.) In humans, the evidence is solid, and growing. In a review of existing literature by Alan J. Budney and coworkers, published in 2004 in the *American Journal of Psychiatry*:

> Regarding cross-study reliability, the most consistently reported symptoms are anxiety, decreased appetite/weight loss, irritability, restlessness, sleep problems, and strange dreams. These symptoms were associated with abstinence in at least 70% of the studies in which they were measured. Other clinically important symptoms such as anger/ aggression, physical discomfort (usually

stomach-related), depressed mood, increased
craving for marijuana, and increased sweating and
shakiness occurred less consistently.

Today, scientists have a much better picture of what anandamide does in the body that they did a few years ago. This knowledge helps explain a wide range of THC withdrawal symptoms. Among the endogenous tasks performed by anandamide are pain control, memory blocking, appetite enhancement, the suckling reflex, lowering of blood pressure during shock, and the regulation of certain immune responses. These functions shed light on common hallmarks of cannabis withdrawal, such as anxiety, chills, sweats, flu-like physical symptoms, and decreased appetite. At Columbia University's Substance Abuse Division, where a great deal of NIDA-funded research takes place, researchers have found that abrupt marijuana withdrawal leads to symptoms similar to depression and nicotine withdrawal.

What treatment measures can help ameliorate marijuana withdrawal and craving in heavy users who wish to quit? To date, there is no effective anti-craving medication approved for use against marijuana withdrawal syndrome. Nonetheless, many addiction researchers believe that "cannabis withdrawal is clinically important and warrants detailed description in the DSM-V and ICD-11." It seems increasingly likely that many more people are trying—and failing—to quit marijuana than researchers have previously suspected.

Serzone (nefazodone), an antidepressant, has been used to decrease some symptoms of marijuana withdrawal in human subjects who regularly smoked six joints per day. Anxiety and muscular discomfort were reduced, but Serzone had no effect on other symptoms, such as irritability and sleep. Serzone is another antidepressant, a modest inhibitor of serotonin and norepinephrine, but it is not in the SSRI or tricyclic families. Serzone has also been looked at for use in the treatment of pathological gambling, and a few small, controlled trials have shown promise there, too, as reported in the *Journal of Clinical Psychiatry*. More studies would be needed to determine if the gambling reductions were a function of antidepressant effects.

But no such studies are likely take place, on gamblers or marijuana addicts. At this writing, Serzone has been recalled in Canada due to the discovery of liver failures associated with its use. This action will be followed by its recall in the U.S. as well. The experience with nefazodone does point to the possibility of future serotonin-active drugs that might be of use in withdrawing from protracted marijuana smoking.

Dronabinol, sold as Marinol, is a synthetic version of THC used in chemotherapy relief, not always successfully. It has not been extensively tested as a methadone-style treatment for marijuana addiction. It does block most cannabis withdrawal symptoms, since it produces an approximation of the marijuana high—although Marinol users have complained that synthetic THC in pill form is far more sedating than smoked marijuana.

Lithium, used to treat manic-depression, curbed marijuana withdrawal symptoms in preliminary animal studies. But another drug for mania and epilepsy did not show any benefit in human trials. Depakote (divalproex), a drug that increases GABA levels in the treatment of epilepsy and manic depression, has been tried against marijuana withdrawal, without result. A related compound, valproic acid, is also being investigated.

Since stimulation of THC receptors has homologous effects on the endogenous opioid system, various investigators have also speculated that naltrexone, the drug used as an adjunct of heroin withdrawal therapy, may find use against symptoms of marijuana withdrawal in people prone to marijuana dependence. Further research is needed on the reciprocal relationship between THC and opioid receptor systems.

Since difficulty sleeping is one common symptom of withdrawal, prescription sleep aids or anti-anxiety medication may be indicated for short-term use in the case of severe marijuana withdrawal. Some researchers have reported that even brief interventions, in the form of support group sessions, can be useful for dependent pot smokers.

The use of marijuana by abstinent alcoholics and substance abusers may heighten the risk of relapse. In a study of 250 patients at a psychiatric/substance abuse hospital in New York, "postdischarge cannabis use substantially and significantly increased the hazard of first use of any substance and strongly reduced the likelihood of stable remission from use of any substance"

It is surprising to note the relative paucity of previous clinical data the researchers had to work with in the case of alcohol and marijuana. "The gap in the literature concerning the relationship of cannabis use to the outcome of alcohol dependence was surprising," according to one researcher. "We were unable to find a single study that examined the effects of cannabis use on post-treatment outcome for alcohol dependence, despite the fact that the majority of patients now in treatment for alcoholism dependence also abuse other drugs. Clearly additional studies of this issue are warranted."

Above all, it is time to move beyond the common mistake of assuming that if marijuana causes withdrawal in some people, then it must cause withdrawal in everybody. And if it doesn't, it cannot be very addictive. This thinking has been overtaken by the growing understanding that a minority of people suffer a chemical propensity for marijuana addiction that puts them at high risk, compared to casual, recreational drug users. Most people do not become addicted to pot, and do not suffer from marijuana withdrawal. In this, marijuana withdrawal does not differ greatly from alcoholism—the vast majority of recreational users and drinkers will never experience it. For those that do, however, the withdrawal symptoms of marijuana abstinence can severely impact their quality of life.

Addiction researcher Barbara Mason of the Scripps Research Institute of La Jolla, California, is overseeing a four-year study of the neurobiology of marijuana dependence under a grant from NIDA. The comprehensive project will involve both animal and human research, and will make use of state-of-the-art functional brain imaging. The federal grant will also be used as seed money for the new Translational Center on the Clinical Neurobiology of Cannabis Addiction at the Scripps Institute.

Mason told reporters in San Diego that the research, which will also be conducted at several universities, is important work: "People are deciding every day whether to use or not to use marijuana, for medical purposes or otherwise, and there is little scientific information to advise this decision."

Benzodiazepines

Due to the GABA affinities of alcohol and opium, many of the same drugs being tested for those addictions are also being looked at for addiction to benzodiazepines like Valium, as well as sedatives like Seconal. In current medical practice, Valium, Xanax, and Klonopin addicts are tapered slowly, without the use of medications. Unfortunately, benzodiazepine addiction remains, like methamphetamine addiction, short on promising anti-craving drugs for withdrawal and abstinence. Trazodone—the tricyclic antidepressant—is being investigated.

Ibogaine for Everything

In an unexpected mid-1990s return to the psychedelic solution, an odd assortment of ex-hippies, AIDS activists, addiction treatment experts, and maverick scientists fell in behind the use of the African plant drug Ibogaine as a powerful agent for "addiction interruption." Ibogaine, a drug that Hunter S. Thompson made famous when he joked that it might have been responsible for the downfall of Edmund Muskie's 1972 presidential campaign, has been cited by some scientists for its ability to free certain cocaine and heroin addicts from their cravings. Initial underground experimentation was aimed at heroin addicts, but the hallucinogenic plant was also tried on alcoholics, cigarette smokers, and cocaine addicts. Recognition of anti-craving potential for this drug was understandably slow to reach the mainstream science world. A bunch of earnest amateurs had stepped forth to restate the initial Psychedelic Proposition: the need to study the use of entheogenic serotonin agonists as a way of breaking the hold of addictive drugs and alcohol. But this time they were talking about a different drug than LSD, and a different mechanism, and they were not touting it as some sort of cure-all. The anti-craving effects of a trip on Ibogaine wore off, they claimed, and another session six months or a year down the road was usually necessary to bolster abstinence. They were petitioning legitimate institutions to perform legitimate research. (The unlikely saga of Ibogaine is related in *The Ibogaine Story*, self-published by Paul De Rienzo and Dana Beal).

Emerging insights in the brain sciences had changed the field considerably, and, unlikely as it may seem, the proponents of Ibogaine, unlike their LSD counterparts 35 years earlier, managed to catch NIDA's ear this time around. They also got a running start on some straightforward clinical research from Dr. Deborah Mash of Miami University, who gained approval for preliminary clinical trials of Ibogaine for the treatment of heroin addiction. In this one area of research, the whole business had come full circle. It was the beginning of an unlikely renaissance in the study of psychedelic drugs.

For all the receptorology involved, Ibogaine still carried with it a rather wigged-out reputation, given the penchant Beal and other proponents had for insisting that "Ibogaine turns the serotonergic and cholinergic pathways into a super-augmented, 'stereoscopic' entity, capable of scanning ancestral memory in the non-nucleated genetic material of your cells." Ibogaine targets the cerebellum—too much so, according to some research, which showed cerebellum nerve damage in rats.

But Ibogaine wasn't the only psychedelic being targeted for a second look, now that serotonin receptor action was better understood. Clearly, psychedelics were never going to become daily maintenance drugs for anyone. But by 2002, dozens of psychedelic drug trials were underway, including, for the first time in decades, clinical studies of LSD and peyote. Most of them were conducted outside of the United States, since a DEA license is required, along with FDA approval, for research on hallucinogens. These are notoriously hard to come by. But at least one study is looking into the effect on alcoholism of participation in the peyote rituals of the Native American Church. And in 1993, the FDA finally gave permission to proceed with clinical trials of Ibogaine on volunteer patients. This decision made Ibogaine the second psychoactive drug to begin the journey toward FDA approval. MDMA (Ecstasy) was the first.

Before stepping down as NIDA director, Alan Leshner told the *New York Times* he believed it was now possible to study psychedelic drugs for evidence of beneficial as well as harmful effects. "Morphine works for pain, but it's horrendous when used in an addictive way," Leshner said. "The same may or may not be true for hallucinogens. It's a mistake to confuse the two issues." The active ingredient in Ibogaine did not produce a classic psychedelic high, even at peak dosages. It is a state more like waking REM sleep, accompanied by hypnagogic images. Some users felt nothing at all, except intense nausea, palsy, and the sound of rushing water in their ears.

Ibogaine gained attention in the usual way—by attenuating alcohol intake in various strains of alcohol-preferring rats. A little-noticed article in the journal *Brain Research* in 1994 detailed the results of work with Ibogaine and harmala at Albany Medical College in New York. These mysterious alkaloids—Ibogaine in particular— decreased the self-administration of cocaine in rats, too—presumably through effects on the "dopaminergic mesolimbic system." It was later determined that Ibogaine also exhibited a weak affinity for one of the less common opiate sites, the kappa opiate receptor.

There was evidence of norepinephrine involvement, and Ibogaine interacted with NDMA receptors, bringing glutamate into play. Lest we forget, Ibogaine is also a potent inhibitor of serotonin uptake, just like LSD and Prozac.

In the *Journal of Neuroscience*, researchers reported that ibogaine substantially decreased alcohol consumption in alcohol-preferring rats. It did so by increasing the levels of a brain protein known as GDNF, or glial cell line-derived neurotrophic factor. "By identifying the brain protein that ibogaine regulates to reduce alcohol consumption in rats, we have established a link between DGNF and reversal of addiction," according to Dorit Ron, a principal investigator of the study.

"On the basis of word of mouth, the ibogaine scene has quadrupled in the last five years," Ken Alper of the New York University School of Medicine told Brian Vastag at *Science News*. Alper reported that an estimated 850 people had taken ibogaine in 2001. By 2006, the number had risen to almost 5,000, says Alper—and almost 70 per cent of users had taken the drug for its antiaddiction properties.

Over the past 15 years, competing scientific papers have flown back and forth on Ibogaine. There were serious concerns expressed about the sheer weirdness of the daylong Ibogaine trip. With its auditory and visual hallucinations, muscle tremors, and vomiting (or "extraordinary cleansing," depending upon your point of view), Ibogaine's symptoms were somewhat similar to the effects of ingesting peyote, the psychedelic cactus hailed by some Native American healers and shamans as an effective treatment for alcoholism. The ayahuasca preparation used by shamans in the Amazon basin turns out to be another example of prescient aboriginal plant use. This potent psychedelic beverage is composed of one part liana bush, containing compounds from the beta-carboline/Ibogaine family, and a plant containing DMT.

One surprising aspect of the FDA's decision to move forward with Ibogaine research was that it followed on the heels of a study in which high doses of Ibogaine caused neural damage in rats. There is also a potential for fatal reactions if Ibogaine is combined with the opiates or the amphetamines. Despite earnest and well-intended lobbying by Ibogaine activists, this plant drug will have difficulty garnering FDA approval for clinical testing in humans beyond the limited work already done. Ibogaine has shown an affinity for acetylcholine receptors in the brain stem and medulla, meaning that the danger of fatal overdose does appear to exist.

Finally, Ibogaine, like Ecstasy and LSD, is, well, entheogenic. All three drugs are hallucinogens. To take the drugs is to experience a version of the classic drug trip produced by LSD, mescaline, and peyote—altered perceptions of time and space, intense emotional experiences, and sustained visual and audio distortions that seriously disorient and frighten some users. These drugs exhibit the drawback of being potentially harmful to people with mental illnesses, or to people who are dosed without their knowledge and consent. Taking Ibogaine or any other psychedelic is a *strenuous* undertaking, involving altered mental states wholly unlike other drug experiences There has never been anything predictable about the results of a psychedelic trip. Since outcomes can vary so markedly, depending upon set and setting, personality, and behavioral traits, studies are difficult to design, and always have been.

Recognition of anti-craving potential for this drug has been understandably slow to reach the mainstream science world. For one thing, Ibogaine remains illegal in the United States. No so in Canada, Mexico, and other countries, where Ibogaine clinics have begun to appear.

Since outcomes can vary so markedly, depending upon set and setting, personality, and behavioral traits, studies are difficult to design, and always have been. Frank Vocci, director of anti-addiction drug development at NIDA, told *Science News* that "The idea of trying to push this into pharmaceutical development is a tough nut."

The psychedelic drugs, new and old, are not only among the most powerful ever discovered, but are also tremendously difficult to study and utilize responsibly. Nonetheless, these drugs have always played an important part of the story, even though they are not addictive. LSD, mescaline, DMT, psilocybin, Ibogaine, ayahuasca—none of these appeal to lab rats as a drug of abuse. Psychedelics have been exhorted, and occasionally deployed, as specific anti-craving medications for more than 50 years now. The psychedelic experience seems to assist some addicts in their efforts to remain sober and abstinent. However, the risks of casual experimentation with these substances should be obvious. Recent research on Ecstasy only makes this point more emphatically.

Psychedelics or entheogens are not reliable recreational drugs or therapeutic drugs. Occasional use of psychedelics has not proven to be irreparably harmful. Overindulgence, however, can trigger serious difficulties. If you are going to experiment with psychedelics, perhaps the best advice is to prepare in advance to limit yourself to a handful of experiences, with the understanding that further experimentation simply results in trips of reduced intensity, compared to the original experiences. Perhaps the most mind-altering drugs known to man are powerful for a reason, and perhaps that reason is to protect against overindulgence.

By the mid-1990s, rumors about Ecstasy (MDMA) toxicity were everywhere. Unlike Prozac, but very much like LSD, Ecstasy not only blocks serotonin uptake, but also causes the release of additional serotonin, much the way cocaine and amphetamine cause the release of extra dopamine. A study conducted by neurologist George Ricaurte at John Hopkins University under NIDA sponsorship seemed to show conclusive evidence of neurotoxic damage to the serotonin 5-HT receptors in the brains of monkeys given large doses of MDMA. A follow-up study of 30 MDMA users (existing users, since researchers didn't have government permission to give MDMA to test subjects) showed 30 per cent less cerebrospinal serotonin, compared to a control group. However, the Johns Hopkins team did not have any baseline measurements for the MDMA users, and other neurologists raised technical objections about various aspects of the study, including dosage levels. As was often the case in such studies, the monkeys had been given a whopping dose, compared to the typical raver's dose. Ricaurte insisted that the amount of MDMA consumed by a typical user in one night of raving was possibly enough to cause permanent brain damage. The government estimates that 10 million Americans have taken Ecstasy.

That would seem to be the end of the story, and a sobering lesson for today's youth—but that is not how it turned out. A few years later, Dr. Charles Grob, psychiatry professor at the UCLA School of Medicine, received the first FDA approval ever given for the administration of MDMA to human volunteers. The result of Grob's testing was that *none* of the volunteers showed any evidence of neuropsychological damage of any kind. In testimony before the U.S. Sentencing Commission, which was considering harsher penalties for MDMA possession in 2001, Dr. Grob seriously questioned the methodology of the Ricaurte studies: "It is very unfortunate that the lavishly funded NIDA-promoted position on so-called MDMA neurotoxicity has inhibited alternative research models which would better delineate the true range of effects of MDMA, including its potential application as a therapeutic medicine." A prominent neurologist quoted in this book has alleged that Dr. Ricaurte at Johns Hopkins runs "a cottage industry showing that everything under the sun is neurotoxic." *Science* retracted its coverage of the Ricaurte findings. And it was eventually discovered that Dr. Ricaurte's monkeys had been injected with amphetamine, not with MDMA—a discovery that also nullified four other published papers. Dr. Ricaurte explained that some labels had been switched, and a Johns Hopkins spokesperson called the whole thing "an honest mistake." The basic questions about Ecstasy remain unanswered. Is there a line that separates a conceivably therapeutic dose of Ecstasy for mental ills or addictive ills from a possibly brain-damaging run of several dozen high-dosage trips? Perhaps the permanently altered receptor arrays, if they exist, don't affect cognition or emotions in any significant way over the long run. Still, the risks of overindulgence appear to be at least potentially higher than the risks of overindulging in LSD or Ibogaine. All of the psychedelics tend to be more self-limiting than other categories of psychoactive drugs, anyway. After two or three days, even the most die-hard raver or LSD head is usually ready to take a break.

Rick Doblin and others are now working with government investigators to pursue MDMA for the treatment of post-traumatic stress disorder. There are reports that very low doses of LSD sometimes have an antidepressant effect. One thing we know for certain is that people on SSRI medications or MAO inhibitors report that their experiences on LSD or Ecstasy are shorter and far less powerful than is typically the case. There appears to be some competition for receptor sites when Zoloft meets LSD. In contrast to the diminished psychedelic experience while on SSRIs, the older norepinephrine-active tricyclics like Tofranil and Norpramine reportedly serve to potentiate the LSD or MDMA experience. None of these combinations is a wise idea, due to uncertainties about the interactions.

Even DMT, which experienced trippers compared to being shot out of a cannon, has returned as a legitimate study subject. Dr. Rick Strassman, then with the University of New Mexico's School of Medicine, received approval for clinical testing of DMT. Strassman was drawn to the subject because of the molecule's natural occurrence in the brain (which makes every man, woman, and child in America a drug criminal, chemically speaking). He gave DMT to 60 human volunteers over a study period of five years. Strassman was primarily interested in near-death experiences and mystical experiences. None of the supervised DMT sessions evidently resulted in any detectable harm to the participants. Strassman presents his views on the medical use of DMT in his book, DMT: The Spirit Molecule.

Many other anti-craving drugs, tailored to produce specific neurotransmitter changes for specific addictions, are being developed and tested. Older compounds are being reexamined for their anti-craving properties. Some researchers are adding serotonin and dopamine precursors such as tryptophan and tyrosine to produce a "therapeutic cocktail" to redress alterations along the reward pathway caused by addiction. One way or another, said Dr. James Halikas, the anti-craving drugs are here to stay. "Whether we find one anti-craving drug that works for all patients, or whether we find a series of drugs which are useful in different populations, I'm game either way. Maybe we'll end up going from drug to drug with a given patient, just like we do with antibiotics, with blood pressure medication, with antidepressants."

"It really does two things for us," said Ovide Pomerleau. "It will allow us to offer something that wasn't available before, and therefore reach more people, and it will allow us to tailor treatment for particular problems."

Behavior has deep roots in the brain, and as knowledge of the conditioned cues and cravings involved in addiction becomes more comprehensive, it is even easier to see why will power, and a just-say-no resolve, are not the answer. They are, instead, additional tools available to an addict. "Anti-craving drugs can be empowering drugs," said Dr. Halikas. "They put responsibility back in the hands of the patient. They takes some of the craving away, and then the person can make a decision, and for that they need all of the aspects of the psychosocial rehabilitation model, the Twelve Steps, AA, and all the rest of it."

In *Brainwork*, a neuroscience newsletter, Markus Heilig, a psychiatry professor at the Karolinska Institute in Sweden, offered a vision of the transformation now taking place: "What's going to happen is we're going to find some drugs that will fit some patients and other drugs that will fit others. That's the way most fields in medicine have developed, and this development has now started in the field of addictive disorders." We are witnessing the early years of a new medical discipline, but much work needs to be done. There are few medical approaches to the abuse of psychedelics or inhalants. Caffeine and benzodiazepines are still in the "taper and grit your teeth" stage. Despite ongoing research, there is no known medical treatment for marijuana addiction.

"Congeners" are drugs specifically designed to be similar in molecular structure to a given addictive drug, but unlike designer drugs, different enough not to be addictive themselves. Methylphenidate, or Ritalin, is a congener of amphetamine, for example. It has a lower abuse potential, and for all its problems, on balance it is generally safer than speed or cocaine. Ronald Siegel of UCLA has emphasized the potential of congeners, and has called for more research on "good" designer drugs of this kind. Such drugs would not modify cravings, however. They would be a more benign form of substitute addiction, which is a solution, but not an answer.

Psychiatric drugs such as the newer antidepressants and anti-craving medications are designed to influence specific receptors in the neurotransmitter pathways of the brain. They are the results of joint efforts in biology, chemistry, genetics, and neurology spanning many years of intense investigative work.

"The efficacy of [newer] treatment approaches for addictive disorders is surprisingly good," writes Dr. Charles O'Brien in *Science*, "and comparable with the results found with other chronic disorders such as diabetes or asthma." O'Brien pointed to studies showing that "for every $1.00 invested in the treatment of substance abuse, there are [long-term] cost savings of $4 to $12 depending on the type of drug and the type of treatment." Future ramifications may not be limited to drugs that treat brain diseases, but may also include drugs that enhance memory or sharpen the performance of certain kinds of cognitive tasks. The fact that we will be facing such treatment choices is amazing, disturbing, and a little scary. No one should feel altogether comfortable risking any long-range predictions about the outcome of this new brand of medicine under the sun. But the new therapeutic drugs will keep coming. The possibility of a major breakthrough can never be ruled out. Despite the well-tempered warnings about magic bullets and gold rings, such a miracle cure, an all-purpose medication for the cravings produced by addiction to a specific drug, is no longer completely beyond the bounds of scientific imagination.

TWELVE: CONSUMERS AND
THE NEW MEDICINE

"The proper object of this work... is to enumerate and elucidate the various causes which have most materially obstructed the improvement of medicine... 1) The fallacy and danger of hypothetical or theoretical reasoning. 2) The diversity of constitutions. 3) The difficult of appreciating the efforts of nature, and of discriminating them from the operations of art. 4) Superstition. 5). The ambiguity of language. 6) The fallacy of testimony [and] excessive deference to authority and fashion."

– **Gilbert Blane**, *Elements of Medical Logic,* 1819

The early neurobehavioral research on addiction has been vindicated by the development of anti-craving drugs and new drugs for depression. From heroin to alcohol, from marijuana to meth, from premenstrual syndrome to bulimia, new treatments are here—and more are on the way.

By the end of the 1990s, Enoch Gordis, the former director of the National Institute on Alcohol Abuse and Alcoholism (NIAAA), could say to *Newsweek* with some pride that anti-craving drugs "herald a whole new era in the treatment of alcoholism. The medications five to ten years from now," said Gordis, "will be even better."

On the other hand, the psychopharmacology of addiction is not much studied in med school, and all but unknown among the general populace. Even the treatments now in existence are woefully underutilized. Moreover, there are good reasons to question whether these drugs are being prescribed with sufficient care and forethought in cases where they are being used. Legitimate, unanswered questions exist about pharmacotherapy for addictive disorders. The most important effect—the reregulation of brain receptor arrays with time—is little understood. And we cannot say with certainty whether messing with Mother Nature's receptors, in some cases, might disrupt other finely tuned immunological or neurological systems in the body. Finally, there is the possibility of side effects years down the road, which obviously cannot be predicted based on current studies. What we already know is that the "bodymind," as Candace Pert refers to it, is a delicate and astonishingly complicated piece of organic machinery. Researchers are confronted with the perpetual dilemma of designing out, or designing down, the side effects of any new class of drugs. The historical record of drugs like Thorazine, and darker cases like Oraflex and thalidomide, are reminders of the potential pitfalls of development races and corner-cutting practices in the pharmaceutical industry. The pharmacological sciences and the people who work in them are inextricably linked to the drug companies that sell the end products of any neurochemistry that yields marketable new medications. It cannot be otherwise: Market considerations drive much of the research. By the end of the 1990s, the American pharmaceutical industry had far surpassed the federal government's National Institutes of Health as the world's principal source of biomedical research and development funding. One of the stiffest challenges facing managed health care in the future will be the matter of evaluating the effectiveness of medications for addiction.

Fighting fire with fire brings scientists face to face with the problems posed by the blood-brain barrier, that superfine mesh of cells that protects the brain from unwelcome molecular intruders. Bacteriologists discovered the barrier more than two centuries ago, when they learned that dyes injected into the body stained all the organs except the brain. Normally, the capillary-rich barrier of cells is so densely packed that the only way to penetrate the tight junctions between them is by means of special transporter molecules. These specialized molecules act as chauffeurs for the amino acids, hormones, and other compounds that must pass regularly and consistently into the brain. These transporter molecules can be fussy about riders, and the only way around that is to use molecules so tiny that they are measured in units of atomic mass called "Daltons." Knowing this, biochemists have worked toward discovering extremely small molecules, and this is partly why so few effective psychoactive drugs come along. While scientists have had some luck with small-molecule approaches to treating epilepsy, schizophrenia, and certain mood disorders, there is no reason to assume a small molecule can always be found to fit the bill. Current work centers on tricking existing transporter molecules into ferrying artificial cargos into the brain. Pills that easily penetrate the blood-brain barrier are rare, special, and capable of causing a host of problematic side effects. If Zyban demonstrated that there were good reasons to be hopeful about future anti-craving drugs, then Redux and "phen-fen" demonstrated to critics of the drug industry what seemed to be a reversion to type—unsafe drugs released to the public without sufficient attention to dangerous side effects. Eli Lilly's earlier caution about moving forward with serotonin boosting drugs as anti-obesity medications—as anti-craving drugs for food addicts—soon came to look like a wise decision. For consumers, and specifically, for patients with addictive disorders taking receptor-active anti-craving medications, the matter is complicated by interactions with other drugs, dosage, and individual drug sensitivities.

Weight Loss Redux

It took many years to bring depression and its treatment into the rational light of day. Addiction in the mid-1990s was in the process of undergoing a similar medical transformation. Even so, scientists were wary of pronouncing that overeating was in some cases a treatable chemical disorder. Obesity, in any form other than pituitary cases, was not typically considered a medical disorder at all. In a 1998 interview with MIT's student newspaper, *The Tech*, neurology professor Richard Wurtman recalled that ten years earlier, the major drug companies had shown little interest in a drug treatment for obesity: "They thought that if you were obese, it was your fault." It was the same view that had prevailed concerning depression, alcoholism, and other drug addictions. Bulimia and carbohydrate craving were no different: a simple failure of will was once thought to explain them all.

In truth, Eli Lilly and Company *did* move forward with efforts to win approval of high-dose Prozac for weight loss. That petition had been languishing in the FDA pipeline for years under the trade name Lovan. Back in the late 1980s, when Eli Lilly scientists were investigating rats that consumed fewer calories on fluoxetine, the company called upon Dr. Richard Wurtman, the MIT brain scientist who specialized in the connection between serotonin levels and carbohydrate intake. Scientists at Lilly had become increasingly concerned that the weight loss from Prozac was short-lived, and the mechanism of action remained maddeningly imprecise. For more than a decade, Eli Lilly had pursued Prozac along three separate but related lines of development: depression, weight control, and alcoholism. If you took it for depression, and it worked, you might also lose a few pounds, and drink less. If you took it for bulimia or weight loss, you might also feel better emotionally, and drink less. When the FDA made encouraging noises about Prozac as a new front-line treatment for bulimia in 1994, Eli Lilly followed that indication to market, and again chose not to follow up on weight loss or alcoholism.

Eli Lilly was no longer interested, but Richard and Judith Wurtman were undeterred. As it happened, the couple had already patented a serotonin-active drug of their own—dexfenfluramine—which French laboratories had been testing as a weight loss pill. The Wurtmans went public with a new company, Interneuron Pharmaceuticals, and filed with the FDA to market their weight-loss remedy. The Wurtmans became instant millionaires on paper.

"Diet pills" had always had a somewhat unsavory reputation. Typically, they were amphetamines, or the near-beer equivalent, ephedrine—and neither compound was anything like a healthy long-term answer to chronic overeating. The serotonin-active drugs were a new class of medications altogether. Dexfenfluramine wasn't addictive, any more than Prozac was addictive. Moreover, fenfluramine was specifically intended for use by people suffering from carbohydrate-craving obesity. But would doctors be able to resist the demands of other patients who just wanted to trim off a few pounds?

Initially, the Wurtmans licensed the serotonin-active weight loss drug to several marketers in Europe, where it met with initial success. After a few small-scale studies, Rochester University in New York published a report showing that the weight loss effect was enhanced when fenfluramine was combined with a drug called phentermine. The resulting combination was widely known as "phen-fen." As with Prozac, dexfenfluramine was tested as an antiobesity medication at dosages several times higher than the amount typically prescribed for depression. Early red flags were raised when Johns Hopkins researchers reported some cases of neurological toxicity in monkeys on dexfenfluramine, but MIT, which shared patent rights with the Wurtmans, was understandably enthusiastic when Redux, as dexfenfluramine became known, won full FDA approval in 1996.

Redux was the first drug ever approved in the U.S. for the long-term treatment of obesity. And for many people, it worked. In the first six months after its approval, physicians wrote at least two million prescriptions for Redux. The phen-fen combination swept the weight loss industry. Estimates of total users of phen-fen ran as high as six million in the U.S. alone. Doctors and weight loss clinics sometimes prescribed Redux, sometimes the phen-fen combination. Initial earnings estimates were running as high as $600 million a year for the Redux portion of phen-fen, netting MIT between one and five per cent of the royalties.

The euphoria didn't last long. By the time Redux made the cover of *Time*, researchers were already rumbling about continued reports of high toxicity and hypertension in rat studies. In addition, the serotonin surge associated with the use of dexfenfluramine caused concerns about pulmonary hypertension. In August of 1997, doctors at the Mayo Clinic in Minnesota reported serious heart valve abnormalities in 24 women taking the phen-fen combination.

A month later, at the FDA's request, phen-fen and Redux were permanently pulled off the market. In 2002, American Home Products settled a class action suit on behalf of almost 300,000 phen-fen users for $3.75 billion. As class action suits go, this put it right between the $2.4 billion Dalkon Shield settlement and the $4.5 billion breast implant accords.

What went wrong? Researchers now believe that the two drugs, which were never offered for sale as a single pill, should never have been combined in the first place. Somehow the fact that the phen part of the combination allegedly acted as an MAO inhibitor, and hence should not have been combined with yet another serotonin-enhancing medication, escaped notice. The combination of the two drugs apparently raised blood plasma levels of serotonin to abnormal levels. Too much serotonin in the bloodstream can damage blood vessels in the heart and lungs. Other suspected MAO inhibitors, like St. John's Wort, or the Chinese herbal remedy ma huang, would not have combined well with Redux or phen-fen, either. Referring to the casual use of Ecstasy, Dr. Rick Doblin drew a parallel with phen-fen in the autumn 1995 issue of the *Multidisciplinary Association for Psychedelic Studies* (MAPS):

> This use of MDMA, though not conducted in the context of a scientifically controlled experiment, does provide an opportunity for a very large epidemiological study. Similarly, over fifty million people have tried a prescription drug called fenfluramine, a diet aid prescribed for daily use for months or years at a time that causes the same kind of neurotoxicity in animals as does MDMA.

The phen-fen disaster highlighted the need to investigate drug synergies thoroughly before combining them as a pharmacotherapy. The phen-fen heart and lung damage may have been related to a potentially toxic condition known as "serotonin syndrome."

And the Wurtmans? Ironically, Richard and Judith Wurtman had patented the use of Prozac for severe PMS years earlier, and ultimately sublicensed the rights back to Eli Lilly for several million dollars. Eli Lilly disguised the fact that their PMS drug was a case of old wine in new bottles. As Wellbutrin had become Zyban, so Prozac metamorphosed into Serafem, when prescribed for premenstrual syndrome.

Too Much Substance H

Serotonin syndrome is a rare but potentially deadly condition that results from the combination of two or more serotonin-boosting drugs. Taken in sufficient quantities, the drugs can lead to a serotonin overdose. The symptoms of serotonin syndrome range from mild flushing, muscle jerks, and rapid pulse to fever, hypertension, disorientation, respiratory problems, destruction of red blood cells, seizures, and kidney failure. No one knows exactly how often it occurs, since most cases are thought to resolve without further problems within 24 hours after discontinuation of the serotonin-boosting drugs in question. Serotonin syndrome was characterized in animal models years ago, and is probably rare enough to merit little more than a passing notice if not for the variety of serotonin-boosting drugs and medicines continually coming to market. Demerol, the pain reliever, and dextromethorphan, the cough remedy, are another good example of a bad serotonin combination. There is also concern about combining serotonin drugs with over-the-counter diet suppressants. Large hits of Ecstasy or LSD are not recommended, either, although Prozac has long been used informally as a "morning after" drug following a long night on Ecstasy. (Self-prescribing of this kind is foolish and dangerous.) Other problematic combinations include SSRI antidepressants and any of the following: Selegiline (used for Parkinson's), Linezolid, Risperidone, Haldol, the analgesic Tramadol, Hismanal, St. Johns Wort, certain forms of antiretroviral therapy, and Sumatriptan for migraine.

The most dangerous combination of all is an SSRI medication taken with a strong MAO inhibitor. There have been reports of fatal interactions between SSRIs and MAOIs. MAO inhibiting drugs themselves do not combine well with a long list of other drugs, and there are dietary restrictions that go with taking any monoamine oxidase inhibitor. Here again, prescribers and drug makers have not always taken sufficient care to explain these basic facts to users of prescription MAOIs like Marplan, Parnate, and Nardil. St. John's Wort and Ecstasy also inhibit monoamine oxidase. Similar problems can occur when MAOIs are combined with stimulants like speed or cocaine.

Foods containing high levels of the amino acid tyramine stimulate the release of norepinephrine, and this buildup can lead to a form of norepinephrine overdose—a hypertensive reaction caused by interaction with MAOIs, which block the reabsorption of nor-epinephrine. The syndrome is marked by intense headache, nausea, and soaring blood pressure. Serious cases lead to cardiac failure, or intracranial hemorrhage. Foods on the danger list for users of MAO inhibitors include, but are not limited to, large amounts of the following: Chianti wine, vermouth, bean curd, dietary pro-tein supplements, certain cheeses, smoked or aged fish and meat, sausages, sauerkraut, miso soup, and Brewer's yeast. Drugs to be avoided, in addition to the aforementioned, include Ritalin, asthma inhalers, Tegretol, psuedoephedrine, ephedrine, and others. (As al-ways, check with your doctor about drug combinations).

Not all physicians are familiar with the presenting symptoms of serotonin syndrome (or the details of the MAOI diet). In an emergency, cyproheptadine or propranolol, which are serotonin-blocking drugs, can be administered. Though rare, it is possible to cause serotonin syndrome in drug-sensitive people with high doses of a single serotonin-boosting drug.

The CYP2D6 Factor

Drugs are broken down into their constituent waste products by specific sets of enzymes. A subset of the human population, variously estimated at 3% to 7%, are categorized as "poor me-tabolizers." For them, a drug's recommended dosage is often far too high. The culprit is a genetic variant that codes for a liver en-zyme called cytochrome P450 isoenzyme 2D6, known in short-hand as CYP2D6. Poor metabolizers produce less of this crucial enzyme, which means that drugs are broken down and excreted at a much slower pace. In these people, the recommended dose results in higher drug concentrations. This obviously can make a crucial difference in how a person reacts to the drugs.

About one out of 20 people has a mutation in the 2D6 gene that causes a lack of the enzyme, according to UC-San Francisco biochemist Ira Herskowitz. "Those people are really getting a whopping dose." In addition, if a person with normal CYP2D6 levels is taking several drugs that are broken down by CYP2D6, then the enzyme's ability to degrade one drug can greatly inhibit its ability to degrade the others. This increases the possibility of adverse drug interactions, particularly among the elderly, who may already be suffering from liver disease or impaired renal function. Drugs of abuse severely complicate these enzymatic issues, since addicts and alcoholics are not known for volunteering information about their condition to medical or hospital personnel. Poor metabolizers often have little or no reaction to codeine-based medications. Screening tests for CYP2D6 variations are becoming cheaper and more widely available.

Enzyme interactions can work the other way, too. St. John's Wort, for example, is suspected of activating another drug breakdown enzyme, CPY3A, thereby *accelerating*, rather than retarding, the destruction of other drugs. The herb can alter the metabolization of Phenobarbital, tamoxifen, oral contraceptives, and antiviral medications. Drugs must be combined with caution, and people need to monitor dosages, because of the tremendous degree of metabolic variation that exists.

"Start low and go slow" is still the best advice. A 2002 report from Georgetown University's Center for Drug Development Science found that the dosage recommendations of 21 per cent of the drugs coming to market from 1980 to 1999 were later revised. Fully 80 per cent of those revisions involved a reduction in the original recommended dose. A related survey undertaken in Europe by the World Health Organization obtained similar results. "It's long been known that for individual subjects the dosage listed on a drug label is not necessarily the right one," said one of the authors of the Georgetown study. Typically, the recommended dosage is set early in the testing process, after analyzing results from a limited number of volunteer subjects. A more rigorous analysis of initial data would help get the dosage right the first time. Metabolic profiles that screen for CYP2D6 mutations will greatly assist this process.

Serotonin Discontinuation Syndrome

The medical community as a whole gets a big black eye, to say the least, for its belated handling of dosage and side effect issues related to receptor-active drugs. Doctors and drug makers clearly failed to spell out for the public how best to discontinue certain psychoactive medications. Non-addictive drugs can still cause withdrawal effects. Prescribing physicians are supposed to know this. But in the case of the SSRIs, the nature of withdrawal did not generally include specific cravings for the drug in question, as a desired means of relief. To mark the distinction (and there is a difference), neurologists coined the term "discontinuation syndrome."

There are often side effects associated with discontinuing certain drugs, just as there are side effects at the starting end. Stop taking a daily antihistamine, and be prepared for withdrawal in the form of a rebound effect—stuffy nose, runny nose, sneezing. Fluoxetine, sertraline, and paroxetine—Prozac, Zoloft, and Paxil, respectively—have long half-lives, which means that when a patient discontinues one of these medications, traces of the drug will remain in body tissues for several weeks. Withdrawal effects are not nearly as unpleasant when the patient fully understands what is happening, and that the effect is temporary. Prozac, with its long half-life, is least likely to cause these effects, and Paxil is the worst offender. All the other SSRIs fall somewhere in between.

One major withdrawal syndrome in particular, common to all the SSRIs, went all but unnoticed for years until patients complained long enough and seriously enough to garner some attention from the medical community. The so-called "shock effect," or "lightning-bolt syndrome" is an unpleasant phenomenon often associated with discontinuing an SSRI. It manifests itself as transient dizziness and brief but unpleasant buzzing sensations, particularly when turning the head—exactly the kind of proprioceptive back-and-forth glancing which characterizes, say, the act of driving. (Driving may be less safe for some people in the first few weeks after discontinuing an SSRI.) It is a short-lived, concentrated version of "paresthesia"—a burning or tingling feeling in the head, face, arms, or legs. Often called "Paxil head," in honor of the primary culprit, these vestibular shock episodes can sometimes be quite intense, and can occur intermittently for the first two to eight weeks of abstinence from SSRIs. (There are ongoing lawsuits over the matter of Paxil's addictiveness, argued on the basis of its withdrawal effects.)

The *Journal of Clinical Psychiatry* published some of the first citations in the professional literature of this withdrawal syndrome. The withdrawal shock effect was an anecdotal report that proved to be clinically true. It was not until the late 1990s that the word began to get out in a more comprehensive way, but the SSRI discontinuation syndrome is still not widely known or publicized. Many patients have reported that their doctors often attribute these SSRI shock sensations to psychosomatic causes, or to a return of the depression for which the medication was first prescribed. Thankfully, there are doctors who keep up with the literature and are aware of the problem. Doctors and patients report that the shock effect can be mitigated in some cases by taking a small dose of Prozac whenever the sensations become too uncomfortable or incessant.

In addition to the shock-like sensations, other common symptoms of discontinuation syndrome include nausea, fatigue, headache, unstable gait, and trouble sleeping—another "flu-like" collection of withdrawal symptoms. (It is important to remember that the bulk of SSRI users notice few withdrawal effects, if any, when they quit.)

Years of experience involving millions of users testify strongly to the need for tapering off SSRI drugs, rather than going cold turkey. Physicians who prescribe SSRIs have been badly remiss about providing basic information to patients concerning the consequences of quitting all at once. The fact that the electric shock effect was so poorly characterized by health providers in the early going does not make for an inspiring story.

Downregulation and Other Side Effects

The brain, as always, bats last. It compensates, reregulates, and adjusts. One of the major ways it accomplishes this is through the neuroadaptive phenomenon called downregulation. The brain compensates for the artificial flood of serotonin by cutting back on its own production, and the receptors on the cell surfaces ultimately degrade. This is, in fact, what can happen in a case of active addiction, or with the habitual use of any receptor-active drug. The concern with downregulation is that, over time, chronic use of serotonin reuptake blockers leads to both a decrease in the number of receptors and a desensitization of existing receptors. After sustained treatment with a Prozac-style drug, patients could end up with a supersensitivity to, or a deficit of, serotonin. In that case, the receptors on the postsynaptic side are either too numerous or too sensitive to stimulation by neurotransmitters stalled in the synaptic gap. The brain does not stay idle during these artificial rains of neurotransmitters. As explained by Peter Kramer in *Listening to Prozac*: "The chronic, constant, reliable presence of high levels of neurotransmitter causes the cell to downregulate—reducing the number of receptors, by drawing them back into the cell membrane, where they become inactive, or by otherwise uncoupling them from further events."

The brain adjusts to the medicine—just as the brain adjusts to the constant bombardment of addictive drugs. Downregulation and upregulation are not well understood. If significant downregulation takes place, then conceivably, there could be a rebound effect. Even withdrawal from non-addictive drugs can be difficult and stressful, as the brain upregulates to account for the new biochemical dispensation. Drugs of abuse, and the drugs used against them, share one important trait—they both illustrate the adage that too much of a good thing is a bad thing.

The entire field of addiction medicine has its detractors, of course. In particular, the SSRI medications have been a prominent target since their inception. Dr. Peter Breggen, Dr. Joseph Glenmullen, and other critics have been particularly vocal in their objections to the use of serotonin-active drugs. They argue that psychoactive drugs cause assorted brain dysfunctions, and that such medications do far more harm than good. For more information on what might be called the "Prozac: Threat or Menace?" school of thought, consult Glenmullen's *Prozac Backlash* or Breggin's *Toxic Psychiatry*.

These jeremiads aside, there are legitimate issues surrounding the use of many of the receptor-active drugs that addicts and alcoholics may encounter, or may request—whether treatment consists of a formal in-patient clinic or an informal arrangement with a family practitioner. Since addiction and mental illness overlap, a percentage of addicts are likely to encounter antidepressant and other psychoactive drugs during treatment. Drawing on work by Robins, Kessler, and Regier, Dr. Lance Longo, Medical Director of Addiction Psychiatry at Sinai Samaritan Medical Center, wrote in 2001: "Approximately half of individuals with bipolar disorder or schizophrenia and approximately one third of those with panic disorder or major depression have a lifetime substance use disorder. In general, among patients with alcoholism, nearly half have a lifetime history of coexisting mood, anxiety, and/or personality disorders."

The optimistic view of anti-addiction drugs says that depressive and addictive episodes feed on themselves. The more you get that way, the more you get that way, so if you can somehow give the brain a giant holiday from being serotonin- and dopamine-impaired, it will naturally adjust, compensate, rewire. It will teach itself. It will learn how not to be addicted and depressed all the time. In this view, what the addict/depressive needs is normalcy, a period of feeling better, a chance to sort things out, adjust behavior, become productive, and build confidence. While all of this is happening, under the influence of an antidepressant or an anti-craving drug, the patient learns to experience a different kind of world on a daily, even minute-to-minute basis. Like training wheels, the medications give the brain its first chance in a long time, possibly ever, to operate

within the normal parameters of serotonin, dopamine, norepinephrine, and GABA metabolism. Taper off the drug, and the brain upregulates, becoming more sensitive again to existing stocks of brain
chemicals. Mood and behavior remain improved, and if there is a
slip back into addiction or depression, the patient goes back on the
meds, and reruns the treatment. Fluoxetine and the other serotonin
boosters do not appear to deplete serotonin as rapidly as addictive
drugs are capable of doing. In people with deficiencies or sensitivities in brain serotonin, these drugs appear to cause serotonin levels
to come back toward normal. After a few days or weeks, the overall
brain concentration of serotonin increases, and remains higher for
as long as the medication is taken.

Of the three most widely known SSRIs—Prozac, Zoloft, and
Paxil—Paxil is the most potent. It binds most tightly to the serotonin transporter as it blocks reuptake. Prozac is the weakest, with
the longest half-life. Zoloft is the most serotonin-selective, and has
the lowest potential for drug interactions with the CYP2D6 enzyme. None of this meaningfully answers the question of which
one is right for any given patient.

At least 14 different receptor subtypes have been identified for
serotonin, so the complete action and potential effects of serotonin uptake blockers is hard to predict. Prospective users of these
drugs should know that approximately one out of every five people cannot tolerate the side effects. During premarket testing and
early clinical trials of most SSRIs, between 10 and 20 per cent
of patients typically dropped out of treatment. The most commonly cited problems were anxiety, nervousness, gastrointestinal
complaints, excessive sweating, insomnia, headaches, and a form of
muscular restlessness known as akathisia. A poorly understood side
effect of serotonin-active drugs, from LSD to Prozac, akathisia is
a condition marked by nervous, restless feelings in the muscles, primarily the legs. Sometimes this is accompanied by sweatiness and
anxiety. Also known as "motor restlessness," akathisia is possibly
due to indirect effects on dopamine pathways. It is sometimes informally referred to as "sewing machine leg," for the characteristic

treadle-pumping foot motion that accompanies it. Akathisia can be highly unpleasant, and it is a significant reason given by patients who discontinue various receptor-active drugs after only a few days.

If prescribing physicians were slow to comprehend the extent and discomfort of "Paxil head," they were even farther afield with respect to sexual side effects. Perhaps the most persistent complaint from even the most successful users of popular SSRIs is difficulty achieving orgasm. What some physicians took to calling the "Zoloft droop" kept many patients away from SSRIs. Anorgasmia, or "retarded ejaculation," is the primary sexual complaint associated with SSRI use. (SSRIs have proven to be useful drugs for premature ejaculators.) For women, the anorgasmic nature of the drugs was equally vexing. In some cases, users report lowered libido as well. Similar problems have plagued the broad family of blood pressure medications. Initial reports from SSRI manufacturers stated confidently that only a small percentage of patients experienced these sexual dysfunctions. As it turned out, the percentage was far higher, possibly as high as 60 per cent. Again, the medical community was reluctant to grapple with the issue, knowing that sexual side effects often lead to patient noncompliance. Sexual side effects are among the least discussed of drug issues. Since these drugs plug into receptor systems designed for survival and reward, it makes sense that side effects can include changes in appetite, sex, and mood. What impressed Peter Kramer about the matter of sexual dysfunction on SSRIs was his patients' "willingness to tolerate anorgasmia" in return for the improvements the medication brought. "Prozac does not feel good to take, and it can cause a discouraging, even embarrassing, form of impotence." Alcoholics and other addicts who have been helped by these drugs are likewise reluctant to discontinue a medicine that effectively diminishes their desire to drink.

Milder, usually transient side effects of the SSRI family include stomach upset and loose bowel movements. This happens because there are serotonin receptors in the gut as well as the brain.

A drug like Zoloft, for example, prevents reuptake and increases serotonin stimulation in the stomach, where it isn't needed, as well as the brain, where it is. An enviable example of receptor selectivity is the widely used anti-asthma drug, Ventolin. This inhaler works by tickling adrenalin B2 receptors in the lungs, while ignoring B1 receptors in the lungs and heart. The result is excellent bronchodilation without the negative cardiac side effects of revved-up heart activity.

Other SSRI side effects can include tinnitus, an intrusive ringing or roaring in the ears. People with existing tinnitus should use the products with care. Additional effects include vivid dreaming, as well as excessive yawning (another serotonin-mediated event). Pfizer, the makers of Zoloft, have released information showing that Zoloft (and presumably other SSRIs) increases mean serum cholesterol by about 3 per cent, and triglycerides by about 5 per cent.

SSRI manufacturers advise pregnant women not to use the drugs, even though the results of a comprehensive 1999 study in Canada, happily, did not find any differences in fetal well being or birth weight between women who had taken an SSRI during the first trimester, and women who had not. Care should be taken when combining SSRIs with the following drugs: other antidepressants, lithium, benzodiazepines, Coumadin, and digitoxin. The interaction between SSRIs and the allergy remedy Seldane was shown to be responsible for rare cardiac arrhythmias, and Seldane was subsequently removed from the market. Finally, there is no evidence thus far from rat studies that any member of this class of drugs is in any way carcinogenic.

A perennial topic at psychopharmacological conferences is the SSRI "poop-out" effect. After a period of use, sometimes as much as three years, the effect of the medicine decreases in certain patients. Since there is speculation that this is due to a dopamine depletion phenomenon in some users, doctors sometimes try to treat this falloff by combining an SSRI with other drugs, usually a dopamine agonist like bupropion, amantadine, or methylphenidate

(Ritalin). The other perennial topic is suicide, and the irony here is inescapable: Drugs created to prevent depressive suicide and treat potentially fatal addictions are seen by some researchers as the source of suicidal impulses—the side effect of last resort.

Suicide

In a sense, suicide is the most controversial drug effect of all. A brief discussion cannot really do it justice. One of the reasons why doctors have been willing to try serotonin medications in so many cases is because patients could not commit suicide very easily by taking too many SSRIs in combination with alcohol.

After a series of glowing reports on Prozac in the media, a publicity backlash set in, as Prozac and the other SSRIs became overprescribed victims of their own success. The initial flash point was the assertion by a Harvard University research psychiatrist that six patients had developed "suicidal thoughts" while taking Prozac. This information, while clearly begging for more systematic verification, was eagerly seized upon by two groups with a clear self-interest in the proceedings: certain trial lawyers, and the Church of Scientology, which opposes all forms of psychiatric intervention. Ironically, the first serotonin research to gain widespread popular press coverage was in connection with suicide. The newsworthy part of the early research was that people who committed suicide had lower cerebrospinal levels of serotonin. It was chronically *low* levels of serotonin that was thought to predispose people toward suicide. The low serotonin-high suicide connection was a valuable clue, and it led neurologists and psychiatrists to consider ways of predicting suicide-prone people. From a sociological point of view, suicide is a hotly contested arena. The only semi-reliable indicators were environmental—the more handguns in someone's immediately vicinity, for example, the more likely they are to kill themselves. Beyond that, all was speculation. But addiction scientists changed most of what we know about suicide. Alcoholics and drug addicts are statistically more likely to commit suicide, or to end up in hospitals, compared to non-addicts. Put simply, addicts and depressives show statistically high rates of suicide, period. Clinically depressed addicts, suffering from "incomprehensible demoralization," are at extreme risk for suicide.

A study of antidepressants and suicide risk published in the *Journal of Clinical Psychopharmacology* in 1992 reaffirmed the original finding, reporting that "the decreased toxicity of newer antidepressants such as fluoxetine and other selective serotonergic drugs makes them an attractive choice for treatment of depressed patients who are at risk for suicide."

In addition to proving the existence of a broad market for psychiatric drugs, Prozac has touched off a brave new world of psychiatric litigation.

One psychopharmacologist, who shall remain nameless, wrote:

> All antidepressants can promote suicidality in
> that, paradoxically, as depression responds, the
> first thing to change—before the despair and
> hopelessness that make the sufferer conclude she
> should end her life—may be her energy, motiva-
> tion and confidence to carry out a suicide plan. It
> is an old chestnut in psychiatric training to watch
> for this problem, a skill that has fallen by the
> wayside with modern prescribing practices.

At this writing, British and American studies have shown a slight statistical increase in suicidal thoughts among adolescents taking SSRIs, with the exception of Prozac. Even though there were no actual suicides in these studies, new warning labels about the possibility of suicidal ideation in teenagers will be the likely result.

Zyban

Years ago, the first round of nicotine patch therapy was hampered by overdose fears after several users fell victim to heart trouble when they combined too many patches with too many cigarettes. For most smokers, however, the situation was just the reverse: one standard nicotine patch was not enough. As Mayo Clinic and other research institutes found, the situation resembled the underdosing problem common to methadone treatment. Better to double the dosage and start with two patches, or double the gum, many doctors now recommend. This problem of suboptimal dosing is widespread in medicine, and stands in contrast to the usual anti-drug message to which Americans are subjected. The idea that in certain cases, patients need *larger* doses for optimum effect cuts against the grain of prevailing wisdom. Only recently have caregivers relaxed enough about addiction fears to begin administering adequate amounts of pain killers to hospitalized children and seniors, despite the obviously low risk of addiction in those two groups.

Zyban, combined with aggressive nicotine replacement therapy, leads to tobacco abstinence rates a year after treatment of roughly 30 per cent. The most common side effects of Zyban are insomnia and tremor. Since Zyban weakly inhibits uptake of serotonin, dopamine, and norepinephrine, some of the side effects we have come to associate with inhibition of norepinephrine uptake, such as dry mouth, indigestion, and orthostatic hypotension (light-headedness when standing) are part of the mix as well. People who are prone to seizures may not want to try it, as previously discussed. All others should stay at or below 300 milligrams per day. Predisposing factors that might lead to an increased risk of seizures include head trauma, cirrhosis, or taking an additional medication that lowers the seizure threshold—such as cocaine, alcohol, sedatives, insulin, L-Dopa for Parkinson's, lithium for manic-depression, theophylline for asthma, certain steroids, and MAOIs, among others. Happily, the reported incidence of sexual side effects is much lower with Zyban than with SSRIs. Some users have reported evidence of a heightened sexual effect with Zyban.

Ritalin

Ritalin is a stimulant in the amphetamine family, with the peculiar property of helping many adults and children who suffer from attention deficit hyperactivity disorder (ADHD). Since amphetamines raise dopamine levels in the brain, it was assumed that dopamine systems were the mechanisms responsible for this effect. Nevertheless, a research team at Duke University Medical Center tried Ritalin on so-called "knockout" mice missing the specific gene for the dopamine transporter, and surprisingly, it calmed them, anyway—by raising serotonin levels in rat brains significantly. One possibility, say the researchers, is that the hyperactive mice get a Ritalin-assisted boost in serotonin, which balances out their already elevated levels of dopamine. Ritalin's effect may be altered if used in combination with amphetamines (obviously), certain anticonvulsants, certain over-the-counter cold remedies, asthma medications, tricyclic antidepressants, MAO inhibitors, cocaine, diet pills, and Zyban. In addition, several herbs do not combine well with Ritalin, most notably ma huang, St. John's Wort, and guarana.

Anti-Craving Drugs

Naltrexone is a potential problem for people with liver disease or hepatitis. It does have the advantage of not being metabolized by CYP2D6, and therefore does not significantly interact with drugs that do. However, naltrexone does have significant side effects. Patients with alcoholism who are also heroin addicts, or who are taking methadone, will be thrown into full-blown opiate withdrawal when they take naltrexone. At very high doses, naltrexone has been implicated in liver damage. More common adverse effects include dizziness, lethargy, and headache. Naltrexone reportedly works best in alcoholics who exhibit very high levels craving, and who have a family history of alcoholism—in other words, in cases that appear wholly biological on the addiction continuum.

Along with Zyban, bupropion is another drug with a dose-related risk of seizure. As a rule, if a drug's package insert lists a maximum dosage that should not be exceeded, chances are the drug has a small range of optimum dosage, and a wide variability in individual reactions. This is known as having a "narrow therapeutic index." A cap on dosage often means that the risk of unpleasant or dangerous side effects trends upward sharply after a certain dose level is reached. We have seen that this is the case with Zyban/Wellbutrin.

One other anti-craving drug, carbamazepine (Tegretol), does not mix well with Tagamet, Clarithromycin, Erythromycin, Prednisone, oral contraceptives, anticoagulants, or MAO inhibitors. Birth defects have been reported in animal studies of carbamazepine. Side effects include restlessness, nervousness, irregular heartbeat, and chest pain. Tegretol combined with tricyclic antidepressants has been known to cause seizures.

Psychedelics

While cocaine and speed were being refined into crack and ice, and the heroin/amphetamine "speedball" was in vogue, the evolution of LSD concentrations took a different path from 1975 to 2000. Compared to average doses of 500 to 1000 micrograms, LSD doses by the 1990s were commonly in the range of 250 micrograms or less—recognition, tacit or otherwise, that yesterday's "heroic" dose was often far too large. Given that LSD can cause noticeable effects in people at dosages of as little as 50 micrograms, or 5/100,000 of a gram, brain damage is a possibility at very high dosages. Under the best of circumstances, overuse of LSD, MDA, and MDMA leads to rapid tolerance—but rarely craving, or withdrawal symptoms, or difficulty quitting. For every other illegal drug of consequence, the method of administration has become more potent, not less, over the past 40 years.

At this writing, Dr. Mash has established a clinic on the island of St. Kitt's in order to continue testing Ibogaine. Frank Vocci, director of antiaddiction drug development at NIDA, has criticized the Ibogaine work as a "vast, uncontrolled experiment." Rick Doblin continues his involvement with Ecstasy research, including MDMA testing on terminally ill cancer patients at McLean Hospital in Massachusetts, and on veterans suffering post-traumatic stress disorder (PTSD) at a South Carolina clinic.

Taking drugs involves taking risks, whether the drugs in question come from the street or the pharmacy. Potential users of these therapeutic drugs must weight the costs and the benefits against the increasing toll of rampant addiction. Put simply, addiction can be fatal. Above all else, this fact should help us approach the new anti-craving drugs with more equanimity. For some people, the risks associated with psychoactive treatments are far less than the known risks of continued addiction. Becoming an informed medical consumer is no longer just a good idea—it is becoming essential.

It would be nice to conclude the chapter—to conclude the book, for that matter—with the pat pronouncement that the perfect anti-craving drugs are right around the corner, and addiction as we know it is about to be routed from the field. Shorn of the obvious hyperbole, I believe that much of that prediction will come true. Nonetheless, we are stuck with the hand we have been dealt, even as anti-craving drugs become better known and better tested, and new ones are developed. At this point, popping the new pill under a doctor's supervision won't automically stop addicts from popping the old pills. For that, we need the other treatment. The old-fashioned kind. We still need the rest of it—for all kinds of new-fangled reasons.

PART IV

THIRTEEN: A.A. AND ALL THE REST OF IT

*"A Sufi physician and his apprentice in the art of medicine saw a
man walking toward them. From a distance, the physician said: "That
man is ill. He needs pomegranates."*
*As soon as the patient arrived at the doctor's doorstep, the apprentice
brought him inside and said to him: "You are ill. Take pomegranates."*
*"Pomegranates!" shouted the patient. "Pomegranates to you—nonsense!
And the patient stalked away.*
*The young man asked his master what the meaning of the interchange
had been.*
*"I will illustrate it the next time we get a similar case," said the Sufi.
Shortly afterwards the two were sitting outside the house when the
master looked up briefly and saw a man approaching.*
"Here is an illustration for you—a man who needs pomegranates."
*The patient was brought in, and the doctor said to him:
"You are a difficult and intricate case, I can see that. Let me see... yes,
you need a special diet. This must be composed of something round,
with small sacs inside it, naturally occurring. An orange...that would
be of the wrong color... lemons are too acid... I have it: pomegranates!"
The patient went away delighted, having gratefully promised to take
his pomegranates.*

*"But Master," said the student, "why did you not say 'pomegranates'
straight away?"*
"Because," said the physician, "he needed time *as well as pomegranates."*

—From *The Dermis Probe,* **by Idries Shah.**

Even if scientists found a magic chemical bullet for the cravings associated with addiction, we would still be left with the fact
that active addiction is a set of behaviors as well as a biochemical
process. Targeted anti-craving drugs may turn out to be as close as
we can come to an insulin shot or a vaccine for addiction. But we
need to extend the diabetes and asthma metaphor, or risk losing
sight of the overall nature of the addictive process.

Like the umbrella term "addiction," the term, "anti-craving
drug" implies that craving has a single dimension, and that this
unified phenomenon is addressable by a single biochemical correc-
tive in pill form. There is more to the matter of effective treatment
than simply taking an anti-craving pill, even if they become safe,
effective, and widely available. There is even more to it than the
matter of deconditioning from environmental cues. The outward
manifestations of these biochemical alterations take place in the
real world, outside of the mind. The many behavioral facets of
craving mean that addiction science can never be simple, straightforward, or noncontroversial, but the day is coming when people
will no longer be admonished to just say no, or be counseled to
believe that personality flaws and problematic relationships with
family members, or lovers, or coworkers, if sufficiently probed, will
bring an end to their addictions.

There is a large gap in our understanding of addiction's time
line. We know very little about what happens in the brain during the
days, weeks, and months following the inauguration of abstinence
from drugs and alcohol. The brain is normalizing and reregulating,
but we do not know exactly how. Our understanding of reward
pathways and serotonin levels and D2 receptors tells us a great deal

about how addictive drugs do what they do. We can even map this process graphically—but none of the animal models, blenderized rat brains, or colorful PET scans has completely explained why some addicted individuals learn to stay clean, and others relapse repeatedly in a never-ending addictive cycle. Producing addicted animals in the laboratory does not speak directly to this particular issue. After suffering through active addiction, followed by the rigors of withdrawal and detoxification—after putting the disorder into remission—why would anyone voluntarily take up these disastrous drugs again? Why would people make themselves *worse* again, once they have succeeded in teaching themselves how to get better?

Relapses are often triggered by environmental cues—but Alcoholics Anonymous is replete with examples of sober alcoholics who suddenly took a drink, on impulse, and relapsed, and did not seem to have the slightest idea of why or how it happened. They did not consciously decide to go back to drinking and drugging—"it just happened." Long-term craving and relapse is the conundrum at the heart of what it means to be actively addicted. In the case of alcoholism, A.A. refers to the sudden onset of withdrawal symptoms long after the alcoholic's last drink as a "dry drunk." A dry drunk is characterized by exactly the kinds of symptoms commonly encountered during withdrawal—shakes, tremors, nausea, etc.

A great deal of future addiction research will be devoted to relapse prevention. It is not that the anti-craving drugs are necessarily meant to replace all forms of psychotherapy. Rather, it is that the drugs sometimes make psychotherapy *possible*. These forms of treatment do have a place in the treatment future—if the new biochemical insights are allowed to inform and deepen the nonmedical treatment community's understanding of addictive behavior. Since addiction is also a set of behaviors and a pattern of daily existence, the talk therapies, the cognitive therapies, and the behavioral therapies are still part of the landscape, even if they cannot get to the root cause of addictive disorders. Diabetes has behavioral and psychological components, too, but we do not usually send diabetics to psychiatrists as a first-line treatment. Nobody routinely says to a diabetic: Please show up for group counseling three times a week. And be prepared to consider the matter of religion. What makes addiction different?

The effort to develop new medications for addiction and mental illness seems at first pass like a major triumph for reductionist thinking; for murdering to dissect. For in the process of laying out the relentlessly biochemical nature of serotonin/dopamine/norepinephrine-mediated disorders like depression and addiction, so inexorably intertwined, something still seems to be missing. Substance H had been identified—more accurately, a cluster of Substance H neurochemicals—and something is still missing. Call it consciousness, or even spirit: Some crucial but intangible element seems to have gotten lost in the rush to catch neurotransmitters in the act. We must attend to the social and psychological aspects of addictive disorders. Can it simply be coincidental that the major faiths—Judeo-Christianity, Buddhism, Islam, and Hinduism—hold firmly against the excesses of the human appetite, such as gluttony and sloth? It could be argued that at least a few of the Seven Deadly Sins are signposts partly to protect us from potentially addictive behaviors. They are about learning to control cravings; about the misery that stems from unchecked appetites.

Once the craving for an addictive drug has been activated, only rarely can a user return to the casual or recreational use of major mood-altering drugs without running the risk of reactivating the neurochemical template of full-blown addiction. When addicts try to quit, or cut back, they must struggle mightily against a physiology that is telling them to do something completely different. Abstinence for addicts after years of chronic addiction is not a moral issue. It is the simplest response to the neurochemical facts of the matter. Just like Dr. Li's rats, practicing addicts have artificially inserted an addictive chemical into the primary survival and pleasure circuitry of their brains. Once they have detoxified, their brains continue to tell them that they must have cocaine, they must have a drink, they must smoke grass. They must do these things; they must have their drugs, or lead a life of misery and die. This is the message of intense craving. True recovery begins when addicts take the first steps toward averting or minimizing the effect of these dire craving signals. Pavlov's dogs must, at some point, cease to salivate when they think about the goodies. Imagine if someone ordered you not to be hungry whenever you saw, or even thought about, a restaurant—especially if you hadn't eaten for days.

While the hard researchers in biomedicine are searching for Lewis Thomas' "switch" in the form of a new pharmacological compound, the soft researchers in alternative medicine are seeking the same switch in organic form, through various nutritional and supplemental therapies. Regardless of how it is accomplished, abstinence is the goal—the central tenet guiding addiction treatment and recovery.

What we eat influences the way our brains function, and researchers have learned that quite subtle differences in behavior can occur with variations in food intake. Dr. Janice Keller Phelps, the nutrition-oriented physician, believes that a striking number of practicing alcoholics are functionally hypoglycemic—they have abnormally low levels of blood sugar. When either sugar or alcohol is consumed, blood sugar levels soar, and the addict feels better, at least for a while. One of the hidden side effects of addiction is bad diet, regardless of class or economic considerations.

Chronic stress and a history of poor diet, combined with the depletion of vitamins and other essential nutrients caused by drug abuse, all combine to retard the functions of the body's own healing mechanisms. For example, cigarette smoking puts additional demands on the body's store of vitamin C. This is another good reason why pregnant women should not smoke. They are probably depriving the fetus of ascorbic acid. Supplemental doses of vitamin C are sometimes recommended for smokers in early abstinence, as a possible way of speeding up the detoxification process.

Since sugar foods and other carbohydrates are frequently resorted to as substitute drugs, they may play a role in keeping cravings alive. Avoiding or reducing the intake of foods high in sugar is considered by some alternative addiction therapists as a way of reducing cravings. To that end, nutrition therapy has become an integral part of treatment at several different treatment centers, including Seattle's Alternatives in Medicine Clinic, and the Haight Ashbury Free Clinics in San Francisco. In fact, Dr. Phelps believed that addiction can be traced to a fundamental error in carbohydrate metabolism; a genetic failure of the body to process simple sugars in the normal way. She also believed strongly that the pain of withdrawal and the stress of associated cravings could be drastically lessened in many addicts through attention to nutritional needs.

Dr. Candace Pert agrees. "Recovery programs," she writes, "need to take into account this multi-system reality by emphasizing nutritional support and exercise. Eating fresh, unprocessed foods, preferably organic vegetables, and engaging in mild exercise like walking to increase blood flow through the liver can speed the process up." Other alternative researchers speak of the body's "natural stimulant capacity," and suggest that drugs and "drug foods" like coffee, chocolate, and sugar be replaced by proteins and raw vegetables.

Alternative therapists see a strong connection between neurotransmitter levels and errors in carbohydrate metabolism, because of the role played by serotonin in appetite control. Normally, after carbohydrates are eaten, serotonin levels rise, and this has the effect of inhibiting the appetite for more carbohydrates. After a sugar-rich meal, most people feel "full," and stop eating. In her book, *The Hidden Addiction*, Dr. Phelps argues that this carbohydrate-serotonin feedback mechanism may not work properly in addictive individuals. It is a flaw, Phelps writes, which leads to a constant physiological craving for addicting substances. Refined sugar is the "hidden addiction" that underlies all others.

Sugar, that old familiar villain, seems too pat and simplistic an answer. The sugar theory seems reminiscent of Ebenezer Scrooge, who attributed his vision of Marley's ghost to an "undigested bit of beef." But if addiction is a chemical imbalance, then steps to redress it logically might include attention to nutritional factors, especially during withdrawal. Dr. Phelps points to experience with hospitalized alcoholics, in which the patients who undertook a rigorous nutritional program in addition to regular treatment stayed sober longer.

Her treatment regimen relies heavily on diet modification and vitamin supplementation. Her controversial approach featured a specific attack on the symptoms of withdrawal and detoxification during the first 30 days of abstinence. Her primary weapon was vitamin C, which she did not hesitate to prescribe in very large doses—typically 4,000 milligrams every three to four hours, sometimes by intravenous infusion. (This is a huge dose, and should only be considered in consultation with a doctor.) She designed specific high-protein nutritional schedules composed of vitamins, minerals, amino acids, adrenal extracts, and protein powders. She recommended the amino acid glutamine for alcohol cravings—but did not hesitate to prescribe antidepressants when indicated.

Practitioners of "complementary medicine" were also beginning to make use of hypnotism, acupuncture, massage, and other forms of reputedly holistic health care. Dr Phelps applauded this, and was disdainful of the idea that there was a single approach to addiction. She chided the mainstream drug and alcohol treatment industry for its habit of treating every addict the same way.

"Insurance companies said that what we were doing was not an accepted form of medical treatment," she told me years ago. "The point I've been trying to make is that there *isn't* any accepted form of medical treatment." In such a vacuum, alternative medicine is bound to gain a hearing. Anecdotal experiments are the rule— whatever works, works, and if someone says it works, we should give them the benefit of the doubt. This is a different kind of endeavor, with different kinds of rules.

Various researchers have been experimenting with amino acid combinations, developing therapeutic "cocktails" composed of precursors for dopamine, serotonin, endorphin, norepinephrine, and other brain chemicals. Kenneth Blum, a co-author of the dopamine D2 studies at the University of Texas, worked with a neurotransmitter restoration cocktail called SAAVE, composed of phenylalanine, glutamine, tryptophan, pyridoxal-5-phosphate, and various enzymes. Unfortunately, tryptophan has been all but unavailable in the U.S. since 1990, when the FDA told consumers to stop taking tryptophan after the supplement was linked to an outbreak of a rare blood disorder called eosinophilia-myalgia syndrome (EMS). The Centers for Disease Control eventually reported 24 deaths. A specific bacillus the Japanese had cultivated to use as a "factory" for the production of tryptophan had gone haywire, and, through a process akin to fermentation, produced a pathogen responsible for the outbreak. Even a "natural" substance as seemingly innocuous as an amino acid in supplement form can have unforeseen effects. If we are what we eat, then it behooves us all to eat a little more carefully—especially since some of the things we eat are either drugs, or else natural substances that exert a similar effect.

By elevating key neurotransmitter levels through amino acid "loading," and by inhibiting the enzyme-induced degradation of these amino acids, SAAVE may be "a useful adjunct to psychotherapy in achieving sobriety, not only in an inpatient setting but as a crucial element for continued recovery," Blum said. Blum eventually sold his patent rights to NeuroGenesis, Inc.

Other researchers say that the ratio of the precursor amino acid to other amino acids present in the body is too complicated, and too little understood, to allow amino acid replacement therapy to be effective at present. Tryptophan, for example, must compete with other amino acids for entry into the brain. The serotonin uptake blockers, on the other hand, apparently produce a decrease in blood concentrations of neutral amino acids, which lessens the competition across the blood-brain barrier. Nonetheless, amino acid replacement therapy is being tried experimentally at clinics around the country

Exercise and Attention

A prescription for aerobic exercise might seem trivial in the face of the life-or-death battle people wage against rampant addiction. But with or without anti-craving drugs, both diet and exercise—two non-pharmaceutical methods of altering neurotransmission—will have roles to play in recovery. As Richard Seymour wrote in *Drug-free*, the book he co-authored with Dr. David Smith, the founder and director of the Haight Ashbury Free Clinic:

> In addition to the production of internal opioids, running and aerobic exercise in general appear to have a dampening effect on the locus ceruleus discharges that various researchers connect to the onset of drug hunger in addicts. Running also seems highly effective in stress reduction on a regular basis. Whatever the mechanism, we have begun prescribing running as a means of decreasing drug hunger during early recovery.

Exercise, attention to diet, and nutritional supplements are only three of the complementary avenues being explored as components of addiction treatment. Successes have been claimed for acupuncture as well. Ear acupuncture, proponents say, allegedly stimulates endorphin production. It is also used for nicotine and other addictions, and some recovering addicts swear by it. Studies performed at the Hennepin County Detox Center in Minneapolis, and at the Acupuncture Clinic of the Lincoln Medical And Mental Health Center in the Bronx, New York, appear to show that, for some addicts, acupuncture can affect an addict's desire to drink or use drugs. It is not clear how long this effect lasts. The same can be said for hypnosis. It has its vociferous claimants, but it has not been widely tested and documented as an addiction therapy.

Meditation, in its many Eastern and Western derivations, is used by some recovering addicts as a means of dampening the panic and anxiety that often accompany detoxification. And again, there is a certain amount of good science behind the notion. Sources as disparate as Maharishi Mahesh Yogi and Harvard's Dr. Herbert Benson have produced evidence that sitting meditation—in which the mind is either purposefully made blank, or else is focused on a mantra (the Maharishi's mantras are Sanskrit, but Dr. Benson maintains that any soft-sounding set of syllables will do)—produces verifiable changes in blood pressure, heart rate, and oxygen exchange. Years ago, Dr. Benson named this phenomenon the "relaxation response." Many addiction clinics use variations on this theme in an attempt to ease withdrawal symptoms.

All of these alternative modalities suffer from the same limitations: a lack of large scale clinical testing due to inadequate funding, and a lack of adequate insurance reimbursements. Nonetheless, almost anything goes in the sprawling treatment and recovery industry. There are, for example, numerous clinics and treatment centers based on the principles of naturopathic and homeopathic medicine. The 3HO SuperHealth program that bloomed in Tucson, Arizona, a "holistic substance abuse facility" inspired by the teachings of the Hindu Guru Yogi Bhajan, was accepted by Blue Cross/Blue Shield and other major insurance providers. (Gaining insurance accreditation is a major factor in the success or failure of many treatment providers and large-scale programs.) There are drug recovery programs based on the spiritual wisdom of American Indians, on the teachings of the German mystic Rudolf Steiner, on assorted holistic health practices such as yoga, guided imagery, lucid dreaming, biofeedback, massage, and other forms of "personal growth" work.

Alternative therapists maintain that recovery from addiction is as much a spiritual voyage of discovery as it is a path back to conventional health and sanity. Traditional psychotherapy in isolation is a frequently ineffective method of treatment, while anti-craving pills, congeners, and replacement therapies are still quite new.

Any treatment that claims to work for all addicts all of the time, under all conditions, should be viewed with extreme skepticism. It is safe to say that any commercial treatment program advertising success rates of 50 per cent or more is very probably engaging in short-term follow-ups, and may be seriously misleading the buying public.

The goal of most for-profit treatment programs is decidedly short-term: to get addicts over the hump of withdrawal and detoxification, preferably during 28 to 40 days of inpatient care, which happens to be the length of stay that most insurance companies are willing to pay for. The addict has to take it from there, which, in many cases, means going home—or else going to AA.

The Three-Headed Dragon

Getting off drugs, or learning to stop drinking, is very often easier than staying off them. As Mark Twain remarked about tobacco, quitting was easy—he'd done it dozens of times. Relapse, the biological imperative, will have its way with most of those abstaining for the first time. Addiction is a psychological disorder with strongly cued behavioral components, whatever its dimensions as a biochemically-based disease.

The three-headed dragon is a metaphor first popularized by alternative therapists at the Haight Ashbury Free Medical Clinic in San Francisco. The first head of the dragon is physical. Addiction is a chronic illness requiring a lifetime of attention. The second head is psychological. Addiction is a disorder with mental, emotional, and behavioral components. And the third head of the dragon is spiritual. Addiction is an existential state, experienced in isolation from others.

Addicts speak of "chasing the dragon" in an effort to catch the high that they used to achieve so easily. It is also drug slang for the use of small metal pipes to catch and inhale the wisps of smoke from a pile of burning opium, crack, or speed. We can picture the dragon chasing his own tail, snapping at it with all three hungry mouths, in an endless escalation of tolerance and need.

"Because of the unique reaction that the genetically addiction-prone individual experiences to his drug of choice, he or she programs his or her belief system with the deep conviction that the substance is 'good,'" writes Richard Seymour. "This is where self-help becomes intrinsic to recovery. Unless one deals with the third head, unless one changes the belief system and effects a turning-about in the deepest seat of consciousness, there is no recovery." The "X" factor in recovery, for many people, turns out to be a form of inner self-awareness; something that includes the attributes of will power and determination yet transcends them through a form of surrender.

And speaking of changing one's belief system, experience has shown that it is a spectacularly bad idea to sit around and do nothing but stare at the wall during the early phase of recovery. Psychologist Mihaly Csikszentmihalyi argues, in *The Evolving Self*, that when attention wanders, and goal-directed action wanes, the majority of thoughts that come to mind tend to be depressive or sad. (This does not necessarily apply to formal methods of meditation, which cannot be described as states marked by wandering attention.) The reason that the mind turns to negative thoughts under such conditions, he writes, is that such pessimism may be evolutionarily adaptive. "The mind turns to negative possibilities as a compass needle turns to the magnetic pole, because this is the best way, on the average, to anticipate dangerous situations." In the case of recovering addicts, this anticipation of dangerous situations is known as craving. The next step is often drug-seeking behavior, followed by relapse.

For a highly motivated addict with a stable social life, a safe and effective medication to combat craving might be all that is needed. For many others, however, attention to the other two heads of the dragon is going to be necessary. An addict's ability to experience pleasure in the normal way has been biochemically impaired. It takes time for the addict's disordered pleasure system to begin returning to normal, just as it takes time for the physical damage of cigarette smoking to partially repair itself. Alternative therapists are fond of referring to recovery as a process, with an emphasis on the importance of time. Medication of any disease, even if successful, does not treat the continuing need for healing. It is now well understood that mood and outlook can have an effect on healing. Positive emotional states can be beneficial to the maintenance of good health. Thoughtful physicians make the distinction between a *disease* and an *illness*. A disease is a chemically identifiable pathological process. An illness, by contrast, is the disease and all that surrounds it—the sociological environment, and the individual psychology of the patient who experiences the disease.

Dissociation

Where does the everyday self go during active cycles of addiction? It is not a simple case of amnesia, or sleepwalking. It is more like a waking trance, or autohypnosis. Psychologically, it is a state of dissociation. For addicts, the three-headed dragon is both a part of them and not a part of them. It is integral to who they are, yet it is estranged from their core selves. When activated, the cycle of addiction leads men and women away from their genuine natures. Their sense of self becomes impaired through the processes of intoxication, denial, neuroadaption, withdrawal, and craving. This impaired sense of self causes behavior that is baldly contradictory to their core beliefs and values. Honest men and women will lie and steal in order to get drugs.

Webster's Unabridged Dictionary defines dissociation, rather vaguely, as "the splitting off of certain mental processes from the main body of consciousness, with varying degrees of autonomy resulting." Recall that in the case of state-dependent memory, if you give a rat a mind-altering drug, and teach him to run a maze, the rat will perform this maze task more efficiently in subsequent runs if it is under the influence of the same drug. How autonomous were you, consciousness-wise, the last time you got drunk and parked your car somewhere you couldn't remember?

Dissociation may be part of the way consciousness itself adapts to chronic drug use. Richard S. Sandor, a thoughtful Los Angeles physician, helped to clarify many of these issues in an excellent essay in *Parabola* magazine:

> ...the inability to satisfy a physical craving or psychological compulsion will produce all kinds of unusual behavior, but this is true for natural drives and appetites as well as for created ones. What might one not do to avoid starvation? Such behavior alone cannot be used as evidence for a pathological personality type. The failure to recognize this point has led to a considerable amount of confusing retrospective research—deducing a personality type after the addiction had developed. But in fact, a dependence on a substance or activity condemned by society as illegal or immoral leads the addict to act in antisocial ways; and this is the case far more often than that drug addiction results from an antisocial personality type.

Secondly, Sandor points to the inability of prevailing behavioral models to produce a comprehensive framework for effective treatment. "None of the current treatment methods based upon the positivist scientific paradigm—be it psychodynamics (Freud, et al.) or behavioral (Pavlov, Watson, Skinner)—has demonstrated any particular superiority in the treatment of the 'addictive disorders,'" he writes. "Many psychoanalysts readily admit the uselessness of that method for treating addicted individuals (the patient is regarded as being 'unanalyzable')."

Thirdly, says Sandor, "It appears that the most successful means of overcoming serious physical addiction is abstinence— very often supported by participation in one of the twelve-step groups based on the Alcoholics Anonymous model.... The basis of recovery from addiction in these nonprofessional programs is unashamedly spiritual."

The problem for the addict, as Sandor realizes, is not so much the matter of quitting, as it is the matter of not starting again. The resolve to quit is often present, but the resolve not to start again can be interfered with in a variety of ways. All addictions, Sandor argues, more closely resemble "the whole host of automatisms that we accept as an entirely normal aspect of human behavior than to some monstrous and inexplicable aberration." Bicycle riding is a good example of an automatism, because once learned, "...it no longer requires the subjective effort of attention; more importantly, once learned, it cannot be forgotten. It is as though the organism says to itself, 'Riding this thing could be dangerous! It's much too important to trust that Sandor will pay close attention to it.'"

So what does the mind do? It creates a new state called bicycle riding:

> Number one priority in this state (after breathing and a few other things, of course) will be *maintaining balance*. In much the same way, the organism recognizes that mind-and mood-altering chemicals disturb the equilibrium of functions and are therefore potentially dangerous. In response, it may form a new state in which the ability to function is restored, but in which a new set of priorities exerts an automatic influence. Just as one's only hope of not riding the bicycle again (if for some reason that is important) is to never

again get on one, once a particular addictive state has developed, there is no longer any such things as "one" (drink, hit, fix, roll, etc.). Addicts begin again when they forget this fact (if indeed they have ever learned it) and/or when they become unable to accept the suffering that life brings and choose to escape it without delay. Addictions can be transcended—not eliminated.

Sandor ultimately concluded that "The only modern Western psychologies that can aid us in our search to become truly human are, like AA, frankly spiritual or transformational in nature (e.g., those of Gurdjieff, Jung, Frankl)."

Sandor compares the addictive state to a form of hypnosis accompanied by posthypnotic amnesia. This automatism, this subsequent amnesia about the drugged "I" on the part of the sober "I," is highly reminiscent of the consequences produced by state-dependent memory:

A hypnotized subject is instructed to imagine that helium-filled balloons are tied to his wrist; slowly the wrist lifts off the arm of the chair. The subject smiles and says, 'It's doing it by itself!' The 'I' that lifts the arm is unrecognized (not remembered) by the 'I' that imagines the balloons.... One part denies knowledge of what another part does. A cocaine addict, abstinent for a year, sees a small pile of spilled baking soda on a bathroom counter and experiences an overwhelming desire to use the drug again. Who wishes to get high? Who does not?

"Interestingly," Sandor says, "this type of amnesia is very similar to that seen in the multiple personality disorder (see Jekyll and Hyde), in which one entire 'personality' seems to be unaware of the existence of another. Even more interesting is the fact that confabulation, rationalization, and outright denial are also prominent features of the addictive disorders." Dissociation, then, can occur without the intervention of anything as dramatic as hypnosis. The common quality is automaticity, the experience of "it doing it by itself."

Does A.A. Work?

"Step One: We admitted we were powerless over alcohol, that our lives had become unmanageable.

Step Two: Came to believe that a Power greater than ourselves could restore us to sanity.

Step Three: Made a decision to turn our will and our lives over to the care of God as we understood him."

—from *Twelve Steps of Alcoholics Anonymous*, 1939.

The drawbacks to inpatient hospitalization for addiction treatment are obvious. There is a disruption of normal family and professional ties, an absence of conditioned cues for habituating, and an enforced self-help mentality not suitable for all personality types. In addition, a patient can disguise his or her addiction from a therapist in a clinical setting for a very long time.

Despite recent progress in the medical understanding of addictive disease, the amateur self-help group known as Alcoholics Anonymous, and its affiliate, Narcotics Anonymous, are still regarded by many as the most effective mode of treatment for the ex-addict who is serious about keeping his or her disease in remission. A.A. and N.A. now accept anyone who is chemically dependent on any addictive drug—those battles are history. In today's A.A.

and N.A., an addict is an addict. A pragmatic recognition of pan-addiction makes a hash of strict categories, anyway.

Nonetheless, under the biochemical paradigm of addiction, we have to ask whether the common A.A.-style of group rehabilitation, and its broader expression in the institutionalized form of the Minnesota Model, are nothing more than brainwashing combined with a covert pitch for some of that old-time religion. As Dr. Ludwig has phrased it, "Why should alcoholism, unlike any other 'disease,' be regarded as relatively immune to medical or psychiatric intervention and require, as AA principles insist, a personal relationship with a Higher Power as an essential element for recovery?" The notion is reminiscent of earlier moralistic approaches to the problem, often couched in strictly religious terms. It conjures up the approach sometimes taken by fundamentalist Christians, in which a conversion experience in the name of Jesus is considered the only possible route to rehabilitation. But if all this is so, why do so many of the hardest of hard scientists in the field continue to recommend A.A. meetings as part of treatment? Desperation? Even researchers and therapists who don't particularly like *anything* about the A.A. program often reluctantly recommend it, in the absence of any cheap alternatives.

In 1939, Bill Wilson and the fellowship of non-drinkers that had coalesced around him published the basic textbook of the movement, *Alcoholics Anonymous*. The book retailed for $3.50, a bit steep for the times, so Bill W. compensated by having it printed on the thickest paper available—hence its nickname, the "Big Book." The foreword to the first printing stated: "We are not an organization in the conventional sense of the word. There are no fees or dues whatsoever. The only requirement for membership is an honest desire to stop drinking. We are not allied with any particular faith, sect or denomination, nor do we oppose anyone. We simply wish to be helpful to those who are afflicted."

In short, it sounded like a recipe for complete disaster: naïve, hopeful, objective, beyond politics, burdened with an anarchical structure, no official recordkeeping, and a membership composed of anonymous, first-name-only alcoholics.

In the words of one long-term A.A. participant:

> Alcoholics Anonymous is a fellowship designed and administered by a bunch of ex-drunks whose only qualification is that they can't hold their booze and don't want to learn how. It has no rules, dues, or fees; nothing that any sensible organization seems to require. At meetings, the speaker starts on one subject and winds up talking about something entirely different and concludes by saying that he doesn't know anything about the program except that it works. The groups are always broke, yet always seem to have money to carry on. They are always losing members but seem to grow. They claim A.A. is a selfish program but always seem to be doing something for others. Every group passes laws, edicts, rules, and pronouncements which everyone ignores. Members who disagree with anything are privileged to walk out in a huff, quitting forever, only to return as though nothing happened and be greeted accordingly. Nothing is ever planned 24 hours ahead, yet great projects are born and survive magnificently. Nothing in A.A. is according to Hoyle. How can it survive? Perhaps it is because we have learned to live and laugh at ourselves. God made man, He made laughter too.... we are trying to be nobody but ourselves. We don't know how it works but it does and members keep receiving their dividend check from their A.A. investments.

Amid dozens of case histories of alcoholics, the Big Book contained the original Twelve Steps toward physical and spiritual recovery. There are also Twelve Traditions, the fourth one being, "Each group should be autonomous except in matters affecting other groups or A.A. as a whole." As elaborated upon in *Twelve Steps and Twelve Traditions*, "There would be real danger should we commence to call some groups 'wet' or 'dry,' still others 'Republican' or 'Communist'.... Sobriety had to be its sole objective. In all other respects there was perfect freedom of will and action. Every group had the right to be wrong. The unofficial Rule #62 was: "Don't take yourself too damn seriously!"

As a well-known celebrity in A.A. put it: "In Bill W.'s last talk, he was asked what the most important aspect of the program was, and he said it was the principle of anonymity. It's the spiritual foundation." Co-founder Dr. Bob, for his part, believed the essence of the Twelve Steps could be distilled into two words—"love" and "service." This clearly links the central thrust of A.A. to religious and mystical practices, although it is easily viewed in strictly secular terms, too. *Alcoholics Anonymous* recounts a conversation "our friend" had with Dr. C.G. Jung. Once in a while, Jung wrote, "...alcoholics have had what are called vital spiritual experiences.... They appear to be in the nature of huge emotional displacements and rearrangements." As stated in *Twelve Steps and Twelve Traditions*, "Nearly every serious emotional problem can be seen as a case of misdirected instinct. When that happens, our great natural assets, the instincts, have turned into physical and mental liabilities."

Alcoholics Anonymous asserts that there are times when the addict "has no effective mental defense" against that first drink.

Bill Wilson wrote:

Some strongly object to the A.A. position that alcoholism is an illness. This concept, they feel, removes moral responsibility from alcoholics. As any A.A. knows, this is far from true. We do not use the concept of sickness to absolve our members from responsibility. On the contrary, we use the fact of fatal illness to clamp the heaviest kind of moral obligation onto the sufferer, the obligation to use A.A.'s Twelve Steps to get well.

(For A.A. detractors, see Stanton Peele's *The Diseasing of America*, Herbert Fingarette's *Heavy Drinking*, or *Seven Weeks to Safe Social Drinking* by Donna Cornett.)

This excruciating state of moral and physical sickness—this "incomprehensible demoralization"—is known in A.A. as hitting bottom. Asks Dr. Arnold Ludwig:

Why is it that reasonably intelligent men and women remain relatively immune to reason and good advice and only choose to quit drinking when they absolutely must, after so much damage has been wrought? What is there about alcoholism, unlike any other 'disease' in medicine except certain drug addictions, that makes being *in extremis* represent a potentially favorable sign for cure?

Hitting bottom may come in the form of a wrecked car, a wrecked marriage, a jail term, or simply the inexorable buildup of the solo burden of drug-seeking behavior. While the intrinsically spiritual component of the A.A. program would seem to be inconsistent with the emerging biochemical models of addiction, recall that A.A.'s basic premise has always been that alcoholism and drug addiction are diseases of the body *and* obsessions of the mind.

When the shocking moment arrives, and the addict hits bottom, he or she enters a "sweetly reasonable" and "softened up" state of mind, as A.A. founder Bill Wilson expressed it. Arnold

Ludwig calls this the state of "therapeutic surrender." It is crucial to everything that follows. It is the stage in their lives when addicts are prepared to consider, if only as a highly disturbing hypothesis, that they have become powerless over their use of addictive drugs. In that sense, their lives have become unmanageable. They have lost control.

A.A.'s contention that there is a power greater than the self can be seen in cybernetic terms—that is to say, in strictly secular terms. As systems theorist Gregory Bateson concluded after an examination of A.A principles in *Steps to an Ecology of Mind*:

> The 'self' as ordinarily understood is only a small
> part of a much larger trial-and-error system
> which does the thinking, acting and deciding...
> The 'self' is a false reification of an improperly
> delimited part of this much larger field of inter-
> locking processes. Cybernetics also recognizes
> that two or more persons—any group of per-
> sons—may together form such a thinking-and-
> acting system.

Therefore, it isn't necessary to take a strictly spiritual view in order to recognize the existence of some kind of power higher than the self. The higher power referred to in A.A. may simply turn out to be the complex dynamics of directed group interaction, i.e., the group as a whole. It is a recognition of holistic processes beyond a single individual—the power of the many over and against the power of one. Sometimes that form of submission can be healthy. Addicts seem to benefit from being in a room with people who understand what they have been through, and the changes they are now facing. It is useful to know that they are not alone in this. "The unit of survival—either in ethics or in evolution—is not the organism or the species," wrote Bateson, "but the largest system or 'power' within which the creature lives." In behavioral terms, A.A. enshrines this sophisticated understanding as a first principle.

No matter how we look at it, addiction has always been viewed as a disease with a strong metaphysical aspect. Is this just a hangover from the days when rummies and drug fiends were seen as morally bankrupt? While there is a strong spiritual element in the A.A. program, newcomers are not forced to undergo a traditional religious conversion experience as a means of escaping from alcohol and other drugs. Other recovering addicts have formed A.A.-style groups that do not refer to higher powers at all. Perhaps one day we will find that the critics are right when they attribute so much of A.A.'s success to the placebo effect. If an addict believes that a higher power, however configured, can aid in recovery, then it just might. It is true that A.A. refers explicitly to God in the Twelve Steps, and sometimes closes meetings with a recitation of the Lord's Prayer. The co-founders of A.A. anticipated the possibility that the group's practices might be seen by many as a disguised version of dogmatic Christianity. In an appendix to the Big Book, they note:

> The terms "spiritual experience" and "spiritual awakening" are used many times in this book... Though it was not our intention to create such an impression, many alcoholics have nevertheless concluded that in order to recover they must acquire an immediate and overwhelming "God-consciousness" followed at once by a vast change in feeling and outlook. Among our rapidly growing membership of thousands of alcoholics such transformations, though frequent, are by no means the rule. Most of our experiences are what the psychologist William James calls the 'educational variety' because they develop slowly over a period of time... We find that no one need have difficulty with the spirituality of the program.

> Willingness, honesty and open mindedness are the
> essentials of recovery. But these are indispensable.

In place of the simple admonition, "I must not drink," which is central to the will power approach, many addicts learn to make use of other mind-control strategies, including thought substitution, thought distraction, and thought manipulation. As Ludwig observes, these are precisely the kind of mind-control techniques employed by Buddhist monks for centuries to control intrusive thoughts and resist bodily temptation. In one of his letters to Bill Wilson, C.G. Jung described intoxication as the "equivalent of union with God," an analogy also used by Islamic mystics. These characterizations are certainly not meant as exhortations to find God in a bottle. They point to the perceived connection between intoxication and the realm of spiritual feelings. "You see, 'alcohol' in Latin is 'spiritus'... the same word for the highest religious experience as well as for the most depraving poison," Jung pointed out. "The helpful formula is: *spiritus contra spiritum.*"

The biochemical view of addiction does not preclude a belief in God, spirit, or soul. On the other hand, a religious conversion experience is not the only available means of release from a presently incurable and potentially fatal disease. Like the spontaneous remissions sometimes seen in cases of cancer, the spontaneous conversion experience that sometimes frees addicts from their addiction remains, at bottom, a mystery not presently amenable to scientific inquiry.

Independent Alcoholics Anonymous groups keep no formal records, and engage in no follow-ups. A.A. does have a world headquarters in New York, which is responsible for what few statistics are available. We know that one out five A.A. participants is under the age of 30, and nearly a third of its members are women. Its success rate with regard to long-term sobriety is variously rumored to be anywhere from one in three to one in 35.

We also know, as one study of A.A. concluded:

"Spiritual change is conceptualized as central to recovery in AA's literature... However, spiritual change is not universal among 12-step participants today, with anywhere from one-third to four-fifths of members reporting no significant changes in spirituality.... In short, in AA it may be less spiritual beliefs than the living out of those beliefs in practical action that benefits members, which is probably what the organization's designers hoped."

A.A. and N.A. meetings are by no means completely drug-free environments, although there are now smoke-free meetings in many locales. Coffee and cigarettes continue to play a significant role in the atmosphere of most meetings. Do they contradict themselves? Very well, then, they contradict themselves.

While Dr. Robert Smith, the Ohio alcoholic who co-founded the program, was one of the disease model's early proponents, A.A. has no official position on the causes of addiction. It deals with addiction as it is, not with how it happens. A.A. devotes its energies almost exclusively to the job of helping its members abstain from the use of alcohol and other drugs one day at a time. Members are often given commemorative pins or badges after various periods of abstinence.

One of the program's greatest strengths, strange to say, is its complete independence from the professional drug and alcohol treatment establishment. A.A. has maintained a degree of autonomy and a studied lack of professionalism that is refreshing. It is strictly a peer group. When addicts enter a meeting, they find themselves, often for the first time in their lives, among a group of people who are exactly alike in one crucial respect. A meeting typically consists of a group of alcoholics and other drug addicts who take turns sharing their experiences of hitting bottom and achieving sobriety. Anyone is welcome to attend. No formal record of attendance is kept, except for court-mandated attendees. A.A. does not make organized efforts at recruiting new members. Other than local phone numbers in the Yellow Pages, the group does very little direct advertising.

There is nothing to prevent a member from lying about being sober, of course. Group psychotherapy, as practiced by A.A., suffers from the same opportunities and limitations as any other form of behavioral or insight-oriented therapy. The strategies practiced on unwitting therapists by addicts are legion—denial, outright fabrication, shifting blame to others, and so on. A.A. deals with this problem quite uniquely: There is no regular authority figure, no official counselor or therapist in the A.A. meeting structure. There is no distinction made between therapist and patient. There is no authority figure to deceive, evade, or placate. No one is in charge. There is a refreshing lack of "chemical-free" cant. Different A.A. members rotate through as group leaders from session to session. It is meant to be a society of equals; a peer group in the strictest sense of the term. When the group structure is composed exclusively of addicts, the situation becomes untenable for the addict who hopes to mislead others about his or her condition. As an active member of A.A. put it: "It's hard to bullshit a roomful of bullshitters."

The overall emphasis is on the present. Newcomers are discouraged from making sweeping promises. The idea is not to drink or take drugs today, the day of the meeting—and to do the same thing tomorrow. Alcoholics Anonymous and Narcotics Anonymous members generally use first names only, a form of anonymity that conduces toward group awareness and away from excessive displays of personal vanity. The collective narrative is a shared story in which members can participate without having to sacrifice all of their personal privacy. The overall atmosphere militates against dissociation, in favor of group awareness and engagement. Many of the cryptic sayings of A.A. point obliquely toward this matter of dissociation. Just bring your body to the meetings, and your mind will follow. Or this: It's possible to be too smart for A.A. Your best thinking got you here; don't you want to try something else?

Studies indicate that many alcoholics attending A.A. meetings still engage in episodes of drinking, followed by periods of sobriety—the basic cyclic pattern of addiction. "Slips," as these episodes of relapse are called, are of course discouraged, but tolerated. The addict is encouraged to start where he or she left off, before the relapse—to begin again immediately with a one-day-at a-time avoidance of addictive drugs other than nicotine and caffeine.

A.A. is a popular target for chic detractors; a sort of muddled Jesus freak love fest; the kind of setup where you might want to call in the deprogrammers. A.A., where everyone admits to the God of their choice that they are powerless over Demon Rum or Demon Dope. After everything science has taught us, what could possibly be of interest about the dynamics of a roomful of old men hacking on cigarettes and slurping bad coffee? A.A. and all the rest of it, as Dr. Halikas says. If addiction is a medical problem, and is treatable through medical means, then do addicts really *need* all the rest of it?

Some of the public criticisms of AA betray a measure of class-consciousness. There is the subtle but widely-shared belief that, as one A.A. member put: "AA-land is inhabited chiefly by people who have plastic pink flamingos in their front yards and plastic gold crucifixes over their beds." Judging by the disparity of looks, lifestyles, and incomes represented at meetings, this portrayal of the organization as a haven for the lower socioeconomic classes does not stand up to scrutiny. It never did, given the professions and salaries of the organization's founders.

In A.A., sobriety is referred to as a gift. "I forgot to be grateful," in the parlance of the group, is a way of viewing relapse that transcends the idea that the addict simply gave up, or got lazy. It might be taken to mean, in psychological terms, that something akin to post-hypnotic amnesia triggered a return to drinking. In neurological terms, adaptation to an artificial state created by active addiction precipitated the onset of drug-seeking behavior.

Addicts in "the program" trade anecdotes about the basic dissociative state that everyone experiences from time to time, but which addiction puts into dramatic play. We are all a bundle of different "Is." If addicts are lucky, they learn that the addictive "I," the thing that seems to be in control, is not their essential self. ("It wants me to drink," one member said, "but it's a liar.")

As Richard Sandor commented:

> What from the outside may well look like mind-less obedience (and may even feel like it for a while) is really, at its best, a voluntary surrender to forces that transcend and can transform the self. I am not referring here to a sudden conver-sion based upon a new belief, but rather to a long and difficult work towards awakening. Only a blind man needs to *believe* that the sky is blue; a man, who can see, *knows*. The fellowship of AA, like the older spiritual traditions, in its principle of 'growth through attraction, not promotion,' has recognized the relative lack of value of 'belief.'

The organization is commonly thought to have evolved from the Moral Rearmament Society and other temperance movements of the past. Observers like Sandor, however, see in A.A. an echo of earlier spiritual traditions and practices. Mystical traditions and re-ligions around the world emphasize the coming together of a group of seekers or sufferers for the purpose of enhancing individual self-awareness through group exercises. The explosion of group therapy and communal forms of "awareness training" that swept the field of humanistic psychology in the 1960s and 1970s were examples of this laudable but often misguided human impulse.

It is not so much the Moral Rearmament Society that stands behind A.A. in a historical sense, but rather the figure of C.G. Jung. A.A. is a brand of humanistic psychology that will appeal to some people and not to others. The fact that it does work—for some people, some of the time—is beyond dispute. If the timing is right, and if the addict is willing to make the attempt, almost any treatment, including the go-it-alone approach, might actually be effective—if not always permanently so.

Despite significant strides in the direction of greater understanding of addiction, the bottom line has not changed: Most people in A.A., or any other treatment program, will ultimately relapse. This return to drug taking may be a transient phase in a longer cycle of sobriety, or it may be a permanent plunge back into long-term addiction.

One of the purposes of self-help and other forms of group therapy is to remind hard-core addicts why they are unlikely to be successful in attempts to return to controlled use. Will power means carrying out decisions through strength of mind; the mobilization of mental energy in a head-to-head battle with drug cravings. Will power is usually the first line of attack taken up by hard-core addicts—and the first to fail. Addicts report, to their surprise, that attempting to fight cravings head-on only seems to fuel the fire. Psychiatrist Arnold Ludwig, in *Understanding the Alcoholic's Mind*, puts it in more formal terms: "The I-want-a-drink versus You-can't-have-a-drink battle becomes a dialectic without resolution—thesis, antithesis, but no immediate synthesis." Repeated failures by addicts to force themselves into a state of abstinence through the application of will power can sometimes bring them face-to-face with a critical existential dilemma (Another example of hitting bottom). It is a classic double bind; a predicament that the characters in Samuel Beckett's *Waiting For Godot* might have appreciated. "I can't go on," says a character in the Beckett play. "I'll go on."

The addict cannot continue to use, but cannot find a way *not* to use. He has set one part of himself against another. The impossible choice for the addict, in Ludwig's memorable phrase, "is between going mad and dying or going mad and dying."

In the tug-of-war between the survival commands of the midbrain and the rational oversight of the cortex, a form of selective amnesia does seem to function at times. One of the founders of

A.A. used to counsel alcoholics to give controlled drinking a try, believing that until a drinker attempted to control his drinking, and failed disastrously, he would not be sufficiently open to what A.A. had to offer. Many addicts, in attempting to establish and maintain a pattern of controlled use, have sought to shed their addictions by changing or rearranging the outward circumstances of their lives—moving to a new geographic locale, for example, or changing jobs. In the case of hard-core addiction, this strategy is rarely successful.

Often, the addict has no experience, no picture, of what successful abstinence might be like. He or she may no longer have, or may never have had, a self-image that includes healthy abstinence. As addiction unfolds and deepens, part of the losing battle involves the need to extract an ever more elusive feeling of normality from drug use. Malcolm Lowry, in his telling novel about alcoholism, *Under the Volcano*, refers to the drinker's efforts to strike "the fine balance between the shakes of too little and the abyss of too much."

We have seen that hard-core addicts cannot be frightened or bullied into producing long-term abstinence on demand. The biology can sometimes be confusing, the maze of neurotransmission can look like an indecipherable rat's nest at times, but the essential point can be summarized in one word: Neuroadaption. The changes are real, and, if not always completely reversible, than at least treatable through abstinence. For strongly addicted individuals with some degree of biological predisposition behind their addiction, abstinence and withdrawal must be followed by long-term recovery practices, in order to minimize the likelihood of serious relapse. The combination of treatment approaches that will best reinforce abstinence in a specific addict is likely to vary tremendously, depending upon the mix of biological and environmental influences, and the degree of self-awareness and openness the addict possesses. Some addicted individuals may find that the best approach for them is to go it alone, cold turkey, without benefit of formal intervention or therapeutic assistance. These may be addicts who cannot or will not respond to the formal dictates of a more structured, interventionist approach. Nonetheless, many addicts I spoke with felt that, as a minimum, some form of structured self-help therapy was almost always essential in the first three or four months of hard-fought abstinence. This is the period during which new and better anti-craving drugs could be immensely helpful. It also takes time to realize that it is not necessary to justify addiction, or feel ashamed of it. What *is* necessary is to treat it.

The feud between A.A. partisans and non-A.A. therapy programs need not concern us here. It is up to individuals to make that choice. It is enough to observe that addicts and alcoholics often find that they benefit from an affiliation with outside social groups. Therapists say this can serve as a counterpoint to the sense of alienation and distance that frequently constricts an addict's normal social life as the disorder progresses. One very strong point in A.A.'s favor is economic. There are no dues, fees, or medical insurance requirements. (Meetings usually have a form of pass-the-hat donations.)

Are A.A and N.A. for everyone, or not? Since the umbrella organization does not do scientific studies, the simple answer is: No way to find out unless you try it.

"A.A. is a non-tested treatment," Professor Pomerleau said. "The problem is, it works for those for whom it works. What we don't know is, how broadly applicable is it? And how effective is it in comparison with other possible approaches?"

As Dr. Arnold Ludwig concludes in *Understanding the Alcoholic's Mind*, "The answer seems to be that not everyone is ideally suited to become a member of this organization and make the kind of commitment necessary to obtain optimal results. Because of its special nature, the organization seems best suited to highly motivated individuals with strong affiliative needs."

One of the few things addictionologists and the treatment community at large seem to agree on is that a stable, nurturing family environment or network of friends can make a major difference. Psychologist Robert Ornstein and others have shown that an effective network of social support plays a positive role in healing, whether the wound is mental or physical. Additional research supports the contention that positive social interaction positively affects the immune system. Social affiliations, whether in the form of A.A., a church, or a service organization, can themselves be a form of higher power. In the absence of such a social support structure, many addicts find a substitute family in A.A. or N.A. If Alcoholics Anonymous also functions as a substitute family, and a source of new friendships, there is certainly nothing blameworthy in that.

Long-term recovery often does mean A.A. or N.A. or Hazelden, and all the rest of it. To paraphrase, there are as many paths to abstinence—as many ways of beheading the dragon—as there are souls of men.

The Minnesota Model

The prevailing mode of clinical treatment in America was pioneered in Minnesota by the non-profit Hazelden Foundation. Hazelden provides a wide range of services related to chemical dependency. Based in large part on the self-help approach of Alcoholics Anonymous, the Minnesota Model, as the Hazelden treatment is known, emphasizes the traditional disease concept of alcoholism and other addictions. It leans heavily on the idea of the Twelve Step self-help group as the optimal means by which addicts can acquire better self-knowledge of their situation. Hazelden makes no secret of having adopted the Alcoholics Anonymous Twelve Step structure as the underpinning of its program, but officials tend to bristle when their treatment centers in Center City, Minnesota, West Palm Beach, Florida, and Newberg, Oregon, are referred to as "just" Twelve Step programs. The Twelve Steps of Alcoholics Anonymous include taking "moral inventory" of oneself, making amends to people one has harmed through one's addictive behavior, and vowing to be of use to fellow addicts by bringing the principles of A.A. to their attention. Anyone who has genuinely "worked" the

Twelve Steps has engaged in some serious psychological and behavioral work on oneself.

Hazelden began in 1949 as a "guest house" for alcoholic men, at a time when there were no alternatives other than jails, psych wards, or the streets. The Minnesota Model, as shaped and refined at Hazelden was, for all practical purposes, a social reform movement. It combined the Twelve Step moral imperatives of A.A. with the need to provide humane alternatives to existing state and federal treatment wards. The original rules posted at Hazelden were elegantly straightforward: "Behave responsibly, attend lectures on the Twelve Steps of Alcoholics Anonymous, talk with the other patients, make your bed, and stay sober."

The primary motivation at Hazelden was to move alcoholics out of their life of isolation, and integrate them successfully into a social setting. Today, the Minnesota model employs addiction counselors, one-on-one therapists, physicians, psychologists, dieticians, and fitness experts. Addicts who need a more structured environment and less immediate temptation often find these tailored programs useful. Hazelden and the clinics modeled on Hazelden feature cognitive therapy, group therapy, supervised detox, recreation activities, healthy meals, mental health services, spiritual advisors, and educational lectures. The overall campus-like atmosphere of Hazelden and other centers is more like a health spa than the cramped room in the church basement typical of A.A. meeting quarters. The Minnesota Model is an attempt to treat body, mind, and spirit at the same time, as the image of the three-headed dragon suggests. When the typical 28 to 48 day stay is over, "alumni" are farmed out to their local chapters of Alcoholics Anonymous or Narcotics Anonymous, where there aren't any doctors, and there aren't any weight rooms. At Hazelden, where treatment outcomes are monitored and analyzed, roughly half of its patients are said to be drug- and alcohol-free a year after treatment.

Hazelden, The Betty Ford Center, and other clinics that adhere to the Minnesota Model favor the practice of "structured intervention"—a controversial approach whereby friends and family confront the addict during a planned session, and gently but firmly attempt to convince him or her of the need for treatment. Alternatively, as critics view it, a drinker with some problems is brainwashed and love-bombed by well-meaning friends and therapists into believing he has a disease. (There is no reason to suppose that it doesn't happen that way sometimes.)

Proponents of the Minnesota Model see structured intervention as frequently necessary in order to break through the fabric of "denial and rationalization" that addicts tend to weave around themselves. The emerging neurological and medical views of addiction are sometimes used in intervention scenarios as a means of convincing addicts that their disorder is not a sign that they are mentally ill, or that they are failures as human beings.

The Minnesota Model has been widely emulated by hospital outpatient clinics and treatment centers across the country. In some clinics, the treatment program is basically A.A. in a high-priced residential setting, with doctors on call.

The multidisciplinary Minnesota Model, with its shared emphasis on long-term peer support, has penetrated dozens of countries. Russia has shown interest in the Minnesota Model, after decades of their own brand of "medical" treatment for alcoholism. The Soviets have historically categorized alcoholism as a physical disease caused by mental or emotional disorders. In practice, they dealt with it as a mental illness. Registered alcoholics, usually late-stage alcoholics with accompanying mental problems, were treated in "narcology clinics," which either resembled psychiatric hospitals or locked dormitories. Soviet doctors and psychiatrists have used antagonist drugs to block the alcoholic "high" of drinking, and they have also dabbled in hypnosis. Lately they have experimented with the dissociative drug ketamine. The overall success rate of this activity has not, apparently, been enviable.

Alexey Kampov-Polevoy, a Soviet physician and former researcher-in-residence at Hazelden, told the *Minneapolis Star Tribune*: "A straight medical model offers less follow-up support for patients than the Minnesota Model, because the Minnesota Model uses the activity of patients themselves, who organize into self-help groups." Kampov-Polevoy said the American concept of addiction holds some surprises for Russian addicts. "Our patients are very disappointed to learn in A.A. meetings that alcoholism is incurable."

In China, the situation is equally confusing. After two years of a nationwide "people's war" against drug addiction in China, government authorities claimed major accomplishments in 2007—but treatment, which is mostly compulsory, remains limited and largely ineffective, Chinese doctors say.

The Chinese surge against drugs was credited with numerous successes almost before it had begun. Zhou Yongkang, Minister of Public Security, told the official news agency Xinhua that officials had seized more than two tons of methamphetamine, and three million "head-shaking pills" —otherwise known as Ecstasy tablets. Two years later, in June of 2007, Minister Yongang, claimed that the number of drug abusers in China had been cut from 1.16 million to 720,400 due to compulsory rehabilitation measures. "The effort has yielded remarkable results," Yongang told the *China Daily*. (Other drug experts estimate the number of Chinese drug addicts to be 3 million or more.)

However, a recent paper co-authored by several Chinese physicians, published in the *Journal of Substance Abuse Treatment*, suggests that things are not so rosy. The report, titled, "Attitudes, Knowledge, and Perceptions of Chinese Doctors Towards Drug Abuse," paints a dismal picture: Less than half the Chinese doctors working in drug abuse had any formal training in the treatment of drug addicts, the report found. Moreover, less than half of the treatment physicians believed that addiction was a disorder of the brain. (One cannot help wondering whether the percentage for American doctors would be any higher.)

The study could find no coherent doctrine or set of principles for drug rehabilitation being employed in China, beyond mandatory detox facilities. In the Chinese government's White Paper on "Narcotics Control in China," the practice of "reeducation-through-labor" is considered to be the most effective form of treatment. Another name for this form of treatment would be: prison.

There are perhaps as many as 200 voluntary drug treatment centers as well. These centers emphasize treating withdrawal symptoms, and feature more American-style group interaction and education, but observers say such centers are often used by people evading police or running from their parents.

In addition, the lack of formal support from the Chinese government has led to the closing of several such facilities after only a few months. The American origins of such treatment modalities have not helped sell such programs to government officials. Pharmaceutical treatments for craving remain unavailable in China.

The Great Coffee Debate

In the mid-1990s, the Hazelden Foundation became enmeshed in the Great Coffee Debate. As anyone who has ever attended an A.A. meeting knows, coffee and cigarettes are an integral part of A.A. tradition. Dr. Bob and his coffeepot comprise one of the indelible images in the A.A. tradition. Perhaps it was inevitable, given the general thrust toward a "drug-free" America, that counselors at Hazelden would eventually decide that coffee was a stimulant drug, and that it was being used and *abused* right there on the premises during treatment. Counselors decided that it had to stop. The edict went out, and the coffee stopped dripping. Patients at Hazelden began brewing their own clandestine coffee. Many and varied are the ways of field-slurping a fast cup of strong coffee. In the end, the fundamentalists lost, and the use of coffee was reinstated.

There is a more serious side to this debate, of course. With the coffee battle as background, consider the difficulty attendant upon making decisions about the use of selective serotonin reuptake inhibitors. "My belief is that today, you should be put in jail if you refuse to prescribe SSRIs for depression," Alan Leshner, former head of NIDA, told the *New Yorker*. "If someone says never, ever use medication I can't understand that at all." The prescription drug issue mattered greatly to Hazelden and the rest of the treatment industry. With the trend toward managed health care, insurance money available for rehab stays has dwindled, while at the same time, many treatment centers have been revealed as shoddy, substandard insurance mills. (In fairness, a low cancer recovery rate at Sloan-Kettering Hospital is rarely cited as a reason to cut funding.) After the client uprisings, Hazelden lost the fight over coffee, and not long after that, decided to allow the use of Prozac, Zyban, and other receptor-active drugs. By 2001, Hazelden was designing studies to test acamprosate. The famed Minnesota Model—the Twelve Step approach combined with clinical counseling—was finding room for "good" drugs after all.

The God Receptor

It often seems as if the proponents of the biological view are offering a take-it-or-leave-it view of human nature and behavior. The gene proposes and the neuropeptide disposes. But one important attribute of the brain's receptor systems is that they are not static. The number and density of receptor fields, the sensitivity of individual receptors, and the "stickiness" of the cell membranes themselves all differ at different times. We have come a long way in our understanding of "unconscious" bodily processes. Yogis demonstrated decades ago that such internal states as breathing rate, blood pressure, and the generation of certain brain waves, once thought to be impervious to volitional control, could in fact be "mentally" influenced. With the proper five-minute introduction, most people can learn to change the surface temperature of their hands by a few degrees using simple biofeedback techniques. Many spiritual growth techniques center on breathing exercises, for the same reason that diet and dietary restrictions are frequently emphasized: Such activities release different neurotransmitters in the brain, the gut, and the respiratory center, and these changes can alter consciousness. Many spiritual techniques that are physical in nature were designed to produce specific changes in brain state. We do not need to soar into the metaphysical to see the wide-ranging role of neurotransmitters. Neurotransmission via receptors is clearly an evolutionary strategy well preserved in the larger scheme of things.

Nonetheless, from A.A. to Ibogaine, alternative treatments are frequently suffused with spirituality, if not outright religiosity. All the way out there, on the edge of speculation, is the notion that a disordered reward pathway might be the impetus for the religious quest, the search for existential meaning, the artistic struggle to create. God is a neuropeptide, Candace Pert once mischievously suggested. Was Martin Luther serotonin- and dopamine-deficient? How about Joan of Arc? Or Michelangelo? Is love, or hate, any less real for having neuropharmacological substrates, microscopic chemical correlates, in the brain and body? This all sounds funny, or blasphemous, or nonsensical—but it may be the metaphorical key to A.A.'s modest successes for more than sixty years. We know with certainty that depression and addiction are deeply linked disorders. What has begun to emerge at the edges of depression and addiction literature is that religious faith, or a spiritual belief system of some kind, can be of value in the battle against depression, drugs, and drink. This does not mean that any sort of correlation between recovery and prayer, or between decreased depression and frequency of church attendance has emerged. Nevertheless, feelings are not just feelings. Emotions influence our health, our evolutionary fitness, our learning, and our decision-making. There is the recurrent suggestion in some of the work that the additional factor at play is something researchers call "intrinsic religiosity." Here is Substance H in a completely different guise—much more metaphorical, and incorporeal. People recover from all sorts of mental and physical afflictions and frequently give credit to their religious beliefs. Whatever we choose to call it, successful recovery from serious illnesses of the mind and body frequently seem to call for a fundamental shift in mental processes. If God is a molecule, and if a powerful addictive drug is a molecule, then, at least figuratively, God and the drugs compete, sometimes, for the same set of receptors. One of the behavioral transitions that puts addicts on the road to abstinence is the heightening of the spiritual impulse in the spaces of the mind formerly occupied by the drug impulse.

In *Why God Won't Go Away*, Andrew Newberg and Eugene D'Aquili describe their use of state-of-the-art SPECT cams (single photon emission computed tomography cameras) to hunt down and identify the specific portions of the brain involved in spiritual and religious experiences. Having studied pictures of brains during or shortly after episodes of ecstatic prayer, mindful meditation, and group rituals like Sufi dervish dancing, the authors conclude:

> ...no matter how unlikely or unfathomable the accounts of the mystics may seem, they are based not on delusional ideas but on experiences that are neurologically real.... religions persist because the wiring of the human brain continues to provide believers with a range of unitary experiences that are often interpreted as assurances that God exists.... we believe that evolution has adopted this machinery... because religious beliefs and behaviors turn out to be good for us in profound and pragmatic ways.

Newberg and D'Aquili locate this impulse in the "posterior superior parietal lobe." V.S. Ramachandran and other brain scientists believe that the limbic system is more likely to be the chemical locus of religious experience. Regardless of the neurology of the matter, how do we define the religious impulse? For Newberg and D'Aquili, "It only means that humans have a genetically inherited talent for entering unitary states, and that many of us interpret these states as the presence of a higher spiritual power."

Or, you could put it this way, and call it Step Two: Came to believe that a power greater than ourselves could restore us to sanity.

Dr. Earle, a beloved early figure in the A.A. fellowship, told his story in the pages of the Big Book:

> What is this power that A.A. possesses? This curative power? I don't know what it is. I suppose the doctor might say, "This is psychosomatic medicine." I suppose the psychiatrist might say, "This is benevolent interpersonal relations." I suppose others would say, "This is group therapy."
> To me it is God.

Step Eight: Made a list of all persons we had harmed, and became willing to make amends to them all.

In its commentary on this step, *Alcoholics Anonymous* sums up what can happen when the required paradigm shift is accomplished: "Our real purpose is to fit ourselves to be of maximum service to God and the people about us."

FOURTEEN: REDUCING HARM

"Everybody was so young they still smoked cigarettes."

—Patty Larkin

Genes are about risk, not about destiny. All drug use is not abuse; all drug abuse is not addiction. Statistics teach us that the casual use of illegal drugs falls off drastically after the age of 35. We could even suggest this hypothesis: People in their 40s and 50s who *do* use illegal drugs regularly are quite possibly addicted to them.

If we take what we know about impulsive behavior and add it to what we have learned about carbohydrate craving, we can begin to sketch a theoretical profile of young people who may be possible candidates for future drug trouble. We cannot yet be certain that what we are identifying is a tendency to become addicted, rather than simply a desire to experiment and rebel. Current youth programs treat all young people as if they are at equal risk. Distinctions of this nature, which it is now possible to make, are in danger of being lost in the fog of perpetual drug wars.

Considering the fact that most addictive drugs score such a direct hit on the reward pathways in the human brain, it seems logical to wonder whether anyone could be truly "protected" against the ravages of addiction. The insidious alteration of neurotransmitter levels seems to imply that anyone who uses these drugs would end up unfailingly addicted—or else nobody would. Yet, most people understand that daily drinkers are not necessarily addicted to alcohol. Frequency of use and amount of intake, as we have seen, are not infallible indicators of addiction. This is easy to understand when the subject is booze, for such users are all around us. However, many of these same people have trouble extending that perspective to heroin, cocaine, and marijuana. The whole idea of so-called "hard" drugs may not, in the end, shed much more light on the process of addiction than does the attempt to make distinctions between physical addiction and psychological addiction.

A great deal of the confusion is semantic. To paraphrase former president Clinton, it depends on what your definition of "addiction" is. This book is an attempt to update the definition of addiction in light of recent research. The metaphor with which this book began—the search for an "insulin shot" against addiction—is getting closer to reality.

Certainly there will be addicts for whom the anti-craving drug, or the vaccine, will be enough. Breaking the grip of craving, or blocking the euphoriant effect of the drug for a period of time, will enable some people to gain sufficient traction for a run at abstinence. There are marvelous breakthroughs in the making. There has never been a better time in history to attempt breaking free.

On the other hand, John Walters, the drug czar under George W. Bush, appeared content to stay the course. He has denounced the idea that addiction treatment has any kind of central role to play in the national drug war. Mr. Walters favors—can you guess?—stricter law enforcement and greater interdiction efforts at U.S. borders.

Drug wars never work. No amount of Viet Nam-style escalation or sheer military firepower is capable of preventing people from getting their hands on illegal drugs. Addicts always know how to find the drugs, even when finding them requires an enormous amount of time, effort, and money. Drug wars tend to increase prices in the short run, which theoretically makes the product less available. But there is a catch. "Cocaine isn't scarce and can't be made scarce," argues Mark A.R. Kleiman of Harvard's John F. Kennedy

School of Government. "Thus we can't create a shortage because Adam Smith is more powerful than [drug czars]." Writing in *The New Republic*, Kleiman argues that none of the "currently fashionable approaches to increasing the price of cocaine imports—eradication, substitution, pre-emptive buying, or interdiction—have any prospect of doubling import prices." Kleiman believes this is equally true of "techno-thriller approaches such as releasing coca-eating caterpillars," a strategy which once made the rounds as a topic of discussion in Washington, D.C.

"It is obvious by now that we can't keep illegal aliens out, and an alien is substantially harder to hide than a kilogram of cocaine," Kleiman wrote. "Every time we seize a kilogram of cocaine, someone in Colombia sells another kilogram to the importers. From the viewpoint of the South American drug lords, a kilogram seized is about as good as a kilogram snorted or smoked."

Alcohol and nicotine inflict more damage than all illicit drugs combined. We know this already, but we don't really let this knowledge *mean* anything. Back in 1990, while the U.S. government was continuing to pour time and energy into the battle with Colombian drug cartels, Philip Morris, the U.S. corporation, announced an agreement to supply the Soviet Union with a minimum of *20 billion cigarettes* annually—the largest single export order in the company's history.

The government's own studies estimate that fully 50 per cent of all legal alcohol purchased in the United States is consumed by only 10 per cent of the drinking population. This suggests that practicing alcoholics may account for as much as half of the total liquor sales in the nation. It is little wonder, then, that certain alcoholic beverage manufacturers were only too happy to offer cheap, high-alcohol wines like Thunderbird and Night Train—fortified wines that some health authorities maintain are nothing more than "designer drugs" for poverty-stricken, late-stage alcoholics. And then there are the newer teen drinks; starter kits for amateur drinkers.

The category called illegal addictive drugs is no longer a sustainable myth. Stephen Jay Gould, the best-selling Harvard professor of paleontology, argued in *Dissent* that the drug crisis is best understood as a taxonomy problem:

> For reasons that are little more than accidents of history, we have divided a group of nonfood substances into two categories: items purchasable for supposed pleasure (such as alcohol) and illicit drugs.... Too rarely, in our political criticism, do we look to false taxonomies, particularly to improper dichotomies, as the basis for inadequate analysis. Our drug crisis is largely the product of such a false dichotomy.

I once asked Dr. Li which two drugs he would choose to legalize, if the whole historical experiment could be run again. He picked alcohol and nicotine. Alcohol, because overall it is less tenaciously addictive than cocaine and amphetamine and heroin. Nicotine, because it is less socially disruptive, though deadly—a side effect Dr. Li would attack by hooking smokers on nicotine gum instead of cigarettes. As for marijuana, Dr. Li pleaded insufficient data.

Perhaps, as has been suggested, there are valid neurological reasons why human societies have frequently sanctioned the use of alcohol and nicotine. Historically, it may be a social reflection of the fact that they are among the most "plastic" of mind-altering drugs, in terms of their wide-ranging grab bag of possible effects. Perhaps they really *are* the lesser of all possible addictive evils. But would they be just as popular if they were illegal? Other cultures and countries have had their own local favorites, and throughout history, the same drug has sometimes been assigned to the legal category, at other times to the illegal one.

The recognition that drug wars create crime is long overdue. More than fifteen years ago, a study of the economics of street drug dealing by the Rand Corporation confirmed that most drug dealers make more money illegally than they could possibly make through any form of legitimate employment. That equation has not changed. Unless drugs can be made less lucrative, the simple offer of a job will not necessarily be sufficient to lure adult dealers out of the trade. For minors, drug dealing is without a doubt the best-paying job available to them.

The effort to combat drugs has poisoned our relationships with other countries. Farmers in Latin America, Southeast Asia, and Afghanistan are not the source of the drug problem. The danger of concentrating on the interdiction of foreign shipments is that it breeds the fantasy solution—a belief that the nation's drug problem can be solved offshore, if the barriers and borders of the United States are vigorously defended. In terms of the war on drugs, where the stuff is coming from isn't really the point. Wherever it comes from, there has always been a demand for it in the U.S.

Drug wars weaken the force of law at home. Minor drug laws are flouted with impunity, while basic civil rights are under attack in the name of national security. Drug wars ask a lot from citizens: weakened rules of evidence, the erosion of the doctrine of probable cause, and an end to the presumption of innocence, for starters. Increasingly, it seems, we are prepared to give up what the drug wars demand of us. "The war on drugs also serves the interests of the state, which, under the pretext of rescuing people from incalculable peril, claims for itself enormously enhanced powers of repression and control," writes Lewis Lapham in *Harper's*, "...more jails, more judges, more arrests, more punishments, more people serving more millennia of 'serious time.'" Drug users and dealers are being attacked by evictions, raids, street sweeps, anti-loitering laws, and confiscation of Medicaid and food stamp identity cards.

A different strategy would obviate the need for these enhanced powers of repression and control. Drug wars foster a form of social hypocrisy. Many of the country's finest doctors, scientists, judges, and legislators have routinely used illegal drugs in their past. Yet their lives were not irreparably damaged, their futures thrown on the trash heap. Millions of productive citizens now in their 40s and 50s know that youthful drug use need not be permanently deleterious. They dare not speak up, of course. The people who have the most experience with these drugs have been systematically excluded from the public debate.

The new model of addiction calls into question almost every aspect of drug wars as they have been historically waged. After a well-meaning start on the project by Richard Nixon, the Reagan administration, in concert with Nancy Reagan's "Just Say No" campaign, launched the biggest drug war in American history. It has been continued by every president since then, and principally supported by a well-meaning public.

For many Americans, the use of alcohol, cocaine, or any other addictive drug is a matter of personal recreational choice. None of the strategies employed in the drug wars of the past four decades has been able to override the fact that prohibition can only be effective with the cooperation of the citizenry. Without voluntary compliance, the only recourse is federal coercion; some Orwellian nightmare of detection, control, forced detoxification, and detention.

Ordinary citizens, in addition to facing the potential erosion of civil protections noted above, are also subject to drug testing in the workplace. Only a fraction of the nation's corporations had drug-testing programs in place in 1990, but the number has climbed dramatically ever since. Job applicants are being tested more often than existing employees are, and government employees in "sensitive" positions are under the greatest pressure for testing of all. Inaccuracies and false positives have bedeviled drug-testing programs from the outset. Ibuprofen, available over the counter as Advil or Motrin, registers on some tests as positive for marijuana. Cold remedies such as Nyquil, Allerest, Contac, Dimetapp, and Triaminicin all contain a substance, phenylpropanolamine, which sometimes shows up as positive for amphetamine. The list of potential false positives is a long one.

Many drug testing programs do not test for alcohol, and even if such constitutionally dubious testing programs were unerringly accurate in what they *do* test for, there would still be valid reasons not to adopt them. Few people would insist that the presence of alcohol metabolites in the bloodstream is incontrovertible proof of incompetence on the job. But we frequently make this assumption in the case of illegal drugs, in part because the drug tests themselves are not refined enough to reliably distinguish between casual use and consistent abuse. There is no urine test for addiction.

Banks, insurance companies, and employers will all be faced with these conflicting notions of personal privacy, set against the demands for public health and safety. Pregnant women are finding themselves under attack for their drug use. If they test positive, should they be imprisoned for the safety of the unborn child? Despite the fact that drug testing cannot distinguish use from chronic abuse, cannot determine whether drugs were used on the job, does not always concern itself with alcohol, and has been found unconstitutional by the Supreme Courts of several states, the issue will not be going away soon. Testing human hair, or taking a swab of perspiration from a person's forehead, are much more reliable forms of assay than urine testing.

The Case for Legalization

People need the truth about drugs—the story thus far. What they have been getting is a series of titillating scare stories from sports heroes and TV stars. (Janice Keller Phelps refers to this as "drug education abuse.") It will take years to dig out from underneath the mound of misinformation that has passed for drug education in thousands of anti-drug campaigns and public service TV spots. In the long run, scaring people doesn't work. What children and young adults need is basic information. For a large number of adolescents, the norm is not drug abstinence at all. The norm is a certain amount of drug experimentation. Prohibitionists and the "Just Say No" crowd are unwilling to concede that this can be the case for any but a very few deeply disturbed souls. Study after study has shown, however, that drug experimentation is not simply a haven for the most troubled and disaffected of our nation's youth. To the contrary, many students who dabble with drugs are bright, motivated, creative young people.

A drug education program based on the contention that abstinence is the norm for young people is already off to a bad start. Extremism in the pursuit of abstinence sends the wrong signal. Kids are being taught that only life's losers and dropouts are hooked on drugs, and yet the media constantly demonstrate that the upper classes, life's moneyed winners, are obsessed with liquor, cocaine, and cigarettes. When children grow older, experiment with drugs, and find that drugs sometimes make them feel good, not bad, their trust in the need for abstinence or even for controlled use is weakened. Drug abstinence is a choice, and many young people make that choice. But to call abstinence a norm is an attempt to make it so by fiat. In late high school and early college, abstinence from alcohol could be characterized as an aberration, rather than a norm.

Given the potential behaviors often associated with young people at increased risk for addiction—the traits that Henri Begleiter, Robert Cloninger, Marc Schuckit, and other researchers made a career of studying—it seems likely that traditional drug awareness campaigns may have their greatest impact on young people at lowest inherent risk for addiction in the first place. The desire to stamp out the urge to experiment with mind-altering drugs is understandable in many ways. It is also misguided and impossible; a desire built on an erroneous taxonomy of drugs, fueled by an amalgam of myths, half-truths, and debatable moral precepts.

The alcoholic in A.A. and the cocaine addict on the street share a common appetite. This shared appetite, and the behaviors that come with it, are played out in a larger social context. For a practicing addict, the world is filled with risks, and some of these risks are

invariably connected with the web of prohibitive laws and legislation governing the sale and use of addictive drugs. The movement
for drug legalization, which began to coalesce about fifteen years
ago, is a collection of public voices spanning a variety of political
and cultural points of view. Many prominent voices in the ranks
of the legalization movement are public officials who have become
disillusioned with the current state of affairs, and are now convinced that the present system is doing more harm than good. Federal District Court Judge Robert Sweet of New York City, former
Secretary of State George Schultz, economist Milton Friedman,
former Baltimore mayor Kurt Schmoke, and the late conservative
commentator William F. Buckley are among the well-known figures
who have publicly argued on behalf of legalization over the years.
The medicalization of addiction requires people to consider the
possibility that drug *abuse* is less of a problem than drug *crime*, and
that drug crime can be attacked differently. Very few of legalization's adherents can be considered "pro-drug."

Police chiefs around the country estimate that their depart-
ments spend too much time trying to enforce the drug laws. As
former FBI Director William Webster told the *Los Angeles Times*, in-
terdicting drug traffic "brings with it the enormous capacity to
corrupt those charged with enforcement of the law." Is anybody
really getting his or her money's worth? We are asking law enforcement officers to assume an unfairly large portion of the burden in
the war against drugs. Nearly twenty years ago, at a hearing of the
House Select Committee on Narcotics Abuse and Control, Con-
gressman Charles Rangel asked officials from the Customs Service,
the Treasury Department, and the Justice Department whether a
tripling of law enforcement resources would put a significant dent in
the availability of drugs on the street. According to the account in
the *Los Angeles Times*, not a single official said yes.

William F. Buckley has argued that legalization would drive
down prices, so that addicts would not have to resort to property
crimes to meet the financial demands of their addiction. Misguided drug laws create crime and drive up prices, just as Prohibition

created millionaire crime boss Al Capone. Long ago, the *Economist* in London editorialized: "Legalising the drug trade would be risky. Prohibition is worse than risky. It is a proven failure, a danger in its own right." Opponents of legalization argue that they are not prepared to consign millions to drugged oblivion, while advocates counter that putting drug users in prison in record numbers is not likely to solve their problems, either. Does it make sense to put addicts in jail?

Drug prohibition itself is a major part of the reason why the more potent and problematic refinements of plant drugs keep taking center stage. Since crack cocaine is more potent, more profitable, and more difficult to detect in transit, it replaces powdered cocaine, which, in its turn, replaced the chewing of cocoa leaves. Just as bootleggers switched from beer to hard liquor, so international drug dealers switch from cannabis to cocaine whenever the U.S. enforcement engine lumbers off in the direction of marijuana interdiction and eradication.

The results of even a partial move toward legalization would be profound. It would be a drastic policy switch, and it is not hard to view it as a frightening idea. What percentage of cocaine users would become addicted if cocaine were legal? What percentage of users would become addicted to "glass," if smokable methamphetamine were widely available? Would the ultimate number of addicts and abusers be more or less of a problem than the drug-related violence and economic disruption of today?

The essential argument against legalization is that some drugs are not bad because they are illegal—they are illegal because they are bad. If alcohol and tobacco are legal, and we are only now beginning to come to terms with the health implications of that historical decision, it is insane to add heroin and marijuana and everything else to the list.

The sticking point, for many people otherwise disposed toward considering better alternatives, is that legalization would be morally wrong. Harvard psychiatrist Robert Coles, a specialist in working with children, holds that legalization would be tantamount to a "moral surrender of far-reaching implications about the way we treat each other." Such an act, Coles believes, would signal an acceptance of the pursuit of hedonism for its own sake.

The celebrated "Deaver defense," in which attorneys argued that Reagan White House aide Michael Deaver was far too drunk, most of the time, to know whether or not he had committed criminal acts, was one colorful example in a long line of morally dubious "diminished capacity" defenses involving alcoholism and other addictions. While the fact of addiction may be beyond the addict's control, addicts nonetheless have a responsibility to do something about it. From a legal point of view, the biochemical model of addiction does not change the basic proposition that, with few exceptions, people must be held responsible for the crimes they commit. In time, it may be possible to separate out the criminals suffering from concrete biochemical abnormalities, so that they can receive medical treatment as well as a prison sentence.

Punish the crime, treat the disorder.

The compressed essence of the war on drugs, however, is simply to put as many people in jail as possible. Obviously, long prison terms will not cure addicts of their condition, any more than long prison terms for diabetics would cure their condition. As a forced cold turkey treatment for addiction, perhaps we could view prison as harsh but necessary. Yet drugs are known to be widely available within the nation's federal prison system. As an inmate in an Oklahoma federal prison wrote in a letter to *Time* magazine: "If the Government cannot stop people from using drugs in a few fenced-off acres over which it has total control, why should Americans forfeit any of their traditional civil rights in the hope of reducing the drug problem?"

The direction taken by the American Civil Liberties Union shades toward the basic libertarian contentions toward personal freedom. Drug use may not be a wise practice in most cases, but should it be illegal? Is it self-evident, for example, that the social contract is more impaired by the use of marijuana than by the extensive use of alcohol?

Ethan Nadelmann, an assistant professor of politics and public affairs at Princeton University's Woodrow Wilson School of Public and International Affairs, has charged that as many as 40 per cent of federal prison inmates are serving sentences for drug dealing. In the end, what percentage of the U.S. population do we want to put behind bars? Does it matter that experts say that at least half of the women in federal prison are there because of drug charges? Clearly, a high percentage of the men and women in prison today are drug addicts. More are on the way. The Sentencing Project, a Washington-based group that promotes alternatives to jail time, said recently that as of 2002, 45 per cent of all drug arrests were for marijuana. Simple possession is the rule—only one-sixth of the imprisonments involved charges of marijuana trafficking.

For the first time in American history, according to a study released by the Pew Center on the States, more than one in every 99.1 adult men and women are now in prison or in jail. States spent a total of $49 billion on prisons in 2007, compared to $11 billion 20 years ago. The United States incarcerates a larger percentage of its population than any other country. China ranks second.

"For all the money spent on corrections today, there hasn't been a clear and convincing return for public safety," according to Adam Gelb, director of the Pew Center's Public Safety Performance Project. The report says that higher incarcerations rates have not been caused by increased crime or a corresponding surge in population numbers. Rather, stricter sentencing policies, such as "three-strikes" laws, as well as longer sentences, are behind the surge.

Data collected by Columbia University's National Center on Addiction and Substance Abuse, and cited in *Women Under the Influence*, show that women convicted of drug-related offenses represent the fastest growing subset of America's prison population. More than 2.5 million women abuse or are dependent on illegal drugs. Women are almost 50 per cent more likely to be prescribed a narcotic or sedative, and teenage girls are more likely than teenage boys to abuse prescription drugs, with dramatic increases among 12 to 17 year old girls. Fully three-fourths of these incarcerated women are mothers, and that fact is at the heart of the difficulties women face when they seek treatment.

Put simply, millions of women who need treatment for addiction to alcohol and illegal drugs do not receive it. This has been true throughout American history. Women were not admitted to meetings during the formative years of Alcoholics Anonymous, and there is evidence that the 19th Century practice of performing hysterectomies on alcoholic women as a last resort quietly persisted until the 1950s.

A.A. soon opened its doors to women, who now comprise roughly one third of its membership. But when it comes to rehab centers, the treatment gap has not closed: "For women with small children, lack of childcare is a serious obstacle to seeking treatment.... For some women, fear of losing their children to the child custody system upon admission that they have a problem makes them apprehensive about entering treatment."

The Pew study reveals that addiction is as firmly criminalized as ever. Obviously, long prison terms will not cure addicts of their condition, any more than long prison terms for diabetics would cure that condition.

The American criminal justice system cannot support the burden of a continual flood of minor drug possession cases. Plea-bargaining—the accommodation that keeps the legal edifice afloat—becomes the rule of the day. The legal system would break down in gridlock if every drug defendant insisted on his constitutional right to a jury trial. Prison sentences are bartered and sold like pork futures, and the jury trial has become an unaffordable luxury. For those accused of drug possession, pleading innocent sometimes looks like a risk they cannot afford to take.

If addicted crack dealers sometimes receive stiffer sentences than wanton murderers (and they do), then it is a double irony, since people convicted of drug offenses are often good candidates for rehabilitation. However, public treatment programs are overbooked, and private programs are out of reach for those with little or no health insurance.

The drug war, in the opinion of many, really *is* the drug problem. Greater availability of addictive drugs will not inevitably lead to a drastic increase in the population of drug users. Michael Gazzaniga of Dartmouth Medical School, a noted neuroscientist in the field of split-brain research, has gone on record with his belief that legalization would decrease crime, but would not increase drug abuse. "The casual-to-moderate user very clearly wants to stay in that category," Gazzaniga told *National Review.* "Illegality has little if anything to do with drug consumption…. There is a base rate of drug abuse, and it is achieved one way or another."

Neo-Prohibition

Even though it seems incumbent upon those opposed to limited forms of legalization to martial some brilliant new argument for maintaining the status quo, we could of course go in the other direction. We could choose to clamp down harder still.

Those who work in the drug and alcohol treatment industry do not tend to look favorably upon the idea of legalization. Neither do average citizens, if polls are given any credit. Even though federal prohibition of alcohol has been tried in various guises, it seems to have had the opposite effect from what was intended—it encouraged crime, discouraged addicts from seeking treatment, and made commerce in alcohol almost unbearably profitable. Nevertheless, is there an argument to be made for Neo-Prohibition?

"I wouldn't want to put another [addictive drug] on the market," said Dr. James Halikas. "I have become a neo-prohibitionist. Years ago, I was doing marijuana research in St. Louis and I was publicly debating in favor of legalization. And I now believe we ought to get rid of all the damn drugs—get rid of alcohol, get rid of cigarettes."

The frustration Dr. Halikas feels is understandable, though few voices have been publicly raised on behalf of Neo-Prohibitionism. This alternative to legalization would make alcohol and tobacco (and possibly coffee) illegal. Rather than widening the net, this would narrow it as restrictively as possible, by banning all potent forms of addictive chemicals already on the market.

This issue has never gotten the serious discussion it deserves. Neo-Prohibitionism is often dismissed as impractical—the same charge commonly leveled against legalization. General social custom, in the end, may prevent us from ever again taking people's alcohol away. And if we prohibited tobacco for the first time in our national history, would there be shooting wars in the growing fields of Kentucky and North Carolina?

These are valid considerations, but the hurdles to be crossed on this particular road seem no more or less formidable than they are for widespread legalization. Neo-Prohibitionism, it is safe to say, would spark a major illicit trade in these commodities, complete with the equivalent of booze houses (formerly known as speakeasies), burglaries to get money for black-market cigarettes, and perhaps even coffee-dealing drug lords rising to power in South America.

Even the quixotic goal of Neo-Prohibitionism sometimes sounds preferable to the haphazard, hypocritical style of modern drug enforcement. Defenders of the status quo urge us to keep on doing what we are doing, only better: Squeeze the pipelines at their sources, and arrest anyone who possesses any amount of prohibited drugs. Retain the goal of absolute abstinence—alcohol, nicotine, and coffee exempted. Neo-Prohibitionists, in common with advocates of legalization, ask us to reexamine the overall ideology upon which we base our approach to drug wars in the first place. At least Neo-Prohibitionists have the courage to view alcohol and tobacco as the drugs they are.

Harm Reduction

Legalization versus Neo-Prohibition: At times, it sounds like a battle between Timothy Leary and Carrie Nation. Society, culture, the rule of law—all these influences form patterns that are not always logical and consistent, and cannot be made so overnight.

There is a third alternative, typically referred to as decriminalization, a cumbersome word for an attitude toward drugs that falls squarely between zero tolerance and 100 per cent permissiveness. It calls for selective enforcement of the drug laws. Ethan Nadelmann has suggested the term "normalization."

Decriminalization of certain drug offenses is one of the goals of a loosely organized movement called harm reduction. While it neither ignores the dangers of addictive drugs, nor advocates their use, harm reduction is a limited step that calls for making distinctions between major and minor classes of drug crimes. Above all, it is a practical approach. According to the International Harm Reduction Association: "In many countries with zero tolerance drug policies, funding for drug law enforcement is five to six times greater than funding for prevention and treatment." In place of that scenario, harm reduction strategies aim for the creation of non-coercive, community-based recovery programs and resources for drug users. The association defines harm reduction as follows: "Policies and programs which attempt primarily to reduce the adverse health, social, and economic consequences of mood altering substances to individual drug users, their families and their communities."

From a harm reduction point of view, it is shocking to discover that most regions of the United States do not have needle exchange programs or over-the-counter syringe sales. Nationwide, drug treatment programs are underfunded to the point of starvation. At least ten states do not offer any methadone treatment at all. We could start by offering free hygienic needles to heroin users, and legalizing the possession of small amounts of marijuana. The harm avoided in these two cases? Pointless jail time in the latter and the possibility of contracting AIDS from dirty needles in the former.

Harm reduction strategies do not call upon the government to eradicate the drug problem. Nor would they ultimately lead to cocaine and heroin being sold in government-owned versions of mom-and-pop drugstores. The limited step of decriminalization would mean that cigarette manufacturers, as well as the federal government, would still be prohibited from opening a marijuana store on the corner of 4th and Main. Under decriminalization, it would still be possible to maintain harsh penalties for selling or trafficking large amounts of speed or heroin, but it would eschew the sort of approach typified by, say, the Gramm-Gingrich National Drug and Crime Emergency Act of 1990, which would have declared a national state of emergency, with drug prisoners assigned to work farms, and those convicted of selling any amount of marijuana receiving five year prison terms without the possibility of parole.

The key to decriminalization is reducing penalties at the margin, while retaining the overall structure of legal disapproval. This is not an easy task. It calls for judgment and discrimination on the part of law enforcement agencies, judges, juries, lawyers, and everyday citizens. At first glance, decriminalization seems to be saying that we can have our cake and eat it, too. But in fact, we do this sort of thing all the time. It may be tricky, but it isn't impossible.

We have to ask whether it is wise to have major felony laws on the books which large portions of the populace routinely disobey. The same argument could be made, of course, against the existence of speed laws on the nation's highways, since they are so frequently violated. But a closer look at the speed limit analogy suggests that speeding has not been so much prohibited as it has been decriminalized. Highway Patrol officers frequently approach violations in relative and situational terms. They engage in a form of harm reduction on the highways.

The decriminalization of speeding laws is a smart idea. The policy of limits is still backed by the force of law, and flagrant violators are dealt with harshly. No one gets off with a warning ticket

for going 90 miles per hour in a school zone. By reducing or otherwise discouraging a strict letter-of-the-law approach to marginal violations, law enforcement officers are free to concentrate resources
where they are most needed. They recognize that if everyone who
technically exceeded the speed limit were to be arrested and jailed
in a ramped-up "war on speeding," the legal system would soon
grind to a halt. Citizens understand and for the most part accept
that there is a grey area. There is a difference between major and
minor violations of a law. Offenders are often released, even in
cases where the technical violation of the law is not in doubt. Has
the law been flagrantly ignored? Have law enforcement personnel
failed to perform their duties? Most people would probably say no
to these questions. In short, everyone is urged to be sensible about
the matter.

Marijuana offers U.S. policy makers a unique opportunity for
experimenting with harm reduction strategies. One option would
be to continue the legal ban on imported marijuana, while allowing
for small-scale domestic possession. Unlike the market for refined
cocaine and heroin, marijuana's status as a plant drug means that
almost any level of domestic consumption could be accommodated
through personal cultivation. It isn't necessary to import marijuana
in order to meet domestic demand. Pitched battles between D.E.A.
enforcement agents and marijuana growers from California to Kentucky serve as evidence that domestic supply is not only possible,
but already an existing fact.

With marijuana, all we have to do is recognize the situation
as it now exists: Millions of Americans use modest amounts of
marijuana privately in their own homes. For now, we could leave
it at that. No marijuana smoking in public, no use by minors, no
advertising, no large-scale legal sales. The cultivation of a specified
number of marijuana plants on private property, for private consumption, would be officially overlooked. It would still be illegal
to sell a pound of marijuana to anybody. Would this seemingly
modest step produce a nation of marijuana addicts? Back in 1975,
the Alaska State Legislature didn't think so. It reduced the penalty

for marijuana possession to a civil fine of $100. The State Supreme Court extended the law to cover possession of small amounts of marijuana in the home. Ultimately, the Alaska law became the most liberal marijuana law in the nation, making it legal for adults to possess up to four ounces of marijuana for personal use.

State legislators ultimately decided they were under an obligation to "send a message" to the youth of the state, in the form of stiff jail time for simple possession. Alaska, once the state with the most liberal pot laws in the nation, became a state with one of the nation's most stringent policies toward marijuana. There is little or no evidence to suggest that the Alaska experiment went horribly wrong, or that it drastically increased the level of crime and drug abuse in the state as a whole. The epidemic of note in Alaska is, and always has been, alcoholism.

The decriminalization of minor marijuana crimes is a small first step. Consider the case of cigarettes. Most people don't like smoking, and don't care to be around it, even though it is still legal in many public places. Adult smokers are now frequently lectured by their children about the hazards of smoking. The declining use of cigarettes proves that public health campaigns can be effective, even in the absence of beefed-up law enforcement.

The medicalization of addiction itself, and harm reduction strategies sensibly applied to small-scale drug crime, can be seen as the broader goal. At the same time, we need to design strong social disincentives for discouraging the use of heroin and the highly refined, smokable end products of cocaine and amphetamine. There are still distinctions to be made, even if the present ones make very little sense. Furthermore, we should continue to put a legal hold on the possession of PCP and other drugs that can cause direct violence. Such a list would include Lariam, a non-addictive prescription anti-malarial strongly implicated in dozens of episodes of violent behavior, and, inexplicably, still in use by the U.S. Army. There is no reason at all to consider legalizing or decriminalizing drugs like PCP or methamphetamine. It is possible to argue from a sound scientific basis that PCP is a more dangerous drug than marijuana, and in such cases, harm reduction strategies dovetail with the greater aims of the prohibitionists. Such distinctions are possible if we allow for greater discrimination, something that cannot be achieved under the current catchall categories of illegal drugs.

No one can deny that there are significant health drawbacks to the use of marijuana. A serious new discussion of marijuana decriminalization might have the effect of sparking additional research funds for this odd drug out. Some of the same hazards encountered in cigarette smoking apply to marijuana smoking, and the mismatch between the data collected from animal models and the data from human experiments means that the yellow flag is out.

Nevertheless, millions of Americans have used marijuana for several generations now. There is quite clearly a widespread demand for it; a demand which far exceeds, in sheer numbers, the demand for the far more socially disruptive cocaine and amphetamine. But as things stand now, the marijuana trade is inextricably linked with the cocaine and amphetamine trade. By cracking down on marijuana, state and federal governments simply help to expand the market for cocaine and amphetamine as dealers, denied the former, shift to the latter. "I was going to the airport in Hawaii after a conference on drugs," one addiction researcher told me. "A cab driver picked me up, and he started talking spontaneously about the danger and the violence, and how Honolulu had changed. And he attributed it to smokable speed. And then he said, 'you know, when everybody was smoking marijuana, we didn't have these problems. And then the government had operation Green Harvest, or whatever they called it, and got rid of all the marijuana.' This driver thought it was part of a conspiracy to bring in smokable speed, and hook everybody on a more addicting substance."

Jamaica also became submerged in its own version of crack and glass hell. Visitors to Jamaica say crack and speed have replaced marijuana as drugs of choice in parts of the country, causing subsequent social and behavioral disruptions that were not previously in evidence. From the harm reduction point of view, these are matters to consider whenever state and federal governments decide to undertake massive marijuana eradication campaigns.

The harm reduction approach outlined here has its own inherent set of flaws, some of them potentially serious. If the laws were loosened, how many new American citizens would be hooked? How many new addicts would decriminalization or harm reduction strategies produce? Nothing is easy or consistent when it comes to the regulation of mind-altering and addictive drugs. There may be a base rate of addiction, which cannot be drastically exceeded or diminished, no matter what a society chooses to do. A certain number of people will find their way to the drugs, and become addicted to them. These people will very likely include a large number of individuals who are biogenetically predisposed toward addiction. Legalization will not solve their problems for them, and neither will prohibition. There is no law we can pass that will solve their problem. We can create laws that conduce toward personal recovery, and reward efforts at finding better methods of treatment. Or we can continue to make an outlaw caste of addicts, criminalize their condition, hound them, and throw them in jail in record numbers until they come to their senses.

The debate has polarized scholars and policy analysts of every persuasion. The controversial Dutch experiment with harm reduction is often the focal point of such discussions. In 1976, the Dutch made a misdemeanor out of the sale of up to one ounce of cannabis. In the Netherlands, possession of marijuana and heroin is illegal, but there are certain well-defined exceptions, such as the Amsterdam coffee houses, where marijuana and hashish may be freely purchased and consumed. The coffee houses pay taxes on their marijuana sales, just as they do with sales of beer. The price of marijuana and hashish available in the shops is reasonably low, which cuts back on the need to commit crimes in order to pay for it, and lowers the profits available to street dealers. "If we kept chasing grass or hashish, the dealers would go underground, and that would be dangerous," a senior Dutch police officer told *The*

Economist. The Dutch officer insisted that the Dutch do not intend to reverse course, as happened in Alaska. "The Americans offer us big money to fight the war on drugs their way. We do not say that our way is right for them, but we are sure it is right for us. We don't want their help."

Dutch police still possess strong enforcement powers when it comes to hard drugs, but they have been instructed to view the issue as a public health problem. Heroin addicts are tolerated, but steered in the direction of treatment. By some accounts, 75 per cent of Dutch heroin addicts are involved in one treatment program or another. Local officials complain that some of their drug problem can be traced to a flood of young people coming in from other countries where stricter drug laws are in force.

Endless rounds of debate have been devoted to the potential economic and legal consequences of this form of limited legalization. There is little use trotting out the studies and statistics on this topic. The decriminalization of drugs works splendidly in Amsterdam, or doesn't work at all, depending upon the interests of the people making the assessments. The Dutch model is not proof that harm reduction strategies reduce drug use and crime. But here in the U.S., such an approach could hardly make matters worse. Whenever the Dutch experiment comes up, U.S. drug officials tend to brush off the query, maintaining curtly that "it doesn't work." But there is no lack of evidence for supposing that it does.

The Dutch experiment rests on the belief that drug addiction is a medical problem, and that medical problems cannot be solved within the structure of the criminal justice system. The lifetime prevalence of cannabis use in the Netherlands for 10- to 18-year-olds is about 4 per cent, compared with a figure in U.S. High Schools of approximately 30 per cent.

When former president Clinton appointed retired Desert Storm General Barry McCaffrey as his "drug czar" in 1996, McCaffrey brought the ethos of his lifelong profession to the job of directing the Drug Control Policy Office. An example of the approach that so infuriates the Dutch was provided by Barry McCaffrey on the eve of his official fact-finding visit to the Netherlands. After misstating Dutch and American murder rates, McCaffrey concluded, "The overall crime rate in Holland is probably 40 per cent higher than the United States," a difference he blamed on drugs. In conclusion, he branded Dutch harm reduction "an unmitigated disaster." None of this was true (the American murder rate was at least four times the Dutch murder rate at the time of McCaffrey's statements), but it was typical of American reaction to Dutch drug policy.

I have lived and worked in Amsterdam on two recent occasions. Guns and hard drugs are not tolerated. The cannabis coffee shops cause no social harm or disruption in the neighborhoods where they are located. Reports of violence or trouble of any kind are rare, and usually involve minors. The establishments are for ages 18 and up, and purchases are limited to less than five grams per day. The primary behavioral dysregulation on display in the coffee shops themselves seems to short-term memory loss. Patrons leave personal objects—coats, hats, umbrellas, money, papers, and other personal articles—only to return sheepishly a few minutes later in search of the lost and found. In recent years, the Dutch have been quietly experimenting with so-called "smart shops," which purvey herbs, incense, and small quantities of psychedelic mushrooms.

In truth, it makes little difference whether Republicans or Democrats control the White House and Congress—drug policy always comes out looking more or less the same. Interdiction and arrest always take precedence over treatment. Education, another budgetary watchword, usually means large and costly anti-drug media campaigns—a favorite of drug czars ever since the "this is your brain on drugs" commercials. (Ronald Siegel has noted that in medieval Muslim society, "One sage placed a quantity of hashish on a piece of liver and let it stay there for a while. Soon the liver was full of holes like a sponge. This was a silly experiment but an impressive demonstration that would stick in the minds of the masses...")

The U.S. might also consider a controlled return to certain aspects of the British experiment with the medicalization of heroin addiction. Recall that British physicians used to involve themselves in the clinical maintenance of opiate and barbiturate addiction, in order to lessen crime and lay the groundwork for possible recovery. (Some of Norman Zinberg's pioneering work on heroin addiction was done in Great Britain.) We could decide to decriminalize heroin. An interesting case can be made for its blanket legalization. Like cigarettes today, but even more so, there is a high level of awareness about its dangers, and there is a history of educating the populace about its public health implications, including the hazards of contracting AIDS and other communicable diseases through contaminated needles. It does not seem outlandish to suppose that a large segment of the adult U.S. population, exposed to heroin on demand, would not be remotely inclined to give it a try. The base level of heroin addiction in the population may already have been achieved, and would grow only marginally under legalization. The idea that Mom, Dad, Bud, and Sis would all be lined up at the local drugstore, itching to buy a few packets of newly-legalized heroin, seems counterintuitive, to say the least.

Alan Dershowitz, the Harvard law professor, has even called for the free distribution of heroin by mobile emergency vans to anyone who is a medically certified heroin addict. Beyond the initial reaction of disgust conjured up by the picture of a government or a society actively aiding heroin addiction, such a scheme might drastically reduce drug-related crimes in neighborhoods heavily populated by heroin addicts. Would neighbors living next door to heroin addicts feel more secure under the present policy, or under the Dershowitz scheme? A medical program of this type would definitely save lives. People overdose on heroin primarily because they don't always know what they're getting. Drug quality and potency both vary too much for the present situation to be considered safe. Obviously, saving lives qualifies as harm reduction.

Only a small fraction of America is biologically and environmentally at high risk for heroin addiction. And there is no reason to suppose that every practicing alcoholic or nicotine addict in America would suddenly substitute heroin as their drug of choice—although some of them might. The heroin addiction problem can be contained and managed as a public health problem, not a legal one. Some people would go through a period of experimentation, possibly even abuse, before moderating or stopping altogether. Even fewer would likely become long-term heroin addicts because of this new availability.

Critics often take harm reduction advocates to task for avoiding the specifics, the details of how it would all play out. But this feature of decriminalization is one of its greatest strengths. Will there be packets of cocaine, heroin, and marijuana on the shelves of every pharmacy in America? Perhaps so. But is it not at least as likely that harm reduction would not evolve that way at all? By limiting what can happen at the outset, harm reduction proponents say that these questions concerning the ultimate outcome do not have to be answered in advance—which is impossible, anyway.

The black market economics that support violent drug lords and drug dealers worldwide can be reduced through harm reduction approaches. We cannot do full justice to those issues here, but the fact that they are being seriously raised helps nudge the discussion toward the public health arena, and away from law enforcement.

By any system of measurement, cigarettes kill more people, and alcohol disrupts more lives, than any other drugs we use. Regardless of the drug in question, advocates of harm reduction are not seeking to change human nature, but to exercise a measure of control over the consequences of drug abuse. If we teach our children to hate and fear all drugs, and to pursue a nonexistent state called "chemical-free," then what message are we sending them about drugs and addiction? We can readily observe that our national suspicion of drugs runs headlong into our desire for a quick fix in pill form, and our guilty avoidance of the social mayhem and private abuse caused by alcohol. If ever there existed a culture exhibiting a perfect love/hate relationship with drugs, it must be our own.

In an important sense, everything an individual addict needs to know in order to recover is available—if not always perfectly available. We do not know everything, but in important ways, we know enough.

As we have seen in the cases of depression, schizophrenia, and addiction, evidence for a strong genetic influence is not the same thing as the discovery of a specific gene or genes responsible for that influence. In the same way, the existence of drugs to combat some forms of craving does not mean that the magic pill is just around the corner. The cure for addiction awaits greater understanding of reward pathways, as we discover more effective ways to disrupt the drug-seeking behavior that motivates addicts.

An Example of Harm Reduction

After a successful pilot program in Boston, the Massachusetts Department of Public Health embarked on the state-sponsored distribution of heroin overdose kits in 2007. Noting that heroin overdoses kill more people in Massachusetts each year than fire-arms, Dr. Peter Moyer, medical director of Boston's fire, police and emergency services, applauded the state's decision to offer addicts an overdose reversal kit. The package contains two nasal doses of naloxone, known as Narcan, a drug that reverses heroin overdose and saves uncounted lives (many victims of heroin overdose never see a hospital) when administered quickly enough. "It's a remark-ably safe drug," said Dr. Moyer. "I've used gallons of it in my life to treat patients."

Approved by the Food and Drug Administration (FDA) 35 years ago, Naloxone, or Narcan, is the standard emergency room treatment for heroin overdose. Naloxone instantly reverses life-threatening overdoses by crowding out heroin molecules at the brain receptor sites where they bind.

Since the first trial run in Chicago several years ago, efforts to provide heroin addicts with naloxone overdose kits has gained ground in Baltimore, New York, Boston, and several other cities and states. Predictably, the Office of National Drug Control Policy in the White House does not support the Massachusetts program. Drug Policy officials do not like the idea of addicts medically treating other addicts and have argued repeatedly against distribution of the naloxone kits, claiming that distributing the Narcan antidote will only encourage heroin use and delay treatment. But the move among states and cities for direct naloxone distribution to addicts continues to gain momentum. At the New York State Health Department, which oversees 20 naloxone distribution programs in New York City, Dan O'Connell told the *New York Times* that from a public health perspective, heroin overdose kits were "a no-brainer." O'Connell, director of the department's H.I.V. prevention division, said: "For someone who is experiencing an overdose, naloxone can be the difference between life and death."

Wisconsin, Minnesota, Connecticut, New Mexico, Rhode Island, and several other states are also embarking on naloxone distribution programs. Thousands of lives are likely to be saved if the idea continues to gain ground.

According to figures reported by the Harm Reduction Coalition, 3,691 California drug users died of overdose in 2003, the latest year of official records. This represents an increase of 42 per cent since 1998, resulting in an annual death rate greater than that from firearms, homicides, and A.I.D.S

But so far, states are on their own, as Federal drug policy officials continue to maintain that naloxone should only be prescribed and administered by doctors. And yet, many doctors refuse to treat heroin addicts, on the grounds that there is nothing that can be done for them, or that they are recalcitrant patients.

A Global Harm Reduction Challenge

The World Health Organization (WHO) estimates that 100 million smokers died of tobacco-related causes in the 20th century, making cigarettes the leading preventable cause of death worldwide.

The agency estimates that as many as a billion people will die from tobacco in the 21st century, if present trends continue. "The shift of the tobacco epidemic to the developing world will lead to unprecedented levels of disease and early death in countries where population growth and the potential for increased tobacco use are highest and where health care services are least available," the report concluded. The eradication of tobacco use will be as difficult as fighting insect-born diseases, WHO officials say. The WHO analysis strongly asserts that "partial bans on tobacco advertising, promotion and sponsorship do not work."

In a forward to the report, noting that 5.4 million people a year die from lung cancer and tobacco-related heart diseases, WHO Director-General Margaret Chan wrote that the world has reached "a unique point in public health history as the forces of political will, policies and funding are aligned to create the momentum needed to dramatically reduce tobacco use and save millions of lives by the middle of the century."

What are cigarette makers doing to combat these grim revelations? Focusing on promising Third World markets, and moving offshore to escape lawsuits.

The new medicines will make an immeasurable difference. Millions of addicts in America want effective treatment, and cannot get it. Funds for research and treatment are still scarce, compared to money for interdiction and law enforcement. What would happen if we took the billions spent on interdiction and let it flow into addiction research and treatment? What if money specifically earmarked for the enforcement pillar of the drug war were freed up for other social programs, such as pre- and post-natal care, Head Start programs, and the like? What would happen if we gave people truthful, accurate information about drugs, and trusted them to make intelligent decisions more often than stupid ones? Can it end up any worse that the present state of affairs?

Susan Sontag's warnings about the danger of disease as metaphor still ring true. In modern American society, heart disease, cancer, AIDS, alcoholism, and cigarette addiction account for millions of deaths. They are all disease entities with strong psychological and behavioral components—complicated, multicellular, multi-organ disorders. But they have all been associated, at one time or another, with negative personality traits and moral flaws. The less we know about the mechanics of a human disorder, the more likely we are to view its external symptoms as signs of laziness, or neuralgia of the spirit, or as a form of damage caused by specific kinds of thoughts and emotions. Without a doubt, all kinds of flaws are sometimes expressed in the behavior of people who have these disorders. Yet none of these flaws can be considered the root cause of the diseases.

Addiction is being added to the roster of physical disorders once thought to be symptoms of insanity, but which are now seen to be physiological disease entities with mental components. It is long overdue. As Professor Felton J. Earls of the Harvard School of Public Health argued almost twenty years ago: "Until we have an Institute of Addictive Behaviors, we are not going to get very far on the public-policy issues because we will not have our science-policy issues properly aggregated and organized in order to move forward on the issues in any meaningful way."

The genuine drug war is being fought in the arena of biomedicine. The New York State Division of Substance Abuse Services in Albany has estimated that the annual bill for successfully treating a single drug addict is $3,850, compared with $14,000 in estimated annual expenses— health, welfare and law enforcement costs—associated with one untreated addict. The real crisis is the indisputable fact that there exists today an appalling shortage of funds for biomedical research—ironically one of the fields of scientific endeavor in which the U.S. holds a clear lead. The cause of the dilemma is a fundamental misunderstanding among politicians and the public about how diseases can be understood and conquered. Cross-fertilization among scientific disciplines yields unexpected results. Targeted research, such as the much-ballyhooed war on cancer, or the crash program to find a cure for A.I.D.S., is not necessarily the most desirable way to proceed. Insights come from unexpected places, in serendipitous ways. As the scientific understanding of cells and receptors deepens, diseases and disorders once thought to have unrelated causes are seen to have common and entirely unanticipated origins. Research into the viral mechanisms of the common cold may ultimately yield more insights into AIDS then all of the directed research now underway. In biomedicine, there is no guarantee that goals can be reached through the front door, by a systematic assault akin to an engineering project. We cannot, for example, hope to cure addiction, or even the common cold, by means of the same methods we used to put a man on the moon.

There are, however, certain things we can begin to do immediately, if, as a nation, we are serious about drug abuse. As a society, Americans have not done a very good job of laying the groundwork for an objective look at addiction and recovery. There is an abundance of underbrush that needs to be cut away. To begin with, we can attend to the staggering number of drug-related deaths, injuries, and hospitalizations caused by the abuse of prescription medications. The government itself has proven the case for this contention in numerous reports issued by the National Institute on Drug Abuse and other official bodies. According to the U.S. Department of Health and Human Services, "Older Americans account for more than half of all deaths from drug reactions," leading one to suspect that the majority of drug fatalities stem from accidentally fatal overdoses by heavily medicated senior citizens. Our national fixation on illegal drugs has blinded us to certain verifiable facts about prescription drug abuse.

We also need to recognize the problem of underprescribing morphine and other addictive painkillers for children and adults in hospital settings. If we continue to stringently prohibit the use and sale of synthetic and designer drugs like methadone, morphine, amphetamines, and barbiturates, we will have to make one important exception: pain abatement in medical applications. One of the great scandals to come out of the drug war is the growing understanding that potent painkillers are not being offered in sufficient amounts to patients suffering intractable and agonizing pain.

"There's a certain amount of hysteria about narcotics among doctors," maintains one researcher.

At least half of all cancer patients seen in routine practice report inadequate pain relief, according to the American College of Physicians. For cancer patients in pain, adequate relief is quite literally a flip of the coin.

A September 10 *New York Times* report highlights studies by the World Health Organization which amply document the ongoing scandal in pain management. At least 6 million cancer and AIDS patients currently receive no appropriate pain treatment of any kind. In addition, WHO estimates that four out of five patients dying of cancer are also suffering severe pain. The numbers of untreated patients suffering intractable, unrelieved pain from nerve damage, burns, gunshots, sickle cell anemia, and a host of other medical conditions can only be guessed at.

Figures gathered by a different U.N. agency, the International Narcotics Control Board, make clear that "citizens of rich nations suffer less." To put it starkly, the use of morphine per person in the United States is 17,000 times higher than per person usage in Sierra Leone. Doctors in Africa paint a grim picture of patients hanging themselves or throwing themselves in front of trucks as an alternative to life without pain relief. The U.S., Canada, Britain, France, Germany, and Australia together account for roughly 80 per cent of the world's medicinal morphine use. Other countries, particularly the poor and undeveloped nations, scramble for what's left.

The ironies fly thick and fast: Studies show that 70 per cent of patients present with painful conditions. Typically, non-addicted patients take morphine therapeutically for pain at doses in the 5 to 10 mg. range. But experienced morphine addicts regularly take several hundred milligrams a day—a huge difference. In many cases, pain relief is the one thing doctors can offer their patients, and the one thing they withhold

This outcome, rather than flashy cocaine seizures at the border, represents the lasting fruits of the drug war. Another correctible result of the war without end is that doctors are not always free to prescribe marijuana or THC in instances where it is medically indicated, such as glaucoma and the nausea associated with intensive chemotherapy.

We can also put tobacco advertising on the same regulated footing as hard liquor. By treating cigarette addiction as a public health matter, and not strictly as a criminal issue, American society has already proven that drug use and addiction can be modestly influenced downward, without the need for broad criminal sanctions. Further restrictions on advertising are not likely to have a dramatic effect on demand either way, but the money saved from advertising budgets could be banked by the tobacco industry against a growing number of product liability suits. If the industry will drop its huge public disinformation campaign, the expenditures can be redirected toward the corporate scramble to diversify, now that tobacco markets are becoming smaller and more competitive.

Addicts are the possessors of a biochemical disorder for which, at present, there is no reliable lifetime cure. Hard-core addicts must "treat it for life," as the commercials say about high blood pressure. Drugs are everywhere, and yet drugs are not precisely the problem. The problem is the wide scope of reactions that they produce in people. The reason the reaction varies so much is that people are different from one other. Nervous systems vary. Metabolic chauvinism will get us into trouble, just like chauvinism of any other kind.

Combination therapies will be the norm in the future, consisting of pharmaceutical intervention in the form of anti-craving drugs; behavioral intervention in the form of attention to cues and cravings; and group psychological intervention in the form of talk therapies, A.A., or other structured self-help groups. The specific mix of these three components will depend upon the addict, the typology of his addiction, and the diagnostic skills of the practitioners involved. Combination treatments, and greater skill at separating out the subcategories of addiction, will mean that particular addicts can be matched to a particular mix of treatment modalities in order to boost the success rate of recovery efforts. At present, it sometimes seems as if the only grounds for optimism about recovery rates is that there is so much room for improvement.

One of the nearly universal constants in human behavior is the urge to alter consciousness. It can be done in any number of ways. The experience of altered consciousness may be only another name for, or another way of looking at, the human drive for spiritual transcendence. Mind-altering drugs represent both the aspiration toward higher religious experience, and the physical and emotional enslavement produced by addiction.

The high and the low.

"That was extremely empowering, Terry," a man says to a bartender in a *New Yorker* cartoon. "I believe I'll have another."

Addicts, and those who love them, are beginning to discover that the biochemical models of addiction are profoundly empowering notions all their own. They stand against denial, and lead in the direction of treatment and recovery.

No other approach holds out such promise.

Notes

Introduction

Burroughs quote — Burroughs, William. *The Soft Machine.* (appendix). New York: Grove Press, 1961, rev. 1966. p.130.

3 "came across a study" — Hingson, Ralph, et. al. "Age at Drinking Onset and Alcohol Dependence." *Archives of Pediatrics and Adolescent Medicine.* July 2006.

8 "as if you had cancer" — author interview, Janice Keller Phelps.

8 "a sign of my general bankruptcy" — Sontag, Susan, *Illness as Metaphor.* New York: Farrar, Straus and Giroux, 1978. p.44.

8 "incarcerating them for extended periods" — In Miller, William, and Kathleen, Carroll, Eds. *Rethinking Substance Abuse: What the Science Shows, and What We Should Do About It.* New York: The Guilford Press, 2006. p.263.

11 "Addiction is a disease entity" — Seymour, Richard B., and Smith, David E. *Drug Free.* New York: Facts On File Publications, 1987. p.19.

11 "a thousand funerals a day" — C. Everett Koop interviewed on "Sonya Live," CNN, November 15, 1989.

12 "twenty times as many people as 'hard drugs'" — Hingson, Ralph, et. al. "Age at Drinking Onset and Alcohol Dependence." *Archives of Pediatrics and Adolescent Medicine.* July 2006 160. p.7.

13 "The exciting implication.... not a bad speculaton" — author interview, Steven Paul.

Chapter I

Sontag quote — Sontag, Susan. *Illness as Metaphor.* p.55.

all quotes by T.K. Li in this chapter from author interviews.

22 "after the Robins study" — Robins, Lee N. "Lessons from the Vietnam Heroin Experience." *Harvard Mental Health Letter.* December, 1994.

25 "risk of long-term addiction" — Bower, Bruce. "Drugs of Choice." *Science News.* December 16, 1989 136. p.392.

25 "social setting in which the drug was used" — Zinberg, Norman, and Jacobson, R. "The Natural History of 'Chipping,'" *American Journal of Psychiatry.* 1976 133. p.37.

26 "genetically different from addicted smokers" — Shiffman, Saul. "Tobacco 'chippers'—individual differences in tobacco dependence." *Psychopharmacology.* 1989 97. p.539.

29 "probably because of genes" — Goodwin, Donald W. *Is Alcoholism Hereditary?* New York: Ballantine Books, 2nd Ed. 1988. p.168.

29 Jellinek material from Jellinek, E.M. *The Disease Concept of Alcoholism.* New Haven, CT: Hillhouse Press, 1960.

29 "death by liver failure" — Roizen, Ron. "E.M. Jellinek and All That!" *H. Thomas Austern Lecture.* San Francisco, October 20, 2000. http://www.roizen.com/ron/jellinek-pres.htm.

30 "excessive appetite for alcohol" — Williams, Roger J. *Alcoholism: The Nutritional Approach.* Austin: University of Texas Press, 1959. p.106.

30 "the craving that dope addicts possess" — Williams, p.16.

33 "distinctly *pharmacological* is going on here" — "Liquor-loving mice." *Science.* September 6, 1966 273. p.1341.

Chapter 2

Lincoln quote — Goodwin, Donald W. *Is Alcoholism Hereditary?* 2nd Edition. New York: Ballantine, 1988. p.27.

35 "seed pods of the poppy plant" — Bower, Bruce. "Deceptive Appearances." *Science News.* July 15, 1995 148. p.40.

37 "ruined morally and otherwise" — Brecher, Edward M., and Editors of Consumer Reports. *Licit and Illicit Drugs.* Boston, Toronto: Little, Brown and Co., 1972. p.42.

37 "twelve hundred pounds of opium" — Brecher, p.4.

37 "in the early 1900s" — Ornstein, Robert, and Thompson, Richard. *The Amazing Brain.* Boston: Houghton Mifflin, 1984. p.85.

38 " have taken to rum" — Brecher, p.85.

39 "all over the world" — Mann, John. *Murder, Magic and Medicine.* Oxford: Oxford University Press, 1992. pp.62-64.

39 "Jimson weed" — Mann, p.29.

40 "as far as 1715 B.C." — "New light on ancient smokers." *Science News.* April 11, 1998 153. p.238.

41 "hardly be restrained therefrom" — Brecher, p.210.

41 "Russia, Prussia, and Turkey" — Schama, Simon. *Embarrassment of Riches.* New York: Vintage Books, 1997. pp.194, 213.

41 "relinquished the practice voluntarily" — Brecher, pp.211-227.

42 "sustain morale" — Siegel, Ronald K. *Intoxication: Life in Pursuit of Artificial Paradise.* New York: E.P. Dutton, 1989. p.256.

44 "moral evil" — Levine, Harry G. "The Discovery of Addiction: Changing Conceptions of Habitual Drunkeness in America." *Journal of Studies on Alcohol.* 1979 15. p.493.

44 "its patron saint" — Levine, p.493.

45 "with drug addicts" — Brecher, p.50.

46 "rather than lessen it" — Brecher, p.45.

46 "smoking in public" — Siegel, Ronald K., pp.271-272.

47 "drunk or violent" — Brecher, p.57.

47 "informer for the FBI" — Brecher, p.58.

47 "Bill of Rights" — Brecher, p. 59.

47 "but the jazz type" — *Harry J Anslinger.* http://www.cannabis. net/prohib/.

48 "quickening the imagination" — Schleiffer, Hedwig. *Narcotic Plants of the Old World.* Monticello. New York: Lubrecht & Cramer, 1979. pp.68-70.

48 "during abdominal surgery" — Schleiffer, p.85.

49 "addicted to amphetamine" — Gorman, Michael. "Speed Use and HIV Transmission." *UCSF Aids Health Project*, 1996.

49 "a powerful and addictive barbiturate" — Post, Jerrold M. "Drunk with Power." *Washington Post National Weekly Edition*, February 5, 1990. p.39.

50 "more or less homosexual way" — William C., ed., *Problems in Addiction: Alcoholism and Narcotics.* New York: Fordham University Press, 1962. p.68.

51 "wholly psychogenic disorder" — William, p. 68.

54 "not recognized as an illness" — adapted from an obituary by Gerrit DenHartog published in the *"A"Team*, Missouri Division of Alcohol and Drug Abuse, 1996.

54 "one afternoon in 1943" — Steven, Jay. *Storming Heaven: LSD and the American Dream.* New York: Harper and Row, 1987. p.81.

55 "from the world of religion" — Stanislav Grof prologue in Stolaroff, Myron J. *The Secret Chief.* Charlotte, NC: Multidisciplinary Association for Psychedelic Studies. 1997. pp.11-12.

58 "traditional psychoanalytic techniques" — Lee, Martin, and Shlain, Bruce. *Acid Dreams.* New York: Grove Press, 1985. Ch.2.

58 "effects may be " — Wilson, Bill. *"Pass It On": The Story of Bill Wilson and How the A.A. Message Reached the World.* New York: Alcoholics Anonymous World Services, Inc., 1984. pp.374-375.

60 "for more than twenty years" — Lee, Ch.1. See also: http://www.frankolsonproject.org/Statements/FamilyStatement1975.html.

62 "LSD, DMT, and psilocybin" — Hewitt, Kim. "A Biochemical Bridge to the Embodied Psyche: LSD Research 1945-1965." *Bulletin of the Multidisciplinary Association For Psychedelic Studies.* Spring 1999. pp.30-34.

62 "and, possibly, hallucinations" — Schleiffer, p.49.

64 "a complete disaster" — Farr, Bill, and McGraw, Carol. "Drug Enforcers Losing Nation's Cocaine War; Massive Government Eradication Efforts are 'Overwhelmed by the Bad Guys,' Official Says." *Los Angeles Times.* September 21, 1986.

64 "comfortable TV viewers' neighborhood" — Diamond, Edwin, et. al. "Is TV News Hyping America's Cocaine Problem?" *TV Guide.* February 7, 1987. p.7.

65 "no lasting successes to report" — Kramer, Michael. "Clinton's Drug Policy Is a Bust." *Time.* December 20, 1993.

66 "across time and species" — Siegel, pp.209-210.

69 "new science 'receptorology'" — Pert, Candace B. *Molecules of Emotion: Why You Feel the Way You Feel.* New York: Scribner, 1997. p.28.

Chapter 3

Jon Franklin quote — Franklin, Jon. *Molecules of the Mind.* New York: Dell, 1987. pp.144-145.

75 "hospitalization for alcoholism" — Goodwin, p.105.

75 "imitate their [non-biological] parents" — Cloninger, C. R. "Neurogenetic adaptive mechanisms in alcoholism." *Science.* April 24, 1987 236. p.412.

76 "smooth and wrinkled peas" — Powledge, Tabitha. "The Inheritance of Behavior in Twins." *BioScience.* June 1993 43. p.362.

77 "neighborhood, and so on" — Kendler, Kenneth, et.al. "A twin-family study of alcoholism in women." *American Journal of Psychiatry.* May, 1994 151. pp.707-715.

77 "than male alcoholics do" — Bower, Bruce. "Alcoholism: Nurture may often outdo nature." *Science News.* February 1, 1992. p.69.

77 "30 per cent for male writers" — "Madness and Creativity Revisited." *Science.* December 2, 1994 266. p.1483.

78 "sensitivity to nicotine" — author interview, Neal Benowitz.

78 "differences in susceptibility" — author interview, Ovide Pomerleau.

78 "of the substances abused" — Cadoret, Remi J., et al. "An Adoption Study of Genetic and Environmental Factors in Drug Abuse." *Archives of General Psychiatry.* December, 1986 43. p.1131.

79 "not so well recognized" — Phelps, Janice Keller, and Nourse, Alan E. *The Hidden Addiction.* Boston: Little, Brown and Company, 1986. p.29

79 "useful in anticipating risk" — author interview, Edward Sellers.

82 "Cravings had a biological basis" — Seymour and Smith, p.129.

83 "Ernest Noble speculated" — Bower, Bruce. "Gene in the Bottle." *Science News*. September 21, 1991. p.19.

83 "than non-gamblers" — Comings, D.E., et.al. "A study of the dopamine D2 receptor gene in pathological gambling." *Pharmacogenetics*. June, 1996. pp.223-224.

84 "Begleiter told *Science* magazine" — Holden, Constance. "A Cautionary Genetic Tale: The Sobering Story of D2." *Science*. June 17, 1994 264 p.1696.

85 "one researcher said bluntly" — Holden, Constance. "Alcoholism Gene: Coming or Going?" *Science*. October 11, 1991 254. p.200.

85 "in the kids of alcoholics" — author interview, Henri Begleiter.

85 "tobacco in later years" — Berman, S. M., et al. "P300 in boys as a predictor of adolescent substance use." *Alcohol*. 1993 10. pp.69-76.

86 "predisposition to many diseases" — author interview, Henri Begleiter.

87 "glutamate and acetylcholine receptors" — "COGA Suggests Genetic Loci for P3 Brain Wave Abnormality." NIAAA Press Office. National Institute on Alcohol Abuse and Alcoholism. May 20, 1998.

88 "experience a normal life.... manifestation of the disease" — author interview, Henri Begleiter.

93 "the primary culprit." — Bower, Bruce."Schizophrenia gene: A family link fades." *Science News*. June 10, 1989. p.359.

93 "diseases are 'complex illnesses'" — Andreasen, Nancy C. *Brave New Brain: Conquering Mental Illness in the Era of the Genome.* New York: Oxford University Press, 2001. p.113.

93 "not just a brain disease" — Leshner, Alan. "Addiction Is a Brain Disease, and It Matters." *Science.* October 3, 1997 278. p.46.

93 "the lifetime of the cell" — Saey, Tina Hesman. "Ch-ch-ch-changes." *Science News.* July 19, 2008 174. p.14.

94 "rewarding responses to cocaine" — Kumar, A, et. al. "Chromatin remodeling is a key mechanism underlying cocaine-induced plasticity in striatum." *Neuron.* Oct 20, 2005 48. p.303.

Chapter 4

William James quote — James, William. *The Principles of Psychology.* Ch. 28. http://psychclassics.yorku.ca/James/Principles/prin28.htm

96 "other information substances" — Pert, p.139.

99 "and.... sexual reproduction" — Ornstein, p.28.

100 "displaces adaptive behaviors" — Nesse Randolph M., and Berridge, Kent C. "Psychoactive Drug Use in Evolutionary Perspective." *Science.* October 3, 1997 278. p.63.

101 "survival of the organism" — Bozarth, M.A. "New perspectives on cocaine addiction: Recent findings from animal research." *Canadian Journal of Physiology & Pharmacology.* 1989 67. pp.1158-1167.

102 "spiraling distress" — Koob, Georg F., and Moalo, Michel Le. "Drug Abuse: Hedonic Homeostatic Dysregulation." *Science.* October 3, 1997 278. p.55.

104 "poisons change things" — author interview, James Halikas.

106 "most notably denial" — Goodwin, p.144.

106 "those who use another" — Tsuang, Ming.T et al. "Co-occurrence of Abuse of Different Drugs in Men." *Archives of General Psychiatry.* 1998 55. p.967.

106 "same in every case" — author interview, Janice Keller Phelps.

107 "tend to be alcoholics" — Lambert, Craig. "Deep Cravings." *Harvard Magazine.* March-April, 2000. p.60.

108 "reward—the jackpot" — Shizgal, Peter, and Arvanitogiannis, Andreas. "Gambling on Dopamine." *Science.* March 21, 2003 299. p.1856.

108 "interest in gambling before" — "Parkinson's drugs 'fuel gambling urge.'" BBC News Online. August 11, 2003. http://news.bbc.co.uk/.

110 "prolonged drug use.... infection or a broken bone" — Leshner, p.46.

112 "an insufficient explanation.... core paradox in addiction" — Nesse, pp.64-65.

113 "it's what happens after" — author interview, James Halikas.

114 "reward pathways of the brain" — Gazzaniga, Michael S. *Nature's Mind.* New York: Basic Books, 1992. p.157.

PART II
Chapter 5

David Lenson quote — Lenson, David L. *On Drugs.* Minneapolis, MN: University Of Minnesota Press, 1995. p.71.

117 "the entire body hurts" — author interview, Steven Paul.

119 "what neurotransmitters may be involved" — author interview, Steven Paul.

119 "armamentarium of addictive pharmaceuticals" — "Alcohol Facts." Addiction Science Research and Education Center, College of Pharmacy, University of Texas at Austin. March 20, 2000. http://www.utexas.edu/research/asrec/

119 "enhanced reward effect in the rats" — author interview, T.K. Li.

120 "naturally selected it" — author interview, Steven Paul.

120 "high in GABA" — author interview, T.K. Li.

121 "have therapeutic implications" — author interview, Steven Paul.

122 "it isn't heart disease" — Talan, Jamie. "The Search for Genetic Keys to Alcoholism." *Los Angeles Times.* October 21, 2001.

122 "greater than that found in men" — Wuethrich, Bernice. "Does Alcohol Damage Female Brains More?" *Science.* March 16, 2001 291. p.2077.

123 "alcohol-related violence" — Vaillant, George, *The Natural History of Alcoholism Revisited.* Cambridge: Harvard University Press, 1983, 1995. p.124.

123 "drug-by-drug basis" — National Center on Addiction and Substance Abuse at Columbia University. *Women under the Influence.* Baltimore: The Johns Hopkins University Press, 2006. pp.5-7.

124 "alcohol by that age.... alcohol abuse than men" — National Center at Columbia, pp.45-47.

124 "a history of alcohol abuse." — National Center at Columbia, p.51.

125 "lower levels of alcohol intake.... ads until 1958" — National Center at Columbia, pp.46, 61.

125 "recorded thalidomide births" — National Center at Columbia, pp.116-118.

126 "both disease and behavior disorder" — Vaillant, p.206.

127 "2 percent die every year" — Vaillant, p.15.

127 "when hospitalized" — Lambert, p.60.

127 "drugs other than alcohol" — Vaillant, p.201.

127 "compared to other drinkers" — Vaillant, p.169.

127 "three times as likely to be depressed" — Vaillant, p.210.

128 "the efficacy of specific treatment" — Vaillant, p.187.

130 "between diagnosis and name-calling" — Vaillant, p.21.

130 "fraternal twins have different levels" — Gold, Mark S., *The Good news about Depression*. Toronto, New York: Bantam Books, 1986. p.208-209.

130 "shortly after withdrawal from alcohol" — Bower, B. "Early Alcoholism: Crime, Depression Higher." *Science News*. March 25, 1989 135. p.180.

131 "reduced levels of platelet MAO" — Tabakoff, B., et. al., "Differences in platelet enzyme activity between alcoholics and nonalcoholics." *New England Journal of Medicine*. January 2, 1988 318. p.134.

131 "It goes like this" — Ewing, J.A. "Detecting Alcoholism: The CAGE Questionnaire." *Journal of the American Medical Association*. 1984 252. pp.1905-1907.

134 "constipation in opiate addicts" — Bewley, T.H., et. al. "Maintenance Treatment of Narcotic Addicts." *The International Journal of the Addictions*. 1972 7. p.597.

134 "Centers for Disease Control" — Cato Institute Policy Analysis, May 25, 1989, # 121.

135 "as good as morphine" — Snyder, Solomon H. *Drugs and the Brain*. New York: Scientific American Library, 1996. p.59.

135 "compulsive drug self-administration" — Swan, Norman. "Myths About Heroin Addiction." Radio National, Australia. October 15, 2001.

136 "if you have it within you" — Heinz, A., et al. "Serotonergic dysfunction, negative mood states, and response to alcohol." *Alcoholism: Clinical and Experimental Research*. 2001 25. p.487.

Chapter 6

Luis Buñuel quote — *My Last Sigh: The Autobiography of Luis Buñuel*.

137 "same thing cocaine or amphetamine is doing" — author interview, Neal Benowitz.

138 "the skeletal muscles" — Snyder, p.22.

138 "in a gasoline factory" — author interview, Ovide Pomerleau.

139 "for smokers to smoke more" — Dubey, Anita. "Alcohol acts on nicotine receptor, scientists find." *Addiction Research Foundation Journal*. January/February, 1997.

139 "more addictive than any other drug" — author interview, James Halikas.

140 "under control conditions" — Vaillant, p.78.

140 "totally different reasons" — author interview, Henri Begleiter.

141 "taking a shot of heroin" — Lenson, p.161.

141 "the method or the motivation" — Glassman, A.H., et. al. "Heavy smokers, smoking cessation, and clonidine: Results of a

double-blind, randomized trial." *Journal of the American Medical Association.* May 20, 1988 259. p.2863.

142 "definitely complicates their lives" — author interview, Ovide Pomerleau.

142 "risks than non-smokers do" — *Science News.* January 16, 1999. p.47.

142 "painful menstrual cramps" — Raloff, Janet. "Smoking out a source of painful menses." *Science News.* October 21, 2000. p.269.

143 "add up to relapse" — "In the mood for a smoke." *Science News.* August 27, 1994. p.143.

143 "by a factor of ten" — "Federal Survey counts female smokers." *Science News.* November 9, 1991. p.140 .

143 "Catching up to the Marlboro Man" — National Center at Columbia. *Women under the Influence.* p.23.

144 "compared to non-smoking women.... supermodels have demonstrated" — National Center at Columbia. pp.18-29.

144 "worldwide disease prevention" — Patel. J.D., et. al. "Lung cancer in U.S. women: A contemporary epidemic." *Journal of the American Medical Association.* April 14, 2004 291. p.1767.

144 "a convincing link" — Glassman, Alexander, et.al. "Smoking, smoking cessation, and major depression." *Journal of the American Medical Association.* September 26, 1990 264 p.1541.

144 "severely depressed smokers" — "Depression puffs up lung cancer." *Science News.* January 4, 1997. p.15.

145 "characteristic of Parkinson's disease" — "Smoking may offer one health benefit." *Science News.* July 2, 1994. p.15.

145 "according to Dr. Glassman" — Gordon, Laura. "Smoker's Addiction Not Caused by Nicotine Alone." *Medical Tribune News Service.* February 21, 1996 16.

146 "symptoms in the test rats" — "Source of withdrawal pangs found in brain." *Science News.* September 10, 1994. p.166.

147 "snow storms and rainstorms" — Nowak, Rachel. "Key Study Unveiled—11 Years Late." *Science.* April 8, 1994 264. p.197.

147 "animal model years earlier" — Nowak, p.196.

148 "with the usual skepticism" — Seppa, N. "Exploring a genetic link to smoking." *Science News.* March 7, 1998 153.

148 "to treat effectively" — Majewska, M.D. "Cocaine addiction as a neurological disorder." National Institute on Drug Abuse monograph. Rockville, MD, 1996.

149 "tried unsuccessfully to quit" — Schelling, Thomas C. "Addictive Drugs: The Cigarette Experience." *Science.* January 24, 1992 255. p.430.

149 "quitting requires determination" — Schelling, p.432.

150 "for all the usual reasons." — Nagourney, Eric. "Smokers' Ethnicity May Make Difference." *New York Times.* January 29, 2002.

150 "genetic archaeology" — Seppa, N. "Nicotine metabolism shows ethnic bias." *Science News.* January 19, 2002 161. p.38.

151 "drank no coffee at all" — Kawachi, I., et. al. "A prospective study of coffee drinking and suicide in women." *Archives of Internal Medicine.* March 11, 1996 156. p.521.

152 "withdrawal is often depression" — Bashin, Bryan Jan. "The Jolt in Java." *San Francisco Chronicle.* February 28, 1988.

153 "advised not to drink it" — Gladwell, Malcolm. "Java Man." *The New Yorker.* July 30, 2001. p.76.

153 "60 countries around the world" — "Caffeine and conservation." *Science.* April 25, 2003 300. p.587.

154 "as other stimulants" — Nehlig, A. "Are we dependent upon coffee and caffeine? A reivew of human and animal data." *Neuroscience and Biobehavioral Review.* Mar 23, 1999 4. p.563.

155 "with that nicotine patch" — Holden, Constance. "Caffeine Link in Parkinson's Bolstered." *Science.* May 18, 2001 292. p.1295.

Chapter 7

Jonathon Ott quote — Ott, Jonathan. *Pharmacotheon: Entheogenic drugs, their plant sources and history.* Natural Products Company, 1993.

156 "either amphetamine or cocaine" — author interview, Robert Post.

158 "heightened perception of pain" — Dubey, Anita. "Cocaine Cravings Linked to Body's Opiate System." *Addiction Research Foundation Journal.* January/ February, 1997. p.7.

158 "heroin plus cocaine" — Zernig, G. "Nicotine and Heroin Augment Cocaine-induced Dopamine Overflow in Nucleus Accumbens." *European Journal of Pharmacology.* October 15, 1997. p1.

158 "not quite clear how that works" — author interview, T.K. Li.

159 "much milder concentrations.... depressed, moody, and so on." — author interview, James Halikas.

160 "during actual episodes of craving" — Netting, J. "Memory may draw addicts back to cocaine." *Science News.* May 12, 2000 159. p.292. See also Nestler, Eric J. "Total Recall—the Memory of Addiction." *Science.* June 22, 2001 292. p.2266.

161 "Chinese herb, ma huang.... when preparing for examinations" — Snyder, p.131.

162 "the war against Iraq" — Groopman, Jerome. "Medical Dispatch: Eyes Wide Open." *The New Yorker.* December 3, 2001. p.52.

163 "the actual time that they're using it" — author interview, Edward Sellers.

164 "other places where *abusers* surface" — Siegel, p.305.

164 "inextinguishably fat and happy" —Wickelgren, Ingrid. "Getting the Brain's Attention." *Science.* October 3, 1997 278. p.35.

164 "origin after firing" — Bower, Bruce. "Drugs, depression and molecular ferries." *Science News.* October 26, 1991. p.261.

Chapter 8

Campbell quote — Campbell, J.M. "On the Religion of Hemp." Indian Hemp Drugs Commission, 1893."within the range of perception" — Lenson, p.72.

169 "been conserved in evolution" — author interview, Miles Herkenham.

169 "the pain of a difficult delivery" — Mestel, Rosie. "Cannabis: the brain's other supplier." *New Scientist.* July 31, 1993 1884. pp.21-23.

169 "a high-brow receptor" — author interview, Miles Herkenham.

169 "this ancient psychoactive substance" — Pennisi, Elizabeth. "Immune cells sport marijuana receptor." *Science News.* September 11, 1993. p.165.

169 "if it just made us stupid" — "UCSF researchers move in on role of brain's naturally occurring marijuana." Press release, University of California, San Francisco. March 29, 2001.

170 "like the alcohol-Valium system.... the parts affected by chronic stress" — author interview, Miles Herkenham.

172 "similar doors in the brain" — Mestel, Rosie. "Cannabis: the brain's other supplier." *New Scientist.* July 31, 1993. p.21.

172 "neurons containing GABA and glutamate" — "UCSF researchers move in on role of brain's naturally occurring marijuana." Press release, University of California, San Francisco, March 29, 2001.

172 "calmer porcine state of mind" — McFraling, Usha Lee. "Natural Form of Marijuana in Humans a Medical Mystery." *The Chicago Tribune.* December 18, 1998.

173 "discovered in dark chocolate" — Piomelli, D, et al. "Brain Cannabinoids in Chocolate." *Nature.* July 11, 1996 382. pp.677-678.

173 "third leading killer in the United States" — Brainard, J. "Marijuana chemical tapped to fight strokes." *Science News.* July 11, 1998. p.20.

174 "before embryo implantation" — Yang, Z.M., et.al. "Activation of brain-type cannabinoid receptors interferes with preimplantation mouse embryo development." *Biology of Reproduction.* 1996 55. p.756.

174 "cortical function in infants" — Strobel, Gabrielle. "Young brain sports marijuana receptors." *Science News.* November 27, 1993. p.367.

174 "unpleasant neuromuscular side effects" — Ungerleider, J.T., et.al. "Cannabis and Cancer Chemotherapy: A Comparision of Oral Delta-9-THC and Prochlorperazine." *Cancer.* August 15, 1982 50. pp.636-645.

174 "brains of Huntington's sufferers" — Fackelmann, Kathy. "Marijuana and the Brain." *Science News.* February 6, 1993 143. pp.88+

176 *"National Academy of Sciences"* — McDonagh, S. "Switching Off Pain." *Science News.* August 16, 2003 164. pp.99-100.

177 "the motor aspects of it" — author interview, Miles Herkenham.

178 "It's a complicated molecule" — author interview, James Halikas.

179 "along the limbic reward pathway" — Ameri, A. "The Effects of Cannabinoids on the Brain." *Progressive Neurobiology*. July, 1999 58. pp.315-348.

179 "dependence on illicit drugs" — Hall, Wayne, et.al. "The Health and Psychological Consequences of Cannabis Use." Monograph Series No. 25. Prepared for the National Task Force on Cannabis Australia, 1999.

181 "seek substances like heroin" — Wickelgren, Ingrid. "Marijuana: Harder Than Thought?" *Science*. June 27, 1997 276. p.1967.

181 "alcohol to the list" — *Science*, letters. August 8, 1997 277. p.749.

Chapter 9

Tuchy Palmieri quote: Palmieri, Tuchy. *The Food Contrarian: Quotes For People Recovering From or Dealing with Eating Issues*. BookSurge Publishing, 2007. p.11.

182 "self-administration of a psychopharmacologic agent" — Hooper, Judith. "All In the Mind." *Whole Mind Newsletter*. November, 1988. p.2.

182 "serves as a precursor for dopamine" — Zeisel, S.H. "Dietary influences on neurotransmission." *Advances in Pediatrics*. 1986, 33. pp.23-47.

183 "Florida College of Medicine" — Knowlton, Leslie. — "Gold Forecasts and Describes Cocaine Vaccine, Smoking Addiction Research." *Psychiatric Times*. July, 1997. p.14.

185 "the abuser's health and appearance" — Wurtman, Richard, and Wurtman, Judith. "Carbohydrates and Depression." *Scientific American*. January, 1989 260. p.68.

185 "binge on sugar foods" — Wurtman, J.J., et. al. "Effect of nutrient intake on premenstrual depression." *American Journal of Obstetrics and Gynecology*. November, 1989 161. p.1228.

186 "a factor in addiction to food." — Hernandez, L., and Hoebel, B.G. "Food reward and cocaine increase extracellular dopamine in the nucleus accumbens as measured by microdialysis." *Life Sciences*. 1988 42. p.1705.

188 "genetic predispositions toward bulimia" — "Serotonin and Bulimia." *Science*. July 13, 2001 293. p.205.

188 "it sure looks like a binge" — Bashin, p.8.

189 "as painful as withdrawing from it." — Phelps, p.75.

190 "preference they had previously shown" — Nesmith, Jeff. "Brain Chemical Linked to Smoking, Weight." *San Francisco Chronicle*. June 29, 1988. p.10.

190 "Universidade do Porto in Portugal" — Andrews, Zane B., and Horvath, Tamas L. "Tasteless Food Reward." *Neuron*. March 27, 2008 57. p.806.

191 "told *Science News*" — Maxman, Amy. "Calorie kick: Desire for sweets not only a matter of taste. *Science News*. March 29, 2008 173. p.13.

191 "to thank for that.... reward signal in the brain" — Callaway, Ewen. "'Diet' foods may not fool the brain." NewScientist.com News Service. March 2008. p.17

191 "vulnerable to compulsive eating" — "Yale Hosts Historic Conference on Food and Addiction." Yale University Office of Public Affairs. July 9, 2007. http://www.yale.edu/opa/newsr/07-07-09-01.all.html

191 "so why look at biology" — Hathaway, William. "Can Food Hook You? Experts Chew Over Eating As Addiction." *Hartford Courant*. July 11, 2007.

192 "same reward system in the brain" — Hathaway, July 11, 2007.

192 "picked up from alcoholic parents" — Rovner, S. "Dramatic overlap of addiction, mental illness." *Washington Post Health*. November, 1990. pp.14-15.

192 "common feature of drug addiction and withdrawal" — Bower, Bruce. "Drug Abuse tied to 'fatal despondency.'" *Science News*. May 27, 1989 135. p.332.

192 "a depression they didn't even know they had" — Phelps, p.24.

Part III
Chapter 10

Lewis Thomas quote — Thomas, Lewis. *The Medusa and the Snail*. New York: Viking Press, 1979. From Goodwin, p.165.

196 "naturally in our bodies" — Mihaly Csikszentmihalyi. *The Evolving Self*. New York: HarperCollins, 1993. p.35.

196 "you pay for it later" — Moyers, Bill. "Moyers on Addiction: Close to Home." Public Broadcasting System (PBS). March 29, 1998.

198 "pharmacotherapies for the future" — Kreek, Mary Jeanne, et. al. "Pharmacotherapy of Addictions." *Nature Reviews*. September 2000 1. p.710.

199 "lost productivity, wages, etc" — Kreek, p.710.

200 "and relapse is frequent" — Duenwald, Mary. "A Fresh Look at a Quick Fix for Heroin Addiction." *New York Times*. December 4, 2001.

200 "seriously ill after a drink or two" — Jha, Dr. Shashi Kant, and Mortensen, Ole. E. Editorial. *CNS Forum*. http://www.cnsforum. com/

201 "Mitigate its intensity, at least" — Bronson, Gail. "The Doors of Perception: Psychiatric Drug Development and New Knowledge About Brain, Spinal Cord." *Forbes*. December 14, 1987. p.222.

201 "Pennsylvania VA Medical Center.... resistance to this change" — O'Brien, Charles P. "A Range of Research-Based Pharmaco-therapies for Addiction." *Science*. October 3, 1997 278. pp.66-70.

202 "principle methadone researchers at Rockefeller" — Kreek, Mary Jeanne, et. al. "Pharmacotherapy of Addictions." *Nature Reviews Drug Discovery*. 2002 1. p.710.

202 "through negative-reinforcement mechanisms" — Kreek, p.710.

203 "normal stress responsivity" —"Brain scans confirm hunch about methadone's effect." *Rockefeller University News and Notes*, December 15, 2000 12. p.12. www.rockefeller.edu/pubinfo/news_notes/121500e.html

205 "National Heart Institute in Bethesda, MD." — Carlsson, Arvid. "A Paradigm Shift in Brain Research." *Science*. November 2, 2001 294. pp.1021+

207 "monoamine hypothesis of mental illness" — Nemeroff, Charles. "Depression." *Scientific American*. September 5, 1998. p.42. See also Bozarth, M.A. "Drug addiction as a psychobiological process." From Warburton, D.M. (ed.). *Addiction Controversies*. London: Harwood Academic Publishers, 1990.

208 "under different circumstances and conditions" — author interview, Ovide Pomerleau.

208 "a Nobel Prize of his own" — "The Julius Axelrod Papers." *Profiles in Science.* Bethesda, MD.: National Library of Medicine. 2007. http://profiles.nlm.nih.gov/HH/Views/Exhibit/narrative/neurotransmitters.html.

208 "a parking space would be nice" — Andreasson, p.242.

209 "their mechanism of action. — Gazzaniga, Michael S. *Nature's Mind.* New York: Basic Books, 1992. p.145.

210 "potentially lethal side effects" — Carlsson, p.1022.

211 "and developed Prozac" — Carlsson, p.1023.

212 "began in the 1950s and continues today" — Snyder, Solomon H. *Drugs and the Brain.* New York: Scientific American Books, 1996. p.3.

214 "days the drinkers were completely abstinent" — Naranjo, Claudio, et. al. "Zimelidine-induced variations in alcohol intake by nondepressed heavy drinkers." *Clinical Pharmacology and Therapeutics.* March, 1984 35. pp.374-381.

214 "weight loss in most of the test subjects" — Naranjo, Claudio, et. al. "The Serotonin Uptake Inhibitor Citalopram Attenuates Ethanol Intake." *Clinical Pharmacology and Therapeutics.* March, 1987 41. pp.266-274.

214 "uncertainty about the striking results" — Liskow, Barry, and Goodwin, Donald. "Pharmacological Treatment of Alcohol Intoxication, Withdrawal and Dependence: A Critical Review." *Journal of Studies on Alcohol.* 1987 48. p.356.

214 "behavior of the P-line rats" — Li, T.K., et. al. "Alcoholism: Is it a model for the study of disorders of mood and consummatory behavior?" *Annals of the New York Academy of Sciences.* 1987 499. p.239.

215 "intake of carbohydrates in animal studies" — Kim, S.H, and Wurtman, R.J. "Selective effects of CGS 10686B, dl-fenfluramine

or fluoxetine on nutrient selection." *Physiology and Behavior.* 1988 42. p.319.

215 "rise 28 per cent this year" — "Who Has The Next Wonder Drug?" *Fortune.* September 28, 1987. p.8.

216 "applications start to manifest themselves.... justify the investment" — author interview, Edward Sellers.

217 "only through private entrepreneurship" — Paul, Steven. "Why I'm Leaving Government for a Drug Firm." *Wall Street Journal.* March 9, 1993.

218 "Serotonin sets tone" — Kramer, Peter D. *Listening to Prozac.* New York: Penguin Books, 1993. p.134.

219 "should have attended to long ago" — Kramer, p.182.

219 "in their ordinary social pursuits" — Kramer, p.265.

220 "lifelong problems with drug abuse" — Longo, Lance P. and Bohn, Michael J. "Alcoholism Pharmacotherapy: New Approaches to an Old Disease." *Hospital Physician.* June, 2001. p.33.

221 "serotonin in the central nervous system" — Galla, John P. and Donnini, Joyce L. "Serotoin Reuptake Inhibitors and the Treatment of Bulimia Nervosa-A Comprehensive Review." *Proceedings of the April 6, 1995 Conferences of the National Social Science Association.*

222 "other twin was diagnosed with the disorder" — Jones, Lee. "Reducing Symptoms in Bulimia Nervosa and Binge Eating Disorder Through Drug Treatment." Vanderbilt University Psychology Department, Health Psychology Home Page. www.vanderbilt.edu.

223 "secondary effect on dopamine release" — Lemberger, Louis, et. al. "Effect of fluoxetineon psychomotor performance, physiologic response, and kinetics of ethanol." *Clinical Pharmacology & Therapeutics.* June, 1985 37. pp.658-664.

224 "essential components of physiological functioning" — author interview, Robert Post.

225 "usually much sooner" — Kreek, p.710.

225 "psychotropic hedonism" — Kramer, p.370.

Chapter 11

Goodwin quote — Goodwin, p.195.

226 "and hit the craving" — author interview, T.K. Li.

228 "after the discontinuation of the injections" — Restak, Richard. *The Mind.* Toronto, New York: Bantam Books, 1988. p.125.

229 "how important it really is.... the desire to use goes up" — author interview, Edward Sellers.

230 "that stimulates craving" — author interview, James Halikas.

231 "both natural and chemical rewards" — Childress, Anna Rose, and O'Brien, Charles P. "Dopamine receptor partial agonists could address the duality of cocaine craving." *Trends in Pharmacological Sciences.* January, 2000 21. p.8.

231 "when enough is enough" — Mihaly, p.4.

232 "glutamate-modulating antianxiety drugs" — Holden, Constance. "Excited by Glutamate." *Science.* June 20, 2003 300. pp.1866-1868.

232 "down the road to relapse" — "Progress Made in Understanding Neurobiological Basis for Relapse to Cocaine Abuse." *NIDA Addiction Research News.* May 21, 2001. http://www.drugabuse.gov/MedAdv/01/NS-6.html. See also: Holden, Constance. "Zapping Memory Center Triggers Drug Craving." *Science.* May 11, 2001 292. p.1039.

233 "because they induce psychosis" — Holden, "Excited by Glutamate." p.1867.

234 "either LAAM or high-dose methadone" — Johnson, Rolley E., et.al. "A Comparison of Levomethadyl Acetate, Buprenorphine, and Methadone for Opioid Dependence." *New England Journal of Medicine.* November 2, 2000 343. pp.1290-1297.

234 "allows a more normal lifestyle" — "High Succes Rates For Variety of Heroin Addiction Treatment Medications." NIDA news release. Bethesda, MD: National Institute of Drug Abuse. November 1, 2000.

235 "using the drug for several years" — Fox, Maggie. "Addiction Treatment to Be Available At Doc's Office." *Reuters.* October 9, 2002.

235 "can see myself getting off everything" — Perez-Pena, Richard. "New Drug Promises Shift in Treatment for Heroin Addicts." *New York Times.* August 11, 2003.

235 "mainstream medical practice" — Thomas, Josephine. "Buprenorphine Proves Effective, Expands Options for Treatment of Heroin Addiction." *NIDA Notes.* May, 2001 16 p.2.

236 "activity along norepinephrine pathways" — Gold, Mark, and Pottash, Carter. "The Neurobiological Implications of Clonidine HCL." *Annals of the New York Academy of Sciences.* 1981 362. p.191.

237 "clonidine shuts off norepinephrine firing" — author interview, Robert Post.

238 "writes Charles O'Brien" — O'Brien, p.66.

238 "when opiate receptors are blocked" — Vaillant, pp. 370-371.

239 "during the course of the study" — "Opioid Antagonists and Alcoholism Treatment." *CNS Spectrums.* 2000 5. p.49.

239 "told *Psychiatric Times*" — Knowlton, Leslie. "Gold Forecasts and Describes Cocaine Vaccine, Smoking." *Psychiatric Times.* July, 1997 14 p.7.

240 "original indication, heroin addiction" — Sales brochure for Revia from Dupont, cited in O'Brien, p.66.

241 "legally exercise those rights" — Rosack, Jim. "Once-Promising Alcoholism Drug Runs Into FDA Roadblock." *Psychiatric News.* September 5, 2002 37. p.24.

241 "abstinence days in alcoholic subjects" — O'Brien, p.66.

242 "helps them get through all that" — Morrow, David J. "Merck unit ponders selling anti-alcohol drug in U.S." *New York Times.* July 31, 1998.

242 "later published in *Lancet*" — Johnson, B.A., et.al. "Oral topiramate for treatment of alcohol dependence: a randomised controlled trial." *Lancet.* May 17, 2003 361. p.1677.

243 "medications that act on multiple sites" — "Topiramate: a potential new medication for treating alcoholism." University of Texas Press Release. The University of Texas Health Science Center at San Antonio. August 15, 2004.

243 "compared to a placebo group" — Johnson, B.A."Topiramate for Treating Alcohol Dependence: A Randomized Controlled Trial." *Journal of the American Medical Association.* October 10, 2007 298. p.1641.

243 "its use in migraines" — Willenbring, Mark. "Medications to Treat Alcohol Dependence." *Journal of the American Medical Association.* October 10, 2007 298. p.1691.

243 low level of drinking or zero drinking" — Ostrow, Nicole. "Johnson & Johnson's Seizure Drug May Fight Alcoholism." *Bloomberg News.* October 9, 2007. http://www.bloomberg.com.

244 "unapproved use of Topamax (topiramate) for treating alcoholics" — Wolfe, Sidney. "Letter to the FDA urging action against a campaign promoting the unapproved use of Topamax for treating alcoholics." (HRG Publication #1825) October 9, 2007.

http://www.citizen.org/publications/release.cfm?ID=7546&secI D=1666&catID=126.

244 "most drug companies are not interested in it" — "Drug to curb smoking also cuts alcohol dependence." University of California, San Francisco. UCSF News Office. July 9, 2007. http://pub.ucsf. edu/newsservices/releases/200707063/

245 "in a study of 25 detoxified alcoholic inpatients" —George, David T. "Neurokinin I Receptor Antagonism as a Possible Therapy for Alcoholism." *Science.* March 14, 2008 319. p.1536

245 "eliminated opiate use in animal studies" — Ripleya, Tamzin L., et. al. "Lack of self-administration and behavioural sensitisation to morphine, but not cocaine, in mice lacking NKI receptors." *Neuropharmacology.* December 2002 43. p.1258.

245 "in humans, at least one earlier study" — Furmarka, Tomas, et. al. "Cerebral Blood Flow Changes After Treatment of Social Phobia with the Neurokinin-I Antagonist GR205171, Citalopram, or Placebo." *Biological Psychiatry.* July 15, 2005 58. p.132.

246 "more nicotine-dependent" — author interview, Ovide Pomerleau.

246 "some slight, early weight loss" — "Study Shows Antidepressant May Fight Obesity." *Associated Press.* July 17, 2002.

246 "delivering the drug to pharmacy shelves" — Preskorn, Sheldon H. "Bupropion: What Mechanism of Action?" *Journal of Practical Psychiatry and Behavioral Health.* January, 2000. p.272.

247 "subsequently approved for use" — Castleman, Michael. "Wonderful Wellbutrin?" *Salon.* September 26, 2000. http://archive.salon.com/sex/feature/2000/09/26/wellbutrin/

247 "compared with smokers in control groups" — Jorenby, Douglas E., et. al. "A Controlled Trial of Sustained-Release Bupropion, a Nicotine Patch, or Both for Smoking Cessation." *New England Journal of Medicine.* March 4, 1999 340. p.610.

248 "Glassman of Columbia University" — Noble, Holcomb B. "New Therapy Helping Smokers Quit." *New York Times.* March 2, 1999.

248 "Chantix outperformed both placebos and Zyban" — Tonstad, Serena. "Effect of Maintenance Therapy With Varenicline on Smoking Cessation: A Randomized Controlled Trial." *Journal of the American Medical Association.* July 5, 2006 296. pp.64-71. See also: Gonzales, David, et.al. "Varenicline, an alpha4beta2 Nicotinic Acetylcholine Receptor Partial Agonist, vs Sustained-Release Bupropion and Placebo for Smoking Cessation." *Journal of the American Medical Association.* July 5, 2006 296. pp.47-55.

248 "roughly a year later" — "Varencline (marketed as Chantix) Information." *FDA Alert.* U.S. Food and Drug Administration. February 1, 2008. http://www.fda.gov/cder/drug/infopage/varenicline/default.htm

249 "strongly appearing to be related" — Johnson, Avery. "Pfizer Heightens Chantix Warning." *Wall Street Journal.* January 18, 2008.

249 "summed up by the *San Francisco Chronicle*" — Tansey, Bernadette. "Doctors warned about epilepsy drugs' risks." *San Francisco Chronicle.* February 1, 2008

250 "recent studies published in *Nature*" — Chanock, Stephen J., and Hunter, David J. "Genomics: When the smoke clears ..." *Nature.* April 3, 2008 452. pp.537-538.

250 "kind of a double whammy gene" — Callaway, Ewen. "Double-whammy gene keeps smokers hooked." *New Scientist.* April 2, 2008. p.10.

250 clearly biologically based." — Borenstein, Seth. "Genetic link tied to smoking addiction." *Associated Press.* April 3, 2008.

251 "to prevent cocaine relapse" — Childress, Anna Rose and O'Brien, Charles P. "Dopamine receptor partial agonists could address the duality of cocaine craving." *Trends in Pharmacological Sciences.* January, 2000 21. p.6.

252 "a similar product for cocaine addiction" — "Nicotine Vaccine Shows Promise For Combating Tobacco Addiction." NIDA News Release. National Institute on Drug Abuse. December 17, 1999. http://www.nida.nih.gov/MedAdv/99/NR-1217.html

254 "brain damage from the drug" — author interview, James Halikas.

255 "kindling theory for alcohol withdrawal.... anti-craving potential of carbamazepine" — author interview, Robert Post.

255 "how well carbamazepine will ultimately pan out" — Lima, A.R., et. al. "Carbamazepine for Cocaine Dependence." *Cochrane Review*. February 5, 2004.

256 "nucleus accumbens seems to be the common factor" — Assadi, Seyed Mohammad, et. al. "Baclofen for maintenance treatment of opioid dependence: A randomised double-blind placebo-controlled clinical trail." *BMC Psychiatry*. 2003 3. p.16.

256 "not to hot, not to cold--just right" — For more, see Childress, Anna Rose. "What Can Human Brain Imaging Tell Us About Vulnerability to Addiction and to Relapse?" In Miller, p.53.

256 "gender research coordinator" — Williams, Jill Schlabig. "Animal Studies Show Sex Differences in Impact of Efforts To Reduce Drug Seeking." *NIDA Notes*. March, 2003 17. p.6.

257 "first few months of treatment." — Gawin, Frank H. "Cocaine Addiction: Psychology and Neurophysiology." *Science*. March 29, 1991 251. p.1580.

258 "promising candidates for further study" — Kampman, Kyle M. "The Search for Medications to Treat Stimulant Dependence." *NIDA Addiction Science and Clinical Practice*. National Institute of Drug Abuse. June, 2008 4. p.28.

258 "a secondary effect on dopamine" — Shankar, R.P. et.al. "Effect of the 5-HT3 Receptor Antagonist Ondansetron on

Amphetamine-Induced Hyperactivity and Stereotypy in Rats." *Indian Journal of Physiology and Pharmacology*. July, 2000 44. pp.355.

260 "14 years of daily pot smoking" — "Chronic Marijuana Users Become Aggressive During Withdrawal." NIH News Release. National Institute on Drug Abuse. April 20, 1999.

260 " a history of cannabis withdrawal symptoms" — Schuckit, M.A., et.al. "Clinical implications for four drugs of the DSM-IV distinction between substance dependence with and without a physiological component." *American Journal of Psychiatry*. 1999 156. p.41.

260 "college age and mid-50s" — Somers, T. "Study aims to clear haze surrounding pot addiction." *San Diego Union-Tribune*. March 14, 2008.

260 "shakes that give them away" — Lichtman, A.H. and Martin, B.R. "Marijuana Withdrawal Syndrome in the Animal Model." *Journal of Clinical Pharmacology*. 2002 42. p.20s.

261 "sweating and shakiness occurred less consistently" — Budney, Alan J., et. al. "Review of the Validity and Significance of Cannabis Withdrawal Syndrome." *American Journal of Psychiatry*. November, 2004 161. p.1967.

261 "and decreased appetite" — Khalsa, Jag. H. et. al. "Clincial Consequences of Marijuana." *Journal of Clinical Pharmacology*. 2002 42. p.7S.

261 "warrants detailed description in the DSM-V and ICD-11" — Vandrey, R.G., et.al. "A within-subject comparison of withdrawal symptoms during abstinence from cannabis, tobacco, and both substances." *Drug and Alcohol Dependence*. January 1, 2008 92. p.48.

261 "six joints per day" — Haney, Margaret."Nefazodone decreases anxiety during marijuana withdrawal in humans." *Psychopharmacology*. January, 2003 165. p.157.

262 "as reported in the *Journal of Clinical Psychiatry*" — Pallanti, S., et. al. "Nefazodone treatment of Pathological Gambling: a Prospective Open-Label Controlled Trial." *Journal of Clinical Psychiatry.* November, 2002 63. p.1034.

262 "in preliminary animal studies" Cui, S.S., et.al. — "Prevention of cannabinoid withdrawal syndrome by lithium: involvement of oxytocinergic neuronal activation." *Journal of Neuroscience.* December 15, 2001 21. p.9867.

262 "marijuana withdrawal in human trials" — Haney, Margaret."Marijuana Withdrawal in Humans: Effects of Oral THC or Divalproex." *Neuropsychopharmacology.* 2004 29. p.158.

262 "in people prone to marijuana dependence" — Tanda, G., et. al. "Cannabinoid and Heroin Activation of Mesolimbic Dopamine Transmission by a Common μ1 Opioid Receptor Mechanism." *Science.* June 27, 1997 276. p.2049.

263 "useful for dependent pot smokers" — Copeland, J., et. al. "Clinical profile of participants in a brief intervention program for cannabis use disorder." *Journal of Substance Abuse Treatment.* January, 2001 20. p.45.

263 "remission from use of any substance" — Aharonovich, E., et. al. "Postdischarge Cannabis Use and Its Relationship to Cocaine, Alcohol, and Heroin Use: A Prospective Study." *American Journal of Psychiatry.* 2005 162. p.1507.

263 "additional studies of this issue are warranted"—Aharonovich, p.1512.

264 "scientific information to advise this decision" — Somers, T., "Study aims to clear haze surrounding pot addiction." *San Diego Union-Tribune.* March 14, 2008.

265 "by Paul De Rienzo and Dana Beal" — De Rienzo, Paul, and Beal, Dana. *The Ibogaine Story: Report on the State Island Project.* New York: Autonomedia, 1997.

266 "a mistake to confuse the two issues" — Blakeslee, Sandra. "Scientists Test Hallucinogens for Mental Illness." *The New York Times.* March 13, 2001.

266 "various strains of alcohol-preferring rats" — Rezvani, A.H., et al. "Attenuation of alcohol intake by ibogaine in three strains of alcohol-preferring rats." *Pharmacology Biochemistry and Behavio*r. November, 1995 52. p.615A.

266 "the journal *Brain Research* in 1994" — Glick SD, et.al. "Effects of iboga alkaloids on morphine and cocaine self-administration in rats: Relationship to tremorgenic effects and to effects on dopamine release in nucleus accumbens and striatum." *Brain Research.* 1994 657. p.14.

267 "a principal investigator of the study" — He, Dao-Yao. "Glial Cell Line-Derived Neurotrophic Factor Mediates the Desirable Actions of the Anti-Addiction Drug Ibogaine against Alcohol Consumption." *Journal of Neuroscience.* January 19, 2005 25. p.619.

267 "for its anti-addiction properties" — Vastag, Brian. "Addiction Alleviator? Hallucinogen's popularity grows." *Science News.* January 5th, 2008 173. p. 6.

268 "a tough nut" — Vastag, p.6.

270 "the typical raver's dose" — Gasser, Peter. "Psycholytic Therapy with MDMA and LSD in Switzerland." *Newsletter of the Multidisciplinary Association for Psychedelic Studies.* Winter 1994-1995 5. p.3.

270 "10 million Americans have taken Ecstasy" — McNeil, Donald G., Jr. "Research on Ecstasy is Clouded by Errors." *New York Times.* December 2, 2003.

270 "everything under the sun is neurotoxic" — McNeil, *New York Times*, December 2, 2003.

271 "less powerful than is typically the case" — Bonson, K.R., et. al. "Chronic administration of serotonergic antidepressants

attentuates the subjective effects of LSD in humans." *Neuropsycho-pharmacology.* June, 1996 14. p.425.

271 "to potentiate the LSD or MDMA experience" — "Psyche-delics and Psychiatric Drugs: NIMH Update." *Newsletter of the Mul-tidisciplinary Association for Psychedelic Studies.* Summer 1994 5. p.1.

271 "DMT: The Spirit Molecule" — Strassman, Rick. *DMT: The Spirit Molecule.* Rochester, VT: Park Street Press, 2000.

272 "tailor treatment for particular problems" — author interview, Ovide Pomerleau.

272 "AA, and all the rest of it" — author interview, James Halikas.

272 "a neuroscience newsletter" — May, Thomas S. "New Vistas in Addiction Treatment: Easier Access, Greater Choice of Medica-tions." *BrainWork.* November-December 2003 13. p.6.

273 "the type of drug and the type of treatment" — O'Brien, p.66.

Chapter 12

Blane quote from Huth, Edward J., and Murrary, T. Jock. *Medicine in Quotations: Views of Health and Disease Through the Ages, Second Edition.* American College of Physicians. January 27, 2006. p.226.

276 "will be even better" — Kalb, Claudia, "Can this Pill Stop You from Hitting the Bottle?" *Newsweek.* February 12, 2001.

276 "biomedical research and development funding" — Cook-Deegan, Robert, et. al. "World Survey of Funding for Genomics Research." *Final Report to the Global Forum for Health Research and the World Health Organization.* September 2000.

http://www.stanford.edu/class/siw198q/websites/genomics/finalrpt.htm

277 "ferrying artificial cargos into the brain" — "Breaking Down Barriers." *Science*. August 16, 2002 297. p1116.

278 "if you were obese, it was your fault" — Chow, Christina. "New Study Supports Use of Embattled Obesity Drug Redux." *The Tech*. April 14, 1998 118. p.1.

279 "monkeys on dexfenfluramine" — "Serotonin and Eating Disorders." *Medical Sciences Bulletin*. October, 1994. http://pharminfo.com.

279 "full FDA approval in 1996" — "Redux story sheds light on drug development process." *MIT Tech Talk*. February 5, 1997.

281 "as does MDMA" — Doblin, Rick. "MDMA Neuorotoxicity: New Data, New Risk Analysis." *Newsletter of the Multidisciplinary Association for Psychedelic Studies*. Autumn 1995 6. p.1.

281 "to Eli Lilly for several million dollars" — "Interneuron Receives Milestone Payment From Lilly." Press release. Interneuron Pharmaceuticals, Inc. January 6, 1999.

282 "discontinuation of the serotonin-boosting drugs in question" — Roan, Shari. "Dangerous Combinations: Doctors are Seeing the Consequences of Misuse of Antidepressants." *Los Angeles Times*. January 14, 1997.

283 "psuedoephedrine, ephedrine, and others" — Savinelli, Alfred, and Halpern, John. "MAOI Contraindications." *Newsletter of the Multidisciplinary Association for Psychedelic Studies*. Autumn 1995 6 p.1.

284 "getting a whopping dose" — Vogel, Gretchen, "How the Body's 'Garbage Disposal' May Inactivate Drugs." *Science*. January 5, 2001 291.

284 "get the dosage right the first time" — Zuger, Abigail. "Caution: That Dose May Be Too High." *New York Times.* September 17, 2002.

286 "of this withdrawal syndrome." — Zajecka, J., et al. "Discontinuation symptoms after treatment with serotonin reuptake inhibitors: a literature review." *Journal of Clinical Psychiatry.* 1997 58. p.291.

287 "in Listening to Prozac" — Kramer, p.133.

288 "wrote in 2001" — Longo, Lance P., and Bohn, Michael J. "Alcoholism Pharmacotherapy: New Approaches to an Old Disease." *Hospital Physician.* June, 2001. p.33.

291 "side effects of revved-up heart activity" — Mann, p.191.

291 "and women who had not" — Potvin, W. and Evans, M.F. "Outcome of Pregnancy Following Mothers' Use of New SSRIs." *Canadian Family Physician.* June, 1999 45. p.477.

293 "depressed patients who are at risk for suicide" — Molcho, A., and Stanley, M. "Antidepressants and suicide risk: issues of chemical and behavioral toxicity [review]." *Journal of Clinical Psychopharmacology.* 1992 12(2Suppl). p.13S.

295 "heightened sexual effect with Zyban" — Castleman, Michael. "Wonderful Wellbutrin?" *Salon.* September 26, 2000. www.salon.com.

297 "at a South Carolina clinic" — Conant, Eve. "A Possible New Role for A Banned Club Drug." *Newsweek.* May 2, 2005.

Chapter 13

Idries Shah — Shah, Idries. *The Dermis Probe.* London: Jonathan Cape, 1970. p.72.

304 "stems from unchecked appetites" — Mihalyi, p.45.

306 "the liver can speed the process up" — Pert, pp.299-300.

306 "proteins and raw vegetables" — Finn, Kathleen, "Nutrition Builds Path To Recovery From Addictions." http://asktomnaturally.com/articles/addictions.html

307 "any accepted form of medical treatment" — author interview, Janice Keller Phelps.

308 "for continued recovery, Blum said" — Blum, Kenneth, "Improvement of inpatient treatment of the alcoholic as a function of neurotransmitter restoration: a pilot study." *International Journal of the Addictions*. 1988 23. p.991.

308 "patent rights to NeuroGenesis, Inc." — Blum, p.998.

309 "drug hunger during early recovery" — Seymour, p.153.

312 "there is no recovery" — Seymour, pp.112-113.

314 "essay in Parabola magazine" — all Sandor quotes from Sandor, Richard S. "A Physician's Journey." *Parabola*. Summer, 1988. p.16+. Reprinted by permission.

318 "an essential element for recovery" — Ludwig, p.83.

318 "helpful to those who are afflicted" — *Pass It On...The Story of Bill Wilson*. New York: Alcoholics Anonymous World Services, Inc. 1984. pp. 204-206.

319 "dividend check from their A.A. investments" — author unknown.

320 "too damn seriously" — *Twelve Steps and Twelve Traditions*. Hazelden, 2002. p.149.

320 "love and service" — *Dr. Bob and the Good Oldtimers*. New York: Alcoholics Anonymous World Services, Inc. 1980. p.77.

320 "emotional displacements and rearrangements" — *Alcoholics Anonymous*, p.27.

320 "physical and mental liabilities" — *Twelve Steps and Twelve Traditions*, pp.42-43.

320 "against that first drink" — *Alcoholics Anonymous, Third Edition*. New York: Alcoholics Anonymous World Services, Inc. 1976. p.43.

321 "Twelve Steps to get well" — Wilson, Bill. *As Bill Sees It: The A. A. Way of Life*. New York: Alcoholics Anonymous World Services, Inc. 1967. p.32.

321 "potentially favorable sign for cure" — Ludwig, p.77.

322 "thinking-and-acting system" — Bateson, Gregory. *Steps to an Ecology of Mind*. New York: Ballantine Books, 1972. p.331-332.

324 "But these are indispensable" — *Alcoholics Anonymous, Third Edition*. pp.569-570.

324 "spiritus contra spiritum" — Ludwig, p.82.

325 "what the organization's designers hoped" — Miller, pp.270-271.

329 "but no immediate synthesis" — Ludwig, p.95.

329 "going mad and dying" — Ludwig, p.157.

330 "the abyss of too much" — Ludwig, p.77.

331 "in comparison with other possible approaches" — author interview, Ovide Pomerleau.

331 "with strong affiliative needs" — Ludwig, p.67.

333 "successfully into a social setting" — "Hazelden—The Minnesota Model of Treatment." Hazelden web site. www.hazelden. org.

333 "drug- and alcohol-free a year after treatment" — www. hazelden.org.

335 "that alcoholism is incurable" — Anderson, Daniel J., "Soviets wage fight to curb alcohol use." *Minneapolis Star Tribune.* May 29, 1990.

335 "Chinese drug addicts to be 3 million or more" — "Anti-Drug Campaign Yields Result." *China Daily.* June 16, 2007. http://www.china.org.cn.

335 "American doctors would be any higher" — Tang, Yi-Lang., et. al. "Attitudes, Knowledge, and Perceptions of Chinese Doctors Towards Drug Abuse." *Journal of Substance Abuse Treatment.* 29. p.215.

336 "running from their parents" — Fan, Maureen. "U.S.-Style Rehabs Take Root in China as Addiction Grows." *Washington Post Foreign Service.* January 19, 2007.

337 "I can't understand that at all" — Samuels, David. "Annals of Addiction: Saying Yes to Drugs." *New Yorker* March 23, 1998. pp.48-49.

337 "substandard insurance mills" — Samuels, p.52.

337 "finding room for good drugs after all" — "Fresh research and shifting views of treatment are opening new fronts in a deadly struggle. (Special Report)." *Newsweek.* February 12, 2001.

338 "in the brain and body" — Koob, George, and Le Moal, Michel, "Drug Abuse: Hedonic Homeostatic Dysregulation." *Science.* October 3, 1997 278. p.55.

339 "in profound and pragmatic ways" — Newberg, Andrew and D'Aquili, Eugene. *Why God Won't Go Away: Brain Science and the Biology of Belief.* New York: Ballantine Books, 2001. p.129.

340 "presence of a higher spiritual power" — Newberg, p.140.

340 "To me it is God" — *Alcoholics Anonymous*, p.308.

Chapter 14

Patty Larkin lyrics from "Do Not Disturb," on *Angels Running*. High Street/Windham Hill Records, 1993.

343 "as good as a kilogram snorted or smoked" — Kleiman, Mark A. R. "Snowed In." *The New Republic*. April 23, 1990, p.14.

343 "in the company's history" — Cockburn, Alexander. "Viewpoint." *The Wall Street Journal*. September 27, 1990.

344 "product of such a false dichotomy" — Gould, Stephen Jay, "The War On (Some) Drugs." *Harper's Magazine*. April, 1990. p.24.

345 "best-paying job available to them" — Epstein, Aaron, "Drug dealing nets better pay, study show." *Knight-Ridder*. July 11, 1990.

345 "more millennia of 'serious time'" — Lapham, Lewis. "A Political Opiate." *Harper's Magazine*. December, 1989. p.43.

350 "a danger in its own right" — "It doesn't have to be like this; Colombia is fighting a war against drugs; America is losing one; the rest of the world will lose too, if its weapon is prohibition." *The Economist*. September 2, 1989. p.21.

351 "hedonism for its own sake" — "Thinking the Unthinkable." *Time*. May 30, 1988. p.16.

351 "reducing the drug problem" — "Letter to the editor." *Time*. October 16, 1989. p.12.

352 "because of drug charges" — "Women In Jail: Unequal Justice." *Newsweek*. June 4, 1990. p.51.

352 "China ranks second" — "Pew Report Finds More than One in 100 Adults are Behind Bars." Pew Press Release. The Pew Center on the States. February 28, 2008. http://www.pewcenteronthestates.org/news_room_detail.aspx?id=35912

353 "apprehensive about entering treatment" — Columbia Center, p.145

354 "achieved one way or another" — Gazzinaga, p.157.

355 "get rid of cigarettes" — author interview, James Halikas.

356 "their families and their communities" — International Harm Reduction Association. www.ihra.net

356 "any methadone treatment at all" — Harm Reduction Coalition. www.harmreduction.org

357 "without the possibility of parole" — Lehrman, Karen. "The Dope on Dana." *New Republic.* November 5, 1990. p.20.

362 "We don't want their help." — "War by other means." *The Economist.* February 10, 1990. p.50.

362 "approximately 30 per cent" — Korf, Dirk. "Dutch coffee shops and trends in cannabis use." *Addictive Behaviors.* November-December, 2002 27. p.851.

363 "stick in the minds of the masses" — Siegel, p.150.

366 "to treat patients" — Smith, Stephen. "Addicts to receive overdose antidote." *The Boston Globe.* November 2, 2007.

367 "the difference between life and death" — Hurley, Dan. "Emergency Antidote, Direct to Addicts." *New York Times.* December 11, 2007.

367 "leading preventable cause of death worldwide." — "WHO Report on the Global Tobacco Epidemic, 2008." Tobacco Free Iniative. World Health Organization. February 7, 2008.http://www.who.int/tobacco/mpower/en/index.html

369 "in any meaningful way" — Earls, Felton J., et. al.. "Should Some Illegal Drugs Be Legalized?" *Issues in Science and Technology.* Summer, 1990. p.43.

369 associated with one untreated addict. — "Principles of Drug Abuse Treatment for Criminal Justice Populations." New York State Office of Alcoholism and Substance Abuse Services. Albany,

New York. http://www.oasas.state.ny.us/hps/grants/news/NID-ACriminalJustice.cfm

370 "other official bodies" — "Comprehensive approach needed to help control prescription drug abuse." Project DAWN Annual Report. Rockville, MD: National Institute on Drug Abuse, 1984.

370 "heavily medicated senior citizens" — *Associated Press.* February 16, 1989.

371 "literally a flip of the coin" — Kuehn Kelly, Christine. "Managing the fifth vital signs: your patient's pain." *ACP-ASIM Observer.* College of Physicians-American Society of Internal Medicine. April, 2001.

371 "scramble for what's left" — McNeil Donald G. Jr. "Drugs Banned, Many of World's Poor Suffer in Pain." *New York Times.* September 10, 2007.

373 "I believe I'll have another" — *New Yorker,* April 29, 1991. p.91.

SELECTED BIBLIOGRAPHY

Aharonovich, E., et. al. "Postdischarge Cannabis Use and Its Relationship to Cocaine, Alcohol, and Heroin Use: A Prospective Study." *American Journal of Psychiatry.* 2005 162: 1507-1514.

Alcoholics Anonymous. New York: Alcoholics Anonymous World Services, Inc., 1976.

Altenau, Brooke. "Bulimia Nervosa and the Effect of Antidepressant Drugs." *Health Psychology Home Page.* Vanderbilt University Psychology Department, www.vanderbilt.edu.

Ameri, A. "The Effects of Cannabinoids on the Brain." *Progressive Neurobiology.* July, 1999. 58: 315-48.

Anderson, Daniel J. "Soviets wage fight to curb alcohol use." *Minneapolis Star Tribune.* May 29, 1990: 4E.

Andreasen, Nancy C. Brave New Brain: Conquering Mental Illness in the Era of the Genome. New York: Oxford University Press, 2001.

Andrews, Zane B., and Horvath, Tamas L. "Tasteless Food Reward." *Neuron.* March 27, 2008 57. 806.

Bagot, K.S., et. al. "Tobacco craving predicts lapse to smoking among adolescent smokers in cessation treatment." *Nicotine & Tobacco Research.* 2007 9. 647–652.

Bashin, Bryan Jay. "The Jolt in Java." *San Francisco Chronicle*. February 28, 1988.

Bateson, Gregory. "The Cybernetics of Self: A Theory of Alcoholism." In *Steps To An Ecology Of Mind*. New York: Ballantine Books, 1972.

Begleiter, H., et. al. "Auditory recovery function and P3 in boys at high risk for alcoholism." *Alcohol*. July-August, 1987. 315-21.

Begleiter H. and Porjesz, B. et.al. "Auditory brainstem potentials in sons of alcoholic fathers," *Alcoholism*. October, 1987. 477-80.

— "Potential biological markers in individuals at high risk for developing alcoholism." *Alcoholism*. August, 1988. 488-93.

— "Event-related brain potentials in boys at risk for alcoholism." *Science*. September 28,1984. 1493-6.

Berg, Paul. "Cocaine's Deceit." *Washington Post*. May 14, 1986. 12.

Blakemore, Colin. "Hysteria over cannabis is getting in the way of truth." *The Observer*. May 4, 2008. http://www.guardian.co.uk

Blakeslee, Sandra. "Scientists Test Hallucinogens for Mental Ills." *New York Times*. March 13, 2001.

Blum, Kenneth. "Improvement of inpatient treatment of the alcoholic as a function of neurotransmitter restoration: a pilot study." *International Journal of the Addictions*. 1988 23. 991-998.

Blum, Kenneth, and Trachtenberg, Michael C. "Alcoholism: Scientific Basis of a Neuropsychogenetic Disease." *International Journal of the Addictions*. 1988 23. 781-796.

Bower, Bruce, "Drugs of Choice." *Science News*. December 16, 1989 136: 392-393.

— "Early Alcoholism: Crime, depression higher," *Science News*. March 25, 1989 135: 180.

— "Schizophrenia gene: A family link fades." *Science News*. June 10, 1989. 359.

Braverman, Eric R., and Pfeiffer, Carl C. *The Healing Nutrients Within*. New Canaan, CT: Keats Publishing, 1987.

Brecher, Edward M., and Editors of Consumer Reports. *Licit and Illicit Drugs*. Boston, Toronto: Little, Brown and Co., 1972.

Budney, Alan J., et. al. "Review of the Validity and Significance of Cannabis Withdrawal Syndrome." *American Journal of Psychiatry*. November, 2004 161: 1967.

Cadoret, Remi J., et. al., "An Adoption Study of Genetic and Environmental Factors in Drug Abuse." *Archives of General Psychiatry*. December, 1986 43: 1131-1136.

Callaway, Ewan. "'Diet' foods may not fool the brain." *New Scientist*. March 26, 2008: 17.

— "Double-whammy gene keeps smokers hooked." *New Scientist*. April 2, 2008: 10.

Carlsson, Arvid. "A Paradigm Shift in Brain Research." *Science*. November 2, 2001 294: 1021+.

Chanock, Stephen J., and Hunter, David J. "Genomics: When the smoke clears ..." *Nature*. April 3, 2008 452: 537-538.

Childress, Anna Rose, and O'Brien, Charles P. "Dopamine receptor partial agonists could address the duality of cocaine craving." *Trends in Pharmacological Sciences*. January, 2000 21: 6-9.

Cloninger, C. R. "Neurogenetic adaptive mechanisms in alcoholism." *Science*. April 24, 1987: 410-6.

Cloninger, C.R., et.al. "Psychopathology in adopted-out children of alcoholics—The Stockholm Adoption Study." *Recent Developments in Alcoholism*. 1985 1: 37-5

"COGA Suggests Genetic Loci for P3 Brain Wave Abnormality." *NIAAA Press Release*. May 20, 1998.

Comings, D.E., et.al. "A study of the dopamine D2 receptor gene in pathological gambling." *Pharmacogenetics*. June, 1996: 223-4.

Copeland, J., et. al. "Clinical profile of participants in a brief intervention program for cannabis use disorder." *Journal of Substance Abuse Treatment*. January, 2001 20: 45-52.

Cowen, P., et al. "Abstinence Symptoms After Withdrawal of Tranquilizing Drugs: Is There a Common Neurochemical Mechanism?" *Lancet*. August 14, 1982: 360-2.

Crawford, John. "Public Attitudes to the Disease Concept of Alcoholism." *International Journal of the Addictions*. 22: 1129-1138.

Csikszentmihaly, Mihaly. *The Evolving Self*. New York: HarperCollins, 1993.

Cui, S.S., et.al. "Prevention of cannabinoid withdrawal syndrome by lithium: involvement of oxytocinergic neuronal activation." *Journal of Neuroscience*. December 15, 2001 21: 9867.

de Fonseca, F.R., et.al. "Activation of Corticotropin-Releasing Factor in the Limbic System During Cannabinoid Withdrawal." *Science*. June 27, 1997 276: 2050.

Deitrich, R.A., and Meichior, C.L. "A critical assessment of animal models for testing new drugs for altering ethanol intake." In Naranjo, C.A., and Sellers, E.M, *Research Advances In New Psychopharmacological Treatments for Alcoholism*. Amsterdam: Excerpta Medica, 1985: 23-43.

De Rienzo, Paul, and Beal, Dana. *The Ibogaine Story: Report on the State Island Project*. New York: Autonomedia, 1997.

De Ropp, Robert S. *Drugs and the Mind*. New York: Grove Press, 1957.

Dennis, Richard. "The Economics of Legalizing Drugs." *The Atlantic Monthly*. November, 1990: 26+.

Diamond, Edwin, et. al. "Is TV News Hyping America's Cocaine Problem?" *TV Guide*. February 7, 1987: 4-10.

"Drug to curb smoking also cuts alcohol dependence." University of California, San Francisco. UCSF News Office. July 9, 2007. http://pub.ucsf.edu/newsservices/releases/200707063

Dubey, Anita. "Cocaine Cravings Linked to Body's Opiate System." *Addiction Research Foundation Journal*. January-February, 1997: 7.

Duenwald, Mary. "A Fresh Look at a Quick Fix for Heroin Addiction." *New York Times*. December 4, 2001.

"FDA Approves Novel Medication for Smoking Cessation." *FDA News*. U.S. Food and Drug Administration. May 11, 2006. www.fda.gov/bbs/topics/NEWS/2006/NEW1370.html.

Fingarette, Herbert. *Heavy Drinking: The Myth Of Alcoholism as a Disease.* Berkeley, CA: University of California Press, 1988.

Franklin, Jon. *Molecules of the Mind.* New York: Dell, 1987.

Galla, John P., and Donnini, Joyce L. "Serotoin Reuptake Inhibitors and the Treatment of Bulimia Nervosa-A Comprehensive Review." *Proceedings.* Conferences of the National Social Science Association. April 6, 1995.

Gawin, Frank H. "Cocaine Addiction: Psychology and Neurophysiology." *Science.* March 29, 1991 251: 1580-6.

Gazzaniga, Michael S. *Nature's Mind.* New York: Basic Books, 1992.

George, David T. "Neurokinin I Receptor Antagonism as a Possible Therapy for Alcoholism." *Science.* March 14, 2008 319: 1536.

Gladwell, Malcolm. "Java Man." *The New Yorker.* July 30, 2001: 76.

Glassman. A.H., et. al. "Heavy smokers, smoking cessation, and clonidine: Results of a double-blind, randomized trial." *Journal of the American Medical Association.* May 20, 1988 259: 2863-2866.

Glassman, Alexander and Helzer, John, et.al. "Smoking, smoking cessation, and major depression." *Journal of the American Medical Association.* September 26, 1990 264: 1541-1545.

Glenmullen, Joseph. *Prozac Backlash.* New York: Simon and Schuster, 2000.

Gold, Mark S. *800-COCAINE.* Toronto: Bantam Books, 1984.

—— "Clonidine: A safe, effective, and rapid nonopiate treatment for opiate withdrawal." *Journal of the American Medical Association.* 1980 243: 343-346.

—— *The Good News About Depression.* Toronto, New York: Bantam Books, 1986.

Goldberg, Rachel Joan. "The Politics of Alcoholism." *Omni.* December, 1988.

Goldstein, Avram and Kalant, Harold. "Drug Policy: Striking the Right Balance." *Science.* September 28, 1990: 1513-1521.

Gonzales, David, et.al. "Varenicline, an alpha4beta2 Nicotinic Acetylcholine Receptor Partial Agonist, vs Sustained-Release Bupropion and Placebo for Smoking Cessation." *Journal of the American Medical Association.* July 5, 2006 296: 47-55.

Goodwin, Donald W. *Is Alcoholism Hereditary?* New York: Ballantine Books, 2nd Ed. 1992.

Grof, Stanislav. *LSD Psychotherapy.* Alameda, CA: Hunter House Publishers, 1994.

Hall, Wayne, et.al. "The Health and Psychological Consequences of Cannabis Use." *National Task Force on Cannabis Australia.* Monograph Series No. 25. 1999.

Haney, Margaret, et.al. "Abstinence symptoms following smoked marijuana in humans." *Psychopharmacology.* February, 1999 141: 395.

—— "Marijuana Withdrawal in Humans: Effects of Oral THC or Divalproex." *Neuropsychopharmacology.* 2004 29: 158.

— "Nefazodone decreases anxiety during marijuana withdrawal in humans." *Psychopharmacology.* January, 2003 165: 157-165.

Hathaway, William. "Experts Chew Over Eating as Addiction." *The Hartford Courant.* July 11, 2007

He, Dao-Yao. "Glial Cell Line-Derived Neurotrophic Factor Mediates the Desirable Actions of the Anti-Addiction Drug Ibogaine against Alcohol Consumption." *Journal of Neuroscience.* January 19, 2005 25: 619-628

Heinz, A., et al. "Serotonergic dysfunction, negative mood states, and response to alcohol." *Alcoholism: Clinical and Experimental Research.* 2001 25: 487-495.

Hernandez, L. and Hoebel, B.G. "Food Reward and Cocaine Increase Extracellular Dopamine in the Nucleus Accumbens as Measured by Microdialysis." *Life Sciences.* 1988 42: 1705-1712.

Hingson, Ralph, et. al. "Age at Drinking Onset and Alcohol Dependence." *Archives of Pediatrics and Adolescent Medicine.* July 2006 160: 7.

Holden, Constance. "A Cautionary Genetic Tale: The Sobering Story of D2." *Science.* June 17, 1994 264: 1696.

— "'Behavioral' Addictions: Do They Exist?" *Science.* November 2, 2001 294: 980-982.

— "Caffeine Link in Parkinson's Bolstered." *Science.* May 18, 2001 292.

— "Excited by Glutamate." *Science.* June 20, 2003 300: 1866-1868.

—— "In Search of an Addiction Gene." *Washington Post*. January 23, 1985: 16 Health.

—— "Zapping Memory Center Triggers Drug Craving." *Science*. May 11, 2001. 292: 1039.

Horgan, John. "Your Analysis is Faulty." *The New Republic*. April 2, 1990: 2

"It doesn't have to be like this." *The Economist*. September 2, 1989: 2

Jellinek, E.M. *The Disease Concept of Alcoholism*. New Haven, CT: Hillhouse Press, 1960.

Johnson, Avery. "Pfizer Heightens Chantix Warning." *Wall Street Journal*. January 18, 2008.

Johnson,B.A., et.al. "Oral topiramate for treatment of alcohol dependence: a randomised controlled trial." *Lancet*. May 17, 2003 361: 1677-85.

—— "Topiramate for Treating Alcohol Dependence: A Randomized Controlled Trial." *Journal of the American Medical Association*. October 10, 2007 298: 1641.

Kampman, Kyle M. "The Search for Medications to Treat Stimulant Dependence." *NIDA Addiction Science and Clinical Practice*. National Institute of Drug Abuse. June, 2008 4: 28. http://www.nida.nih.gov/ascp/Vol4No2Refs.html

Kendler, Kenneth, et.al. "A twin-family study of alcoholism in women." *American Journal of Psychiatry*. May, 1994 151: 707-715.

Kennedy J.L., et. al. "Evidence against linkage of schizophrenia to markers on chromosome 5 in a northern Swedish pedigree." *Nature.* November 10, 1988: 167-70.

Khalsa, Jag. H., et. al. "Clincial Consequences of Marijuana." *Journal of Clinical Pharmacology.* 2002 42: 7S-10s.

Knowlton, Leslie. "Gold Forecasts and Describes Cocaine Vaccine, Smoking." *Psychiatric Times* July, 1997 7: 14.

Koob, George, and Le Moal, Michel. "Drug Abuse: Hedonic Homeostatic Dysregulation." *Science.* October 3, 1997 278: 52-58.

Kouri, E.M. "Does Marijuana Withdrawal Syndrome Exist?" *Psychiatric Times.* February 1, 2002 19. www.psychiatrictimes.com.

Kramer, Michael. "Clinton's Drug Policy Is a Bust." *Time.* December 20, 1993.

Kramer, Peter D. *Listening to Prozac.* New York: Penguin Books, 1993.

Kreek, Mary Jeanne, et. al. "Pharmacotherapy of Addictions." *Nature Reviews* September 2000 1: 710-726.

Krough, David. *Smoking: The Artifical Passion.* W.H. Freeman & Company, 1992.

Kumar, A, et. al. "Chromatin remodeling is a key mechanism underlying cocaine-induced plasticity in striatum." *Neuron.* Oct 20 2005 48: 303-314.

Lambert, Craig. "Deep Cravings." *Harvard Magazine.* March-April, 2000.

Lapham, Lewis. "A Political Opiate." *Harper's Magazine*. December, 1989: 43-48.

Lee, Martin, and Shlain, Bruce. *Acid Dreams*. New York: Grove Press, 1985.

Lenson, David L. *On Drugs*. Minneapolis, MN: University Of Minnesota Press, 1995.

Leshner, Alan. "Addiction Is a Brain Disease, and It Matters." *Science*. October 3, 1997 278: 46.

Levine, Harry G. "The Discovery of Addiction: Changing Conceptions of Habitual Drunkeness in America." *Journal of Studies on Alcohol* 1979 15: 493-506.

Leviton, Richard. "Staying Drugfree Naturally." *East West*. March, 1988: 36-46.

Li, T.K., et. al. "Alcoholism: Is it a model for the study of disorders of mood and consummatory behavior?" *Annals of the New York Academy of Sciences*. 1987 499: 239-249.

— "Pharmacology of alcohol preference in rodents." *Advances in Alcohol and Substance Abuse*. 1988. 7: 73-86.

— "Progress toward a voluntary oral consumption model of alcoholism." *Drug and Alcohol Dependency*. 1979 4: 45-60.

Lichtman, A.H., and Martin, B.R. "Marijuana Withdrawal Syndrome in the Animal Model." *Journal of Clinical Pharmacology*. 2002 42: 20s-27s.

Lohmeier, Lynne. "The Hidden Addiction." *East West*, March, 1988: 47-50.

Longo, Lance P., and Bohn, Michael J. "Alcoholism Pharmacotherapy: New Approaches to an Old Disease." *Hospital Physician*. June 200: 33-43.

Ludwig, Arnold M. *Understanding The Alcoholic's Mind*. New York: Oxford University Press, 1988.

Majewska, M.D. "Cocaine addiction as a neurological disorder." *National Institute on Drug Abuse Monograph*. Rockville, MD. 1996.

Mann, John. *Murder, Magic and Medicine*. New York: Oxford University Press, 1992.

McBride, William J., et. al. "The Role of Serotonin in Ethanol Preference." *Recent Developments in Alcoholism*. 1988: 7.

McDonagh, S. "Switching Off Pain." *Science News*. August 16, 2003 164: 99-100.

McKenna, Terence. *Food of the Gods*. New York: Bantam Books, 1992.

McNeil, Donald G. Jr., "Research on Ecstasy is Clouded by Errors." *New York Times*. December 2, 2003.

Miller, William, and Kathleen, Carroll, Eds. *Rethinking Substance Abuse: What the Science Shows, and What We Should Do About It*. New York: The Guilford Press, 2006.

Moore, Theresa H.M., et. al. "Cannabis use and risk of psychotic or affective mental health outcomes: a systematic review." *Lancet*. 2007 370: 319.

Moorhouse, Mona, et.al., "Carbohydrate Craving by Alcohol-Dependent Men During Sobriety: Relationship to Nutrition and Serotonergic Function." *Alcoholism.* May 2000: 635-43.

Nadelmann, Ethan A. letter. *Science.* December. 1, 1989: 1104.

Nagourney, Eric, "Smokers' Ethnicity May Make Difference." *New York Times.* January 29, 2002.

National Center on Addiction and Substance Abuse at Columbia University. *Women under the Influence.* Baltimore: The Johns Hopkins University Press, 2006.

Naranjo, C.A., and Sellers EM; et. al. "The serotonin uptake inhibitor citalopram attenuates ethanol intake." *Clinical Pharmacology & Therapeutics.* March, 1987: 266-74.

Naranjo, C.A., and Sellers, EM, et. al. "Modulation of ethanol intake by serotonin uptake inhibitors." *Journal of Clinical Psychiatry.* April, 1986: 16-22.

Nehlig, A. "Are we dependent upon coffee and caffeine? A review of human and animal data." *Neuroscience and Biobehavioral Review.* March 23, 1999 4: 563-76.

Nemeroff, Charles. "Depression." *Scientific American.* September 5, 1998.

Nesse, Randolph M., and Berridge, Kent C. "Psychoactive Drug Use in Evolutionary Perspective." *Science.* October 3, 1997 278: 63-65.

Nestler, Eric J. "Total Recall—the Memory of Addiction." *Science.* June 22, 2001 292: 2266+.

Newberg, Andrew, and D'Aquili, Eugene. *Why God Won't Go Away: Brain Science and the Biology of Belief.* New York: Ballantine Books, 2001.

Nutt, D., et. al. "Development of a rational scale to assess the harm of drugs of potential misuse." *The Lancet.* 24 March 24, 2007 369: 1047–1053.

O'Brien, Charles P. "A Range of Research-Based Pharmacotherapies for Addiction." *Science.* October 3, 1997 278: 66-70.

Ornstein, Robert, and Thompson, Richard. *The Amazing Brain.* Boston: Houghton-Mifflin, 1984.

Ostrowski, James, "Thinking About Drug Legalization." *Cato Institute Policy Analysis No. 121.* May 25, 1989.

Pallanti, S., et. al. "Nefazodone Treatment of Pathological Gambling: A Prospecive Open-Label Controlled Trial." *Journal of Clinical Psychiatry.* November, 2002 63: 1034-9.

Patel. J.D., et. al. "Lung cancer in U.S. women: A contemporary epidemic." *Journal of the American Medical Association.* April 14, 2004 291: 1767.

Perez-Pena, Richard. "New Drug Promises Shift in Treatment for Heroin Addicts." *New York Times.* August 11, 2003.

Pert, Candace B. *Molecules of Emotion: Why You Feel the Way You Feel.* New York: Scribner, 1997.

Phelps, Janice Keller, and Nourse, Alan E. *The Hidden Addiction.* Boston: Little, Brown and Company, 1986.

Pomerleau, Ovide F., and Pomerleau, Cynthia S. "Neuroregulators and the Reinforcement of Smoking: Towards a Biobehavioral Explanation." *Neuroscience and Biobehavioral Reviews.* 8 198: 503-513.

Pomerleau, Ovide F., and Rosecrans, John. "Neuroregulatory Effects of Nicotine." *Psychoneuroendocrinology.* 1989 14: 407-423.

Post, Jerrold M. "Drunk With Power." *Washington Post National Weekly Edition.* February 5, 1990: 39.

Preskorn, Sheldon H. "Bupropion: What Mechanism of Action?" *Journal of Practical Psychiatry and Behavioral Health,* January, 2000: 272-276.

"Profiles in Science—The Julius Axelrod Papers." *National Library of Medicine.* Bethesda, MD. http://profiles.nlm.nih.gov/HH/Views/Exhibit/narrative/neurotransmitters.html

"Progress Made in Understanding Neurobiological Basis for Relapse to Cocaine Abuse." *NIDA Addiction Research News.* May 21, 2001. http://www.drugabuse.gov/MedAdv/01/NS-6.html.

Reich. T. "Biological-marker studies in alcoholism." Editorial. *New England Journal of Medicine.* January 21, 1988: 80-182.

"Results from the 2006 National Survey on Drug Use and Health: National Findings." Department of Health and Human Services, Substance Abuse and Mental Health Services Administration. Rockville, MD: Office of Applied Studies, 2006.

Ripleya, Tamzin L. "Lack of self-administration and behavioural sensitisation to morphine, but not cocaine, in mice lacking NK1 receptors." *Neuropharmacology.* December 2002 43:.1258.

Robins, Lee N. "Lessons from the Vietnam Heroin Experience." *Harvard Mental Health Letter*. December, 1994.

Rocio, M., et. al. "Suppression of psychoactive effects of cocaine by active immunization." *Nature*. December 14, 1995 378: 727-730.

Roizen, Ron. "E.M. Jellinek and All That!" Thomas Austern Lecture, San Francisco, October 20, 2000.

Saey, Tina Hesman. "Ch-ch-ch-changes." *Science News*. 2008 174: 14.

Samuels, David. "Saying Yes to Drugs." *New Yorker*. March 23, 1998: 48-49.

Sandor, Richard S. "A Physician's Journey." *Parabola*. Summer, 1988: 16+.

Sayette, M.A.,et. al. "A multidimensional analysis of cue-elicited craving in heavy smokers and tobacco chippers." *Addiction*. 2001 96: 1419–1432.

Sayette, M.A., et. al. "The measurement of drug craving." *Addiction*. 2000 95: S189–S210.

Schleiffer, Hedwig. *Narcotic Plants of the Old World*. Monticello, N.Y.: Lubrecht & Cramer, 1979.

Schuckit, M.A., et.al. "Clinical implications for four drugs of the DSM-IV distinction between substance dependence with and without a physiological component." *American Journal of Psychiatry*. 1999 156: 41-49.

— "Genetic and clinical implications of alcoholism and affective disorder." *American Journal of Psychiatry.* February, 1986: 140-7.

— "Genetics and the risk for alcoholism." *Journal of the American Medical Association.* November 8, 1985 14: 26+.

— "Reactions to alcohol in sons of alcoholics and controls." *Alcoholism.* August, 1988: 465-70.

Schuckit, M.A.; Li , T. K; Cloninger, C.R.; Deitrich, R.A. "Genetics of Alcoholism." Clinical conference. *Alcoholism.* December, 1985: 475-92.

Sellers, E.M., and Naranjo, C.A. "Therapeutic use of serotonergic drugs in alcohol abuse." *Clinical Neuropharmacology.* Suppl 4. 1986: 60-2.

Seppa, N. "Exploring a genetic link to smoking." *Science News.* March 7, 1998: 153.

— "Nicotine metabolism shows ethnic bias," *Science News.* January 19, 2002 161: 38.

"Serotonin and Bulimia." *Science.* July 13, 2001 293: 205.

"Serotonin and Eating Disorders." *Medical Sciences Bulletin.* October, 1994. http://pharminfo.com.

Seymour, Richard B., and Smith, David E. *Drug Free.* New York: Facts On File Publications, 1987.

Sherrington, R., et. al. "Localization of a susceptibility locus for schizophrenia on chromosome 5." *Nature.* November 10, 1988: 164-7.

Shiffman, Saul, "Tobacco 'chippers'—individual differences in tobacco dependence." *Psychopharmacology*, 1989 97 :539-547.

Shizgal, Peter, and Arvanitogiannis, Andreas. "Gambling on Dopamine." *Science*. March 21, 2003 299: 1856+.

Shoaib, M., et.al. "Chronic caffeine exposure potentiates nicotine self-administration in rats." *Psychopharmacology*. March, 1999 142: 327-33.

Siegel, Ronald K. *Intoxication: Life in Pursuit of Artificial Paradise*. New York: E.P. Dutton, 1989.

Smith, David E., and Landry, Mim J. "Cocaine, Drug of the 80s." *San Francisco Chronicle*. February 28, 1988: 10

Snyder, Solomon H. *Drugs and the Brain*. New York: Scientific American Library, 1996.

Solomon, David, *The Marihuana Papers*. New York: Signet Books, 1966.

Sontag, Susan. *Illness as Metaphor*. New York: Farrar, Straus and Giroux, 1978.

"Source of withdrawal pangs found in brain." *Science News*. September 10, 1994: 166.

Squires, Sally. "Alcoholism Is the Most Common Addiction." *Washington Post*. November 4, 1986: 17 Health.

Sternbach, Harvey. "Serotonin Syndrome: How to Avoid, Identify, & Treat Dangerous Drug Interactions." *Current Psychiatry Online*. May, 2003 2: 5.

Stevens, Jay, *Storming Heaven: LSD and the American Dream.* New York: Harper & Row Perennial Library, 1987.

Stolaroff, Myron J. *The Secret Chief.* Charlotte, NC: Multidisciplinary Association for Psychedelic Studies, 1997.

Tabakoff B., et. al. "Differences in platelet enzyme activity between alcoholics and nonalcoholics." *New England Journal of Medicine.* January, 21, 1988: 134-9.

Tapper, A.R., et.al. "Nicotine Activation of A4 Receptors: Sufficient for Reward, Tolerance, and Sensitization." *Science.* November 5, 2004 306: 1029+

Thomas, Josephine. "Buprenorphine Proves Effective, Expands Options for Treatment of Heroin Addiction." NIDA Notes. May, 2001 16: 2.

Thompson, Larry. "Is It in the Genes?" *Washington Post.* December 15, 1987: 10 Health.

Tonstad, Serena. "Effect of Maintenance Therapy With Varenicline on Smoking Cessation: A Randomized Controlled Trial." *Journal of the American Medical Association.* July 5, 2006 296: 64-71.

"UCSF researchers move in on role of brain's naturally occurring marijuana." *Press Release.* University of California, San Francisco. March 29, 2001.

Vaillant, G. E., *The Natural History of Alcoholism Revisited.* Cambridge: Harvard University Press, 1995.

Vandrey, R.G., et.al. "A within-subject comparison of withdrawal symptoms during abstinence from cannabis, tobacco, and both substances." *Drug and Alcohol Dependence.* January 1, 2008 92: 48.

"Varencline (marketed as Chantix) Information." *FDA Alert*. U.S. Food and Drug Administration. February I, 2008. http://www. fda.gov/cder/drug/infopage/varenicline/default.htm

Vastag, Brian. "Addiction Alleviator? Hallucinogen's popularity grows." *Science News*. January 5th, 2008 173: 6.

— "Ibogaine Therapy: A 'Vast, Uncontrolled Experiment.'" *Science*. April 15, 2005 308: 345-346.

Weil, Andrew. *The Natural Mind*. Boston: Houghton Mifflin Company, 1972.

Weiss, Gary. "Gilding Lilly: how much weight should be given to its diet drug?" *Barron's*. May 12, 1986: 15+.

Wickelgren, Ingrid. "Marijuana: Harder Than Thought?" *Science*. June 27, 1997 76: 1967-8.

William C., ed. *Problems in Addiction: Alcoholism and Narcotics*. New York: Fordham University Press, 1962.

Williams, Roger J. *Alcoholism: The Nutritional Approach*. Austin: University of Texas Press, 1959.

Willenbring, Mark. "Medications to Treat Alcohol Dependence." *Journal of the American Medical Association*. October 10, 2007 298: 1691.

Wilson, Bill. *"Pass It On": The Story of Bill Wilson and How the A.A. Message Reached the World*. New York: Alcoholics Anonymous World Services, Inc., 1984.

Wise, RA. "The role of reward pathways in the development of drug dependence." *Pharmacology and Therapeutics*. 1987 35: 227-63.

Wuethrich, Bernice. "Does Alcohol Damage Female Brains More?" *Science*. March 16, 2001 291: 2077+.

Wurtman, Richard J., and Wurtman, Judith J. "Carbohydrates and Depression." *Scientific American*. January, 1989: 68+.

— "Carbohydrate craving, obesity and brain serotonin." *Appetite*. 1986 7: 99-103.

Wurtman, J.J., et. al. "Effect of nutrient intake on premenstrual depression." *American Journal of Obstetrics and Gynecology*. November, 1989 161: 1228-1234.

Zeisel, S.H. "Dietary influences on neurotransmission." *Advanced Pediatrics*. 1986 33: 23-47.

Zickler, P. "Study Demonstrates That Marijuana Smokers Experience Significant Withdrawal." *NIDA Notes*. October 17, 2002: 17. Bethesda, MD: National Institute on Drug Abuse.

Zinberg, Norman, and Jacobson, R. *Drug, Set, and Setting: The Basis for Controlled Intoxicant Use*. New Haven, CT: Yale University Press, 1984.

INDEX

INDEX

52–53
Alles, Gordon, 48
Alliance for a Drug-Free
America, 66
Alper, Ken, 267
ALS (Lou Gehrig's disease), 87
Alzheimer's disease, 145
American Civil War, 36
amines, 101
amino acids, 182, 307–8
Amish, 92
Amos, Christopher, 250
amphetamine
overview of, 48–49, 51
anticraving drugs, 258–59
cocaine and, 157
cravings and, 157
depression and, 162
dopamine and, 156–58,
163, 186, 223, 295
marijuana eradication and,
360–61
mechanics of, 156–65
neurotransmitters and,
157–59
rats and, 258
reward pathway and,
157–58
tolerance for, 162
withdrawal, 159, 162
see also Benzedrine; Dex-
edrine; Ecstasy
(MDMA); metham-
phetamine

amphetamine psychosis, 163
amygdala, 98, 180
anandamide, 172–74, 261
Andreasen, Nancy, 93
Angel Dust. see PCP
animal models, 18–22, 177,
206–7
see also rats; other animals
anorexia nervosa, 187, 221
Anslinger, Harry J., 47–48
Antabuse (disulfiram), 121,
200–201, 226, 253,
258
antagonists
for addiction treatment,
121, 199–200, 334
definition of, 5, 68
dopamine, 146, 251,
256–57
glutamate, 233
heroin, 199
H2 receptors, 224
opioid receptors, 67,
238–39
serotonin, 258
anticoagulants, 296
anticraving drugs, 231–74,
294–96
see also specific addictive substances
antidepressant drugs, 144, 164,
209–10, 252, 257, 273,
288, 293
see also MAO (monoamine
oxidase) inhibitors;

Made in the USA
Lexington, KY
05 August 2010